PERFORMING FOLKLORE

PERFORMING

RANCHOS FOLCLÓRICOS

FOLKLORE

FROM LISBON TO NEWARK

KIMBERLY DACOSTA HOLTON

INDIANA UNIVERSITY PRESS
Bloomington & Indianapolis

This book is a publication of

Indiana University Press
601 North Morton Street
Bloomington, Indiana 47404-3797 USA

http://iupress.indiana.edu

Telephone orders 800-842-6796
Fax orders 812-855-7931
Orders by email iuporder@indiana.edu

The paper used in this publication meets the minimum requirements of American National Standard for Information Sciences—Permanence of Paper for Printed Library Materials, ANSI Z39.48-1984.

Manufactured in the United States of America

Library of Congress Cataloging-in-Publication Data

Holton, Kimberly DaCosta.
Performing folklore : ranchos folclóricos from Lisbon to Newark / Kimberly DaCosta Holton.
p. cm.
Includes bibliographical references and index.
ISBN 0-253-34631-2 (cloth : alk. paper) — ISBN 0-253-21831-4 (pbk. : alk. paper) 1. Folklore—Performance.—Portugal. 2. Portugal—Social life and customs. I. Title.
GR72.3.H65 2005
398'.09469—dc22
2005011536

1 2 3 4 5 10 09 08 07 06 05

IN MEMORY OF

DWIGHT CONQUERGOOD

CONTENTS

ACKNOWLEDGMENTS

This project has involved the generous efforts and energies of many people on several continents. First, I would like to thank all the folklore performers and enthusiasts in Estremadura, Portugal, and Newark, New Jersey, for their patient answers to my questions and for sharing their wisdom and warmth over the course of many years. I am forever grateful to Olinda, Carlos, and Ricardo Pereira; Fátima, Luis, Joana, and Filipa Carvalho Santos; Helena Marques dos Santos; Isidro and Manuela da Cruz; António Luís and Ana Pereira; Aníbal and Fátima Salvador; José Hermínio Carvalho; António Reis; Vítor, Fátima, Claudia, and Ana Luís; Crispim Luís; João and Vina Murteira; Luís and Lídia Ventura; João and Lourdes Mendes; Joaquim and Tiago da Costa; Manuel, Dulce, Ana, and Teresa Anacleto; Fernando, Maria do Carmo, and Glória Rodrigues; Miguel Oliveira; Manuel Martins; Luís Rema; Tony Cardoso; Joe, Mena, and Jeff Cerqueira; Jessica Moreira; Melissa Gonçalves and Brian Santos; and especially Armindo, Fátima, Lucília, Fernando, Acácio, and Alexandre Rodrigues, who became my adopted Portuguese family in Alenquer.

I am thankful for the unflagging support of several teachers and mentors who guided this project to fruition. Dwight Conquergood, to whom this book is dedicated, was an unfailing source of inspiration and a dear friend. He read and commented on endless drafts of this manuscript, gently pushing me to cross disciplinary borders and to situate ethnographic readings within broader ideological contexts. His ebullient spirit has profoundly marked this project. I would also like to thank Margaret Thompson Drewal, Tracy C. Davis, and Paul Berliner for their critical advice and encouragement in the early stages of fieldwork and writing. Tremendous thanks to Caroline Brettell, who reviewed this manuscript with care and offered me incisive critiques and support throughout many rounds of revision. Finally, heartfelt thanks to Salwa Castelo Branco, who initially suggested the topic, critiqued the manuscript, helped facilitate contact with Portuguese academics, and offered me many uplifting afternoons of tea and company in Portugal.

In the beginning stages of my research, I spoke with several scholars who were instrumental in focusing my work. I would like to thank Barbara Kirshenblatt-Gimblett, Diana Taylor, Fernando Rosas, Tomaz Ribas, Nélia Dias, Rubem de Carvalho, António Firmínio Costa, and António Costa Pinto. I would also like to thank João Soeiro Carvalho, Susana Sardo, and Francisco Melo, who shared their unpublished manuscripts with me.

At the *Instituto Nacional para Aproveitamento dos Tempos Livres dos Trabalhadores,* I am grateful to Henrique Rabaço for sharing his knowledge and for furnishing me with key primary documents and rare books. I am also grateful to Augusto Gomes dos Santos, of the *Federação de Folclore Portuguese,* who spent many days captivating me with accounts of FFP history and his vast knowledge of Portuguese folklore. I thank Luís Rema of the *Câmara Municipal de Alenquer* for his assistance in accessing primary documents in the *Câmara* archives and for sharing his knowledge of the *Feira da Ascenção.* Thanks to Rita Galo in Lisbon 94's promotional department for her inside view of the L94 ad campaign. Finally, I am grateful to Fernando dos Santos and Maria do Carmo Pereira of the *LusoAmericano* newspaper in Newark for their help in accessing back issues and for their interest in this project.

During the writing stage, several friends and colleagues offered moral support and insightful commentary on chapter drafts: thanks to Dorothy Noyes, Nélia Dias, Helena Correia, Catherine Cole, Regina Bendix, Elizabeth Traube, Bela Feldman-Bianco, João Leal, João de Pina Cabral, Mary Fonseca, David Jackson, Anna Klobucka, Liza MacAlister, Maureen Mahon, Joyce Powzyk, Elpidio Laguna-Diaz, Rick Shain, Alan Sadovnik, Margaret Campbell-Harris, Josephine Grieder, Nancy Diaz, Fran Bartkowski, Clem Price, Charles Russell, Edward Kirby, Annette Juliano, Steve Diner, Max Herman, Beryl Satter, Jamie Lew, Sherrie-Ann Butterfield, Laura Lomas, Jenifer Austin, Anna Stublefield, and especially Marcy Schwartz, António Joel, Asela Laguna-Diaz, Andrea Klimt, and Mara Sidney for their affection and humor and for keeping me afloat during the ups and downs of writing. Finally, I am forever grateful to Luís and Amy Vasconcellos e Souza and Kevin and Cuca Rose, who opened their hearts and homes to me and my family in Lisbon over the course of many months.

I also appreciate the efforts of Sofia Silva and Ana Fonseca in Portugal and Susete Cesário and Jessica Moreira, my dedicated student assistants at Rutgers–Newark, for meticulously transcribing hundreds of hours of taped interviews. I am grateful to Catarina Dias for helping secure foreign copyright permissions. Thanks to Mike Heffley, who transcribed my field recordings into musical notation. Many thanks to Colin Campbell-Harris, Robert Holton Jr., Antonío Joel, Martin Elbl, Tim Raphael, and R. Scott Taylor for helping prepare the visuals for this book.

I owe a huge debt of gratitude to Michael W. Lundell, Richard Higgins, and Elisabeth Marsh at Indiana University Press for believing in this project and for the gentle prodding which enabled its completion.

A different version of chapter 6 was published as "Dancing along the In-between: Folklore Performance and Transmigration in Portuguese Newark,"

Portuguese Studies Review 11, no. 2 (2004): 153–82. Excerpts from chapter 5 appeared in "Dressing for Success: Lisbon as European Cultural Capital," *Journal of American Folklore* 111, no. 440 (1998): 173–96. And a short excerpt from chapter 3 was published as "Fazer das Tripas Coração: O Parentesco Cultural nos Ranchos Folclóricos" in *Vozes do Povo: A Folclorização em Portugal,* edited by Salwa Castelo Branco and Jorge Freitas Branco, 143–52 (Oeiras: Celta Editora, 2003).

This research was made possible through generous grants from Northwestern University's Alumnae Fellowship, from the Joint Committee on Western Europe of the American Council for Learned Societies and the Social Science Research Council with funds provided by the Ford and Mellon Foundations, from Wesleyan University's Center for the Humanities, from Rutgers–Newark Joseph C. Cornwall Center for Metropolitan Studies, and from Rutgers–Newark's Institute on Ethnicity, Culture and the Modern Experience. I am extremely indebted to these institutions for support of my research and writing.

Lastly, I would like to thank my wonderful family, who has provided me with an abundance of humor, good food, company, and love—the late Marguerite and Robert V. Holton, Beatrice DaCosta and the late António DaCosta, Laurie and Roland Pritchett, Rob and Christa Holton, Elizabeth DaCosta Ahern, Tom Ahern, Caitlin Ahern, Linda DaCosta, Ann Wiener, Chad Raphael, Betty Achinstein, Dan and Jennifer Getz, and Monique and Sharesse Houston. And to my extraordinary parents, Robert and Judyth Holton, whose generosity of spirit and passion for knowledge has been infectious, who took my children on extended adventures so that I could work, and who provided me with unflagging inspiration and encouragement, I thank you. To my spirited children, Noah Lisbon and Antonia Maya, joyous creatures full of affection and wonder, who put up with several stretches of my computer-bound absence and kept me sane with invitations to play, I thank you. And lastly, to my husband, Tim Raphael, muse and companion, who shouldered the burden of extra domestic labor, who uprooted himself twice to accompany me to the field, and whose insights on countless drafts of this manuscript were crucial to the development of this project, I am forever in your debt.

ABBREVIATIONS

CCB	*Centro Cultural de Belém* (Belém Cultural Center)
CCP	*Conselho das Comunidades Portuguesas* (Council of the Portuguese Communities)
CGD	*Caixa Geral dos Depósitos* (General Savings Bank)
EC	European Community
ECC	European Cities of Culture Programme
EEC	European Economic Community
EN	*Estado Novo* (New State)
ER	*EuroRSCG* (L94 French Advertising Firm)
EU	European Union
FFP	*Federação de Folclore Português* (Federation of Portuguese Folklore)
FNAT	*Fundação Nacional para a Alegria no Trabalho* (National Foundation for the Joy in Work)
GFB	*Grupo Folclórico de Belas* (Folklore Group of Belas)
INATEL	*Instituto Nacional para Aproveitamento dos Tempos Livres dos Trabalhadores* (National Institute for the Productive Use of Workers' Leisure Time)
IOHP	Ironbound Oral History Project
IPT	*Instituto de Promoção Turística* (Institute for Tourist Promotion)
JCCP	*Junta Central das Casas do Povo* (Central Council for the Houses of the People)
KdF	*Kraft durch Freunde* (Strength through Joy)
L94	*Lisboa 94* (Lisbon 94)
MFA	*Movimento das Forças Armadas* (Movement of the Armed Forces)
MP	*Mocidade Portuguesa* (Portuguese Youth)
NUTE II	*Nomenclatura de Unidade Territorial para Fins Estatísticos* (Nomenclature for Territorial Units for Statistical Ends)
P/C	*Publicis/Ciesa* (L94 French Advertising Firm)
PCP	*Partido Comunista Português* (Portuguese Communist Party)
PIDE	*Polícia Internacional de Defesa do Estado* (International Police for the Defense of the State)
PTC	*Plano Trabalho e Cultura* (Work and Culture Plan)
PS	*Partido Socialista* (Socialist Party)
PSD	*Partido Social Democrata* (Social Democratic Party)

RFA	*Rancho Folclórico de Alenquer* (Folklore Group of Alenquer)
SCE	*Serviço Cívico Estudantil* (Student Civic Service)
SL94	*Sociedade de Lisboa 94* (Lisbon 94 Society)
SNI	*Secretariado Nacional de Informação* (National Secretariate for Information)
SPN	*Secretariado de Propaganda Nacional* (Secretariate for National Propaganda)

PERFORMING FOLKLORE

Introduction

Everywhere and Nowhere

"They're everywhere!" a friend exclaimed at the outset of my preliminary research trip to Portugal in the summer of 1993. "Saturday and Sunday afternoons, they're always performing. Thousands of them, everywhere. Just ask anyone. Go to any public square, anywhere. You'll find them."

I was in search of *ranchos folclóricos*, groups of amateur musicians and dancers who performed late nineteenth-century popular music for, reputedly, throngs of people. Intrigued by their apparent ubiquity, I went to the tourist office in Lisbon to obtain information and schedules. Much to my surprise, the woman at the front desk knew of no upcoming folklore performances in Lisbon or the surrounding areas.

"But are you sure there are no schedules? *Ranchos folclóricos*—don't they perform *everywhere*?"

"Apparently not anywhere near here," she snipped, handing me a brochure for the Algarve's resort beaches.

"But do you know who I could call? Where I might go to find out?"

"Nope. Sorry," she said returning to her paperwork.

The clerk's seeming indifference to my inquiry regarding folklore performance was something to which I would soon become accustomed, not only from people in Lisbon's tourist industry, but also academics, artists, bureaucrats, and other urban sophisticates. In addition to the fact that folklore is still associated with fascist merrymaking, *ranchos folclóricos* are also widely viewed by many Portuguese urban dwellers as *piroso*, or "tacky," as one Lisbon teenager termed them. Slightly daunted, I continued my search.

I was staying with friends in the Alfama, one of Lisbon's oldest and most "popular" neighborhoods, and asked them about *ranchos folclóricos*. Upon mention of the topic, they threw their arms into the air, bent at the elbows, and began twirling right, then left, then right, giggling uncontrollably. This parodic gesture represented what they considered to be the prototypical folklore movement.

"Haven't you seen them? Those *rancho* performers downstairs?" my friend asked, trying to suppress a smile.

"Where?"

"Right downstairs, under our window. Haven't you heard them? The accordions and stuff. They're *always* rehearsing." One friend began the arm gesture again but the other grabbed his elbow and cut him off before the twirl.

"You mean in this building?"

"I don't know. Go down to the street. Ask around. They're right around here. Everyone must hear them."

I couldn't believe my luck! A *rancho folclórico* right here in my own backyard! I began asking people in the corner café, the bus stop, the gift shop, the Laundromat. Everyone had heard their music or seen them on the street in costume, but no one could produce an address. Certainly they're not in the telephone book, I thought, somewhat embarrassed it had come to this. I looked under "r" for "*rancho.*" I looked under "f" for "*folclore.*" I took the telephone book over to the waiter and asked what he would look under if he were trying to locate a *rancho.* The café patrons who had witnessed my inquiry chuckled. Potential solutions to my problem, however, were soon forthcoming. People gave me names of cousins, butchers, violin makers. They suggested I contact the local gym, the embassy, the Secretary of Culture. I took down all their suggestions on paper napkins and prepared for a fresh assault.

Just then, an older woman with a *chá de limão* (lemon tea) dangling gracefully from her fingertips motioned me over to explain *ranchos'* system of institutional affiliation. *Ranchos* are often formed in conjunction with associations, she informed me. Recreational associations, cultural centers, churches, gyms, employee groups in banks, insurance companies, even TransAir Portugal has a *rancho.* The most certain way to locate *ranchos* in Lisbon is to call a *casa do concelho* (literally "county house"), she advised. *Casas do concelho* serve recently arrived Lisboans native to the same Portuguese county or province. These *casas* often sponsor *ranchos folclóricos* so that rural migrants can maintain links with local tradition. I thanked the woman profusely for sharing her wisdom. Several days later I located the *rancho* which rehearsed just a few doors down from my friends' apartment. The group was indeed affiliated with a *casa do concelho* from the northern province of Minho.

Shortly after locating the *rancho,* I attended a performance which took place on the broad sidewalks outside of Lisbon's historic Coliseu. Several *ranchos* from Lisbon's northern suburbs had traveled to the city for an afternoon performance. There was no advance publicity for this event, and at the

Figure 1. *Grupo Folclórico de Belas,* "Entrance March," Lisbon 1994. *Photograph by Tim Raphael.*

designated starting time, no audience members had assembled. Admission was free. Twenty minutes after the show was scheduled to begin, *rancho* performers, who had lined up several hundred yards away from the stage area, began marching and singing in single file, snaking their way through the narrow cobblestone streets which led to the Coliseu. The long, colorful line of performers was led by a young girl dressed in a floor-length gray skirt, white shirt, and red scarf, holding a large wooden sign bearing the name and regional provenance of the group (see fig. 1). Following her were other young performers dressed in turn-of-the-century rural costumes and singing an up-tempo song while showing off the agricultural props—clay urns, pitchforks, hoes, and woven baskets—they held tightly in their hands. Bringing up the rear, middle-aged men and women, dressed in more somber garb, sang loudly, many of the men playing instruments—accordions, a guitar, a bass drum, a triangle, and long, grooved cylinders played with sticks, I later learned were called *reco-recos.* This pre-performance parade acted as spontaneous advertising, prompting neighbors to peek their heads out of open windows, shopkeepers to stand in their doorways, and pedestrians to follow the parade toward the performance area. The *rancho*'s "Marcha de Entrada"

Figure 2. *Grupo Folclórico de Belas,* dancers, Lisbon 1994. *Photograph by Tim Raphael.*

(Entrance March) produced 50 to 60 spectators, who, lured out of their daily routines by the animated music and costumes, had gathered for this seemingly impromptu performance. As the public clapped and swayed to the music, dancers executed precise footwork along Lisbon's rough cobblestone esplanade (see figs. 2 and 3).

Both *ranchos* had their own emcee, charismatic middle-aged men who announced the name of each song, sometimes giving a brief history detailing when and where the song/dance was "collected." Phrases such as "Just like our ancestors sang these songs in the wheat fields of our distant past, our *rancho* performs this number for you" peppered the emcee's prefatory speeches. In between songs, the emcee bantered back and forth with the audience, offering playful lectures about the benefits of performing folklore, not only to "preserve our region's cultural riches" but also "to keep our teenagers, the leaders of tomorrow, off the streets and free from vices, violence, and drugs." Immediately following the emcee's introductory remarks, the musicians, huddled around several tall microphones, began playing loudly. The crowd favorite was called "Fandango Saloio," a showy number where pairs of young men and women executed fast, choppy footwork to infectious syncopated rhythms from the percussion and accordions. For this and other numbers, the young female dancers hiked up their long, heavy wool skirts, revealing legs adorned with hand-crocheted stockings, maneu-

Figure 3. *Grupo Folclórico de Belas,* dancer, Lisbon 1994. *Photograph by Tim Raphael.*

vering adroitly around their partners with precision and grace. After each number the crowd applauded, milling around to get different views of the performers, some audience members leaving, other newcomers joining the crowd. Mothers held children, dancing along the margins of the stage. Older couples chatted and laughed, sometimes shouting out encouragement to the dancers. The audience, surprised by the spectacle dropped in their midst, seemed energized by the amplified melodies and twirling pairs and followed the *ranchos* to large chartered buses, as the performers wound their way back the way they came, singing their final "Marcha de Saída," or Exit March.

Once I became connected to the *rancho* scene in Lisbon and the surrounding areas, I realized how often *rancho* events in this region were promoted through word of mouth and during the performance itself by way of the "Marcha de Entrada," strategically choreographed throughout residential streets and public squares. In this way, it made sense that, initially, *ranchos* had been mysteriously elusive, inaccessible, almost invisible. My first experience searching for *ranchos folclóricos*—that were at once everywhere and nowhere—introduced me to several of the themes which would become pivotal to my analysis of Portuguese revivalist folklore throughout ten subsequent years of research.

Revivalist folklore is indeed ubiquitous in that it is one of Portugal's most popular forms of expressive culture; it is widely performed throughout every Portuguese province and in countless Portuguese emigrant communities around the globe; and hundreds of thousands of spectators attend *rancho* performances every year. At the same time, however, revivalist folklore performance is also inflected by a charged political history and lingering class-based tensions that contribute to folklore's "invisibility" within certain social and geographical contexts. Folklore is also, as the *senhora* in the café first suggested, inextricably linked to migration and the identity-building projects that often accompany deterritorialization. Whether among rural migrants in Lisbon or Portuguese Americans in New Jersey, folklore performance constitutes an essential tool for ensuring cultural reproduction and bolstering regional or ethnic solidarity within alien territory.

Given what I later learned of the complexities of revivalist folklore performance, it is not surprising that the clerk in Lisbon's national tourist office had no listings of folklore performances. Revivalist folklore, as I argue in chapter 5, has been excluded from many of Lisbon's "official" festivals of the late twentieth century. Upon entering the European Economic Community in 1986, Portugal engaged in an aggressive campaign of image overhaul (see Holton 1998a). *Ranchos folclóricos*, viewed by the cultural elite as an embarrassing holdover from the fascist *Estado Novo* regime (1926–74), were to be excluded from many international festival programs. Instead of being harnessed to the national departments of culture and propaganda, as was the case under fascism, revivalist folklore now draws its performers, sponsors, publics, and publicity from an alternative sphere. Hitchhiking on the terminology of Arjun Appadurai (1996), revivalist folklore operates within an international network of contacts, communities, and venues I label a diasporic *performanscape*.[1] As the post-1974 Portuguese nation-state has bowed out of the tasks of explicit social engineering and cultural censorship, newly invigorated spheres of folklore research, performance, and sponsorship have emerged. Concomitant with the general erosion of the nation-state around the world, giving way to globalization and new forms of localisms, Portuguese folklore performance has become both reentrenched in localized community-building projects and, at the same time, operative within expansive networks of Portuguese migrants around the globe. The nation, once the primary referent for revivalist folklore performance, has been upstaged by the dialectical forces of globalization and localization.

My initial research question asked, How and why did revivalist folklore performance survive the downfall of fascism? Folklore performance constituted an important cornerstone of *Estado Novo* cultural policy and became so emblematic of the regime's image that many predicted *ranchos folclóricos'* total demise following the Revolution of 1974. Curiously, however, just the opposite occurred. Since 1974, the numbers of *rancho* performers and publics have increased "exponentially" (Branco, Neves, and Lima 2001).[2] What explains *ranchos folclóricos'* protean adaptation?

My research suggests that revivalist folklore does not serve the nation in the ways it once did. Portuguese revivalist folklore, once the face of the nation, now operates behind the scenes, on the margins of the nation—in the nooks and crannies of regional festivals inaugurated after 1974 to help local merchants connect with local clientele—in the social clubs of Portuguese emigrant communities in Newark, Paris, Johannesburg, and Hamburg, where Luso-descendants celebrate their heritage, mark their ethnic difference, and mobilize folklore to reproduce and recreate Bourdieu's habitus upon the shifting terrain of migratory settlement and "temporary lives" (Klimt 1992, 2000b). Portuguese revivalist folklore performance contributes to local community-building projects while catalyzing transnational contact among Portuguese emigrants around the globe. Fostering "communities of sentiment"—groups of geographically separate individuals and collectives who begin to "imagine and feel things together" (Appadurai 1996, 8)—folklore performance acts as a cultural cohesive for satellite communities throughout the Portuguese diaspora.

Going Glocal

In the late twentieth century, multinational corporations, global markets, information systems, and other intercontinental networks have linked geographical areas transnationally. Globalist discourse argues that the importance of the nation-state as the socioeconomic and political arbiter of place has been superseded by a powerful logic of transnationalism due to the interrelatedness of the world's political and economic systems (Wallerstein 1974, 1984) and increasingly global flows of capital, labor, and information (Castells 1989; Harvey 1989; Jameson 1991). According to some theorists, however, Marxist-inflected globalist discourse tends to proffer a totalizing narrative of "capital-centrism" (Escobar 1998), leaving little room for theorizing what if anything lies "outside" this contemporary order (Williams 1998) or for contemplating autonomous sites of struggle "that do not privilege the nation and are not necessarily defined by class consciousness" (Lowe and Lloyd 1997, 2). Much globalist discourse also tends to establish spatial binaries that essentialize the local as the domain of primitivism, nativism, women, indigenous people, popular culture, nature and pre-modern or anti-modern conditions.

In response, there has been an attempt to theorize place without re-inscribing the old essentialized notions of locality as bounded, isolated, timeless, feminized, and as independent from the influences of political-economic macro forces. By combining research into space and place, and apprehending the local through the prism of the global and vice versa, theorists have posited hybrid configurations such as "glocality" (Wilson and Dirlik 1995), unearthing a distinctly "global sense of place" (Massey 1994). By examining hybrid areas such as "global cities" (Sassen 1996), scholars articulate shifting late twentieth-century relationships of people to territory that is influenced *both* by grounded face-to-face encounters *and* by transnational flows of capital, media, resources, products, information, and populations. Central to these new ways of conceptualizing globalist place is an emphasis on the highly diversified and contested processes which comprise globalism (Sassen 1996, 138),[3] the irregularity that characterizes international capital, and the differentiating processes of advanced global capitalism that generate "significant sites of contradiction" (Lowe and Lloyd 1997, 2). New views of globalist place also theorize locality not as an inert, given category, but as a property of social life, tied to new processes of collective imagination that cross regional and national borders (Appadurai 1996).

The erosion of national borders giving way to an increasingly internationalist logic has been accompanied by a simultaneous and perhaps compensatory increase in expressions of localized belonging. In the context of European unification, as the European Community (EC) attempts to negotiate transnational cultural and economic coherence, this "global-local nexus" is particularly visible. The idea of a Europe without internal boundaries can create anxieties and a sense of cultural disorientation. "One response to these upheavals has been to find refuge in more localized senses of place and identity . . . [and] the flourishing of cultural regionalism and small nationalisms" (Morley and Robins 1995, 3). What this study examines is not what Bruce Robbins describes as the "romantic localism of a certain portion of the left, which feels it must counter capitalist globalization with a strongly rooted and exclusive sort of belonging" (1998, 3), but the complex dialectic between localism and transnationalism—a sense of spatial belonging which involves entrenchment in the particularities of place with an acute awareness of global associations, networks, and macro interdependencies (Rabinow 1986, 258). This book combines the nitty-gritty ethnographic analysis

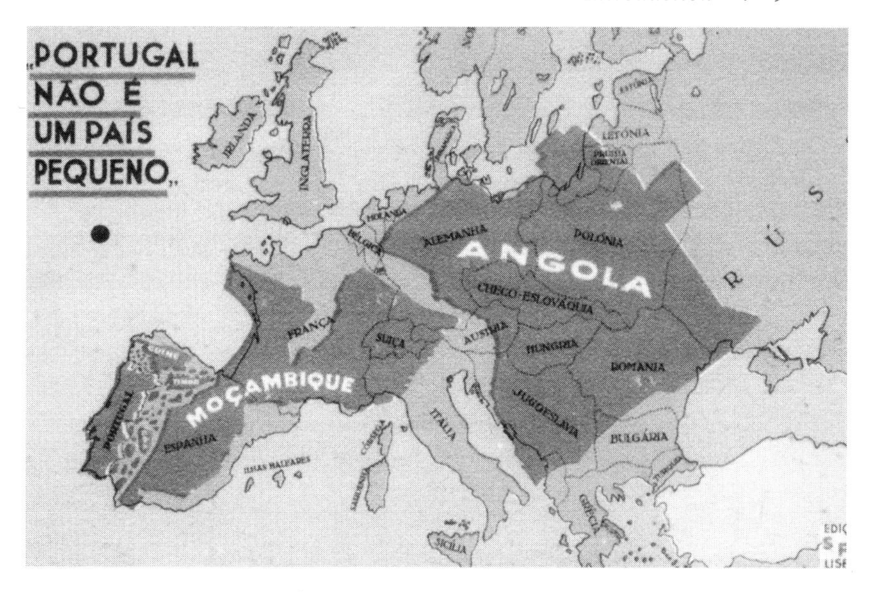

Figure 4. *"Portugal Não É Um País Pequeno"* (Portugal Is Not a Small Country). SPN map of Portugal postcard widely distributed during *Estado Novo*. *Collection of author.*

of *ranchos folclóricos* within the localities of Alenquer, Portugal, and Newark, New Jersey, with an examination of macro forces such as emigration, revolution, and European integration, in order to understand revivalist folklore performance as a "cosmopolitan" cultural form (Rabinow 1986, 258) that produces localized relationships even as it inheres within a global trajectory of Portuguese diaspora.

Portugal constitutes an extremely fertile arena for examining the dynamics of this global-local dialectic due to recent political upheavals that have set in motion a series of transnational contractions and expansions, producing a radical renegotiation of spatial identity. Portugal's global realignment began with the 1974 coup that ended forty-eight years of authoritarianism and some four hundred years of colonial rule, and continued with the 1986 integration into the EC. This dramatic upheaval meant not only a shift from authoritarianism to democracy, but also a dramatic change in socio-spatial identification.[4] Under fascism, Portugal was kept "gagged and bound" (Soares 1990) in a state of strict cultural and political isolation. At the same time, however, dictator António Salazar aggressively promoted the notion of Portugal as a vast multi-continental, pluri-racial nation-state, routinely feeding cartographic images of Portugal's impressive colonial span to Portuguese citizens (see fig. 4). Following the coup in 1974, Portugal's borders shrunk back to their medieval size, and its postcolonial reach moved away from Africa and toward a new "regionalizing Europeanism" (Cruz 1992, 153). These sea changes caused a complex renegotiation of identity, "whose motivation and expression have tended to be articulated in predominantly spatial terms" (Klobucka 2001, xii).

In a very short span of time, Portugal's social imaginary has been buffeted about between several different poles of transnational alignment. This violent shake-up has manifested itself in post-revolutionary literature—newly concerned with issues of history and politics (Kaufman and Klobucka 1997) and heavily reliant on spatial metaphors "to comment on the abrupt changes and discontinuities that have characterized recent Portuguese national experience" (Sapega 1997, 181). Revivalist folklore performance processed the post-revolutionary change in similar fashion. During the *Estado Novo* (1926–74), Salazar harnessed popular culture, particularly revivalist folklore, to policies of social control and national image management. Salazar essentially drained Portugal's "archive" of cultural forms by either driving out modernist innovators,[5] or co-opting traditional forms in the service of fascist ideology. Following 1974, many of the cultural forms controlled by Salazar were seen as tainted goods, inextricably linked to fascism and policies of cultural repression.[6] Popular culture practitioners were, therefore, forced to rehabilitate old forms in order to find a distinctly post-revolutionary voice. Not only have popular genres such as *fado* and revivalist folklore found new performers, expressive vocabularies, and audiences since 1974,[7] but they have plugged into new global circuits of spectatorship and practice. Like the literary authors of the 1980s and 1990s, *ranchos folclóricos* responded to Portugal's transformation in largely spatial terms.

Guided by newly formed cultural institutions such as the *Federação de Folclore Português* (Federation of Portuguese Folklore), many *ranchos folclóricos* replaced the "invented traditions" of fascist nationalism with more accurate historical recreations of songs and dances celebrating decidedly local spheres of reference. In the process of investigating local history, *rancho* performers forged networks of neighbors, friends, and families who together negotiate the unstable social landscape of the present. Following decades of political oppression, many *rancho* performers use ethnographic methodologies not only to build historically responsible repertoires, but also to exercise newly granted rights of civic and social freedom. Folklore can compel *rancho* members to knock on elderly strangers' doors, asking if they remember traditional songs from their childhood. Folklore can motivate *rancho* members to recruit wayward teenagers for youth groups in an attempt to ameliorate social ills perceived as the outgrowth of Portugal's newly found freedom. Folklore can spark the rekindling of local festivals, connecting newly privatized local businesses with folklore nonprofits in relationships of sponsorship and support. *Rancho* performers, publics, and consultants are key catalysts in building local communities according to the exigencies and opportunities of post-revolutionary Portugal.

Revivalist folklore's post-1974 localism, however, is also complemented by an increasingly transnational focus. As more *ranchos* were founded after 1974 and often competed for resources within the same locality, groups searched for ways to distinguish themselves from others. One strategy for increasing the prestige and cultural capital of a *rancho* was to clinch performance engagements as far from home as possible. Performances in distant provinces or, better yet, foreign festivals became an important marker of quality. Foreign engagements impact a *rancho*'s standing in its own community, sometimes facilitating increased funding from local governments and private beneficiaries. Post-revolutionary *ranchos* increasingly celebrate and promote local identity, and the further the reach of this celebration, the better for the home community. As I argue in chapter 4, the issues of travel and hospitality, both domestic and foreign, have become dominant features of *rancho* sociability and self-definition in post-revolutionary Portugal.

The procurement of international performance engagements is also tied into folklore's diasporic performanscape. The 1960s and 1970s witnessed a surge of Portuguese out-migration due to political instability, the colonial wars in Africa, and economic hardship. This "third wave" of Portuguese migration was primarily destined for northern Europe and secondarily to the northeastern United States (Baganha and Góis 1998; Brettell 2003; Mulcahy 2001). Third-wave emigrants, particularly those residing in northern Europe, returned home regularly in the summer months—revivalist folklore's high performance season. Folklore spectatorship in the context of local festivals became an important meeting point for emigrants to renew social bonds and reconnect with local customs and traditions. Pilgrimages home were also recreated on foreign soil, as emigrants began to organize heritage festivals in their adopted homelands, inviting domestic *ranchos* to perform for Portuguese enclaves in France, Germany (Klimt 2000a), Belgium (Santos 1996), and the United States (Holton 2002b), among other diasporic communities. The emerging *rancho* performanscape is composed of cultural collectives, bound by migratory experience and a shared ethnic identity, who interact across vast expanses of terrain. Unlike rock bands who perform in indistinguishable arenas and alight in interchangeable hotel chains throughout hundreds of anonymous cities, traveling *ranchos folclóricos* create a "diasporic public sphere" (Appadurai 1996), where foreign groups are often hosted in private residences and purposeful connectivity yields cultural reproduction, communication, and, sometimes, enduring social relationships.[8]

Diasporic public spheres are also created among *ranchos folclóricos* through the use of global media. After Portugal's political and economic landscape stabilized in the early eighties, out-migration diminished. This left communities of Portuguese emigrants, particularly in the United States,[9] without a fresh stream of foreign nationals to reconnect them to their homeland. It was during this period that many revivalist folklore groups in the United States began to build their own repertoires, costumes, and performance schedules. As conducting ethnographic research into nineteenth-century Portuguese traditions was impractical for emigrants living in the United States, many *ranchos* employed global media as the source for recreating historical songs and dances. Folklore performance reviews appear weekly in the Portuguese emigrant newspaper *LusoAmericano,* where *ranchos* from Newark, New Jersey, can read about groups in Hartford, Connecticut, and Fall River, Massachusetts. Folklore performers in Newark also report taping folklore programs aired on *Rádio Televisão Portuguesa Internacional* (RTPi) and recreating the dances based upon these video sources (B. Santos 2002; Cardoso 2003; Carvalho 1990). Some emigrant groups send performance "scouts" to Portugal to videotape live folklore festivals, order costumes from Portuguese seamstresses, and purchase antique agricultural tools for use onstage as props (B. Santos 2002). In this way, geographical distance is collapsed through the regular consumption of international media and continual travel—both real and imagined—among communities living in and outside of Portugal.

As I argue in chapter 3, the relationships between individuals and collectives bonded by the common practice of performing folklore often concretize into a web of cultural kinship. Global networks of cultural kin indeed foster a new kind of social imagination, as Appadurai suggests. This new type of collective imagination, "now central to all forms of agency, . . . itself a social fact, and . . . the key component of the new global order," is something which the increase in diasporic migration and the development of global media enables (Appadurai 1996, 31). Unlike the dynamic scholars such as Sarah Mahler (1995) document, where members of marginalized migrant groups obstruct one another's socioeconomic advancement due to competition for scant resources, the *rancho* performanscape, spread across vast expanses of terrain, sometimes morphing into cultural kinship systems through the employment of new media, can enable "diasporas of hope" to flourish through vitally imagined ties to a global collective and a sense of extended ethnic belonging.[10]

The concomitant emergence of globalization as a driving force behind the practice and reception of expressive culture worldwide and the specific sea changes in the Portuguese social imaginary produces a fertile landscape for the study of revivalist folklore. This book outlines revivalist folklore's protean adaptation to a dramatically transformed social and political environment, while examining *ranchos folclóricos'* local articulation and global connectivity. At the dawn of the twenty-first century, *ranchos folclóricos* act as barometers of social change. Through an examination of revivalist folklore's post-revolutionary rehabilitation, we can interrogate the legacy of fascism and the future of Portuguese democracy—a democracy which includes a third of its native-born population currently residing abroad. The examination of Portuguese revivalist folklore as a glocal phenomenon uncovers the interworkings of an emergent diasporic public sphere and new forms of post-fascist localism.

New Perspectives on Invented Tradition

Interwoven with an exploration of globalization's effects on popular culture, this book examines how "invented traditions," often analyzed top-down as the creation of nationalist ideologues, effect the grassroots performers and publics involved in the "invention." Hobsbawm and Ranger's (1983) seminal anthology outlined the conceptual parameters of a new and innovative approach to cultural history. Uncovering the relative newness of "ancient" traditions became key for many historians tracing the expressive roots of nation-building projects. Concomitant with the analysis of nations as "imagined communities" (Anderson 1991) came a new awareness of the constructed nature of national traditions presented as primordial, and the role that these constructs have played in commandeering a sense of shared history. The scholarly innovation sparked by Hobsbawm and Ranger has been largely focused on discovering expressive falsity, pinpointing historical artifice, and examining the ideological underpinnings of such performative productions.

Raphael Samuel calls for a push beyond these scholarly boundaries, claiming that historians have become too accustomed to analyzing "commemoration as a cheat, something which ruling elites impose on the subaltern classes . . . , a means of generating consensus . . . by reference to a mythologized version of the past." Samuel argues that by employing a more ethnographic approach, the invention of tradition can be seen as process rather than as event, thereby allowing scholars to "focus on the perceptions of the past which find expression in the discriminations of everyday life" (Samuel 1994, 16–17). Following Samuel, I am particularly interested in a bottom-up approach to invented tradition, examining the grassroots, "backstage" processes (Goffman 1959; Scott 1990) which inflect national commemorations and impact popular perceptions of a shared past. I am interested in the expressive agents involved in the invention—and how, outside of affirming official ideology, this enactment differently impacts the performers and their publics.

This book does *not* deliver the dramatic exposé of *ranchos folclóricos* as "fakelore," nor does it interrogate the degree to which Portuguese folklore performance represents an accurate reenactment of the past. Instead, *Performing Folklore* examines the indigenous criteria for distinguishing folkloric authenticity from fantasy and the historicized forces which have produced these distinctions. More important, though, this book analyzes the social processes behind the creation of what many term "invented tradition." I view revivalist folklore not as a phenomenon consigned to the realm of the symbolic, ideological, or aesthetic, but as a "productive force" in Raymond Williams's realignment of Marx's term—"a body of activities . . . grasped as they are; as real practices, elements of a whole material social process" (1977, 94).

Analyzing *ranchos folclóricos* as a productive force, imbricated in local and transnational processes of sociability, entrepreneurship, and cultural exchange, serves as a corrective to the conventional view of Portuguese folklore performance as a commemorative "cheat" tied up in fascist propaganda, historical inaccuracy, and just plain bad taste. The complex political and cultural stigmatizing of *ranchos folclóricos* by late twentieth-century critics has produced a general trend of scholarly inattention toward what is arguably the most widespread popular performance form in Portugal today.[11] Ambivalence toward folklore performance has characterized the attitudes of many scholars of the Left. Fernando Lopes Graça, a musicologist and composer whose compositions often included adaptations of traditional music, writes in 1953, for example,

> *Ranchos folclóricos* are springing up everywhere. The suppliers of repertoires of light music inundate the market with their "folkloric arrangements," radio programs sparkle in the "folkloric style," restaurants announce their "folkloric culinary specials," there are homemade folkloric furnishings and decoration. Finally, folklore has invaded everything. Folklore has become a mania, a sickness, a way of life. (1973 [1953], 21)

Lopes Graça's statement contains a thinly veiled critique of fascist cultural policy of the day and the suffocating effects it had on habits of cultural production and consumption. Another Portuguese composer, Luís de Freitas Branco, known as "the pioneer of Portuguese musical modernism" (Nery and Castro 1991, 157), writes negatively about Salazar's co-optation of folklore, in this instance with particular concern for the effects of fascist policy on the cultural education of the rural underclass. In 1943, Freitas Branco writes,

> I say here very much in secret that the great length of time I have spent in this country makes me more and more detest popular song and village festivals. . . . All this reminds me of the animal inferiority in which these unfortunate people are kept without their being aware of it, and it arouses in me together with a repulsion for folklore the desire to urge them to more and more truly beautiful and artistic manifestations. Meanwhile as the provinces always copy the Lisbon fashion, the rich boys of the countryside . . . whose parents fifty years ago dressed in Lisbon style and asked about the artist of São Carlos, now, on the merest festive pretext masquerade as harvesters, ox-cart drivers or shepherds and make speeches and greetings in a virtuous and religious language that the true Alentejo workers haven't used for a century and a half. (Unpublished letter quoted in Nery and Castro 1991, 159–60)

Toward the end of the *Estado Novo,* scholarly reflections on folklore performance presented yet another angle of critique. In 1970, anthropologist Jorge Dias condemns folklore performance according to empirical concerns for authenticity: "Where nothing of the past remained, some *rancho* leaders would themselves invent a repertoire, starting with fantastical costumes to music and dance. They started performing in folkloric parades, contests, national and international exhibits, and little by little, even the best groups lost their sense of truth and purity" (1970, 11–12).[12] The attitudes toward *ranchos folclóricos* exhibited in the passages above endure to some extent today, despite Portugal's dramatically changed political and social environment. As some scholars such as Salwa Castelo Branco and Jorge Freitas Branco (2003) contend, however, it is precisely *ranchos'* charged history of political involvement that makes the groups such a rich object of study.

Due to the stigma of fascism and invented tradition, *ranchos folclóricos* have been excluded from several high-profile national festivals of the 1990s, as outlined in chapter 5. The exclusion of *ranchos folclóricos* from select manifestations of "official culture," however, has accompanied the development of alternative circuits of performance forums, including the inter-regional exchanges analyzed in chapter 4 and the emigrant performanscapes analyzed in chapter 6. I would argue that the stigma of "invented tradition" has motivated *ranchos'* aesthetic metamorphosis while broadening their geographic horizons, and only through the careful ethnographic investigation of revivalist folklore as social process rather than symbolic event can these post-revolutionary transformations be grasped in all their richness and complexity.

Historical Background

Ethnomusicologist Salwa Castelo Branco defines *ranchos folclóricos* as

> non-professional instrumentalists, singers, dancers ideally representing on stage, or in other settings outside of the original context, revivals of the music, dance, and costume traditions of their region or specific locale, as they were thought to have existed in the beginning of the century. Representations of *ranchos folclóricos* range from those adhering closely to local traditions, to those presenting new interpretations thereof, or new products inspired therein. (1991, 97)

Recent scholarship concerning the history of Portuguese folklore performance documents the appearance of amateur troupes conforming to the definition above as early as 1850 (Branco 2003a; Branco and Branco 2003). In celebration of the First Fair of Funchal in Madeira, for example, the *Hercúleos Filhos de São Martinho,* comprised of "13 peasants . . . dressed in costumes particular to their country, performed a dance from Madeira called 'A la moda' " (quoted in Branco 2003a, 447–48). The *Pauliteiros da Miranda do Douro,* another troupe dedicated to the performance of popular music and dance, traveled to Lisbon in 1898 to celebrate the anniversary of Vasco da Gama's arrival in India (Mourinho 1983; Branco and Branco 2003). Once thought of as a twentieth-century phenomenon, explicitly staged folklore performance, according to new research, clearly emerges out of the last half of the nineteenth century.

Late nineteenth-century revivalist folklore performance can be linked to literary romanticism (Branco and Toscana 1988), as well as the larger fin de siècle trend across Western Europe involving the intense search for national roots among peasant populations. Portuguese bourgeois society attributed an authenticity to popular culture that they found absent from their own core (J. Cabral 1991b, 15), while "intellectuals all over Europe tended to regard peasants in particular as 'the nation's most adequate representatives' on the grounds that the peasants were the least contaminated by foreign influences and the most in touch with the nation's distant past" (Burke 1992, 297).

Ethnology, associated at that time in both academic and literary circles with the search for national authenticity, allowed bourgeois society to access popular tradition (J. Cabral 1991b, 17). Writing in 1883, ethnographer J. Leite de Vasconcellos, for example, makes an impassioned case for the ethnographic study of folklore and its relevance to the nation:

> At first glance, folklore appears to be destitute of importance, the exclusive property of rough and ignorant spirits. However, the scientific study of popular

> tradition is important . . . because it demonstrates the ways in which society lives . . . Neither the historian nor the psychiatrist can claim to know his country without first having researched its peasant population . . . [they are] an embryo developing . . . and represent one of the most important forces of the nation. (1986 [1883])

In the decades that followed Leite de Vasconcellos's appeal, ethnographic research into and documentation of popular tradition resulted not only in an outpouring of scholarly manuscripts, but also in the constitution of folklore performance groups by "local erudites, folklore enthusiasts, community leaders and tradition carriers" (Branco 2000, 31), aiming to preserve or revive popular music and dance.

Anthropologist João Leal argues that in its development from 1870 to 1970, Portuguese ethnography has sustained a primary interest in popular culture, "monumentalizing" the material and expressive symbols of the rural peasantry to create a national imaginary that "turns the inhabitants of Portugal into Portuguese" (2000, 16). Leal characterizes Portuguese anthropology as participating, above all else, in an "ethnogeneological" discourse of national identity. Following Anthony Smith's (1993) definition, Leal argues that this approach construes "the nation as a community of descendants, underscoring the role of vernacular culture, language, and popular customs in its definition . . . counting anthropologists, ethnographers and folklorists as its 'organic intellectuals'" (2000, 17). It is interesting to note that the temporal boundaries of Leal's study, 1870–1970, cut across a historical period characterized by substantive political and social shifts. Despite such changes, Leal and others (Branco and Branco 2003) argue for a model of continuity regarding popular culture's importance to national identity and its relationship to the practice of ethnography, the academic researchers who have served as its foot soldiers, and the performance troupes it has inspired.

Following its early history, folklore performance became institutionalized during the 1930s as the *Estado Novo* strategized the ruralization of Portugal's image through the Most Portuguese Village Contest, among other initiatives. Chapter 1 examines in depth the uses to which folklore was put and the ways in which dictator António Salazar harnessed popular culture to corporatist ideology. During the 1950s, *ranchos folclóricos* enjoyed an initial "golden age," part and parcel of the burgeoning folklore movement which emerged out of *Estado Novo* cultural policy, sparking the proliferation of performance troupes throughout the country.

Following the Revolution of April 25, 1974, which signaled the end of the *Estado Novo*, some *ranchos folclóricos* disbanded for a short period during the change in regime. Generally, though, revivalist folklore performance not only weathered the change but began gaining force in democratic Portugal, as the number of *ranchos folclóricos* surged to 3,000, today occupying the energies of over 100,000 Portuguese performers of all ages (Branco, Neves, and Lima 2001). The subject of some scholarly disagreement, however, is whether the 1974 Revolution catalyzed a rupture in the content and practice of *ranchos folclóricos.* Chapter 2 outlines the contours of this debate, providing a case study of the effects of the Revolution on the *Rancho Folclórico de Alenquer,* a group founded in 1959 in the Estremadura region of Portugal.

Generally, my ethnographic research points to a shift not only in the master frame which orients *rancho* practice—from a national to a local/transnational frame—but also a substantive transformation of costume and repertoire following the post-revolutionary reforms put in motion by the *Federação de Folclore Português* (Federation of Portuguese Folklore) throughout the 1980s and 1990s. Although my research reveals a shift in *rancho* orientation and practice following 1974, it is difficult to say whether the FFP exerted the same kind of influence in other parts of Portugal, and whether the changes mandated were as dramatic. Such a sweeping study is beyond the scope of this project but constitutes an important vector of inquiry for further pursuit.

Folklore performance, an activity which has accompanied the development of Portuguese anthropology as a discipline, has participated during its first century of existence in nation-building projects spawned from differing ideological matrices. This book focuses on revivalist folklore's more recent evolution, starting with its institutionalization in the 1930s, its movement through the 1974 Revolution, to its present incarnation within local Portuguese celebrations of commerce and sociability and transnational projects of emigrant cohesion and acculturation.

Methodological Considerations

The genesis of this project can be traced back to an ornate, darkly stained table in a working-class neighborhood of East Providence, Rhode Island, where on Thanksgiving Day my grandfather would belt out Portuguese *fado* while carving the requisite turkey. Leaning on vowel sounds until I thought they would shatter, my grandfather's voice ran up and down the scale, pushing melodies into near weeping. On these occasions my sister would often lean over and whisper, "Why do our Thanksgivings have to be so sad, with all this lamenting, all this *fado*?" The fact of the matter was that our Thanksgivings were different from those families who didn't have recordings of Amália Rodrigues wafting out over heaping plates of grilled *chouriço* (savory sausage). The pilgrim's turkey was always a nod to American tradition, the hurry-up course wedged between *caldo verde* (kale soup) and *arroz doce* (rice pudding). My fascination with Portuguese popular music began at the heavy table in my grandparents dining room not far from a piano where my grandfather would plunk out the tunes from his youth in Beira Alta, proving to us that Portugal had "happy music too." It was these childhood get-togethers that inspired my interest in the culturally coded sounds of celebration and sparked my scholarly foray into performed manifestations of national and ethnic difference.

Many decades later as I started my fieldwork, I often announced my Luso-American heritage, as a way of breaking the ice and explaining my interest in Portuguese folklore performance. After describing the lineage—the family of my maternal grandmother from São Miguel and grandfather from Beira Alta—I would wait for nods of recognition and solidarity, which, in the beginning, sometimes came and sometimes didn't. As I spent more time with folklore performers in the Estremadura region, and my personal relationships deepened, I realized what a charged symbol the Portuguese emigrant was (see, for example, Brettell 1993b) and the way in which I, the granddaughter of Portuguese emigrants, sparked a set of preconceived notions about what happened on the distant and somewhat suspect shores of the northeastern United States when scores of Portuguese arrived throughout the nineteenth and twentieth centuries in search of better lives.

Joel Serrão analyzes Portuguese emigration, as a "persistent phenomenon," a "national drama" (1977, 22–23), and a constitutive feature of Portuguese culture, dating back to the colonization of Madeira in 1425 (1970). Maria Baganha and Pedro Góis argue that since 1425, emigration has become "progressively integrated into the mentality of the Portuguese . . . who have developed value systems to support this way of life" (1998, 231). Even though emigration has evolved into a self-perpetuating social phenomenon over centuries of departures and returns, and one-third of Portugal's population currently lives and works abroad, the emigrant is a polyvocal symbol that sometimes carries a negative valence within the borders of Portugal. As I argue in chapter 6, emigration's stigma is partly formed by state policies and ideologies. Other scholars attribute emigration's negative charge to widespread *inveja* (envy) among those left at home (Cole 1991; Brettell 1995). The stereotypical portrait of the twentieth-century emigrant is someone who leaves Portugal with little formal education, strikes it rich elsewhere, returns to Portugal to build a large retirement home of dubious architectural and aesthetic integrity, and, after resettling in Portugal, is visited annually by younger generations of Luso-descendants who speak pidgin Portuguese and demonstrate poor training in Portuguese customs and values.[13]

It is this stereotype which sometimes entered my relationships during fieldwork, and which became the occasion for rich discussions of national difference and ethnic identity. After several years in the field, the context of friendship became the backdrop to a playful process of redressing Portuguese education gone awry in the United States. Throughout my fieldwork, I accepted periodic lessons in customs which, "perhaps her grandparents forgot to teach her"—peeling fruit in one long scroll, asking favors without asking, swaddling infants in intricate wraps, accepting food only on the third insistence, and, of course, dancing folklore.[14] With a nod to recent feminist scholarship that challenges fixed dichotomies between insider/outsider and native/non-native ethnographers (Narayan 1993; Abu-Lughod 1988; Cole 1995), I view my perceived "imperfect" Portuguese-American enculturation as an important driving force behind my relationships in the field, something that, in the words of Victor Turner (1986), "put experience into circulation." The push and pull on either side of the hyphen, a battle for cultural dominance which consistently ghosts debates surrounding the Portuguese-American emigrant, has constituted a felicitous "enactment of hybridity" (Narayan 1993) throughout the course of my project—an enactment which characterizes both my research methods and the ensuing ethnographic text.

Drawing on the fruits of extended periods of fieldwork in Lisbon, Alenquer, and Belas, Portugal, and Newark, New Jersey, this book constitutes a "multi-locale ethnography" (Marcus 1989, 1992; Marcus and Fischer 1986). The fieldwork in Portugal took place during the summers of 1993, 2001, 2002 and throughout twelve months between 1994–96. During initial periods of research in Portugal, I attended rehearsals and performances of the *Rancho Folçlórico de Alenquer, Grupo Folclórico de Belas, Rancho Folclórico da Casa do Povo da Golegã,* and the *Rancho Folclórico de Ceifeiras e Campinos da Azambuja* and conducted informal interviews with the leaders of the *Rancho Folclórico "As Lavadeiras" do Sabugo* and the *Grupo Folclórico "Os Saloios" da Póvoa da Galega.*[15] I decided on the Estremadura region, the home to all but one of these groups, because, it had been historically, overlooked by scholars of folklore, cultural anthropology, and ethnomusicology due to its association with Lisbon and the academic bias against researching urban and suburban areas of demographic flux and cultural change (Branco 2000; Brettell 1993a; Santos 1994). Estremadura also has a history of ambiguity with regard to regional identity (J. Cabral 1991b) which presented intriguing challenges to the post-revolutionary *rancho* practice of "purifying" repertoires according to region. I also chose Estremadura to measure the effects of Lisbon 94 on cultural production within neighboring suburban and rural areas, and to conduct concomitant research on Lisbon 94 programming and promotion.

By 1995, I had focused my ethnographic research solely on the *Rancho Folclórico de Alenquer* (RFA), located in the town of Alenquer, forty kilometers northeast of Lisbon, due to the longevity of the group, the personal rapport I had with its members, and the fact that RFA is one of the few troupes in the region founded during the *Estado Novo.* As a performance studies scholar trained in ethnographic methodologies, I focused my fieldwork on weekly rehearsals, performances, administrative meetings, social gatherings, festival preparations, and other more informal RFA functions. Toward the end of 1996, I conducted lengthy ethnographic interviews with twenty-eight of RFA's thirty-one members, periodically re-interviewing RFA leaders on subsequent research trips.[16] Thirty RFA members also filled out formal questionnaires pertaining to job, income, family composition, and history of *rancho* membership. In addition to work with RFA, I also spent several weeks in 1994 and 1996 interviewing FFP president Augusto Gomes dos Santos and conducting research at the FFP archives in Vila Nova de Gaia.

My ethnographic fieldwork in northern New Jersey began in 2000 and has continued into the present. In addition to participant observation of numerous New Jersey *rancho* rehearsals and performances, I have conducted ethnographic interviews with folklore dancers, musicians, directors, and festival organizers primarily drawn from the *Sonhos de Portugal rancho* of Kearny, New Jersey, and the *Danças e Cantares de Portugal rancho* of Elizabeth, New Jersey. The Newark portion of this project is also informed by research at the Rutgers University–Newark archive of the Ironbound Oral History Project,[17] a store of primary audio, visual, and textual documents containing over one hundred and fifty interview transcripts with Portuguese-speaking immigrants of northern New Jersey.

Throughout this text, I have cited excerpts from ethnographic and oral history interviews as I would any other document, including them in alphabetical order in the works cited list. All of the interviews in Portugal were conducted in Portuguese. When citing short excerpts from these interviews, I have included the original Portuguese first, followed by my translation. For the longer block quotations, I have only used the English translation in the interest of space and readability.

Combining archival research, ethnographic participant-observation, and oral history, the methods used to research this book reflect my commitment to interdisciplinarity and the "nesting" of macro and micro approaches (Marcus 1989). In addition to the field sites enumerated above, much of what I learned about revivalist folklore occurred around strangely familiar dark, heavy tables amid a tumble of accordions, guitars, *caldo verde,* and coffee, where *rancho* performers spoke of music and memory, folklore and festivity.

Ranchos folclóricos, groups of amateur musicians and dancers who perform turn-of-the-century popular tradition, have acted as cultural barometers of change throughout twentieth-century Portugal. The project of this book is to unearth and interpret how macro changes have marked the performance practices of *ranchos folclóricos* from 1926 to the present, and how performers, in turn, have processed, adapted to, and/or contested these markings. *Performing Folklore* embraces "invented tradition" as process rather than event, presenting an ethnography not only of folkloric revivalism, but also of sweeping cultural transformation powered alternately by the motors of authoritarianism, democracy, emigration, and European unification.

1 

Choreographing the Spirit: Fascism, Folklorization, and Everyday Resistance

Throughout the 1930s, as post–World War I Europe witnessed rising social instability brought on by intensifying industrialization, unemployment, and economic crisis, political leaders sought solutions to social unrest. The idea that popular culture and the management of leisure time held the potential to defuse social problems while softening the blow of unemployment became a unifying theme in international meetings across Western Europe in the 1930s and 1940s. At the 1936 International Congress of Leisure and Recreation, for example, an Austrian participant stated, "Popular culture with its spirit of collective community-based creativity, is the natural base for the organization of leisure" (Winkler-Hermaden 1936, 41). In the early forties, the Vichy government hailed folklore as the "official culture of France" and the "only solution for the depraved practices of the popular urban classes and young people" (Valente 1999, 176). Even within democratic countries such as England, folklore became the foundation for state initiatives destined to help "peasants, miners and students, saving them from perdition" (Valente 1999, 175).

European leaders became increasingly attentive to the issue of leisure time management, as the workweek diminished from 70 to 75 hours in the nineteenth century to 40 to 45 hours in the twentieth. With this shift, workers enjoyed an unprecedented increase in free time. Theories popularized at the turn of the century linked worker satisfaction ("joy in work"), productivity, and workplace harmony to the effective use of leisure time.[1] Helping workers manage their free time also piqued the interest of European governments due to the fact that the truncated workweek became an effective means for "absorbing the enormous volume of unemployment that ravaged the Western World" during the 1930s (Valente 1999, 17).[2] The "Joy in Work" movement found an ultranationalist incarnation in the totalitarian governments of Nazi Germany and Mussolini's Italy. Both the German *Kraft durch Freude* movement and the Italian *Opera Nazionale Dopolavoro* provided influential models for Portugal's *Fundação Nacional para a Alegria no Trabalho*—FNAT (National Foundation for the Joy in Work).

Founded in 1935 during the *Estado Novo*'s early period of cultural policy creation, FNAT coordinated recreational activities at the national level, creating large-scale *colónias de férias* (subsidized vacation resorts), *refeitórios económicos* (subsidized cafeteria lunches for workers), seaside camps for children, gymnastics classes for men and women, radio programs, a Worker's Theater, the National Workers Museum, among many other initiatives. Through its *Gabinete de Etnografia* (Ethnography Office), FNAT also conducted research in the form of questionnaires and surveys distributed throughout Portugal's rural populations. In tandem with research into the lifestyle, expressive traditions, and material culture of the countryside, FNAT's *Gabinete de Etnografia* also attempted to oversee and orient folklore performance troupes throughout Portugal.

FNAT's official mission was to "help Portuguese workers utilize leisure time to better their physical, intellectual and moral development" (Kuin 1994). The creation of FNAT reflected Salazarism's totalizing project, which aimed to impose a unified conception of "all levels of civil society—within the workplace, the family, education, culture, and, finally, leisure and recreation—according to nationalist, corporative and Christian imperatives" (Valente 1999, 41). In addition to the mass "spiritualization" of workers through sport, culture, and repose, FNAT dressed ideological indoctrination in the garb of cultural dynamism. Early on in its development, FNAT offered workers adult education classes which contained overt *Estado Novo* propaganda, aimed at neutralizing the threat of communism and providing an ideological barrier between Portugal and Spain, then engulfed in civil war. Employing a politics of surveillance and a geographic fixing of the labor force, FNAT closely monitored associative activity, defusing any event that threatened to mobilize political action (Kuin 1994).

Beginning in the early 1940s, *ranchos folclóricos* operated within both local and national frameworks of institutional influence. Initiatives geared toward the standardization and regulation of rehearsal and performance practices occurred nationally, through FNAT, the *Junta Central das Casas do Povo* (JCCP [Central Council for the Houses of the People]), and the *Secretariado de Propaganda Nacional* (SPN/SNI [Secretariate for National Propaganda/Information]),[3] and locally within *casas do povo* (houses of the people), *centros de recreio popular* (popular recreation centers), and *centros de alegria no trabalho* (joy in work centers).

Casas do povo, decreed into being by the 1933 constitution, quickly evolved into the most vital localized outposts of corporative cultural activity, serving as the platform for *Estado Novo* cultural policies (Melo 2001, 18). Replacing the old rural unions, *casas do povo* were denied any representative function and were frequently controlled by powerful local landowners. Initially designed to provide social assistance, relief services, and community improvement, the *casa do povo*'s main function was to direct and monitor the leisure activities of the rural working class. By offering regular screenings of the *Cinema Ambulante,* productions of the *Teatro do Povo,* and libraries replete with propagandistic texts, António Ferro, cultural policy mastermind and director of SPN, envisioned the *casa do povo* as

> the village center for popular corporative education, a place where rural laborers and country folk can gather after a hard day's work, participating in innocent games, theatrical performances, and choral groups. *Casas do Povo* will facilitate our spiritual rebirth as they become centers of folklore. Folklore, the soul of the people with its songs, dances, rural costumes and traditions, will be constantly aflame. (Ferro 1982, 262)

Punctuated with the rhetoric of social Catholicism, Ferro describes *casas do povo* as spaces for the ideologically infused enjoyment of leisure time, where target activities revolving around the restoration and performance of folklore would keep participants under the watchful eye of local leaders and cultural collectives while the natural beauty and "innocence" of tradition illuminated the path toward moral salvation.

Popular culture, in all of its formal manifestations and expressions, comprised the cornerstone of dictator António Oliveira Salazar's plans for a national culture throughout the *Estado Novo.* Salazar tied the celebration of popular culture to long-term governmental initiatives which cloaked ideological indoctrination in the neutral garb of cultural enrichment. The *Estado Novo*'s ideological foundation was built upon sedimented sociocultural realities rather than revolutionary overhaul, with Catholicism, nationalism, and traditional ruralism comprising the three pillars of Salazarist doctrine (Silva 1991; Melo 2001). Popular culture became the grist for fashioning Portugal's national identity, and, as both fixed symbol and lived activity, the key to social harmony, political stability, and collective moral rectitude.

Salazar and António Ferro focused their attention on two major areas of cultural production and consumption, which can be characterized as "intellectual" and "popular" spheres of activity.[4] Within the intellectual sphere, an emphasis was placed on the restoration of historical architecture and monuments,[5] the creation of large-scale international festivals, and the development of other exportable spectacles, exhibitions, and professional troupes.

Figure 5. Exposição Mundial 1940, Popular Life Pavilion, Lisbon. Revolving disc with movable figurines designed by João Tomé. *Courtesy of Livros Horizonte. Reprinted from* Margarida *Acciaiuoli, Exposiçoes do Estado Novo, 1998, 170.*

Combining the celebration of Portugal's "glory days" (the golden age of the discoveries) with the "convocation of the pre-industrial past," Salazarist ideology depended upon the idiosyncratic blending of two strains of "non-contemporaenity" (Melo 2001, 37). Cultural dramatizations of Portugal's peasant past mingled with allusions to her navigational triumphs in many large-scale spectacles, where the syncretic blending of popular culture and modernist aesthetics formed a new symbolic lexicon. Both the *Verde Gaio* national ballet troupe and Portugal's 1940 World Exhibition bore António Ferro's unmistakable signature; folkloric elements such as regional costumes, rural tools, terra cotta figurines, and turn-of-the-century songs and dances were reassembled using modernist principles of composition and geometric visual economy (see fig. 5). These smartly presented folkloric adaptations always carried an ideological charge, bringing the virtues of the countryside into the potentially corrupted space of the city while transposing popular cultural vocabularies into more sophisticated visual and aural idioms for consumption by the urban elite.[6]

Within the "popular" sphere of activity, the primary focus of this chapter, rural tradition played an even greater role in the communication and realization of Salazar's political and social doctrine. The process of "folklorization"[7] constituted a marked feature of the *Estado Novo* period, and in the late 1930s, as revivalist folklore performance became institutionalized and "endowed with the mechanisms of production and regulation," *ranchos folclóricos* began to appear in increasing numbers (Branco and Branco 2003). Although revivalist folklore troupes existed as early as the mid-nineteenth century, their widespread proliferation occurred throughout the *Estado Novo* in direct response to cultural initiatives such as the Most Portuguese Village Contest of 1938 and as a result of Salazar's corporatist social engineering. *Ranchos folclóricos* came to serve significant functions under Salazar. Folklore performance kept the rural masses in a constant state of festivity while spinning a national image of Portugal as a rural paradise stopped in time.

This chapter exposes the many different forms folkloric performance assumed in order to teach Salazarist principles of social conciliation, defuse political mobilization, and express national identity during the *Estado Novo* period. The chronological trajectory which drives the subsequent chapters will draw on this historical foundation to measure the extent to which the twentieth-century folklore movement can be construed as a practice characterized by continuity and/or rupture. By understanding how and why the *Estado Novo* placed folklore at the center of Portugal's nation-building endeavors and at the service of Salazar's plans for ideological indoctrination, we can better understand the protean adaptation of *ranchos folclóricos* following the regime's collapse in 1974.

This chapter also examines the extent to which Salazarist corporative and propagandistic initiatives took hold at the ground level. Did the *Estado Novo*'s totalizing ambitions in the cultural sphere leave any room for individual creation? Or did Salazar's drive to eradicate the individual for the good of the collective render personal creativity and resistance impossible? Were *rancho* performers simply the vehicle for indoctrinating and distracting Portugal's rural masses while spinning the *Estado Novo*'s target image to those at home and abroad? Or did they serve their communities and themselves in alternative ways? Did *rancho* members comply with FNAT's regulation of folklore practice, or was there intended or inadvertent resistance? Employing ethnographic data gleaned from fieldwork and interviews with the oldest members of the *Rancho Folclórico de Alenquer* (RFA), a group whose lineage dates back to the 1930s, I suggest a broader reading of folklore performance during the *Estado Novo*—one where individual creativity can be glimpsed in the slippage between invented tradition and historical restoration, allowing individuals the opportunity to exhibit virtuoso "shows of strength." This reading hovers along the cleavages and inconsistencies of the *Estado Novo*'s totalizing reach, positing ethnographic research, encouraged by FNAT in order for folklore groups to build repertoire, as an "everyday act of resistance" (Scott 1990), where unsupervised sociability led to an intimate politics of proxemics, and folklore performers and informants mined personal memories, placing the "people's cultural history" (Hall 1981) in the service of individual, autonomous creativity.

Corporatist Ideology, Political Immobilization, and Spatial Tactics

Termed "the ideological combat weapon of the *Estado Novo*" (Paulo 1994, 36), Salazar's unique brand of corporatism has captured the interest of political scientists and historians for several decades (Lucena 1979; Wiarda 1977; Schmitter 1975; Figueiredo 1976; Riegelhaupt 1979, 1967, 1964; Pinto 1995; Martins 1990; and Paulo 1994). Phillip Schmitter offers an aggregate definition of Salazar's corporatism, explaining it as a system of interest representation

> whose constituent structures and interdependent relations differ markedly, if not diametrically, from those of pluralism . . . [and] in which the constituent units are organized into a limited number of singular, compulsory, non-competitive, hierarchically ordered and functionally differentiated categories, recognized or licensed . . . by the state and granted a deliberate representational monopoly within their respective categories in exchange for observing certain controls on their selection of leaders and articulation of demands and supports. (1975, 8–9)

Within this system, the breaking down of social groups into their smallest constitutive bundles was part and parcel of dissipating political power. Joyce Riegelhaupt's ethnographic study of a peasant community in the Saloio region during the 1950s reveals the link between small corporatist units of association and political disempowerment (1964, 1967, 1979). Labor unions and rural associations, ostensibly organized at the local level to represent the interests of the working class, were powerless due to structural inequalities which favored the interests of the economic and political elite and the inability of these isolated local units to mobilize across expansive geographic terrain.[8] Unlike Nazism, Salazarist corporatism opposed mass popular movements. Salazar once stated, "we need neither fawn on the working classes to get their backing, nor provoke their ire only to have them later shot for their excesses" (in Pinto 1995, 178). This ideological belief derives in part from Salazar's personal predilections and leadership style. Unlike Mussolini or Hitler, who Salazar once noted, "like to live an intense, frenetic life," Portugal's dictator maintained an understated public persona—he was "conservative to the core," always preaching the virtues of religion, rurality, routine, modesty, humility and simplicity. Aiming to avoid inspiring "sacred hate toward our enemies" and political agitation, Salazar stated: "I want to normalize the nation. I want to make Portugal live habitually" (in Lucena 1979, 58).

Living habitually meant defusing or preempting mass political action across national terrain by controlling the lives of the Portuguese working class through strategies of socio-spatial containment and by organizing regular cultural activities for apolitical distraction and "spiritual" nourishment. Salazarism exploited the moral controls and the forces of habit that preceded his rule. Riding the coattails of the pervasive Catholic order, Salazarism counted on the self-censorship and auto-repression that had been "plainly established by the so-called social doctrine of the Church" (Carvalho 1995, 107). Salazarism also relied upon the individual family, as both an ecclesiastic and social unit, to become the foundational building block of his disciplined, conflict-free nation. Salazarism utilized concentric circles of socio-spatial control to insure that within domestic households, parents would discipline children; within neighborhood churches, local priests would discipline parishioners; and within the abstract space of the nation, the paternalist dictator would discipline his citizens. Salazar's national corporatist family depended on thousands upon thousands of Portuguese families for its survival. Dividing the country into diminutive familial units paradoxically insured national unity. The neutralization of political dissent through the maintenance of Catholic social doctrine and through spatial fragmentation promoted a silenced but unified national polity.

Moisés de Lemos Martins analyzes the technology of *Estado Novo* patriotism and asserts that corporatist discipline is filtered through localized edification and "cellular division" of familial and corporatist space. Salazar's social control depended on strategic, well-placed "localization of individuals"; his was a regime obsessed with the minuscule, with "the details of the national body" (1990, 177–79), not with the expansive sweep of mass action. Jorge Ramos do Ó refers to Salazar's strategy of demobilization as the "paralyzing of sociability"; the *Estado Novo* severed "the individual from that dangerous area of citizenship and enclosed him in spheres of restricted public opinion, in fragmented units without the possibility of influencing the direction or production of political reality" (1992, 393).

In the above passages both Ramos do Ó and Martins employ spatial terminology to describe Salazar's strategies—"localization," "area," "fragmented units," "enclosed spheres." They characterize Salazar's demobilization of the Portuguese lower class as discursive, social, and political tactics, but not, oddly enough, as *spatial strategy*. During the *Estado Novo*, I would argue, the dialectical maneuvering between fragmentation and unification was a decidedly spatial practice, a practice essential to Salazar's implementation of corporatist education and discipline. Salazar pursued the strict division of geographic space, and the ideological and representational unification of these divisions simultaneously. Satisfying the criteria for the implementation of what Robert Sack (1986) terms "territoriality," Salazar classified geographic and social space, communicated this classification through cartography, and enforced power over area through the construction of social institutions such as *casas do povo,* and through the crafty manipulation of popular culture.

The development of an official national culture became an important means for bonding these spatial fragments, or "cells," together. Influenced by Mussolini's co-optation of culture to elevate the spirit while establishing positive identification with the dictatorship, António Ferro masterminded the *Estado Novo*'s cultural policy, coined *Política do Espírito* (Politics of the Spirit) in 1933. Catalyzing, adapting, and producing folkloric performance and display became an important feature of Ferro's policy. Unlike Salazar's initial desire to concentrate the nation's cultural efforts on the restoration of historical architecture and museum relics, Ferro felt the Portuguese people were in desperate need of artistic animation and expressive outlets. "It's ridiculous to give a man an overcoat when he has no shirt," Ferro quips. "We are a nostalgic people who need music, who need joy, who need human sympathy . . . to shake off our pessimism, our native sadness" (1982, 120–23).[9] In Ferro's view, the best way to fight the Portuguese "passivity," "coldness," and "melancholy" was to develop cultural initiatives for the public expression of nationalist fervor.

Promoting the formation and maintenance of *ranchos folclóricos* during the *Estado Novo* not only served to keep the masses in a constant state of festivity, it also provided the symbolic fodder for nation-building and external propagandizing. Following Mussolini, Ferro recognized the enormous influence organized culture, particularly expressive culture, had on national image construction. Culture, he asserted, is "the great showpiece of a nation, that which can be seen from abroad" (1982, 122). Although Ferro had a personal affinity for modernist aesthetics, he believed that folklore better emblematized the people and ideologies of corporatist Portugal. Like other cultural strategists in Mussolini's Italy, Nazi Germany, and authoritarian regimes throughout Latin America, Ferro recognized folklore's potential for expressing the "the joy of ideas when marched, the joy of ideas when sung" (Rodrigues 1987, xxiii). Colombian playwright and theorist Enrique Buenaventura speaks of folkloric spectacle as "just another trick of the system" (1970, 154). Analyzing Nazi Germany, Dan Ben-Amos argues that folklore and fascism had similar motivating ideas—that of nationalism and primitivism, the idealization of the peasantry, and an avowed interest in community building and the intricacies of expressive representation (1994, x).

Confronting the divergent tasks of building a unified national community and creating a symbolic lexicon for national representation, Salazar and his cultural advisors drew heavily on folkloric forms to meet both challenges. As several recent works argue (Melo 2001; Branco and Branco 2003; Valente 1999), the political demobilization of the urban working class and the erasure of its expressive traditions coincided with the elevation of rural signs, symbols, and practices under Salazar. "Folklorizing initiatives featuring rural and religious contents came to fill in symbolic spaces which had previously been occupied by the labor movement" (Branco and Branco 2003, 11). The larger folklorization of the Portuguese nation also included the reinvigoration of agrarian traditions such as pig killings and other harvest rites, craft-making, local parades, and popular choral singing. *Estado Novo* leaders also established "musical folklore" as a primary expressive outlet for the *Mocidade Portuguesa* (MP [Portuguese Youth]), among other high-profile collectives. Transforming folkloric choral music into a "political language," MP leaders viewed performed folklore as a vehicle for engendering nationalist sentiment within Portugal's youth while disciplining such expressions using military postures and choreographies (Silva 1999; Branco and Branco 2003). During the *Estado Novo,* folklore was both a means toward ideological indoctrination and symbolic representation destined for internal and external consumption.

Folklore's double duty relied heavily on the animating characteristics of performance. As SPN officials stated, "[it is] necessary and beautiful to transform rustic Portugal into a constant live exhibition of popular art. Dolls don't satisfy anymore. We want to see them move, sing and dance!" (quoted in Brito 1982, 530). The SPN's desire for "live dolls" in "constant exhibition" who "move, sing and dance" reveals with chilling clarity how *ranchos folclóricos,* MP choral groups, and other performance collectives were harnessed to corporatist cultural plans in the service of political ideology and nationalist image management. From the vantage point of Salazar's cultural policy makers, folklore performers were easily metamorphosed into "living signs of themselves" (Kirshenblatt-Gimblett 1991, 388), "live dolls" exhibited as national archetypes to be inventoried, celebrated, and reproduced. During the *Estado Novo,* politicians-cum-ethnographers mined Portugal's rural landscape for dramatized representation of Portugal's primordial past, as folklore was transformed into a performative practice which unified the nation's atomized social body and connected a preindustrial past to its corporatist present.

The Most Portuguese Village Contest

In 1938, António Ferro and other SPN officials masterminded a national competition entitled *O Concurso da Aldeia Mais Portuguesa de Portugal* (the Most Portuguese Village in Portugal Contest). The contest would award a prize to the village which through "sculpting clay, intoning songs or simply repudiating foreign and noxious influences, achieve(d) the maintenance of traditional customs" (Brito 1982, 511). This contest, termed the "folkloric and ethnographic rebirth" of Portugal, sought to develop in the Portuguese a sense of regional and local belonging through the reinvigoration of traditional values manifested in public stagings of mass baptisms, weddings, folklore dances, parades, and agricultural demonstrations. The Most Portuguese Village Contest, widely perceived as "the beginning of folklore" (Pestana 2000), became an important vehicle for the development of *ranchos folclóricos* and the exploitation of folklore performance as a means for morale boosting, social control, and the performative articulation of cultural wealth. Designed to enlist the help of all Portuguese in a war against "disturbing ideas that threaten national unity," the Most Portuguese Village Contest developed in the Portuguese the "cult of tradition" while simultaneously "stimulating national regionalism" (Brito 1982, 511). The winning villages served as inspirational exemplars of the aesthetic and social efficacy of folkloric revivalism, and the practices sparked by the contest served as models for a new generation of fledgling *ranchos folclóricos.*

Obsessive media coverage of the Most Portuguese Village Contest gripped the nation over a period of many months, as the country's major newspapers repeatedly portrayed *Estado Novo*'s dictator, António Salazar, as "the great friend of all of the Portuguese villages" (Brito 1982, 526). The contest, according to a press release, demonstrated the government's interest "in the small corners of our country . . . searching to do them justice and pay homage to their natural state of being!" (Brito 1982, 514). According to official contest rhetoric, Salazar, Ferro, and their *compadres* were not to be viewed as authoritarian figures holding the power to limit free speech, censor the media, and imprison political dissidents, but as benevolent friends seeking to honor the rural underclass. Contest rhetoric affirms corporatism's desire to construct a society free of interclass and inter-regional conflict. "If the cultured population shows their appreciation of the modest rural people, then the villagers feel better about who they are and what they represent . . . [Such a dynamic] proves the success of the contest" (in Brito 1982, 521, my insert). Underscoring the regime's "friendly" relationship to all villages, contest rhetoric also recalls Salazar's humble rural beginnings as the "son of country folk" who "cannot live without breathing the smell of the earth . . . without seeing trees, bushes and flowers" (Garnier 1952, 39).

SPN organizers published contest rules in *Diário da Manhã,* one of Portugal's largest national newspapers, on February 7, 1938. Each of the eleven Portuguese *províncias* was to elect a jury of local academicians and administrators, which would in turn nominate two villages for the competition (Brito 1982, 511–12). A central jury comprised of three ethnographers, one musicologist, two humanities professors, and António Ferro would award the victorious village a silver rooster for display in the local church.[10] The central jury would evaluate which locality best fended off "foreign influences and corruption" by "conserving to the highest degree" the purity of (1) habitation, (2) furniture and domestic tools, (3) clothing, (4) arts, (5) forms of commerce, (6) means of transport, (7) poetry, tales, superstitions, games, songs, music, dance, theater, and festivals, and (8) topographical appearance and landscape (Brito 1982, 512).

The announcement of this "patriotic contest" captured the hearts and imaginations of hundreds of thousands throughout the nation. Scores of villages from every corner of the country competed for the title. Local leaders first inventoried their village's arsenal of tradition, explaining what was expected of the village inhabitants while stimulating the local pride necessary for a positive identification with the initiative (Brito 1982, 512). In order to bolster the chance of victory, many villages deliberately accentuated, revived, or even invented "age-old" local traditions. They took up popular craft-making, resurrected outdated agricultural tools, and restored communal treasures such as old fountains, village ovens, wells, churches, and windmills. They revived old systems of economic exchange such as bartering goods for services. They abandoned modern forms of transport in favor of the oxcart. And finally, many collected songs and dances from elderly neighbors and formed *ranchos folclóricos.*

Following six months of evaluation, the regional juries selected a total of twenty-two localities to advance to the next round of competition.[11] On September 9, 1938, the *Diário da Manhã* published a brief article outlining the next phase of the contest. The central jury would visit each of the twenty-two villages, participating in "days of intense, continuous and dazzling programming" (Brito 1982, 517). The article outlined one village's planned programming:

> First the jury will tour the village, then witness a cow milking, they will see grazing cattle, demonstrations of agricultural work, and an exposition of domestic tools. Later the jury will experience a running of the bulls, followed by an open air lunch featuring a culinary menu typical of the region, which will be followed by the performance of songs, dances and local music. (Brito 1982, 517)

As the weeks progressed, more villages announced finalized plans for the central jury's visit. Proposed performances and parades became increasingly elaborate. By the time the central jury began its series of site-specific evaluations, originally conceived as brief afternoon visits to each location, villages had created enough programming to entertain the jury for up to forty-eight consecutive hours.

The central jury narrowed the pool of village finalists to twelve following a long summer of on-site evaluations. In choosing a winner, the judges aimed to

> 1) discover an extraordinary copy of valuable folkloric elements, 2) awaken local pride to the riches that the people unknowingly guard, 3) stimulate the desire for victory and the will to recover lost folkloric treasure for future endeavors 4) publicize an admirable world unknown even to the Portuguese themselves 5) select a village with traditional physiognomy along with the idiosyncrasies of progress to serve forever as the beautiful poster for this old and new Portugal. (Brito 1982, 519)

Keeping in mind that the victorious village will serve as synecdoche for the nation, sensitizing Portugal's citizens across social class and regional divides to the "lost folkloric treasures" lurking in their midst, the judges chose the village of Monsanto located in Beira Baixa as the contest's winner.[12]

The activities inspired by Ferro's 1938 contest provided an important prototype for folkloric revivalism during subsequent decades of the *Estado Novo.* Throughout the 1950s and 1960s, FNAT and JCCP encouraged the formation of *ranchos folclóricos* in tandem with other types of activities such as the ethnographic collection of popular songs, dances, and preindustrial objects, the organization of ethnographic museums, and the resurrection of artisan craftmaking.[13] This amalgam of activities echoed the varied categories erected by contest juries to determine the Most Portuguese Village and the wide array of programming created by village contestants to demonstrate cultural wealth through diversity of folkloric media. *Ranchos folclóricos* became the expressive mouthpiece for a larger plan of integrated folkloric revivalism, which celebrated the existence of a preindustrial past in the present. The Most Portuguese Village Contest illustrated the idealized organic whole, where *ranchos folclóricos* were part and parcel of a multifaceted *complex* of folkloric activities that followed, in its contest incarnation, the living history model of revivalism. *Ranchos folclóricos* represented just the tip of the iceberg within this larger complex. As the most performative manifestation of folklorization, *ranchos* geared their onstage spectacle toward a nonparticipatory public, communicating Salazarism's ruralist doctrine while providing festive entertainment. Although *ranchos* executed overtly "restored behaviors" (Schechner 1985), it was assumed, following the contest prototype, that behind *rancho* spectacle existed a more organic and integrated foundation of traditional activities still moored to a peasant quotidian which legitimated the *Estado Novo*'s consecration of Portuguese villages as spaces of moral purity and cultural authenticity.

In 1939, a newly formed *rancho folclórico,* directed by Father José Augusto Ribeiro from the winning village of Monsanto, performed popular songs and dances to celebrate the award of the Silver Rooster to his Most Portuguese Village. Addressing a select urban public in the sophisticated surroundings of the Teatro Nacional Almeida Garrett, António Ferro introduced the *rancho* as a group of "true peasants traveling out of Monsanto for the first time, having until now only danced and sung for themselves," experiencing today for the first time "light which does not emanate from the sun or the moon, trees which are not genuine and a stage that is not the simple esplanade in front of the [village] castle" (cited in Melo 2001, 226). In this passage, Ferro reveals the inherent tension between acting and enacting or living and performing, otherwise defined as "twice-behaved behavior" (Schechner 1985, 36). The mise-en-scène which frames the performance with overhead lights, sound amplification, faux trees, and a proscenium stage are far from the idyllic image of preindustrial innocence targeted by contest organizers. Contest discourse reveals the conflation of anti-modernism and technological backwardness with cultural wealth and authenticity. Ironically, however, communicating Ferro's politics of rural purity necessitated an engagement with artifice, and this paradoxical tension dogged *rancho* performance throughout the *Estado Novo. Estado Novo* initiatives routinely disengaged expressive culture from its "traditional matrix" (Melo 2001, 187), in order to stimulate cultural dynamism and push folkloric production into the center of public awareness. What Ferro lost in "authenticity" he gained in control over the hegemonic master framing of folklore performance as a vehicle for ideological instruction.

The national uses to which folklore was put during the 1930s, 1940s, and 1950s demanded that target images and sounds be circulated. As the 1938 contest objectives clearly state, the winning village, with all of its folkloric "secrets" revealed, would become an everlasting "poster" for the new and old Portugal. Ferro imagined the Most Portuguese Village as a marketing tool, an "emblem of the nation" (Brito 1982, 523) to be emblazoned in the domestic and perhaps foreign social imaginary. Contest discourse emphasized the importance of "revealing," "unearthing," and "uncovering" hidden folkloric treasure from the nooks and crannies of Portugal's sleepy countryside. However, this revelation had to be followed by widespread dissemination and circulation of village spoils if the contest were to accomplish its purpose.

Of course the print media served this function, as did Ferro's band of modernist artists who in the years following the contest incorporated folkloric iconography into posters, national exhibits, and scenic designs, to international acclaim.[14] However, I would argue that *ranchos folclóricos* most directly and efficaciously put the new aural, visual, and gestural lexicon into domestic circulation. *Ranchos* possessed the power to animate static imagery through performance and satisfy folklore's double duty as corporatist propaganda *and* escapist entertainment. After all, as stated in an SPN publication, "Dolls don't satisfy anymore. We want to see them move, sing and dance!" (quoted in Brito 1982, 530).

The Most Portuguese Village Contest also set in motion the complex transfer between locality-region-nation to achieve what Ferro termed the re-Portuguesation of Portugal. Cultural heterogeneity spoke to Portugal's folkloric wealth, and the contest capitalized on this diversity to reinforce regional stereotypes. Maintaining fixed regional identities constituted an important feature of Salazarist spatial tactics, where official cartographic revisions of Portugal's province boundaries dovetailed with organized cultural initiatives to keep people in their places (Holton 1999). Diverse localities within newly drawn regional borders contributed to national unity, as local specificity and regional generalities were always folded into a *national* matrix of referentiality. Documents from the *Secretariado Nacional de Informação* proclaimed, "Portugal is today an amalgam of provinces which are all identical in the rights and duties conferred to them by the Patria" (cited in Melo 2001, 83). Beira Baixa's Monsanto was chosen not only as Portugal's national stamp, but as the infinitely substitutable image of Portugal's smallest geographical unit and regional representative.

In conclusion, the Most Portuguese Village Contest created a model for the traditional *lifestyle* that Ferro aimed to stoke or reactivate throughout Portugal's rural countryside. The contest's media coverage captured the picturesque features of this lifestyle in vibrant detail. Highlighted activities—communal bread baking, crocheting, cow milking, corn husking, traditional dancing, and storytelling—provided a new visual and aural template for the Portuguese social imaginary and framed a new set of symbolic practices and images around which collective identity could cohere. The contest's identificatory process aimed to sensitize Portuguese citizens to the cultural riches hidden in plain sight, while framing folkloric tradition—evidence of the past in the present—as the nation's primordial base. The drive to uncover, understand, and disseminate folklore stemmed both from endogenous plans for nation-building, and also from the exogenous concern with resisting the noxious modernizing influences that threatened to invade Portugal from abroad. Most important for the purposes of this book, the contest marked what is commonly perceived as the birth of widespread folkloric revivalism. Ferro's 1938 initiative not only spawned several new performance troupes, but it also provided *ranchos* with an integrative model for the restoration, and often invention, of tradition. Greasing the wheels for the subsequent founding of hundreds of *ranchos folclóricos,* the contest demonstrated folklore's multifaceted potential for providing escapist entertainment for Portugal's impoverished rural masses, while creating a set of symbolic images and sounds which would become an expressive lexicon for SPN propaganda and other nationalist celebrations throughout the *Estado Novo.*

Folklore's Institutionalization

Although SPN and FNAT officials had high hopes for the widespread corporatist stimulation and co-optation of folkloric performance, this vision was slow to materialize. Many of the earliest *ranchos* of the *Estado Novo* were explicitly created in order to perform in official large-scale events. The Monsanto group is a good example, founded to mark the awards ceremony for the Most Portuguese Village Contest. Other newly created *ranchos* performed at the 1940 World's Fair.[15] Several *ranchos* marked the alliance between FNAT and the *Kraft durch Freude* (KdF) by performing aboard German ships docked in Lisbon in 1937. And in 1936, 1937, and 1938 Portuguese *ranchos* traveled to Germany to perform during the annual congress of the National-Socialist Organization (Valente 1999, 102–103). In June of 1938 FNAT president Higínio de Queiroz traveled to Hamburg to attend KdF's annual conference and "brilliantly announced his presence with the performance of a *grupo folclórico,* constituted expressly for this effect" (Valente 1999, 176).

Outside of the formation of *ranchos* contrived specifically for the decoration of official governmental occasions, however, the widespread founding of FNAT affiliated folklore troupes did not meet the *Estado Novo*'s high expectations until the 1950s. Although the 1930s witnessed tremendous international enthusiasm for the institutionalization of folklore as a state-subsidized and state-controlled form of structuring worker leisure time, Portugal's FNAT had difficulty putting theory into practice. In 1945, an FNAT report notes that relatively little had been accomplished with respect to the creation of permanent folklore groups: "special reasons, traditions, old habits, local-political interests and the incomprehension of the goals of our initiatives has impeded a determinant number of folklore groups, already formed, from integrating into FNAT's cultural activity" (FNAT, 1945). FNAT's initial difficulty in institutionalizing extant folklore troupes and inspiring the creation of new groups was partly ameliorated in the late 1940s, due to the creation of the *Gabinete de Etnografia* in 1946. Between 1943 and 1949, six folklore groups registered for affiliation with FNAT,[16] among them the highly acclaimed *Grupo Folclórico do Doutor Gonçalo Sampaio* from Braga, the *Rancho das Lavradeiras de Santa Marta de Portuzelo* from Viana do Castelo, the *Rancho Tricanas Serraninhas*, the *Rancho da Casa do Povo de Elvas*, and the *Rancho das Rendilheiras* from Praça de Vila do Conde (Valente 1999, 133–40).

Just as the Most Portuguese Village Contest served as a model for the integrated restoration of diverse folkloric activities, the *Grupo Folclórico do Doutor Gonçalo Sampaio* served as a model for the formulaic constitution of folklore troupes under Salazar and a testament to the efficacy of FNAT's institutional "guidance." Affiliated in 1943, the *Grupo Sampaio* worked tirelessly with personnel from FNAT's Braga outpost to create an authentic duplicate of regional tradition. It is worth noting that the *Grupo Sampaio* represented the region of Minho—widely hailed as folklore's birthplace and the mythic locus of Portugal's primordial core.[17] Entrusted with this substantive symbolic charge, the members of the *Grupo Sampaio* spent a year rehearsing with Professor J. C. Mota Leite, a specialist in music and folklore who "played the role of a cultural intermediary, building a bridge between the world of the government's political elite and the world of the peasant participants" (Melo 2001, 190). This model, which communicated the government's superior ability to "define the specific contents of folklore" as well as the criteria for determining folkloric authenticity, began to bear fruit as the group enjoyed the appreciation of an enthusiastic public during several inaugural performances in 1944 (Melo 2001, 190–91). After proving themselves on their home terrain in northern Portugal, exhibiting a seriousness of purpose which infused their performances with "the true and the genuine" as well as "educational characteristics," the *Grupo Sampaio* was invited to perform at the *Coliseu dos Recreios* in Lisbon on the occasion of the First FNAT Festival in 1946 (Melo 2001, 191–92). With this performance in Portugal's capital and FNAT's home base, the *Grupo Folclórico do Dr. Gonçalo Sampaio* was trotted out as an example par excellence of *ranchos'* formulaic constitution, quickly becoming one of the most "visible faces of corporative culture" (Melo 2001, 192).

It was not until the 1950s, following many years of government-sponsored folklore competitions, that FNAT succeeded in stimulating large-scale interest in the formation of revivalist performance troupes and a companion willingness to pursue centralized affiliation. In 1954, there were seventeen FNAT-registered folklore groups, eight of which belonged to *casas do povo*. By 1958, the number of FNAT *ranchos* had surged to ninety-four, with

43 percent of all *casas do povo* reporting an avowed interest in forming a *rancho folclórico* (Valente 1999, 180; Melo 2001, 192). The 1950s represented "an exceptional moment in the growth and visibility of *ranchos folclóricos.* From the Alto Minho to the Ribatejo . . . it is the decade of *explosion*" (Melo 2001, 193, italics in original). Factors such as tourism, industrialization, and economic growth contributed to the precipitous increase in the number of *ranchos* throughout the fifties. The development of regional festivals also catalyzed the formation of *ranchos folclóricos.* The *Feira do Ribatejo,* for example, served as the impetus for the creation of eight local *ranchos,* in 1954–56, many of which were founded just months before their first public performance in direct response to solicitations from festival organizers.[18]

With the "explosive" proliferation of folklore troupes throughout the 1950s came anxieties on the part of government-endorsed folklore pundits about the abuse of spectacle and the sloppy recreation of "authentic" tradition. As groups began appearing in larger numbers across the entirety of Portugal, FNAT's centralized control became threatened. With only a handful of groups to orient in the 1930s and 1940s, FNAT officials had the time and resources to appoint artistic directors such as Mota Leite who worked with the *Grupo Folclórico do Dr. Gonçalo Sampaio,* and who spent twelve months reorganizing a well-intentioned but perhaps ill-informed group as to the norms of responsible folkloric revivalism. As stated in the Figeira da Foz festival program on the occasion of *Grupo Sampaio*'s public unveiling in 1944, "This first year was a year of preparation, designed to motivate the performers, offering them the instruction necessary for good conduct and helping them integrate into the soul and secrets of folklore. It was a year of internal work, of rehearsal" (in Melo 2001, 190). However, due to the increasing number of groups and their dispersal throughout various regions—many taking only weeks to assemble and rehearse repertoire before performing publicly—the luxury of year-long internal work periods under the strict direction of FNAT advisors seemed to be an unrealistic model, and impossible to enforce during folklore's golden decade and beyond.

Fabricated Arrangements

As *Estado Novo* folklore initiatives began gaining momentum, the desire to recreate authentic local tradition through the duplication of instrumentation, music, lyrics, and choreography from late-nineteenth-century popular songs and dances came into direct conflict with the desire to "stylize" tradition through contemporary artistry and arrangement. On the one hand, folklore scholars such as Mota Leite, Abel Viana, and Jorge Dias, many of whom were aligned with or employed by corporatist institutions, pushed for the maintenance of historically accurate standards of ethnographic restoration. Jorge Dias frequently complained about the spectacular excesses of folkloric performances, and Abel Viana lobbied FNAT to employ stricter criteria for the "approval" of affiliated *ranchos folclóricos,* claiming that many *ranchos* "costume themselves without the least respect for ethnography . . . and instead of building repertoires according to the folklore of their own localities, they imitate songs and dances of foreign areas which results in imperfection and confusion" (Viana 1953, 12). On the other hand, this somewhat academic anxiety over ethnographic truth and spatial purity is balanced by the corporative and propagandistic drive to unify the nation through the syncretic blending of iconographic and expressive forms and the neutralization of potentially dangerous social difference through the creation of a unified cultural whole.

Salazar, Ferro, and FNAT administrators present a divergent and sometimes paradoxical stance with regard to folkloric authenticity. Ferro, for example, well known for his modernist leanings and passion for aesthetic innovation, created the *Centro Regional* section of the 1940 World's Fair employing an in situ display model. Ferro urged visitors to "speak with the laborers of the bride's house, with the lace makers, the weavers, with all of these small people who work and sing in the shadows of your houses" in order to demonstrate that these objects of display were not "figurines" but "authentic peasants" (Ferro 1940). Ferro's drive to exhibit ethnographically "authentic" rural specimens paralleled a conflicting desire to represent regional Portugal as a diminutive "fairy tale," where, upon entering the Village Exhibition Section, "every visitor can have the sensation of closing Portugal in the palm of his hand, like a frightened dove, immediately calmed" (Ferro 1940). Ferro's poetic metaphor telegraphs both the exhibits' immersion in the expressive vocabulary of fiction, while spinning a figurative portrayal of Portugal—split up into hundreds of atomized villages—as a dove in need of the unifying containment of the palm (read nation).

Ferro's curatorial blending of social science and aesthetics, of ethnographic fact with stylized fiction, found many echoes in the corporative discourse and policies regarding *ranchos folclóricos.* On the one hand, FNAT administrators professed the need for folkloric purity. Abel Viana even suggested categorizing all groups according to taxonomies which measured varying quotients of the "invented" versus the "natural" (1954, 12).[19] On the other hand, the recontextualization of folklore performance within the master frame of competition, a favorite strategy of *Estado Novo* leaders aiming to stimulate cultural production, undermined the drive toward authenticity (Holton 1999; Melo 2001). The context of the folklore competition tore expressive culture from its traditional matrix (Melo 2001, 187). During the *Es-*

tado Novo, ranchos competed for prizes at regional festivals which were dislodged from religious or agricultural calendars. The organization of such events impeded the traditional characteristics of "informality and spontaneity." The competition context inspired contemporary tinkering with repertoire, musical tempo, and choreographic stylistics to create crowd-pleasing numbers, often rewarded with contest accolades, local pride, and popularity (Holton 1999).

In sifting through the conflicting discourses and practices surrounding the policing of folkloric authenticity, it is clear that corporatist leaders publicly affirmed strict standards of ethnographic accuracy while turning a blind eye to the manipulation and fabrication of popular tradition. Salazar had a lot to gain from allowing, however quietly, *ranchos'* spectacular excess. Abuses to tradition actually forwarded many of corporatism's social objectives. Portuguese corporatism demobilized political action by dividing the country into its smallest constitutive geographic units. Salazar partitioned off space into discreet "cells," often "paralyzing sociability" (Ó 1992, 393). These fractured cells were gathered up and unified at the level of discourse and representation through cultural initiatives such as the Most Portuguese Village Contest and through thousands of *rancho* contests. *Ranchos folclóricos* played an essential role in representing a unified Portuguese nation. Although *ranchos* ideally mined local tradition for repertoire, in actuality many performed songs and dances from all of Portugal's regions, ultimately serving as mini composites of the nation. The value placed on spectacle—colorful costumes, up-tempo music, and complex choreography—caused *ranchos* across Portugal to alter and ornament tradition, thereby neutralizing local and regional differences. Many folklore groups also showcased versatility by performing songs and dances characteristic of varying regions throughout the whole of Portugal, amalgamating tradition in the service of repertoire variation and crowd appeal. *Ranchos folclóricos* thus often performed along a national-local dialectic, where spatial identification and cultural heritage were in constant flux between the grounded sphere of local residence and the abstract sphere of national belonging.

The initial forming of *ranchos folclóricos* required an inwardly driven community focus. Before creating a *rancho,* members of the group had to gather performance material—choreography, music, costumes, and props. They had to rally participants—instrumentalists, vocalists, dancers, choreographers, directors, administrators, and tailors. Both human and material resources were naturally drawn from local communities. *Rancho* members ostensibly banded together to construct a mimetic representation of turn-of-the-century *local* tradition. These decidedly local activities were, however, always already in dialogue with *national* frameworks for cultural revivalism and folkloric display. Generally, in performing local tradition, *ranchos folclóricos* needed only to nod toward history—what mattered was not the hem of the costume nor the meter of the song, but the gestalt of the performance and the easy co-optation of local custom by a consumptive national culture. *Ranchos folclóricos* needed to reflect local color yet remain indistinct enough to avoid singularity; in this way *ranchos* floated between representational duties to the local and the national. FNAT and SPN initiatives posited *ranchos folclóricos* as interchangeable representations of nation, minimizing qualitative differences between local customs, producing what Kirshenblatt-Gimblett terms "the banality of difference, whereby the proliferation of variation has the neutralizing effect of rendering difference (and conflict) inconsequential" (1991, 433).

Many *ranchos* neutralized differences between the "proliferating variations" of local songs and dances by pursuing the spectacular. In adapting local tradition for public performance, *ranchos folclóricos* blurred genre and period, tinkered with lyrics, rhythm, and melody to augment crowd appeal and choreographic challenge. In the *Rancho Folclórico de Alenquer* (RFA), a group whose *rancho* predecessors began collecting songs and dances in the 1940s, expressive traditions collected from elderly neighbors served as a jumping-off point for the creative efforts of *rancho* choreographers and instrumentalists. Seeking to please both folklore publics and RFA performers, RFA leadership transformed local *recolhas* (songs and dances "collected" from elderly residents) into impressive spectacles, showcasing performers' athletic prowess and musical dexterity. These transformations often entailed speeding up tempo and transposing vocal and instrumental music into higher keys.[20] RFA's president and accordionist, José Hermínio Carvalho, explained, for example, that "Corridinho Serrano," the show-stopping number with which the *rancho* often closed during the sixties and seventies, was played and danced significantly faster than when originally collected. RFA also added a dazzling key change at the beginning of the last verse, where the music was played higher and faster still. "This way," he stated, "we ended with a bang."

Spectacularizing folklore performance also occurred in response to the *Estado Novo*'s favored model of organized cultural competition. The state supported folklore competitions throughout the *Estado Novo,* encouraged *ranchos* to work toward exacting standards of showmanship, frequently at the expense of historical accuracy. The competition paradigm stands in direct contrast to post-revolutionary performance forums, such as *rancho* anniversary festivals, that evoke an ethos of inter-regional cooperation, cultural exchange, and community enrichment. Even though folklore competitions per se are rare in post-revolutionary Portugal, many *ranchos* still tout accolades amassed during the *Estado Novo* as important legitimating credentials.[21]

The competition paradigm not only implied alteration in choreographic and musical style, but also affected repertoire selection. Just as a Western actor is valued for his or her range (ability to play characters far from one's quotidian personae), so too were *ranchos* valued for their versatility. RFA, a *rancho* from the Estremedura region, for example, prided itself on the ability to perform *modas* (numbers) typical of other regions. Throughout the *Estado Novo,* RFA regularly performed *corridinhos* characteristic of the Algarve and a *fandango* typical of the Ribatejo as part of its standard repertoire. RFA also performed a lengthy ten-minute medley, an onstage test of physical endurance, cut and pasted together in a brazen potpourri of excised samples drawn from many different songs and dances. According to RFA performers, this medley, composed by then-director António Dionísio, was a source of great pride, not only because it showcased the dancers' range and versatility, but also because it communicated Dionísio's choreographic and musical artistry.

Song/dance types were and are essential components in the popular construction of regional identity and socio-spatial differentiation. In his book chapter "Popular Portuguese Dances of Today: Elements for a Choreographic Map of Portugal," Tomaz Ribas (1982, 85–93) constructs choreographic taxonomies traced over Portugal's eleven *províncias.*[22] During the *Estado Novo,* regional taxonomies guided social cohesion through disassociative belonging (e.g., "we are Algarvians because we possess cultural traditions distinct from those in the Alentejo; we are Algarvians because we are not Alentejanans"). This logic of social coherence depended directly upon the reinforcement of regional boundaries through the wide-scale distribution and public posting of maps, for which Salazar was famous (Paulo 1994). The task of unifying these disparate regional units fell to *ranchos folclóricos.* Amassing *modas* from varying *províncias, ranchos folclóricos* aggregated spatial fragments into a coherent national whole through the medium of performance. By performing *modas* typical not only of the Estremadura region, but also of the Algarve and the Ribatejo, RFA danced skillfully across geographical boundaries, stepping into the shoes of regional Others, while diversifying its repertoire in the service of onstage pace, plot, and versatility.[23] By featuring *modas* from all corners of Portugal's folkloric terrain, *rancho* repertoires constituted cultural amalgams essential to national unity in the symbolic register, and to the "neutralization of difference and conflict."[24]

Rancho costumes under Salazar also helped represent a unified nation by concealing regional and local differences. Unlike the FFP-approved *rancho* costumes of today—historical recreations of late-nineteenth-century

Figure 6. Photograph of *Rancho Folclórico de Alenquer*, circa 1960. *Used with permission.*

rural dress which vary widely from performer to performer and region to region—many of the costumes Abel Viana (1954) complained about during the fifties and sixties were surprisingly uniform. Figure 6 shows the costume design that RFA featured from the time of its foundation in 1959 until the costume reforms of the mid-1980s. The respective costumes of male and female performers during the *Estado Novo* were essentially identical, with the exception of the women's skirt color that alternated primarily between red and green—aptly, the colors of Portugal's national flag. According to many RFA performers, this prototypical folklore costume, vaguely "citing" northern Portugal's rural peasant dress of the early twentieth century, [25] varied only slightly from town to town and region to region during the *Estado Novo*. RFA dancers Luís Fernando Ventura (1996) and Lídia Maria Ventura (1996) elaborate:

> Luís: In our *concelho* almost all [the *ranchos* had these same costumes].
> Lídia: Short skirt, black stripe, almost always. We still see this costume with the short skirt worn by *ranchos* even today.

Pre-revolutionary *rancho* costumes unified folklore performers while providing visual appeal and enhanced onstage spectacle. The genealogy of the pre-revolutionary folklore costume further underscores the link between *rancho* dress, spectacle, and crowd appeal. According to many RFA performers, *marchas populares* served as the inspiration for *rancho* costume design around the time of their founding in 1959. *Marchas populares,* still performed today, particularly in urban open-air spaces, feature parades or processions that accompany a variety of secular and non-secular celebrations.[26] Many women who perform in *marchas populares* wear short colorful skirts, lace stockings, aprons, and scarves. In some *marchas,* juries award coveted prizes for best costume. According to RFA members, many groups who initially banded together to perform in *marchas populares* later used the same constellation of dancers and the same costumes to form their own *rancho folclórico.*[27]

Although many SPN/SNI reports expressed anxiety over *ranchos folclóricos'* "bastardization" of "genuine" local customs, "the appropriation of popular culture . . . did not aim to (re)create a peasant universe exactly as it exists in reality, but rather to create scenery where the emblematization of the nation is in play for the appreciation of urban or even foreign publics" (Alves 2003, 194). As long as the festive costumes remained tailored to these taste publics in the service of national identity, many corporatist leaders turned a blind eye to tradition's fabricated arrangement. Many pre-revolutionary costumes were thus unmoored from the past, creating a simulacrum of mimetic repetition. Moving laterally across place and genre, *rancho* costumes cited one another; the material referents for *rancho* uniforms were other contemporary popular costumes, not period originals. Often articulating a commitment to spectacular entertainment rather than historical restoration, *ranchos* donned homogenized uniforms of cultural nationalism, borrowing an expressive grammar from a military context (Branco and Branco 2003; Branco 2003b). As Diana Taylor states in her article on political theatrics during Argentina's "Dirty War," consensus-producing spectacles, such as "the endless parades, fairs, ceremonies, and celebrations of the military, relied on repetition" (1996, 307). In the Portuguese case, corporatist folkloric spectacle relied not only on the repetition of performative event, but also on the reiteration of choreographic, musical, and clothing styles across terrain, neutralizing difference and facilitating the easy transfer of local custom to national heritage. The organized control of mimesis is a fundamental strategy of fascist repression (Taussig 1993, 68), and many FNAT and SPN/SNI administrators controlled mimesis through letting historical restoration unfold largely unchecked, despite written complaints about inauthenticity. In contrast to the detail-oriented restoration of material culture during the Most Portuguese Village Contest, the expressive culture of *ranchos folclóricos* was held to another standard because *ranchos* served different social and symbolic purposes. *Ranchos folclóricos* were meant to articulate the broad, impressionistic reminiscence of days gone by. They were meant to entertain, to "express the joy of ideas when sung and danced," to "*fazer a festa*" (throw parties) (Brito 1982), and to perform ornamented and homogenized local tradition in the service of national unification.

The Poetics of Everyday Resistance

Stuart Hall outlines two distinct historiographical approaches that have dominated the analysis of popular culture; cultural historians have either focused on popular culture in a vacuum, as if "purely autonomous," independent of sociopolitical relations of power, or they have focused exclusively on forces of domination, portraying the working classes as "cultural dopes" and popular culture as "totally encapsulated" (1981, 232). Hall argues for an integrated model of cultural struggle, combining the two dichotomous paradigms:

> there is a continuous and necessarily uneven . . . struggle, by the dominant culture . . . to disorganize and reorganize popular culture; to enclose and confine its definitions and forms within a more inclusive range of dominant forms. There are points of resistance; there are also moments of supercession. This is the dialectic of cultural struggle. (1981, 233)

The performative practices of *ranchos folclóricos* unfold along these same complex lines of resistance and acceptance, refusal and capitulation.

In late 1996, after two years of ethnographic fieldwork with the *Rancho Folclórico de Alenquer,* I began questioning the older members of the group about their experiences performing folklore during the *Estado Novo.* Although RFA was officially founded in 1959, the group inherited leaders, administrators, performers, and repertoire from two local predecessors, the *Rancho dos Malmequeres* (1945–59) and the *Rancho do Cacho Dourado* (1937–39). Given this rich history, I was certain I would unearth important historical information. The *Estado Novo* was a delicate topic, and one I broached with caution. For many who lived with the constant anxiety of the secret police, censors, local government spies, political imprisonment, and sometimes torture, self-censorship became an important mode of survival. Even twenty-five years after the Revolution, public expression of views on fascism or politics remains taboo among certain Portuguese communities.[28] Also, although no one in the *rancho* was a fascist sympathizer, opinions of Salazar's government ranged from mild disapproval to palpable hostility. These variations in political persuasion caused the *rancho* to disband for over a year in the early eighties.[29] Current RFA members generally avoid discussion of organized politics and regularly announce that their *rancho* has no religious or political affiliation—"it is for everyone." Following the *ran-*

cho upheaval in the eighties, a tenuous balance had been struck among RFA members of disparate political affiliation, and few want to disrupt this hard-won harmony.

Despite initial reticence, many older RFA performers eventually spoke privately, some even agreed to taped interviews, recounting their experiences as folklore performers during the *Estado Novo* or the experiences of their relatives. Based on many hours of conversations and years of gentle probing, a fuller portrait of RFA folklore practice during the *Estado Novo* began to emerge. This understanding, based on ethnographic testimony, complicated and at times challenged historical analyses based solely on textual sources, which lumped folklore performance into a large grab bag of corporatist initiatives argued to have accomplished the uniform indoctrination and distraction of masses of people. This was indeed the purpose of revivalist folklore under Salazar—we can easily verify this through analyses of primary documents—and no doubt folklore, to a large extent, accomplished the *Estado Novo*'s corporatist objectives. But what about the way in which folklore performance was experienced and perceived on the ground level? Was this ideological indoctrination really so uniform? How did the performers process their roles within the space of the locality and the space of the nation? What and how did the embodied practices of ethnographic collection, arrangement, rehearsal, and performance mean to the performers themselves?

RFA testimony revealed a surprising measure of artistic autonomy during the *Estado Novo*. According to several older RFA members, folklore performers were rarely targets of overt censorship.[30] RFA performers employed a variety of rationales to explain this sense of artistic freedom. Several performers underscored that *rancho modas* reproduced late nineteenth century songs, and escaped the censor's attention due to their distance from contemporary political circumstance. Other performers believed the paucity of written musical or lyrical notation made censorship difficult; most folklore musicians learned *rancho* repertoires by ear in contrast to other popular troupes, such as local *bandas* (small groups of orchestral instrumentalists or marching bands), who relied more heavily on musical notation. Several other performers described folklore music as "light" or "fanciful" and less likely to inspire intense emotion (which could lead to political action), in contrast to the powerful military marches performed by local *bandas*.

In describing the process of ethnographic collection, performers portrayed the transfer of folkloric knowledge as a charged act, a sensual encounter between strangers during a time when networks of secret police and civilian spies inspired intense suspicion among neighbors, curtailed physical mobility, and "paralyzed" sociability. Ethnographic collection was often followed by a process of aesthetic arrangement, where RFA leaders wrote lyrics, composed music, and choreographed dances in order to fill in, adapt, or arrange the original *recolha.* These acts of personal creativity challenged corporatism's ideological eradication of the individual for the good of the collective, and problematized the *Estado Novo*'s celebration of the anonymous peasant mass—guarantors of the treasure trove of expressive traditions *ranchos* were only supposed to "uncover." Finally, RFA performers, particularly proud of their director's complex choreographic arrangements, reveled in the physical challenges that "invented tradition" demanded. Learning and performing the up-tempo footwork generated by RFA directors required rigorous athletic training and instilled in many dancers a new awareness of their own corporeal power—physical potential some glossed as "liberating." Whether through the sensual sociability engendered by the act of ethnographic collection, the individual creations inspired by the process of musical composition, or the virtuoso "shows of strength" demanded by invented choreographies, folklore revivalism during the *Estado Novo* allowed everyday acts of resistance to sprout in the gaps between cultural policy and implementation, between official discourse and grassroots practice, and between historical restoration and fabricated arrangement.

RFA, like many other *ranchos folclóricos* during the *Estado Novo,* gathered performance material through ethnographic research, or *recolha.*[31] For RFA, the process of *recolha* took place over three decades (approximately 1945–75) and yielded over eighty songs and dances. Amassing such an extensive repertoire required years of intense commitment to local networking and ethnographic fieldwork. RFA participants spent countless afternoons with older Alenquer residents socializing, sharing food, and reconstructing oral histories while gathering song lyrics, instrumental melodies, and dance steps to build the *rancho* repertoire.

Many hours of negotiation occurred, however, before RFA actually entered a song donor's home. Unsupervised association was a potentially dangerous activity during the *Estado Novo.* When strangers networked in the name of tradition gathering, an endeavor ostensibly encouraged by the regime, a healthy dose of caution preceded many encounters. Although, arguably, corporatism posited ethnographic research as a vehicle toward panoptic surveillance, *unchecked* tradition gathering was sometimes considered a threat to national security.[32] RFA evolved a formulaic system for garnering ethnographic information and quelling the anxieties of potential informants. Throughout the time António Dionísio, local café worker and one of RFA's founding members, was *ensaiador* (rehearsal master), Alenquer residents would often stop by his establishment to talk folklore. According to many, Dionísio's café was the perfect venue for repertoire acquisition. Dionísio, nicknamed "Muco" for his raspy voice, was a gregarious, generous man with a penchant for making people laugh. By all accounts, he possessed *muito conhecimento de folclore* (great knowledge of folklore). Many people of all ages knew and liked Dionísio. Older Alenquerians with a song to donate would either visit the café themselves or send an interlocutor to make the initial contact. The interlocutor would then describe the song, and Dionísio would carry this information back to the *rancho.* According to Armindo Rodrigues (1996a), current *rancho ensaiador,* arranging an appointment was often a time-intensive task and *"um processo extremamente delicado"* (an extremely delicate process). Dionísio would often visit the elderly Alenquerian as a gesture of respect, while confirming that the song *"tinha interesse"* (was of interest). Another round of scheduling dialogues would ensue until a date was set and Dionísio could assemble his team of RFA ethnographer-performers. Up to six months sometimes passed between the time of the initial contact and RFA's acquisition of a new song or dance.

Lourdes Mendes (1996), a seasoned dancer and often part of Dionísio's ethnographic team, fondly recalls the afternoons of *recolha.* She and her dance partner would accompany Dionísio, founding member Crispim Luís, two accordionists, and another pair of dancers to the elderly neighbor's home. One performer would dance with the elderly neighbor, while the other pair of dancers imitated the steps. RFA's choreographic *recolha* process was an innovative blend of spontaneous performance and systematic reenactment. When asked to dance with an RFA member, the elderly neighbor would often hesitate, claiming that physical ailments, memory lapses, or shyness prevented her from performing the dance properly. But eased into the multiple roles of dancer, instructor, and informant, the neighbor would inevitably rise to the occasion—reexperiencing the dances of her childhood while performing in the moment with fellow Alenquerians half her age.

The *recolha* team employed the same interactive process to learn instrumental and vocal music. Crispim Luís (1996), a septuagenarian who has collected songs for five decades, explained:

> We would bring the recorder they had at the *rancho* . . . in those times they didn't have a video . . . there were no such things as cassettes. It was a recorder with reels . . . Then into the recorder the people sang and danced. The accordionists would then see what the melody was like, then sound it out and then they would record themselves playing. They did this at the time so they'd remember . . . later they might forget.

José Hermínio Carvalho (1996) characterizes this process as a kind of "hunt and peck," or trial and error method. The advanced age of the song donor often hindered his or her ability to sing. José Hermínio would listen, then play part of the tune on his accordion, asking, "Was that it?" The old person would answer, "Almost, but not exactly." And José Hermínio would ask again, "Okay, then how did it go?" This back and forth would continue until the song donor was satisfied that the accordionists had duplicated the melody s/he remembered. According to José Hermínio, it was only the melodic line which was recorded. The RFA instrumentalists composed the percussion parts later during rehearsal. In their collective service to the mimetic restoration of late nineteenth-century popular songs and dances, RFA performers and local residents forged new social bonds and strengthened localist solidarity. These localized social ties were continually renewed and reinforced throughout the life of the *rancho,* as song donors attended *rancho* performances and rehearsals, inspecting the repertoire they helped create, giving advice, critique, and moral support.

The ethnographic process of tradition gathering was both intricate and intimate. *Recolha* began as older Alenquerians contacted younger friends who contacted Dionísio who contacted RFA instrumentalists who contacted dancers who contacted the older Alenquerian who taught the *rancho* a song or dance. This social chain operated like the children's game "Whisper down the Lane," where an originary utterance is passed from one to another to another, the group reveling in the hermeneutic twists and turns that terminate in a metamorphosed "secret." Such a chain requires a seriality of intimate contact to move knowledge forward.

The *recolha* process also unfolded across local terrain—"down lanes," over hills, and through valleys. This mobility challenged Salazarist laws that limited freedom of association and sought to contain social activity within official corporatist institutions such as *casas do povo.* As recorded in my field notes, Armindo stated that during the *Estado Novo:*

> *ranchos* only had competitions where groups performed to win titles. There were no festivals where *ranchos* performed to exchange information, meet new people, and travel . . . It was difficult for RFA to travel to the north. *Ranchos'* physical mobility was limited . . . There were also no social gatherings after performances—no dinners or parties. It was just "perform, exit the stage, get on the bus and go home without a word to anyone" . . . People were afraid to get into discussions with strangers for fear of inadvertently talking to a PIDE spy. (Holton n.d.)

Armindo described the risk involved not only in socializing with strangers but in traversing physical terrain. *Ranchos* were required to report all intra-

concelho performance activities to a regional FNAT representative and invite an FNAT official to attend all formal events (FNAT 1958, article 7). *Ranchos* were also forbidden to travel out of the *concelho* without prior FNAT authorization: "In the case of performances outside of the *concelho,* groups must ask permission to travel, furnishing the request with details [of the trip and anticipated performance]" (FNAT 1958, article 8). During the process of *recolha, ranchos* transgressed socio-spatial regulations, meeting strangers through interlocutors, and crossing borders sometimes into neighboring *concelhos* through series of back-and-forth invitations, arrangements, and escorts.

Under Salazar, *ranchos folclóricos'* tradition gathering resembled a courtship. As Armindo stated, "it was an extremely delicate process," particularly in a political environment that bred suspicion, self-censorship, and enclosure. RFA performers reassured older Alenquerians that childhood memories would be protected, that an encounter with strangers in their own homes would be safe, comfortable, even pleasurable. Once inside, RFA singers strained to recreate the raspy melodies sung by elderly representatives of Alenquer's popular past. As the memories of aging Alenqerians wavered, RFA singers experimented with new tonal progressions and lyrics. The Alenquerian in turn modified these melodic suggestions, tuning them to suit emergent memory. Together RFA vocalists and their older neighbors intoned a patchwork quilt of musical certainty and elliptical filler, an antiphonic call and answer sustained over long afternoons of tea and company. Like C. Nadia Seremetakis's study of Maniat mourners where "lament circulates from mouth to mouth among singers as a shared substance," a substance of "material density" (1994b, 37), RFA vocalists and the older Alenquerians shared song at the brink of mnemonic death and rebirth, passing newly materialized sound from one body to the next, whispering down thc lane toward cooperative sensorial restoration.

During these afternoons of *recolha,* RFA performers danced in the arms of octogenarians, stepping in their steps, guiding their bodies back toward the choreographies of the past. If the older body faltered, the younger body tightened its embrace. If the younger body misstepped, the older body repositioned errant posture and gesture—"the arm should be raised here," "the foot should be flexed," touching ankles, shoulders, hips, and torsos. These dancing bodies kept musical time by pounding out rhythms with heels and palms, kept historical time by resurrecting and transferring once dormant movement from one to another. This erotic dance of cultural transmission involved the shared consumption of history and memory akin to Seremetakis's theory of reflexive commensality: "the exchange of sensory ories and emotions, and of substances and objects incarnating remembrance and feelings" (1994b, 37).

During these visits, according to RFA performers, memories were materialized, tea and pastries consumed, melodies intoned, and secrets passed. Coteries of intergenerational Alenquerians shared languid afternoons of sensory interchange—through touch, smell, and sound they re-embodied expressive history, inhabiting what Henri Lefebvre terms "representational space": "Redolent with imaginary and symbolic elements, they have their source in history—in the history of a people as well as the history of each individual belonging to that people . . . [expressed in] childhood memories, dreams . . . Representational space is alive: it speaks . . . It embraces the loci of passion" (1991, 39–42). The spaces in which *rancho* performers and their older neighbors operated fell outside or beyond the mandated spaces of national corporatism. Traveling from personal home to personal home, evolving an oppositional theater of proxemics, RFA performers gathered dance steps, lyrics, and melodies, garnering the strength and imagination to change and reappropriate cultural history for their own inventive purposes.

The contiguous interplay of bodies across spatial, historical, and mnemonic terrain guarantees a dynamic system of representation built not on the distancing verticality of hierarchized leaps—from village to nation—but on the metonymic linking of person to person. Susan Stewart writes, "we can see the body as taking the place of origin for . . . our understanding of metonymy (the incorporated bodies of self and lover)" (1993, xii). Stewart's depiction of metonymy resonates with Seremetakis's discussion of commensality, a term connoting the ability to "live with, on, or in another" (*Random House Dictionary* 1984, 269). Through the process of *recolha, rancho* musicians, dancers, and their cultural informants formed a chain, an "incorporated body of selves and lovers," inhabiting Lefebvre's "locus of passion," and creating an auto-ethnographic representation of Alenquer, its people and expressive history. Through an erotics of cultural transmission, *rancho* performers took possession of local memory.

Shows of Strength

If, as the etymology of the term *metonymy* suggests, the localized bodies of folklore performers and informants "changed names," they also changed places. Traditional songs and dances were less likely to be performed in basements, fields, patios, or *casas das brincadeiras*.[33] During the *Estado Novo*, folklore performers were placed front and center on proscenium stages throughout the country. This move from basement to proscenium resulted in the augmentation of spectacle. As previously discussed, Salazar's taste for cultural competition and his explicit use of folklore for nationalist propaganda and mass entertainment created change not only in performance venue, but also in performance style; *ranchos folclóricos* under Salazar created colorful, ahistorical costumes and produced spectacular choreographic and musical arrangements.

But how, one might ask, can folklore's place-changing and its resultant change in folklore stylistics, clearly inspired, manipulated, and controlled by Salazarist cultural policies, possibly be construed as everyday resistance? In talking to RFA dancers about their pre-revolutionary experience rehearsing and performing challenging choreographic arrangements, I realized that folklore performance under Salazar was neither "totally encapsulated" nor "completely autonomous," just as Hall theorizes. Folklore spectacle, I learned, demanded rigorous physical training, shows of strength, and the performance of individual corporeal sovereignty.

While Salazar stated otherwise in public speeches, RFA performers claim that physical exercise and self-directed development of corporeal strength were discouraged during the *Estado Novo*. We need only glance at the photographs of FNAT gymnastic groups to understand the importance of collective militarized uniformity, as opposed to the display of virtuoso skill (see figs. 7 and 8). On April 27, 1996, I traveled to Torres Vedras to attend a gymnastics demonstration with Armindo and Fátima Rodrigues. Their thirteen-year-old daughter, Lucília, who had been a junior Portuguese regional champion, was performing. During the five-hour program where gymnastics teams from across the Estremadura and Ribatejo regions showcased new routines, Armindo, Fátima, and I discussed physical education in Portugal. In my field notes, I recorded our conversation:

> Armindo explained that this was not a competition but a demonstration, organized to encourage other young people to participate in gymnastics (and sports in general) . . . Armindo said that physical exercise in and of itself had been discouraged during the dictatorship—"except in competition, with athletes carrying the Portuguese flag and winning a title for the country." Armindo believed that Salazar realized the association between liberation and physical exercise and therefore discouraged it. He said, "to work your body in the morning means you'll have a totally different kind of day. Your attitude will change after you've exercised. But Salazar didn't want that for the people. He wanted to keep them *fechado* (closed) and *embrulhado* (wrapped up or shrouded) so that they wouldn't sense their own strength." (Holton n.d.)

Figure 7. An FNAT women's gymnastics group during a festival performance, July 6, 1941. *Courtesy of INATEL, Edições Colibri. Reprinted from Valente 1999, XI.*

Lourdes Mendes's (1996) anecdote concerning adolescent dancing during the *Estado Novo* illustrates a popular mistrust of exercise that consistently ghosted the physical exertion required for *rancho* participation. When RFA founders first formed the adult *rancho* in 1959, they also created a *rancho infantil* (children's *rancho*) that disbanded after less than a year due to what was perceived as the dangers of rehearsal. Lourdes, who began dancing as a young girl in the late 1950s and was a member of this short-lived *rancho infantil,* explained:

> The children's *rancho* folded because there was a young boy who had been the mascot—he was the smallest—who became ill with cancer. And in those days this was very shocking to people, because the disease was still poorly understood. And because the disease affected such a small boy, people became very emotional . . . So because the boy was sick, the *rancho* broke up temporarily. During the break several children quit . . . and the *rancho* soon disbanded permanently. There was even the feeling that . . . the illness developed because of the dancing.

Given this popular view of exercise as unhealthy, RFA dancers who trained in preparation for performance engaged in oppositional practices of devel-

Figure 8. FNAT women's gymnastic class, August 11, 1940. *Courtesy of INATEL, Edições Colibri. Reprinted from Valente 1999, XVI.*

oping individual, autonomous strength and endurance. Many RFA dancers who participated in the *rancho* during the *Estado Novo* cite physically rigorous rehearsals and performances as responsible for maintaining their strong, even "obsessive" commitment to the *rancho.* Manuel Anacleto (1996) and his wife, Dulce Anacleto (1996), described Manuel's development as a dancer,

> Manuel: I started going to the 1960s *bailes* when I was fifteen.[34] I started going there—I was fourteen years old, almost fifteen . . . Only folklore! It's a bug that gets lodged in your body.
> Dulce: It's an obsession with folklore . . .
> Kim: Is it the music or the dancing?
> Manuel and Dulce: It's the dancing.
> Kim: It's the dancing?
> Manuel and Dulce: It's the dancing!
> Manuel: It's the love of, I think that, it's of, really of folklore and dance. Before [*25 de Abril*] when there was a *baile,* here or there, not one weekend went by when I didn't go to a *baile.*

Manuel describes his love of dancing using terms denoting illness, "a bug that lodges in your body," "an obsession," implicitly evoking the popular suspicion of physical exercise while describing his passion for it. Later in the interview, Manuel states that only by maintaining a strict regimen of physical conditioning including swimming and calisthenics was he able to rehearse and perform RFA's challenging choreography well. Engaging in regular physical exercise fast became a quasi-religious commitment and a source of great pride. The spectacular dances which at the level of representation satisfied a Salazarist need for propaganda and entertainment, at the level of practice gave dancers a vehicle for making a "show of strength," gaining confidence in their corporeal potential and a sense of individual sovereignty over their own bodies.

Manuel Anacleto (1996) and Dulce Anacleto (1996) described how competition during rehearsals and performances distinguished the better dancers:

> Manuel: I don't like to lose, not one bit. I joined RFA with Olinda and Carlos . . . we wanted to see who could dance better . . . Not only who could dance like this [demonstrates the correct posture], but who could dance a little faster and still dance well.
>
> Dulce: If a *corridinho* came up or a *desafio,*[35] we would choose the fastest to prove who could dance better—those who dance better are different from those who can't dance as well. No, no, no it's not by accident that Olinda and Carlos dance well.

The informal contests waged by RFA dancers in rehearsal differed markedly from Salazar's elaborately staged official folklore competitions. Salazarist initiatives framed spectacular choreography and accompanying up-tempo music as *visual* components of nationalistic displays. From this viewpoint, folklore performers became "living signs of themselves," "live dolls on exhibit"; they were apprehended, compared, and judged *visually.* Combining both spectacle and surveillance, "complementary apparatuses . . . central to the maintenance of . . . repressive power in the modern world" (Jay 1993, 383), Salazarism featured folklore performance from within a profoundly "scopic regime."[36] Spectacular choreography for the folklore practitioner, however, according to Manuel and Dulce, facilitated the development and evaluation of physical strength and skill. RFA dancers apprehended the choreography *corporeally*—through tactility, bodily intuition, physical experimentation, and practice. Further, corporeal self-evaluation could only be achieved, as Dulce points out, during the flashiest, fastest *modas, modas* separating those who dance better from those who don't dance as well.

"Dancing better" meant making a show of physical strength and skill—distinguishing oneself from lesser dancers and asserting an individual identity from within the confines of a group. Both of these actions, performing strength and asserting individuality, were oppositional practices within a

Salazarist framework built on harnessing the individual to the corporative collective and maintaining harmony across class through the masking or, in Kirshenblatt-Gimblett's words, the "banality" of difference. Both of these activities also required an alternative, embodied engagement with spectacle as opposed to the Salazarist visual deployment of folklore performance. By allowing choreographic spectacle to showcase one's own physical force and dexterity, Armindo, Manuel, Dulce, Lourdes, and others imply that dancing facilitated a subversive spark between corporeal strength and liberation. In Armindo's words, dancing folklore meant "you'll have a totally different kind of day."

In underscoring the ways in which folklore practitioners resisted Salazar's system of representation and corporatist ideology while researching, arranging, and performing popular tradition, I am not suggesting that folklore performance was an overtly revolutionary practice, or that it ever broke free from Salazarism's master frame. I view the oppositional practices of *ranchos folclóricos* as important components in what James C. Scott (1990, xiii) terms "the theater of the powerless," a theater whose "hidden transcripts" and, in this case, hidden choreographies, creates narratives of autonomy and dignity for those living under repressive authoritarian forces. Mary Louise Pratt's definition of the term *autoethnography,* foregrounding the complicated relationship between hegemonic power structures and popular self-portraiture, relates to the practices of Portuguese *ranchos folclóricos.* She defines *autoethnography* as "instances in which colonized subjects undertake to represent themselves in ways that engage with the colonizer's own terms." Autoethnographic texts are not, Pratt states, "what are usually thought of as 'authentic' or autochthonous forms of self representation . . . Rather autoethnography involves partial collaboration with and appropriation of the idioms of power" (1992, 7). *Ranchos folclóricos'* corporeal engagement with folkloric spectacle opposed while partially collaborating with Salazarist cultural policy, exposing the inherent "instability" of the performance medium, which can "more effectively undermine oppressive forces than other art forms" (Taylor 1991, 4–5). Whispering down the lane toward unsupervised community contact sparked a quiet politics of proxemics, where *rancho* members networked with elderly neighbors beyond the radar of Salazarist socio-spatial surveillance.

Salazar elevated the rural countryside and its popular traditions to the level of national representation. Corporatist policies designed to defuse political action through the atomization of the country into small socio-spatial units and the distraction of the working class through festivity provided an

al platform for the proliferation of *ranchos folclóricos* during the *Es-*
o. Following the example of the Most Portuguese Village Contest
troupes oriented by FNAT consultants, *ranchos folclóricos* emerged according to templates for the restoration and performance of turn-of-the-century tradition. Professing the desire to pursue ethnographic authenticity while turning a blind eye to the increasing incidence of *rancho* artifice and arrangement, *Estado Novo* officials ineffectively policed the invention of tradition. Within the cleavages between historical restoration and invention, *ranchos folclóricos* such as RFA served as the springboard for exercising individual powers of creativity, unleashing virtuoso skill and emancipatory "shows of strength."

2

Battling the *Bonitinho:* Revolution, Reform, and Ethnographic Authenticity

Rupture or Continuity?

An analytical rift has emerged in recent folklore scholarship regarding the degree to which Portugal's 1974 Revolution sparked change in *rancho* practice and ideology. Some scholars argue that *25 de Abril* did not,[1] in general, disrupt the ideological foundation nor the specific practices of *ranchos folclóricos.* Branco and Branco state, for example, "The shift from authoritarianism . . . to democracy did not mean a rupture in the contents [of revivalist folklore], at this level, there is continuity. In terms of folkloric practice, the revolution did not cause alterations in its contents, repertoires, or performative practices" (2003, 15). They argue that *25 de Abril* facilitated the "expansion and reinforcement" of revivalist folklore, emphasizing that although folklore, previously the subject of the nation, moved into the purview of the local, this shift did not alter the ideological or practical content of revivalist performance.

In contrast to this model of continuity, the model of post-revolutionary rupture views *25 de Abril* as the catalyst for a paradigmatic shift in the practices and ideology of revivalist performance troupes. Due to new guidelines promoted by post–revolutionary cultural institutions such as the *Federação de Folclore Português,* this theory argues, many *ranchos* formed after *25 de Abril,* particularly those applying for FFP affiliation, were held to stricter standards of historical verisimilitude in the gathering and recreation of turn-of-the-century popular song, dance, and dress. This shift has resulted in a tension between paradigmatic poles of folkloric activity—what João Vasconcelos (2001) terms the "paradigma da estilização" (stylization paradigm) dominant during the *Estado Novo* and the "paradigma da reconstituição" (reconstitution paradigm) which emerges in post-revolutionary Portugal.

My research supports selected premises drawn from each model. First, the stylization paradigm is based on the assertion that a "visualist" orientation framed folklore performance during the *Estado Novo* (Alves 1997), producing onstage spectacle which marginalized ethnographic research because its "immediate social efficacy was considered less important than or potentially corrosive to the canons of nationalist rhetoric" (Vasconcelos 2001). My case study of the *Rancho Folclórico de Alenquer,* however, reveals that ethnographic research did constitute an important and sustained activity for performers during the *Estado Novo.* In fact, in the case of RFA, all but three or four of their eighty *modas* were collected during the 1960s and early 1970s—meaning that the vast majority of RFA's repertoire, particularly that which was based on ethnographic research, was amassed during the *Estado Novo.* And, as the testimony of RFA performers cited in chapter 1 suggests, the process of ethnographic collection, conducted by amateurs without any formal training in ethnology, the social sciences, or history, was carried out with seriousness of purpose, methodological skill, and technological savvy. Unlike some of the early *ranchos* in northern Portugal, such as the groups trained by Abel Viana and Gonçalo Sampaio, RFA did not possess an FNAT aligned leader, nor an academic consultant. None of RFA's early leaders had university degrees nor specialized training. And still ethnographic collection, capably conducted, formed the foundation of RFA's expressive archive—out of which emerged a repertoire of over eighty *modas.*

The fact that RFA employed ethnographic methods to build repertoire does not mean, however, that group leaders didn't "stylize" *modas.* Ethnographic collection served as a point of departure for individual acts of choreographic and musical composition. In the case of RFA, ethnographic data, evidence of the past painstakingly recorded, became the inspiration for contemporary creativity. And both elements existed side by side in a performative bricolage that aimed to address a multitude of conflicting demands and desires. My research suggests that post-revolutionary *rancho* practice featured both continuity and rupture, as many *ranchos* under Salazar balanced pressures from competing paradigms.

Part of this balancing act resulted from Salazarist cultural policy which contained internal contradictions, leaving *rancho* performers to negotiate a series of subtle double binds. According to RFA performers and leaders, although there was a vaguely centralized pressure to collect songs and dances from local informants during the *Estado Novo,* the sociability necessary to carry out such research remained circumscribed, in the words of Armindo Rodrigues, by fear "that you might be talking to PIDE spies." The desire to celebrate the past through ethnographic restoration was also balanced by conflicting pressures to rally a local audience and satisfy skilled dancers, who always preferred the up-tempo medleys composed by António Dionísio in order to showcase ability and stamina. Salazar's own framework of cultural competition also worked against the reconstitution paradigm. According to RFA performers, judges rewarded spectacle in the form of bright, pleasing costumes, uniform execution of choreography following a militaristic mode of presentation, and flashy numbers which showcased rapid musical phrasing and quick, up-tempo footwork; in short, competition usually rewarded stylization. Finally, the local pride informants reportedly felt at seeing "one of their dances" up on stage conflicted with pressure to use *rancho* performances as a venue for the expression of pride in a distinctly nationalist register. The lyrics of one RFA *moda* celebrate both the town of Alenquer and the Portuguese nation using melodies adapted from the town hymn and the national anthem. This *moda* reportedly invigorated local audiences, because, although it contained almost nothing of Alenquer's peasant past, it invoked an official expression of local and nationalist patriotism Salazar's cultural policies promoted.

In an analysis of RFA's expressive practices prior to *25 de Abril*, I would argue that both the paradigm of reconstitution and the paradigm of stylization inflected *rancho* research, rehearsal, repertoire, and performance. These models existed in tension with one another, producing an amalgam of songs and dances which cited the past using varying degrees of stylized adaptation. Following *25 de Abril*, once the FFP established itself as a centralized force with the power to "discipline" the field of folklore (Vasconcelos 2001, 414), RFA entered a new phase in its protean evolution. With regard to *expressive* practice, this new phase constituted more a repertoire pruning than explicit repertoire reform. With regard to the *material* elements of onstage performance and research, however, RFA sustained momentous changes along the lines of the paradigm shift Vasconcelos theorizes. FFP's post-revolutionary emphasis on material culture, sometimes to the exclusion or neglect of expressive culture, indicates how slippery the medium of performance can be. FFP administrators found it much easier to excise marks of fascist influence from costumes and ethnographic museums than from live music and dance, and this is reflected in the documents produced by FFP consultants following RFA's petition for affiliation. The FFP focus on *rancho* costume reform and the development of less overtly "performative" activities such as object display and explication invokes a historical "anti-theatrical prejudice" (Barish 1981) while articulating folklore's move from showmanship to scholarship in post-revolutionary Portugal.

This chapter examines how and why the concept of "ethnographic authenticity" came to dominate the folkloric field following the 1974 Revolution. The number of Portuguese folklore groups has dramatically increased since 1974, and an astounding quantity of post-revolutionary *ranchos* has expressed an avowed commitment to improving the quality of their groups (Sardo 1990; Santos 1996). According to an ambitious study by Branco, Neves, and Lima (2001), post–*25 de Abril* constitutes a "boom" period for the foundation of *ranchos folclóricos:* 81 percent of "traditional musical groups" were created after 1974. This means that the FFP must meet a double challenge, reforming holdover groups from the *Estado Novo* while inculcating a new generation of *ranchos* according to new standards and expectations. Expressed as a backlash to Salazar's spectacular *bonitinho* (prettiness), FFP's folklore reform aimed to change the public perception of folklore as fascist merrymaking while teaching *rancho* performers the art of responsible research and performative restoration. This chapter tracks the institutionalized definition, management, and enforcement of historical verisimilitude among post-revolutionary folklore practitioners, and the ways in which one *rancho* embraced and at times subverted these pressures to reform. FFP's reform discourse and RFA's embodied response also expose, I argue, collective anxiety over gendered social change and the liberalizing modernization that characterized the transition to a democratic Portugal.

Revolutionary Missions

Backed by the Movement of the Armed Forces (MFA), General António de Spínola, a respected leader in the African wars, led the bloodless coup on April 25, 1974, ending forty-eight years of fascist rule. As president of Portugal, Spínola established a government comprised of members of the Communist, Socialist, and moderate Popular Democratic Party (PPD). He was soon joined by General Vasco Gonçalves, a left-wing leader in the MFA, who became prime minister in July 1974 and remained in power until September 1975. Backed by the Communist Party and the MFA's left wing, Gonçalves's rule saw the revolution reach its zenith. Throughout most of 1974 and 1975, the nation's new leaders radically restructured Portugal's economy by nationalizing banks and insurance companies, empowering labor unions, and collectivizing large agricultural estates. Elections creating a Constituent Assembly in April 1975, where the Socialists obtained 38 percent of the vote, the PPD 26 percent, and the Communists a mere 13 percent, however, signaled a weakening in Gonçalves's support. A failed coup attempt by the MFA's left wing on November 25, 1975, "marked the halt of the radical revolution" (Herr 1992, 12). Moderate political leadership elected to power in the late seventies and early eighties eventually reversed early revolutionary measures, solidifying Portugal's commitment to democracy and insuring the country's acceptance into the EC.[2] The reversal of the collectivist legislation began in August 1982 with the abolition of the Council of the Revolution. Following the constitutional reforms of 1982, private property was gradually restored and steps toward the creation of a free market economy put into place.

Immediately following *25 de Abril,* Portugal experienced a short period of cultural backlash where art, music, and literature associated with the *Estado Novo* became stigmatized, and some artists and musicians suffered a de facto blacklisting. Throughout 1974 and 1975, artistic production from musicians deemed "fascist" was banned from radio waves and retail centers.[3] While many *ranchos folclóricos* experienced a similar backlash, some even disbanding during the revolutionary period, other modes of folkloric research and collection took on new vitality during *O Verão Quente* (The Hot Summer) of 1975. Perhaps the most significant of these post-revolutionary endeavors was ethnographer Michel Giacometti's ambitious program for university students caught up in the turmoil of post-revolutionary educational reform.[4] Giacometti's *Missão* (Mission) involved the energies and efforts of over one hundred college-aged students who formed the *Serviço Cívico Estudantil* (SCE [Student Civic Service]) to carry out what would be termed the *Plano Trabalho e Cultura* (PTC [Work and Culture Plan]) over the course of many months. Akin to a politicized Peace Corps for ethnographic research into rural life and the collection of its material and expressive artifacts, student workers uprooted themselves from Portugal's urban hubs in order to travel the countryside, conducting lengthy questionnaires with the rural poor concerning sanitary conditions in their village, educational resources, social services, and attitudes toward politics, religion, sex, and money.

In addition to compiling a sociological portrait of Portugal's rural interior—an area Salazar celebrated symbolically but neglected in terms of infrastructural modernization and the improvement of social services such as public transport, healthcare, and education—student ethnographers also recorded popular songs, folktales, anecdotes, and proverbs and collected hundreds of agricultural tools, linens, and earthenware.[5] Many of the students involved in this project shared revolutionary ideas and a desire to help the rural poor improve their material existence and come to political consciousness.[6] The collection of folklore became a feature of leftist initiatives after *25 de Abril,* just as it had been a feature of official fascist initiatives before *25 de Abril.* Giacometti's project inaugurated the protean transformation of revivalist folklore performance in post-revolutionary Portugal while recasting urban intellectual interest in popular culture as an activist endeavor concerned with the socioeconomic welfare of Portugal's rural citizens.

Plans for *Rancho* Reform

Concurrent with Giacometti's PTC, a broader movement to transform the leadership structure, costumes, repertoires, and instrumentation of thousands of *ranchos folclóricos* throughout Portugal emerged following *25 de Abril.* The *Federação de Folclore Português* and to a lesser degree INATEL championed these reforms. According to FFP president Augusto Gomes dos Santos, his not-for-profit organization embarked on a mission of *rancho* reform shortly after its inception in 1977.[7] Santos argues that during the later years of the *Estado Novo, ranchos* were offered little official guidance, falling, by 1970, into a state of "startling degradation" (1986b, 5). He attributes this decline to the fact that under Salazar rural folk were left to their own aesthetic devices. Instead of collecting and preserving authentic traditions, *ranchos* fabricated so-called historic costumes and "corrupted" popular songs and dances through creating musical and choreographic arrangements Santos terms "staged fantasies" (Santos 1986b, 1994, 1996).

During the 1970s, Santos and his team of folklore experts began an aggressive plan for reform. They organized regional folklore conferences and offered "in-home" consultations for *ranchos,* as well as weekend retreats and workshops throughout the country. Santos also began compiling a master data bank of extant folklore collectives, their repertoires, costumes, and group histories. This cataloging project metamorphosed into a competitive federation program where *ranchos* could apply for FFP affiliation. Winning FFP's stamp of approval soon became an important objective for many *ranchos* that were serious about folklore.

Implicit in the drive to educate *ranchos* is Santos's populist desire to dignify folklore and its participants, some of whom were the object of harsh critique and condescension during the *Estado Novo.* Vera Marques Alves, for example, outlines a general attitude of "disdain for the behavior of rural people, namely for members of *ranchos folclóricos,*" documented in several communications to SNI leaders (2003, 195). In a letter to SNI, the director of London's "House of Portugal" describes members of the *Rancho do Douro Litoral* who had performed in an English festival in 1955:

> The group from the Douro Litoral, which I came across accidentally in the Paddington train station, . . . presented a deplorable physical appearance. The men were unkempt and unshaven wearing dirty, patched denim overalls and straw caps. The girls also looked like pigs with hair half dyed, and very badly dressed. Together, sitting on the floor of the station, encircled by jugs of old bottles of red wine and other dirty packages, the members of the group presented a shameful appearance. (Cited in Alves 2003, 195)

The FFP program of reform and pedagogical instruction contains a subtextual civilizing mission, where old classist stereotypes of ignorant country bumpkins are replaced with an image of well-trained researchers who, through the medium of performance, disseminate Portugal's expressive treasures both domestically and abroad.

FFP's official goal is to "valorize and defend national folklore" (FFP 1978, 54), and to "improve the quality of *ranchos folclóricos*" throughout Portugal and among Portuguese-speaking emigrants around the globe (Santos 1994). Quality in this case signifies "authenticity." And authenticity can be achieved, according to Santos, by replicating as precisely as possible the popular traditions of dress, music, and dance in Portugal during the period from 1890 to 1920. Santos (1994, 1996) isolates this thirty-year time period for several reasons. First, according to the FFP rationale, traditions of dress and expression underwent dramatic changes with the creation of Portugal's First Republic in 1910, and rural populations began to adopt these changes by 1920. Second, reliable data concerning the period of 1890–1920 is still accessible to *rancho* members through ethnographic research; it is still possible to interview older people who have first-hand knowledge, lived experience, of this period. Santos advocates ethnographic research methods as the most accurate means toward achieving this replication (as opposed, for example, to relying on secondary sources such as scholarly manuscripts). Ethnography also serves to (re)integrate local communities of *rancho* performers and elderly residents, which strengthens the revivalist folklore movement in general.

Santos also believes that local communities can be reunited through a more holistic approach to the revivification of folklore. In addition to collecting, rehearsing, and performing songs and dances, FFP advocates the creation of ethnographic museums and the local collection of objects found in the homes of Portugal's rural peasantry from 1890 to 1920. He also encourages *ranchos* to revive collective agricultural and spiritual rituals such as harvesting parties, pig killings (*matanças do porco*) (see fig. 9), grain grinding (*malhas* or *malhadas*), corn husking (*esfolhadas*), singing traditional carols door to door (*cantar As Janeiras*), New Year traditions of marking neighbors' doorways with symbols (*pintar e cantar Os Reis*),[8] and Lenten traditions (Santos 1994). By reviving these expressive rituals, *ranchos* not only deepen their research into local tradition, they can also invite an audience and diversify their performance portfolio.[9]

Santos's stated objectives for the post-revolutionary reform of *ranchos folclóricos* appear similar to the goals of Salazar's cultural policies during the *Estado Novo*. Indeed, as chapter 1 argues, the Most Portuguese Village Contest encouraged a similar multilayered approach to the celebration of rurality

Figure 9. Advertisement for a pig killing sponsored by a local fire department. This event includes the performance of popular music and feasting on traditional foods used in São Martinho celebrations. Estremadura, Portugal, 1994. *Photograph by author.*

in all of its expressive and material forms. Many of the activities Santos suggests reviving in the 1990s—corn husking, pig killings, communal baking and washing—were the very activities villages "performed" for Salazar's judges in the 1938 Most Portuguese Village Contest. During the *Estado Novo,* FNAT also encouraged *ranchos* to pursue ancillary activities such as the development of ethnographic museums, another important ingredient in FFP's post-revolutionary reform. The difference between what Santos is trying to achieve after *25 de Abril* and what Salazar promoted before *25 de Abril* centers on issues of scale, uniformity, and political engagement.

Implicit in Santos's plan for post-revolutionary *rancho* reform is a critique of Salazar's folkloric exploits during the *Estado Novo.* The *Estado Novo* used *ranchos folclóricos* as a means to "propagate their politics" and "entertain the people" (Santos 1996). Santos believes *Estado Novo* officials ensnared *ranchos* in an agenda of pure nationalism with little concern for the process of historical corruption they had put in motion. Santos wants to eradicate the Salazarist stamp on *rancho* performance, the telltale markings of fascist artifice or *o bonitinho* (prettiness), by providing education for *ranchos* which is entirely divorced from politics. The tutelage FFP provides through on-site consultation, weekend retreats, workshops, and classes acts as a corrective, Santos contends, not only for the political ideology which "corrupted" folklore during the *Estado Novo,* but also for the neglect of "pure learning" propagated by Salazar's censors and propaganda.

FFP folklore reform also differs from *Estado Novo* initiatives in scale and uniformity. Santos reports in 1994, "Eighty percent of the folklore groups in Portugal, and there are almost 2000, are federated. The remaining 350, possessing a lot of quality, still receive free technical assistance. The FFP takes the place of the state in this task, as you can see" (Santos 1994). If Santos's statistics are accurate and by 1994 80 percent of *ranchos folclóricos* had been federated, then FNAT and other Salazarist institutions had far less success in implementing official cultural initiatives and exercising direct influence over folklore practice, as both Melo (2001) and Valente (1999) confirm.[10] The slippage between official cultural policy and ground-level implementation allowed for the blossoming of what I have termed individual acts of composition and creation and what Santos would term *o bonitinho* among *ranchos* under Salazar. The spotty control over folkloric restoration, aided by the fact that the excessive spectacle associated with "invented tradition" actually abetted Salazarist desire to keep the rural masses in a constant state of festive distraction, created an environment of heterogeneous folkloric revivalism, featuring *ranchos* with extremely varied degrees of mimetic proximity to the target "rural past." Starting in 1977, Santos aimed to sheer folklore of its political charge and spectacular "falsity" through the standardization of historical restoration, the uniform and disciplined application of these new standards, and the development of *effective* centralized leadership.

One of the key strategies to encouraging new standards of authenticity, according to Santos, involved selecting teams of folklore experts from each province who would help *ranchos* reform their repertoires and costumes according to the expressive traditions indigenous to each locality. After working with a *rancho,* the FFP team would then judge whether the group was worthy of federation. These teams, termed *Conselhos Técnicos* (Technical Councils), were comprised of local folklore experts who had "lived experience" of popular traditions. Santos (1996) states,

> The members of the Technical Council are experienced people, some with a certain education, others with a knowledge of costume, in the way that we value. Usually [we also have] a musicologist—happily this has not happened recently . . . but . . . we've had musicologists that embark on a study of folklore and strangle it, ruin it, taking the voice away from the people, because they enter it onto a *pauta* [*pauta* can be translated as "music sheet," "guideline," or "schema"] . . . and sometimes science and practice collide.

As Santos explains, the FFP tries to hire folklore evaluators with an expertise in regional practice. They must also reside in the regions they evaluate. Local residence, according to Santos's logic, insures a familiarity with tradition based on practice—attendance at local *bailes* and festivals where traditional music and dance are featured. By working with folklore experts who have *lived* local tradition, FFP attempts to avoid the "collision of science and practice." FFP prefers experiential knowledge to the disembodied investigation of culture that tries to fit musicological data into a predetermined scientific schema, sometimes disregarding the aberrant finding and "taking the voice away from the people."

Santos encourages *ranchos* to embark on a study of culture based on oral history and ethnographic research. He offers classes in ethnographic methodology, teaching *ranchos* not only how to gather songs and dances for their repertoires, but also how to forge social connections with their elderly neighbors:

> I advise them like this: You have to bring a recorder and start talking to the person. [You say] "I'd like to know how things were done in the olden days" . . . Near Lamego there was a group that two years ago [told me] "we can't collect anything, people say they don't know [any old songs or dances] . . . One day I went there and recorded twelve dances. The *rancho* stood there with their mouths open. But I approached the older people in a different way . . . A woman who was eighty some years old . . . I started talking with her. [I said,] "tell me something, have you been here many years?" "I have." "And so you've always lived here?" And she starts in . . . "Look, what do you want?" . . . Because these ladies are always very suspicious, and so I started to tell her who I was . . . "So, could you tell me how you spent your youth, I'm a bit younger than you are, and so I don't know. How did you do things in the olden days?" And she says, "Look, I would go to Mass" . . . And I continued to listen very patiently, and the *rancho* members there [said] "Let's go. We don't have to waste all this time." Sometimes to get just one or two dances takes two or three days or more. And so, very patiently again, "So how did you spend your youth?" (Santos 1996, my inserts)

FFP's drive toward folkloric authenticity hinges on the establishment of local networks of performer-ethnographers and elderly informants. These relationships are forged with patience and perseverance. FFP also encourages *rancho* members not to "rip off the data and run" (Conquergood 1985), but to involve older residents in the overall life of *ranchos folclóricos*, as ongoing consultants and friends.

Consistent with this emphasis on local research and community building is the value placed on enrichment and exchange versus Salazarist entertainment and competition. The FFP encourages *ranchos* to host and participate in annual festivals where *ranchos* from all regions come together not to compete for prizes but to exchange ideas and broaden perspectives based on an informed sense of regional diversity. This ethos of exchange and learning is also reinforced during regional *estágios* (workshops) sponsored by both INATEL and FFP, where *rancho* leaders are invited for weekend retreats to deepen their knowledge of regional tradition in a pedagogical atmosphere of cooperation and amiable intra-regional comparison.[11]

Increased institutional support has contributed significantly to the health of revivalist folklore performance in democratic Portugal. As Sardo's (1990) research suggests, both the *Federação de Folclore Português* and the *Instituto Nacional para Aproveitamento dos Tempos Livres dos Trabalhadores* (INATEL), FNAT's legacy in post–*25 de Abril*, have played important roles in the fiscal and educational support of *ranchos* since 1974. This support has "created a process of *retro-alimentação* (retroactive nourishment) that has not only increased the qualitative level of *ranchos folclóricos* but has also increased the level of support available to them" (Sardo 1990, n.p.).

No longer appendages of corporatist ideology, these cultural institutions serve to relate *ranchos folclóricos* to new socio-political objectives within post–*25 de Abril* Portugal. FFP, for example, is affiliated with the *Instituto de Apoio à Emigração* (Institute for the Support of Emigration) and the *Instituto de Promoção Turística* (IPT [Institute for the Promotion of Tourism]) (Sardo 1990). INATEL also has ties with IPT as well as the *Secretaria de Estado da Cultura* (State Secretariate of Culture) (Sardo 1990). This new constellation of inter-institutional networks links *ranchos folclóricos* to Portugal's changing concerns in the late twentieth century. Objectives such as fortifying ties among Portuguese emigrants throughout the world[12] and developing the foreign tourist industry reflect Portugal's new international focus following decades of corporatist isolationism. Once framed as highly visible emblems of a national identity, *ranchos folclóricos* now reflect the new ideological complexion of contemporary Portugal and the erosion of national insularity. FFP's reform agenda reinforces folklore's new role in post-revolutionary Portugal, encouraging *ranchos* to "clean up their acts," employ ethnographic research as a tool for connecting to local communities, and, once federated, "take their act on the road" to participate in performance programs of regional and international exchange and enrichment.

RFA's Rocky Road toward Reform

Although the goals of FFP's post-revolutionary reform sprang from the well-intentioned drive to educate rural populations, not unlike Giacometti's *Missão,* to encourage community building, and to promote transnational outreach and travel, some of Portugal's older, more established *ranchos* bristled at the imposed changes. In the case of the *Rancho Folclórico de Alenquer,* complaints ranged from a general reticence to "fix something that wasn't broken" to more-specific charges that FFP used authoritarian methods to exact reform. Almost all RFA dancers reported missing their old costumes, and many of the older dancers still wonder aloud why certain *modas* had been excised from the repertoire. According to RFA members, it is not only the performers who question the reform, but Alenquer's local public as well.

RFA applied for FFP affiliation in 1989 by filling out a questionnaire providing the names of RFA leaders, the titles of RFA *modas,* how the *modas* were obtained, the history of the locality, and the history of the group. On May 9, 1989, an FFP *Conselho Técnico Regional* (Regional Technical Council) comprised of two regional folklore experts, Manuela Carriço and Bertino Coelho, visited RFA to observe a costumed rehearsal. Later another member of the *Conselho Técnico,* Carlos Ribeiro, conducted a follow-up visit. According to the *Conselho*'s evaluation, RFA would not be recommended for federation until several "errors had been corrected" (Carriço 1989, 1–2). According to the report, RFA's most egregious errors occurred in the area of costume.

By the time the *Conselho* arrived, most of RFA's female dancers had already retired the short, bright skirts they had worn during the *Estado Novo* (see fig. 6), attempting to anticipate and preempt FFP's critique. They knew that the FFP required female dancers to abandon their old, colorful garb for more historically responsible costumes. *Rancho* costumes had to represent turn-of-the-century rural styles, including workday dress, Sunday best, and rural wedding attire. Further, costumes had to be site specific; a performer could not, for example, dance a *corridinho,* characteristic of the Algarve, while dressed in clothing from the northern province of Minho. Additionally, *rancho* clothing should be varied: each performer should dress differently, thereby displaying the entire spectrum of rural wardrobes.

Like other *ranchos* in the central regions who sought the FFP's stamp of approval, an honor which often brings national prestige, international performance engagements, and monetary support, RFA not only retired the women's short, colorful skirts but also much of their lacy undergarments and white thigh-highs. Instead, the women dressed in more "authentic" period clothing—drably colored long wool skirts, blouses, and jackets with high collars and dark wool tights. RFA dancers balked at the change, while local audience members criticized the dismal appearance of their neighborhood *rancho.* Olinda Pereira (1996) reports, for example, "I was the first person in the *rancho* to change. I cried a lot. I hated it. The skirt was really long and I hated it . . . It didn't feel right . . . and then people (around town) started saying we looked like gypsies, and they didn't like seeing us that way. Still today the people of Alenquer don't like our new costumes . . . They think we look sad." RFA performers and audiences alike responded to the substitution of bright reds, greens, and yellows for browns and grays with melancholy and "sadness." Neutral-colored costumes not only sparked a new range of somber emotions, they also stripped away Salazarist camouflage by unmasking rural hardship. The figure of the gypsy in Olinda's testimony serves as a trope for poverty and marginality. In order to transform rural indigence into a moral virtue, Salazar also had to alter the appearance of poverty. *Ranchos folclóricos,* dressed in vibrant colors accented by bold black stripes and crisp white lace, helped market Salazar's elevation of the humble rural villager by changing the face of material destitution into chromatic opulence and gaiety. The aesthetic alteration of *rancho* costume also signaled a change in the function of folklore performance. After *25 de Abril,* folklore was no longer intended to merely *dar alegria à gente* (bring the people joy), but to inform and educate them about the local history of expressive traditions. FFP reforms framed *ranchos folclóricos* as representatives of living history. Many RFA performers and audience members, however, had already *lived* this history, and judging from their negative response, did not care to revisit it as drably staged naturalism.

Even though RFA dancers had already made a painful costume change, they were asked to make even more-stringent reforms. The *Conselho* noted that "some costumes still featured elements of the '*fardas*'[13] worn during an anterior phase" (Carriço 1989, 2). Not only was RFA's costume reform deemed incomplete, it was also critiqued as inconsistent. "There is a certain carelessness in the way that blouse, skirt and scarf are combined. Some skirts typical of quotidian working garb are worn with blouses reserved for 'Sunday best'" (Carriço 1989, 2). Additionally, RFA had collected several old photographs and pieces of clothing from elderly neighbors, "but these influences were not present in any of the costumes worn by RFA performers" (Carriço 1989, 1–2).

Following the *Conselho*'s initial visit, RFA began making the appointed changes in costume, paying new attention to the fabrics chosen for their revised costumes and the process whereby the clothing was made. FFP encouraged *ranchos* to seek out fabric without synthetics. They also recommended that *ranchos* make their costumes using turn-of-the-century methods. Barbara Kirshenblatt-Gimblett describes a similar "shift in the locus of authenticity" from object to process at the living history museum in Plymouth, Massachusetts,

> Visitors are urged to "browse through the museum's renowned giftshop, where many items created using authentic seventeenth century methods are available for your own private collection." Authenticity is located not in the artifacts per se or in the models on which they are based, but in the *methods* by which they were made . . . It is as if the tool not only animated a hand, but also a total sensibility—and so fully, that using an adze to understand how it works extends from the hand to the body to the mind to the inner state and way of being in the world that constitutes the person who might have used the tool in 1627. (1993, xv)

In Kirshenblatt-Gimblett's example, antiquated production methods insure the authenticity of commodities "available for private collection."

In the FFP example, traditional methods of production also signal cultural authenticity, but to differing ends. Sewing costumes by hand, crocheting socks, and making lace serve not to enhance the exchange value of commodities, but to augment the pedagogical value of "performing" the task necessary to produce the object. In seeking out regional craftspeople who still practice older methods of cloth making, *rancho* performers learn about the activity itself, sometimes apprenticing until they too can perform the activity. Again, social connections are forged between contemporary practitioners of nineteenth-century artistry and folklore revivalists, while *rancho* performers rehearse the fine motor skills of the past. In this way the reconstitution of period dress results not only in an authentically costumed *rancho,* but also in *rancho* members who have deepened their performance research, extending it "from the hand to the body to the mind to the inner state and way of being" of the Alenquerian locals they embody onstage.

Although several RFA members (particularly the leadership) view these changes positively, others view the FFP as an aggressive, alien, even authoritarian force. When asking RFA performers about Salazarist censorship, for example, many would answer, "No, the only times we've ever been censored have been by the FFP" (J. Mendes 1996; L. Mendes 1996). Some disgruntled *rancho* members refer to the FFP as the "Folklore Police." Although the reforms are well intentioned and ostensibly generated by members of the Portuguese rural *povo* (people) themselves, they employ rhetoric and champion cultural regulation in ways strikingly similar to Salazarist cultural policy—policy that the FFP allegedly works against. FFP reform serves as a "systematic cultural intervention," terminology David Whisnant uses with regard to the preservation of Appalachian mountain music (1983, 186). He states,

> Those who consider themselves "seriously" interested in traditional music (that is, those collectors . . . who considered it their mission to conserve and use traditional music for "higher" purposes) perceived the growing commercial pop-

> ularity of mountain music to be a grave cultural problem . . . the forces of industrial . . . modernity were undermining the rural and agricultural base of the traditional music that such people valued; the machine had entered the folk garden, and was wreaking havoc . . . commercial recordings were [also] vulgarizing an ancient treasure. Such an analysis of the cultural dynamics of the late 1920s implied that a fight had to be waged against modernity and the very popularity of a warped version of traditional culture. (1983, 184)

Whisnant's example is strikingly parallel to FFP's "fight" against Salazar's corrupting stamp on revivalist folklore. The musical arrangements and costumes created during the *Estado Novo* have caused "grave cultural problems," according to new FFP standards of authenticity and the campaign to dignify folklore and its practitioners.

By reforming *ranchos folclóricos,* the FFP also "wages a fight" against the effects of Portugal's rapid modernization. Described overtly as a battle against fascist *bonitinho,* in practice, FFP reforms address both threats from the past and threats from the present. Reforms aimed at sensitizing *rancho* performers to the wealth of expressive traditions in their own backyards coincide with an increase in foreign film and television programming throughout Portugal, and a deluge of American and Brazilian music clogging Portugal's previously censored airwaves and retail centers. Augusto Gomes dos Santos (1996) punctuates worries about the *Estado Novo*'s "neglect" of folkloric authenticity with animated claims that "our teenagers don't want to see Hollywood movies! They aren't seduced by Brazilian *telenovelas* (soap operas). They want Portuguese culture. Our culture." Engaging in a rigorous examination of Portugal's rural traditions not only eradicates the fascist stamp on folklore, it also aims to combat American and Brazilian cultural imperialism, newly felt in Portugal as borders have softened following *25 de Abril,* allowing an influx of foreign media, films, music, and other cultural products.

FFP reforms focused on the appearance and behavior of folklore performers can be read not only as an attempt to dignify folklore, challenging classist *Estado Novo*–era disdain for the rural peasantry expressed in the previously cited letter from London, but also as a conservative warning against emulating the risqué behavior modeled by Brazilian *telenovela* actresses and Hollywood film stars, ubiquitous figures now broadcast throughout Portuguese homes. Unlike Whisnant's liberal do-gooders, who couch their intervention in terms of charitable cultural service, FFP drafts stringent criteria for federation, often phrased in the imperative and issued as superior moral advice. For example, in a list of regulations sent to all *ranchos* who apply for federation and published in the FFP bulletin, the FFP informs women:

> You should not twist your torso to twirl your skirt and make it rise, exposing your thighs. You should not wear short skirts and knee socks . . . You cannot abuse the use of white lace stockings as many *ranchos* erroneously do. White stockings were only used by the wealthy . . . Do not wear lipstick, blush or nail polish, and do not pluck your eyebrows . . . While you are wearing your costume, you should not smoke, because the women you are representing did not smoke. You should not chew gum because it is inappropriate and ugly. (Santos 1986c, 24)

Although these regulations are ostensibly meant to unify and improve quality standards with regard to folklore performance, they strike an odd balance between historical instruction and *contemporary* social regulation. Whom does the "you" refer to in the FFP rules, the turn-of-the-century character or the late twentieth-century performer?

FFP's strong-arm rhetoric reminiscent of a regime long buried has caused a backlash of quiet, sometimes invisible insurrection. RFA performers have found ways to enter this fight for authenticity through mimetic counterpoint. If the FFP wants documented proof of local turn-of-the-century costume in the form of old photographs, and if they want precise duplications of these photographed styles, fabrics, and methods of production, why not give them what they really want? Why not perform in period originals?

Olinda performs in an antique lace collar donated to the *rancho* by an elderly neighbor. The collar dates back to the late nineteenth century. Manuel also carries an antique walking stick onstage, donated to him by an Alenquerian local. Also, in preparation for RFA's annual festival, many of the antique linens and costumes displayed in the ethnographic museum must be taken to members' private homes to be washed and ironed. Female performers have told me that these linens sometimes find their way onto tables or bodies, used in the quotidian "real" lives of RFA members. According to RFA, other *ranchos* engage in similar activities. These strategized acts of mimetic rebellion could be justified as "performance research"—extending the object "from the hand to the body to the mind to the inner state and way of being in the world that constitutes" RFA's historical characters. Michael Taussig's discussion of sympathetic magic, where copies assume power from originals through physical contact (1993, 47–57), also applies here.[14] But *rancho* members have also attended enough FFP workshops on museum preservation to know that performing in antiques is taboo. And this, of course, is part of the point.

FFP's costume reform relies on notions of material purity and historical pollution. As Mary Douglas states, "pollution is used as [an] analogy for expressing a general view of social order . . . And ideas about separating, purifying, demarcating and punishing transgression [in this case, the use of Salazarist *fardas*, man-made synthetics, or machines to fashion folklore costumes] have as their main function to impose system on an inherently untidy experience" (1995 [1966], 3–4, my insert). It makes sense that during the 1980s and 1990s, as Portugal endures the naturally untidy experience of political, social, and economic transformation by relinquishing colonial possessions, embracing democracy, and joining the European Union, that centralized cultural reformers are grasping at measures which might soften the blow of change by reordering historical revivalism through the pursuit of authenticity and, in the words of Mary Douglas, "putting matter back in its place."

RFA's Repertoire Reform

In addition to costume, the FFP also critiqued musical and to a lesser degree choreographic repertoire. The *Conselho Técnico* reviewed ten *modas* and deemed seven either *"aceitável"* (acceptable) or *"bom"* (good) (Coelho 1990). Among the seven *modas* that were approved, several needed slight modification. The remaining three *modas* needed significant alteration. The musical reviewer, Bertino Coelho, had two primary areas of critique: geographical attribution of *modas* and musical tempo.

Coelho felt that many RFA *modas* were played too rapidly. His general recommendations call for a "moderation in rhythm" (1990, 2). For the *moda* "Bico e Tacão" (see appendix), he states, "good number, but too fast." For the "Carreirinhas Marcadas" (see appendix) he states, "None of the old instruments could have provided the conditions for this number to be played so fast . . . If it is played much more slowly, perhaps it will do." The "Vira," although not too fast, was judged too high, "played in a key outside of the singers' vocal capacities" (1990, 1–2).

Coelho also reported that several RFA *modas* were in fact musical forms typical of other regions. Although Coelho phrased these comments as gentle critiques, he did not explicitly suggest that RFA cut these *modas* from its repertoire. In his report, for example, Coelho described RFA's "Carreirinhas Marcadas," as "an authentic *corridinho* from the Algarve" (1990, 2).[15] He also categorized the *moda* "Sariquité" as an "Algarvian *corridinho.*" Even though the *corridinho* is not "typical" of the Estremeduran or Ribatejanan regions, Coelho deemed them both "acceptable." His reasoning alludes to Alenquer's complicated geographical and demographic history, where migratory workers from the south most probably brought the *corridinho* to the *concelho* of Alenquer in the mid- to late nineteenth century.[16]

Manuela Carriço of the *Conselho Técnico* states that Alenquer is a difficult place to evaluate "because it falls within a *zona de transição* [literally

Figure 10. Regional map of Portugal's central *Províncias*. Note Alenquer's position on the border between Estremadura and Ribatejo.

'transition zone' or borderlands] with marked influences from the Ribatejo, Estremadura, and perhaps other areas as well" (Carriço 1989, 1, my insert). Alenquer is also considered a *zona das influências* (zone of influences) due to the nineteenth- and twentieth-century influx of people from differing provinces. Alenquer was a favored destination for those seeking industrial employment. By the end of the nineteenth century, Alenquer boasted four large factories manufacturing textiles, paper, and grains and employing over one thousand workers (Melo et al. 1989). Due to Alenquer's somewhat elusive regional character and geographical position on the border between two provinces (see fig. 10), FFP asked three judges from different areas to review RFA: Carlos Ribeiro from Torres Vedras in northern Estremadura, Manuela Carriço from Mem Martins in southern Estremadura, and Bertino Coelho from Santarém in the Ribatejo.

Although Coelho condoned a good deal of inter-regional borrowing in the special case of Alenquer, he recommended that RFA *suprimir* (suppress or withhold) the *moda* "Morna." Coelho states,

> The dance steps have nothing to do with the rhythmic realities of your region and other regions within metropolitan Portugal . . . the musical melody, however . . . falls squarely within the melodic structures of the Ribatejo. This incongruence forces me to classify this *moda* as a distortion or adulteration composed by musicians. We cannot classify this as a *moda* of "the people" . . . This is a complicated subject, but I did not like the *moda* for the reasons outlined above. (1990, 2)

Many RFA performers attribute "Morna's" problem to geography or terminology, rather than to an incongruence between choreography and music. Olinda Pereira (1996) and Lídia Ventura (1996) discuss the change,

> Olinda: We have the "Morna," now called the "Contradança," which was one of the *modas* that the Federation refused to accept because of its name. We had to rename it "Contradança."
>
> Lídia: Because *mornas* are not from here, they're from Cape Verde, and here, around the *rancho* of Alenquer, I think none of the *ranchos* have *mornas.*

Following the *Conselho*'s critique, RFA changed the title to "Contradança" (see appendix) and modified the music and dance steps. The revised "Morna" is now a standard part of their repertoire.

Coelho's report shows that FFP criteria for judging authenticity focuses both on regional affiliation and generic purity. Because Alenquer occupies a *zona de transição* and a *zona das influências, modas* typical of other regions are permitted to enter the RFA repertoire. These *modas,* however, must be "pure" examples of the song and dance forms. *Modas* which display hybridity—differing music and dance types, syncretized song forms, or syncretized choreography—are deemed inauthentic, "adulterated," "distorted," or the product of musician tampering. In addition, aberrant *modas* which explicitly allude to forms outside of Portugal (as is the case with RFA's "Cape Verdean" *morna*) are deemed the work of contemporary composers and not the assimilated traditions of "the people."[17]

The FFP's criteria seems at odds with other historical scholarship. As Tomaz Ribas states, "a great number of Portuguese popular songs and dances of today are, from a musical and choreographic point of view, foreign bourgeois dances imported during the nineteenth century and assimilated by our people according to their own ways and personality" (1982, 54). In addition, Ribas lists other non-European influences:

> It is also important to consider the influence of the colonial expansion on Portuguese popular dances. The sailors and soldiers that spent many long months in foreign lands later returned to their country bringing exotic dances with them from the people overseas . . . By way of the African slaves beginning in the sixteenth century and the Afro-Brazilian slaves in the eighteenth century, Portuguese popular dances gained new rhythms, new steps, and new movements that dramatically altered their traditional physiognomy. (1982, 53)

Given the fact that outside influences on Portuguese popular song and dance forms are so thoroughly documented, perhaps the FFP is less concerned with matters of foreign origin and more with domestic assimilation. Coelho frames the incongruence between the "Morna's" Ribatejanan music and its non-Portuguese choreography as evidence of deliberate "distortion" on the part of RFA musicians. RFA's "Morna" was so aberrant that the "people" could not possibly have "popularized or folklorized" this form (Coelho 1990, 2).

In addition to balking at much of the FFP's repertoire critique, RFA members also claim that they were never in need of ethnographic training, that these methods of research were already present within *rancho recolha* processes. On the cover of their album, *Rancho Folclórico de Alenquer,* for example, Crispim Luís writes, "Without the precious collaboration of the '*velhinhos*' (old folks) and their instruction, friendship and smiles, these *modas* would have disappeared into eternal sleep. Thank you, people of Alenquer, for all that you have taught us" (RFA 1985). This album was recorded in 1985 in celebration of RFA's twenty-fifth anniversary—several years before FFP reform and RFA's candidacy for federation. As their album cover attests, RFA has always relied on the wisdom and memories of Alenquer's *velhinhos* to build their repertoire of over eighty songs and dances. Of RFA's current membership, ten veteran performers have participated in the *recolha* of dances or objects.

Most members also cite RFA's early foundation date (1937, if you include their *rancho* progenitors) as evidence of their profound and superior knowledge of local tradition, as compared to FFP, founded in 1977. As Armindo Rodrigues (1996a) eloquently states, "*Sou como um livro de história, só que não está escrita*" (I am like a book of history, only it's not written down). RFA members proudly underscore their firm position within the popular class. As Armindo often states, "*Nós somos do povo, vivemos esta música, vivemos esta dança*" (We are of the people, we live this music, we live these dances). RFA views the local historians, auto-didacts, and rising middle-class members of FFP's *Conselhos Técnicos,* on the other hand, as having a distant and perhaps dubious connection to popular tradition. RFA's collective lack of formal education and general location outside of the rising class of young (sub)urban professionals, who increasingly find residence along the transport lines from Lisbon to Alenquer, form the basis of a class consciousness which, according to RFA leaders, legitimizes their more "genuine" and "authentic" knowledge of Portugal's peasant traditions.

This is not to say, of course, that RFA performers have not embellished or authored folkloric music and dances. José Hermínio Carvalho (1996) unabashedly reports that *"Grande parte das vezes as próprias pessoas sabiam as letras, outras vezes era o António Muco que arranjava as letras para essas músicas"* (Most of the time the people [the ethnographic informants] knew the lyrics, other times it was António Muco who created lyrics for these musics). In addition to RFA's former president occasionally filling in the gaps of songs collected, he also composed songs in their entirety. José Hermínio Carvalho (1996) recalled that António Dionísio, who often worked the night shift at the café, would wait for the bread to bake with a pencil and paper in hand:

> He would create the verses . . . Then later . . . he would come up to me and say: "I have here something so beautiful." "And how does it go, Sr. António?" But he never told me like that because he knew he couldn't sing, so he spoke [the lyrics]. So he would stand next to me . . . and I would start to invent the music playing accordion. His response was always the same: "It's beginning to sound good. It's beginning to sound good." I would compose the musical part.

Many of these compositions were offered as gifts to other *ranchos,* particularly RFA's *afilhados,* or godchildren. Most of the composed songs and dances featured highly complex choreography and rhythms, and so were used in rehearsal as challenging physical exercises for musicians and dancers alike. Other explicitly composed *modas* such as RFA's signature "Rapsódia," a medley of tunes sometimes lasting for over ten minutes, became famous among local audiences and were performed as encores, gestures of gratitude, shows of strength, or tests of endurance. Many of these composed *modas* never hid behind the guise of "authenticity" but served other important functions within insider *rancho* networks and among local publics.

RFA Response to Repertoire Reform

Paradoxically, since FFP affiliation, RFA has collected neither *modas* to augment their repertoire nor objects for their ethnographic museum. Crispim Luís (1996) attributes this inactivity to the fact that RFA already has an extensive repertoire: *"agora . . . eles não têm trabalho, porque aquilo já está feito, o rancho tem as modas . . . a gente já teve de ir recolhê-las, fomos à tanta terra"* (now . . . they don't have work, because it's already been done, the *rancho* has it's *modas* . . . We already had to go and collect them—we went to so many places). Others feel that there is always more information to collect and are puzzled as to why RFA stopped building their repertoire. Olinda Pereira (1996) states, "*Temos actualmente uma 'Moda a Dois Passos' na Atouguia das Cabras que um senhor ofereceu para a gente lá ir buscar. Até hoje ainda não fomos*" (We've got a "Two-Step Dance" in the town of Atouguia das Cabras that a man offered to teach us. To this day we still haven't gone). Still others, newly sensitized by FFP regulations to the dangers of irresponsible data collection, feel that RFA has stopped collecting *modas* because there are fewer and fewer reliable sources from whom to learn the dances. Following this reasoning, RFA should not compromise its standards of methodological excellence by relying on informants with faulty memories or calling on a younger generation of locals who possess only secondhand knowledge of popular tradition.

Following FFP federation, RFA leaders have focused their energy on improving the *modas* the group currently possesses and convincing RFA members that this new direction warrants their time and commitment. Armindo Rodrigues (1996a) explains the change:

> When the *rancho* was founded there wasn't the preoccupation with . . . finding out why folklore existed, with knowing how the people dressed . . . the preoccupation was, "let's create a dance group with regional music that will perform spectacle" . . . Later . . . when I joined the *rancho* and even before then, Sr. Pires had started this project, the great preoccupation was then, let's make folklore and integrate the spectacle. But now we are the spectacle in terms of folklore. The spectacle is authenticity.

Armindo's argument, positing authenticity as impressive onstage spectacle, convinces some but not others. The dancers with the greatest physical ability and consequently the most flair resist these changes. They appreciate spectacular choreographic challenge, regardless of whether it is the product of pure *recolhas* or the product of embellishment. The oxymoronic "spectacle of authenticity" seems to them, at best, a shabby substitute for RFA's former performative zip and, at worst, an affront to the history and the founders of the oldest *rancho* in Alenquer. António Reis (1996)[18] states, for example:

> Sometimes I become furious thinking about what I have danced . . . We have the "Saloian Bailarico," the "Alenquer Corridinho," the "Rhapsody," we have many that should have been danced. Why aren't they danced? Because they don't have the dancers? They don't have the people who know how to dance? . . . There *is* someone who knows how to dance! [indicating himself].

Negotiating the tensions between creating evocative onstage spectacle and pursuing authenticity via ethnohistorical accuracy has been a gradual and delicate process. In becoming federated, RFA was forced to overhaul its costumes and perform very selectively from its repertoire to pass muster with the *Conselho Técnico.* RFA's leadership has gradually continued this process of selection, by "weeding out" the *modas* which do not faithfully represent the region or are inauthentic due to musical or choreographic doctoring. Presently, only certain *modas* are rehearsed on a regular basis. The repertoire has been segregated into those dances which are rehearsed and performed and those which are, for all intents and purposes, stored. Armindo Rodrigues (1996a) insists that *"não esquecemos o que o António Muco criou, não esquecemos, mas o repertório de todos os dias são puras recolhas"* (we haven't forgotten what António Muco created, we haven't forgotten, but what we perform everyday is pure *recolha*). The *modas* confined to the "storehouse," however, have never been taught to newer dancers. And the older performers, who once knew these dances, are never asked to practice the choreography. Further, there is no written notation of these dances. RFA administrators have, thus, orchestrated a gradual but systematic process of forgetting.

Other RFA dancers explain the repertoire changes in a different way. João Mendes (1996) and Lourdes Mendes (1996) attribute these changes to situational variables. They feel that RFA tailors its performance repertoire to suit the performance venue and the geographic location of the event. João states that during

> festivals and other things we have to dance . . . certain dances . . . those dances that for us really represent our zone. The dances which are more physically demanding that we like more—if we go to a *festa* and have to dance for more time, then we dance these dances. We make a type of selection because there are dances that we like a lot but we know that there are certain situations in which we shouldn't for any reason dance them.

João offers an insightful analysis of the contingencies that influence repertoire selection based on the nature and location of the performance event. He also alludes to the important distinction between "festivals" and "*festas.*"

Almost all *ranchos* with the financial means host an annual festival commemorating the group's inception.[19] These festivals feature five *ranchos* from vastly different regions of the country that perform for twenty minutes each. To a certain extent, the success of the festival is measured in terms of the representativeness of the *ranchos* invited. *Ranchos* that host festivals go to great lengths to insure that there are no two *ranchos* representing the same region.[20] They also invite *ranchos* known for performing the most "typical" *modas* of their respective regions. In turn, RFA chooses only the *modas* which are most representative of its zone for festival performance. Other types of dances associated with locales outside Alenquer would never be performed during a festival. The pressure *ranchos* feel during festival as opposed to *festa* performance to portray regional representativeness through repertoire selection is compounded by the danger of duplicating repertoire of the four other *ranchos* sharing the performance program.

Festa performance is always paid, as compared to festivals, which are performed for free. *Festas,* local fairs which celebrate religious or popular holidays or commemorate civic events, can last for several days. The organization sponsoring the event, usually the *freguesia* (parish) or the *Câmara,* hires, for example, *ranchos folclóricos,* marching bands, magic shows, and/or *fado* singers as *festa* entertainment. As João Mendes explains, *ranchos* are usually asked to "dance for more time"—at least an hour, sometimes longer. In these situations RFA is forced to delve further into its repertoire to fill the allotted performance time. *Festa* performance, therefore, features more of RFA's *danças mais movimentadas*—those physically demanding dances partially or entirely choreographed by António Dionísio.[21] Dionísio's dances can also be performed at *festas* because the primary focus of the event is entertainment as opposed to ethno-geographic representation. Further, *festa* performance usually engages only one *rancho* at a given time, so there are fewer concerns about inter-regional comparison.

In addition to the differing demands of festival versus *festa* performance, another situational variable influences repertoire selection. It is unwise, for example, to perform a *moda* firmly associated with a certain region (e.g., the *fandango* with the Ribatejo) when performing in this region. The fear is that in so doing, the *rancho* will be "shown up." An RFA member explained this rule to me using an analogy—"It would be like an American coming to Portugal to perform *fado,* or a Portuguese going to the States and serving his dinner guests hamburgers." Each region should have exclusive claim to certain *modas.* In the Ribatejo, for example, people come from all over Portugal to see *rancho*-sponsored *fandango* contests. The crowd-pleasing capacity of the *fandango* is notorious, and these contests can continue well into the night. *Fandango* contests not only evaluate the abilities of individual dancers throughout the Ribatejo, but also confirm and celebrate local and regional identity.

The reticence of non-Ribatejanan groups to perform *fandango* exemplifies not only the way in which repertoires are shaped situationally, but also the pressure exerted upon folklore groups by the FFP to maintain static geographic divisions, delimiting rights to cultural property based on region.

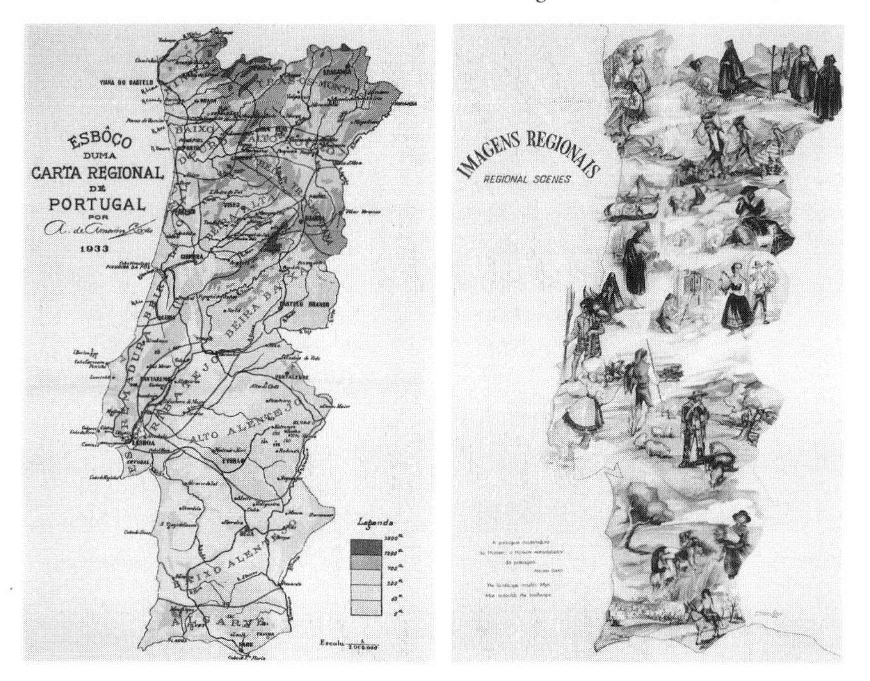

Figures 11a and 11b. Left: Amorim Girão's 1933 map of Portugal, produced during the *Estado Novo.* Right: A map designed in 1958 by Helena Abreu entitled "Imagens Regionais" (Regional Images), combining regional identity with peasant archetypes, many of which find parallel in *rancho* costume and props. *Courtesy of the Instituto de Estudos Geográficos, Universidade de Coimbra, Portugal.*

RFA used to perform *fandango,* a *moda* that was reportedly collected from an elderly person within the *concelho.* However, after becoming federated, the *fandango* was dropped from the repertoire altogether. When I asked about the *fandango* many RFA members would say, "*O fandango não é daqui. É mais p'rá zona do Ribatejo*" (The *fandango* is not from here. It's more from the Ribatejan zone).

The *fandango,* however, is "a men's dance of Spanish origin. In the Tagus River valley it is usually performed by two men who compete to attract a woman's attention by alternating their virtuosic dancing" (Branco 1994). Branco cites the Tagus River Valley as the primary place *fandango* is performed. Such a description reveals the artificiality of regional divisions immortalized by geographer Amorim Girão's provinces portrayed in his 1933 map, and reiterated in pictoral form in 1958 by Helena Abreu (see figs. 11a and 11b).[22] The Tagus River Valley delimits an area along the border of the river, jumbling Girão's provincial delimitations by combining portions of Estremadura and Ribatejo.

Alenquer is located along this strip; as RFA states in its performance resume, Alenquer occupies the *"terra fértil . . . entre a serra de Montejunto e a margem do rio Tejo"* (the fertile land between the Montejunto mountains and the banks of the Tagus River). In addition, Alenquer was once considered part of the Ribatejo, and the town of Azambuja, an important center of contemporary *fandango* performance, once belonged to Estremadura (Santos 1985). Jorge Gaspar affirms that "certain territorial units, such as Estremadura . . . have oscillating borders, reflecting economic and social dynamics, but also the precariousness of prior delimitations" (1993a, 15). The FFP, then, often enforces the *Estado Novo* regional divisions drawn along the lines of Girão's 1933 map, despite contemporary efforts to update cartographic borders according to revised notions of sociocultural and economic coherence.[23]

RFA members also recognize the paradoxes inherent in fixing repertoires according to static, outdated notions of regional identity. João Mendes (1996) and Lourdes Mendes (1996) state:

> João: If you really think about it, we are located in a zone which is both Ribatejo and Estremadura. We have many things, but if you think about it, we really don't have anything which is from here.
>
> Lourdes: This happens a lot in folklore. It's because you have people who came to this zone to work and stayed here for many years . . . they brought a certain tradition of theirs, which they later passed on and which then became [the tradition] of the people who were born here. Things are always carried from one place to another. Because of this there are often similar things (in different places). "But this is ours!" And in the end it might not even be ours. It could have come from the grandparents, the great-grandparents of other people who came from different places . . . Sometimes we go to places outside of our zone and we see, "But this *moda* is ours, how did it come to rest here?"

Lourdes and João discuss the difficulty in assigning bounded geographical areas a finite bundle of traditions. As Lourdes says, "Things always are carried from one place to another," which serves to blur and complicate neat spatial divisions and stringent taxonomic groupings of corresponding traditions. The FFP creates a system of evaluation where folklore is understood in terms of region and where certain signature *modas* act as synecdoches for bounded geographical space. *Ranchos* like RFA located on the border between regions must modify or delete certain *modas* to be understood within such a system. The FFP's enforcement of regional representativity and folkloric localism differs greatly from Salazar's symbolic deployment of folklore as nationalist propaganda. While the FFP encourages *ranchos* to retreat into their local communities to conduct ethnographic research and pare down repertoires according to strict notions of local and regional representativity, many *rancho* repertoires during Salazar amalgamated regional traditions, celebrating and unifying the entirety of the nation.

FFP reform employs models of authenticity and mimesis that assume a static, verifiable original. If *ranchos* work hard enough, contacting the most accurate sources and crafting the most precise replicas, they will succeed in unearthing, copying, and performing traditions identical to "true" originals. FFP's view of mimesis opposes postmodern constructionist ideas which argue that "it is the copying that originates" (Geertz 1986, 380). FFP's model of authenticity and mimesis frames mutations in popular tradition caused by population flux, industrialization, or foreign influences as corrupting features performers should avoid or purge. FFP attempts to purify and insulate regional difference and compartmentalize regional identity according to geographic taxonomies, even though as Gaspar argues, these territorial units have been "precarious" from the start. RFA performers recognize the instability of geographic, cartographic, and cultural classification systems. Most do not endorse FFP's stringent regulation of expressive authenticity. RFA members work around the rules by performing in period originals, tailoring repertoire to performance venues and locales, and struggling to satisfy their desire to perform and perform well despite the dilution of choreographic and musical challenge.

The Revolution of April 25, 1974, sparked a cultural boom in Portugal which, in the field of literature, prompted formal experimentation, an emergent feminist discourse, and the literary engagement with previously taboo themes, such as the colonial wars in Africa, political repression, social disfunctionality, sexuality, and utopia and distopia (Sadlier 1989; Kaufman and Klobucka 1997; Ferreira 1997; Sapega 1997; Ornelas 2002). Expressive culture also experienced a postrevolutionary flowering, characterized by formal experimentation, a proliferation of new practitioners, and the embrace of new thematic foci. After a brief period of postrevolutionary blacklisting, for example, *fado* enjoyed an international renaissance, boasting a new generation of vocalists eager to push the urban ballad form into fresh musical and lyrical territory. And finally, membership numbers in *ranchos folclóricos* witnessed an explosive rise following *25 de Abril,* as centralized organizations such as FFP and INATEL offered support for new troupes and consultation and training for older groups.

It is within this context of cultural awakening that folklore reform occurred. Folklore experts such as FFP president Augusto Gomes dos Santos and the members of his *Conselhos Técnicos* struggled to excise the marks of fascist *bonitinho*, or stylization, by promoting ethnology as the primary methodological vehicle for insuring the authenticity of *rancho* repertoire. FFP reform also sought to standardize revivalist folklore performance through limiting the temporal scope of revivalist *modas* and the geographic provenance of repertoire.

Although the expressive products of *ranchos folclóricos* have been the object of reform, it's the *material* components of *rancho* performance, I would argue, which have claimed the most attention and born the most scrutiny. Aligned with the view that folklore performance participated in Salazar's distinctly visualist initiatives to control and indoctrinate rural populations, reform of visualist elements such as *rancho* costumes took on added importance post–*25 de Abril*. Retiring the short A-line skirts, often in reds and greens—the colors of Portugal's national flag—meant cutting the charged association with Salazar's enforced patriotism and the festive "dressing up" of poverty characteristic of Salazar's corporatist policies.

FFP complemented the reform of costumes with initiatives to promote the development of archives and museums dedicated to the research and display of rural objects from the turn of the century. Collecting objects such as old agricultural tools, clothes, books, photographs, bedpans, linens, utensils, and knitting needles would allow *rancho* performers to understand the material backdrop to the *modas* they collected, so that songs and dances could be contextualized and authenticated by ancillary displays. FFP also encouraged the revivification of activities which animated the objects housed in new *rancho* museums—such as corn husking, weaving, wood working, and cow milking—in order to create a multilayered restoration of historical period and cultural pastiche.

Post-revolutionary folklore reform, framed as a corrective to fascist spectacle, aimed to replace showmanship with scholarship, training rural performers to conduct ethnographic research, understand local history, build community, and experience unencumbered outreach, travel, and exchange. As well intentioned as these objectives may be, many older *ranchos* questioned the way in which reforms were imposed and the legitimacy of FFP's centralized guidance. In the case of RFA, skilled dancers felt the more "authentic" *modas* did not allow them to showcase their skill or stamina. Many RFA dancers also missed the overtly arranged or stylized *modas* composed by António Dionísio—claiming that these dances contained historical value of a different sort. Costumes worn during the *Estado Novo* were also favored by both performers and local publics; the new, drably colored, historically responsible costumes created an image of indigence and marginalization which undercut the euphoric liberation post–*25 de Abril* Portugal was supposed to be experiencing. FFP's focus on the female dancers' appearance, questioning the appropriateness of short skirts, lacy undergarments, make-up, and eyebrow plucking—described in FFP literature as both historically inaccurate and "ugly"—also revealed anxiety about gendered social change and the proliferation of choices in wardrobe, lifestyle, and behavior enjoyed by women throughout post-revolutionary Portugal. *Rancho* performers subverted some of FFPs demands by tailoring repertoire to performance engagement, enabling certain stylized *modas* to stay in circulation, and wearing period originals onto the stage knowing full well this practice was ill advised from the standpoint of historical preservation.

Undergoing the FFP accreditation process and answering to the critiques of judges widely perceived to be geographical outsiders sparked a latent class consciousness among RFA performers, who felt themselves better equipped to judge the authenticity of traditions that their relatives had *lived* as members of Portugal's rural peasantry. The way in which FFP phrased cultural reform in printed literature and mandated change through the *Conselhos Técnicos* also caused RFA members to label FFP as the "Folklore Police" and describe their practices as "authoritarian." In an anachronistic blending of period and political regime, some RFA performers report that the only time their group had been the object of fascist censorship was during the FFP affiliation process.

Concerns over authenticity dominated post-revolutionary reform, acting against the excesses of the past and the present. As chapter 1 demonstrates, the *Estado Novo* employed revivalist folklore performance to aestheticize politics. FFP reform aimed to rid *ranchos folclóricos* of this aestheticization, substituting the material and expressive traces of fascist patriotism with the fruits of grassroots research and the careful restoration of local tradition. By battling Salazarist *bonitinho,* Santos implies that Portugal's rich compendium of rural tradition is plenty *bonito* unadorned by invented arrangements. Stripping performers down to replicas of turn-of-the-century peasant dress makes a spectacle out of ethnographic authenticity, as drab as it may be in some parts of the country. Plunging folklore performers into the pursuits of autochthonous restoration also safeguards against the clear and present danger posed by Portugal's modernization and the post-revolutionary influx of foreign cultures unleashed by EEC membership, a free market economy, and the liberalization of Portuguese society. Disciplining folklore performance according to new standards of ethnographic authenticity attempts to fix Portuguese tradition by staving off the threats of global homogenization and foreign influence.

3

From Intestines into Heart: The Performance of Cultural Kinship

In the twenty-five years following the 1974 fall of the *Estado Novo,* Portugal opened its borders to a flood of new ideas, consumer products, and migrational flows. The media was no longer censored. Foreign programming aired across a proliferation of public and private Portuguese television channels. Lisbon and other urban centers became hubs of immigration. Military personnel and *retornados* returned to their hometowns from years in Africa with stories of alternative ways of life and changed cultural habits. Following 1986, EEC monies helped fund massive infrastructural improvements in highway, rail, and other public transportation systems. Post-revolutionary Portugal experienced new transnational permeability and increasing social, ethnic, and racial heterogeneity within its own borders.

At the same time that Portugal's national borders became more porous, extending into a unified Europe and softening for the mass entrance of postcolonial migrants, its citizens turned with renewed attention toward localized community. A new appreciation for foreign cultural products was balanced with a new desire to understand and document Portugal's *own* popular culture. Although under Salazar, Portuguese popular culture carried an important symbolic valence and rural populations drew the focus and energies of many FNAT, SPN/SNI, and JCCP initiatives, post-revolutionary movements encouraged new kinds of interior explorations with an eye toward developing distinctly post–*25 de Abril* forms of localism. As chapter 2 outlines, the early post-revolutionary interest in researching the expressive and material riches of Portugal's rural communities is exemplified in Michel Giacometti's ambitious 1975 Work and Culture Plan initiative conducted by the Student Civil Service. Giacometti's approach to understanding, documenting, enriching, and aiding rural communities found a depoliticized extension in the reform of *ranchos folclóricos* by the *Feder-*

ação de Folclore Português, also outlined in chapter 2. Instead of sending "outsiders" into the nooks and crannies of Portugal's rural communities, the FFP strived to teach local "insiders" how to use ethnographic methodology to research and record local tradition and re-create these expressive practices through performance.

The FFP's new emphasis on the historical accuracy and regional representativity of folklore repertoire demanded personal interaction with local communities. Employing ethnographic methods to collect late nineteenth-century songs, dances, and material objects meant forging local relationships. In the process, many *ranchos* throughout Portugal have become increasingly integrated into local business initiatives, festivals, and cultural partnerships, which further strengthens community ties and socioeconomic interdependence.[1] The FFP also discouraged the old competition paradigm prevalent during the *Estado Novo,* urging *ranchos* instead to hold folklore festivals meant to facilitate broad cultural interchange among troupes of differing regions. Post-revolutionary *ranchos* have met new fiscal and cultural demands brought on by the hosting of large anniversary festivals by networking with local merchants, entrepreneurs, and political leaders, entering into relationships of corporate sponsorship and reciprocal marketing and promotion. These partnerships mark the new ways in which *ranchos* experience and produce locality post–*25 de Abril.*

The present chapter focuses on the return to the local during a time "where the nation-state faces particular sorts of transnational destabilization" (Appadurai 1996, 178). As scholars of globalism theorize, transnational destabilization has been accompanied by compensatory attempts at small-scale community building, as people try to offset the alienation engendered by larger spheres of alignment through a reentrenchment in the grounded realm of the local. Locality, according to Appadurai, is "an inherently fragile social achievement . . . maintained carefully against various kinds of odds" (1996, 179). Due to the dramatic social, political, and spatial change that has occurred throughout Portugal in the last quarter century, the "odds" against which *ranchos folclóricos* produce locality in post-revolutionary Portugal are particularly palpable. An examination of *ranchos folcóricos* kinship systems provides a compelling example of the ways in which some communities have weathered these changes and built locality following *25 de Abril.*

This chapter contributes to recent anthropological scholarship that has resurrected kinship studies from the ashes of academic disfavor by exploring notions of "relatedness" in new ways (Stone 2001; Franklin and McKinnon 2002; Carsten 2000). Employing the metaphor of kinship as an organizing analytical approach, this chapter examines the machinery of locality production as it is played out within the extended families of *ranchos folclóricos* and the networks of corporate sponsors, "godparents," and "godchildren" which comprise *ranchos'* local support systems.

My research indicates that *ranchos folclóricos* play an important role not only in building new kinds of localized communities, but also in negotiating the social changes which have transformed Portuguese families post–*25 de Abril. Estado Novo* ideology, dominated by Catholic conservatism, favored large families where wives were ideally confined to the domestic sphere and husbands worked outside the home. Divorce and abortion were illegal. Since the collapse of the dictatorship, however, divorce has been legalized, the birth rate has plummeted, and women have entered the workplace in ever-increasing numbers. These challenges to traditional gender roles leave Portuguese families to navigate new social landscapes without the domineering voice of the state providing moralizing policy and prescriptions.[2] In this era of greater autonomy, life choices, and civil rights for Portuguese citizens, particularly women, *ranchos folclóricos* provide an important local forum for the collective negotiation of change.

For the members of RFA, often described as "one big family," the *rancho* serves as a staging ground for processing conflict within individual family units, rehearsing new forms of sociability, and experimenting with roles of power and authority for women. Contemporary struggles are aired and vetted in the process of recreating the past, further contextualizing change by examining it against the backdrop of turn-of-the-century tradition and *Estado Novo bonitinho.* Post-revolutionary struggles endured by RFA at a local level refract and reflect larger societal transformation, providing members with support networks, avenues of communication, and localized spheres of affective belonging. Bonds of "cultural kinship" found within folklore collectives extend outward toward sponsors, supporters, and audience members, which together confront the fragility of achieved locality through an active engagement with expressive culture.

Fascism and the Family: A Historical Backdrop

Families comprised the foundational building block for corporatist social engineering during the *Estado Novo.* Under Salazar,

> Attempts [were] . . . made, through personal and family ties, the *compadrazgo,* and personal identification with the leader, as well as an increasingly elaborate system of corporate associations, to construct various linkages so that a sense of "belonging" [was] engendered, alienation [was] reduced and all [were] integrated into the prevailing structure . . . The national system [was], hence, con-

Figure 12. António Salazar's "Lesson," the trilogy of national education. *Reprinted from Rosas 1990, cover.*

ceived in terms of the family metaphor, implying strong benevolent leadership, assigned and accepted duties, paternalism, a purpose greater than the sum of its individual parts. (Wiarda 1977, 20)

Salazar's famous *lição* (lesson)—*Deus, Pátria, Família: A Trilogia da Educação Nacional* (God, Fatherland, Family: The Trilogy of National Education) (see fig. 12)—expressed in gendered terminology the core values that Portuguese families were meant to uphold.

Figure 12 communicates Salazar's lesson through a colorful portrait of the ideal family. A luminous sunset lights the father's entrance into his simple abode, home from a long day of agricultural labor. A gleaming hoe slung over his shoulder, he greets two small children. The little girl interrupts her game of "playing house," rehearsing for her future maternal role with a doll, pots, pans, and a diminutive bed, to run to her father. The boy, dressed in uniform embodying militaristic discipline and obedience, gets up from a wooden bench, smiling toward the opened door. The mother is literally and figuratively captive within the hearth, holding a large pot, her long skirt almost touching the "home fires" which will speed the arrival of dinner, and perhaps engulf her in the process. An enormous wooden crucifix and a tumble of rakes, barrels, and pitchforks frame the long shadow cast by the entering head of household.

Salazar's cultural ideology hinged on projecting values of Christianity, rurality, and humble lifestyle into the domestic space and onto the nuclear family. The composition of the family and the gendered roles ascribed to its members became the subject of state policies and initiatives. Salazar's traditional family ideally featured an authoritative husband as the head of household, and his wife, confined to the domestic sphere, who needed her husband's written consent to hold a passport, open a bank account, and work outside the home (Lisboa 2002, 129). Salazar elaborated on these points in several interviews in the 1950s and 1960s:

> Women's work outside the family sphere disintegrates home life, separates its different members, and makes them strangers to each other . . . Life in common disappears; the work of educating the children suffers and families become smaller . . . We consider that it is the man who should labor and maintain the family and we say that the work of the married woman outside her home, and, similarly that of the spinster who is a member of the family, should not be encouraged. (Quoted in Sadlier 1989, 2–3)

> The great nations should set an example by confining women to their homes. But these great nations seem oblivious to the fact that the solid family structure cannot exist where the wife's activity is outside the home. And so the evil spreads and each day becomes more dangerous. (Quoted in Sadlier 1989, 3)

Folklore troupes, with their resurrection of outmoded agrarian practices and traditions, celebration of modest living, and performed expression of traditional gender roles, reinforced Salazar's vision for the Portuguese family, and the nation by extension.

If, however, folklore troupes were part and parcel of the symbolic machinery that communicated and enforced Salazar's conservative ideologies, how, then, can *ranchos folclóricos* act as vehicles for processing the liberalizing changes which effect families in contemporary Portugal? Does revivalist folklore, with its static portrayal of archetypal female virgins and strong male field hands—very much the characters Salazar portrays in his "lesson"—simply work to reinstate conservative values and habits among "folklore families" in post-revolutionary Portugal? The bald incongruity between folklore's fascist legacy and the social realities faced by contemporary *ranchos* provides a crucial entrée into the negotiation of post-revolutionary change. My research shows that folklore performance acts as a conservative strategy to protect Portugal's youth from the social ills such as drug use and crime that have come with rapid "modernization." Further, the act of rehearsing and performing folklore in post-revolutionary Portugal, with its emphasis on travel and exchange, actually keeps families together and hinders the traditional gendered segregation of leisure-time activities which characterized family dynamics under Salazar.[3] The *rancho* also acts as an arena for the "rehearsal" of new gendered sociability, as women take on leadership roles and negotiate power within the *rancho* family. At rehearsals, administrative meetings, and social gatherings, the historical trajectory of the *Rancho Folclórico de Alenquer* from its initial appearance in the 1950s to its present incarnation is often discussed, and diachronic changes—in membership, performance schedules, budget, sociability, and morale—are consistently evaluated. Ironically, in coming together to perform the "traditional family," RFA members are able to process a new set of contemporary familial relationships, changing gender roles, and cultural realities. The expressive portrayal of the late nineteenth-century rural family, influenced as it is by layers of fascist cultural policy and propaganda, exists as a historic backdrop, a benchmark against which change is measured, conflict is vetted, and collaboration is achieved among contemporary *ranchos folclóricos* and new coteries of local kin.

The *Rancho Sede* as "Homeplace"

Upon first entering the *sede* (headquarters) of the *Rancho Folclórico de Alenquer* at Forum Romeira, one steps into an open lobby area bounded by a railless staircase on the left and a bar on the right. Directly in front of the lobby is a large dance floor devoid of furniture except for the eight or nine small tables and chairs which ring the rehearsal space. The back wall behind the dance floor features tall windows with homemade green plaid curtains and several glassed bookcases displaying RFA ribbons and trophies. The area around the bar contains shelves of *aguardente* (strong Portuguese brandy), large jugs of wine from neighboring vineyards, water, and soft drinks. Behind the bar is a large poster with beverage prices. The walls are a stark Mediterranean white and the floors, thick planks of sumptuous blond wood. In the far right corner is a small, enclosed office where the *rancho* administrators keep important documents and research books. In the office, large-scale photographs of the *rancho* at various periods throughout its history hang beside shelves of mementos and municipal flags—gifts from other *ranchos.* Beside the door to the office is a bulletin board where an assortment of *rancho* business is posted, from upcoming performance dates to lists of official winners in the ongoing *rancho* drinking game. Up the railless stairs on the second floor is the RFA Ethnographic Museum. Although most of the objects collected by the *rancho* are on display in the museum, some items are stored in the closet above the office, while still others are kept in the private homes of *rancho* members.

All thirty-one members of the *Rancho Folclórico de Alenquer* and their *acompanhantes,* or companions, gather every Wednesday evening for rehearsal at the *rancho sede.*[4] The *sede* is located in a small self-contained corner unit of the massive Forum Romeira,[5] a rose-colored building perched conspicuously at the entrance into Alenquer which houses myriad events throughout the year, including academic conferences, art exhibits, auctions, theater performances, trade shows, concerts, craft sales, bull fights, and local fairs. Although the building is officially titled the Centro Municipal de Exposições (Municipal Exhibition Center), Forum Romeira functions more as a community cultural center and a primary architectural manifestation of Alenquerian neighborhood.[6]

The *sede* at Forum Romeira constitutes RFA's collective home. Upon initial acquisition of the space, *rancho* members installed new lighting and hardwood floors, repaired the staircase and windows, and repainted the walls. Group members regularly water plants, clean and wax floors, restock the refrigerator, and repair leaky faucets. The *rancho* members renovate and contribute to the continual upkeep of the *sede* without receiving monetary compensation. According to many I interviewed, such "domestic" tasks are undertaken with *amor à camisola*—or as a "labor of love."[7] The *rancho sede* is home not only for RFA members and their weekly rehearsals, social gatherings, administrative meetings, and *rancho* archives of fiscal reports, letters, awards, and photographs, but is also home to the material objects and performative practices of the local space of Alenquer. As urban ethnographer Dwight Conquergood states, housing is "an intersection between macro-forces and micro-realities. Housing . . . is situated between the deeply personal and the highly political. Housing is both a physical structure and an ideological construction" (1992, 98). The *sede* contains both the "micro-realities" of RFA's interpersonal relationships as well as the "macro-forces" concerning regional arts funding, the institutionalization of folklore performance, local politics, and the construction of local identity. The *rancho sede* is an architectural space housing both the deeply personal and the highly political.

Although RFA members often refer to their group as "poor" in financial terms, they acknowledge their good fortune at having a large, aesthetically pleasing home base. The fact that the *Câmara Municipal de Alenquer* (Alenquer's Mayoral Office) gave RFA a *sede* in Forum Romeira while other groups must rehearse in basements or garages not only reflects the high quality of RFA—indicated by their status throughout the region as being the oldest group with the largest repertoire and by their official affiliation with the FFP—but also relates to their location in the center of the *concelho.* *Ranchos* that represent localities in the center of a given *concelho* often benefit from a more immediate and intimate relationship with the *Câmara.* RFA profits from its geographic positioning and subsequent familiarity with the *Câmara* by receiving a hefty portion of the cultural department's annual budget, while many other groups in the *concelho* are given less or nothing.

Grupo Folclórico de Belas (GFB), for example, operates within the *Concelho de Sintra.* Unlike Alenquer, however, Belas is located over thirty miles from the *Câmara Municipal.* According to GFB president Miguel Oliveira, the *Câmara* openly favors the *ranchos* headquartered in Sintra. Given the relatively small annual budget devoted to local culture, the groups closest to the *concelho* center often fare better than those who operate along *concelho* margins. Miguel Oliveira spoke of his *rancho*'s geographical misfortune in relation to the group's *sede.* GFB is headquartered in a beautiful historic mansion, centuries old and in desperate need of repair.[8] During a visit in 1994, Oliveira showed me documents listing the monetary sums owed GFB by the *Câmara Municipal de Sintra.* He then took me on a tour of the building, pointing out decaying walls and ceilings, particularly on the second and third floors, stating repeatedly, "This could be a great cultural center for the kids of Belas—a place to keep them off the streets and away from the *vícios* [vices] you see more and more of around here. Instead, we wait and we wait for the money that is promised us. This place *não tem condições*! [is in bad shape!]" (Holton n.d.).

Oliveira's anger at the *Câmara*'s indifference focuses on the unrealized potential of the GFB *sede.* Ideally, the *sede* should function as a home base for Belas youth, but due to its shabby physical condition, it does not. In his conception, the *rancho sede* as home base could provide Belas youth with a refuge from corrupting forces external to this domestic space. GFB administrators also envision the home place as a safe haven from the onslaught of increasing urbanization along the corridor north of Lisbon, where foreign investors buy up and parcel out land for vacation homes and industrial centers, and where overcrowding and poverty lead to *vícios* and danger.

Oliveira speaks of renovating the GFB as a first step toward returning Belas to its permanent residents. Employing terms like "territory" and "occupation," Oliveira speaks of the *sede* as a strategy to "take back the streets" from the northern European vacationers, real estate tycoons, Lisbon commuters, and drug traffickers who have descended upon Belas and transformed it into a community long-time residents barely recognize. Appadurai argues that "all locality building has a moment of colonization, a moment both historical and chronotypic, when there is a formal recognition that the production of neighborhood requires deliberate, risky, even violent action" (1996, 183). Creating a vital GFB *sede,* a "deliberate action" toward the "production of neighborhood," is a grassroots intervention designed to combat Lisbon's urban sprawl and real estate development.

In addition to "re-colonizing" the physical space of neighborhood, the *rancho sede* houses activities perceived to have tangible social value. Many *ranchos* envision their mission as one which awakens local youth to the positive aspects of Portugal's rural past in the face of today's urbanization. Participating in revivalist folklore provides a performative antidote to the negative effects of modernization. In virtually all the *rancho* performances I've attended, for example, the announcer prefaces or concludes the show by underscoring the importance of folklore performance as a cure for today's social ills. Norberto Ribeira, president of the *Grupo de Cantares e Dançares de Montemuro,* introduced the young performers in his group during a performance in Lisbon: "These kids are the men of tomorrow . . . Unfortunately, today there are many problems that afflict our youth—drugs, crime, and more. But I am happy that we have more and more kids that dance folklore. Without any doubt folklore is a good use of their free time. And it is important that our kids continue these cultural activities" (Holton n.d.). In Montemuro, Belas, and Alenquer, parents hope the re-creation of the past through performance will restore a set of values they perceive as fast disappearing. It is not only the physical (architectural) presence of the *sede* as home place or safe haven but also the physical (corporeal) embodiment of turn-of-the-century tradition that has the power to protect against the ill effects of rapid modernization. In this way, the performance of the past is also used as a preemptive social salve.

On the surface, contemporary *rancho* leaders' approach to folklore appears remarkably similar to the *Estado Novo*'s ideological framing of the rural past. The difference, however, lies in modernity's proximity. Mid-twentieth century, Salazar and Ferro employed folklore like a necklace of garlic to keep a safe distance from the corrupting forces of the West. In the 1990s, with Portugal firmly entrenched in Europe as an EEC member state, *rancho* leaders view folklore performance as an interventionist measure against the negative effects of urbanization and modernization *already in their midst.* Many members of RFA and GFB also laud what they view as the positive effects of Portugal's entrance into the EEC and recent steps toward modernization. Older performers cite the construction of roads and highways, school reform, and increased jobs and wages as improvements in their lives and neighborhoods. Folklore performance does not, therefore, reflect a desire to recreate the past in its entirety, but as a corrective for the negative *excesses* of change. Modernity's perceived proximity is extremely significant in explaining *ranchos'* exponential increase and unexpected vitality in late twentieth-century Portugal.

Ranchos folclóricos' ability to install themselves within the built environment of neighborhood relies increasingly in post–*25 de Abril* on their relationship to local government. The acquisition of private property reflects and produces economic and political power, and although RFA members have transformed their *sede* into a collective "home," it will never serve as a completely autonomous site due to issues of ownership. RFA has no legal right to the space. Just as with the *sede* at the slaughterhouse, local development can displace the *rancho* at any moment. RFA's fate with regard to its *sede* is also affected by changes in elected officials each voting period. As Appadurai states, "the capability of neighborhoods to produce contexts . . . and to produce local subjects is profoundly affected by the locality-producing capabilities of larger-scale social formations [in this case, the *Câmara Municipal de Alenquer*] . . . to determine the general shape of all the neighborhoods within the reach of their powers" (1996, 187, my insert). Armindo Rodrigues (1996a) expresses the importance of local government support for RFA:

> The people of Alenquer [are] behind us—this is important, you'll see. Some ten years ago no one knew the Alenquer *rancho,* not even the residents of Alenquer knew us. Twenty years ago, fifteen, they didn't appreciate us. Now today even the municipal government, the *Câmara,* the *Junta da Freguesia*[9] are with us. This is important, you know—it's proof that we're on the right path . . . They give us their support.

Armindo attributes recent local government support to a shift in *rancho* policies, renewed commitment, and seriousness of purpose. The *rancho,* he says, is at a zenith in terms of development and quality of performance, due in part to FFP reforms; this level of performance is hence rewarded by the acquisition of a semipermanent *sede.* In addition to the *rancho* home, the *Câmara* also grants RFA discretionary funds for its annual festival, and use of municipal buses to attend distant performances. The *Câmara*'s 1996 contribution of 160,000 escudos (roughly $1,000 U.S.) toward RFA's annual festival was the largest single donation and accounted for roughly one-fifth of RFA's annual budget (RFA 1996a, 1996b).[10] In addition, RFA's good standing with the *Câmara*'s *Vereador da Cultura* (cultural councilman) has also yielded invitations to appear on national television. In 1996 RFA performed on *Português, Portugal* in an episode dedicated to Alenquer and on Marco Paulo's *Música no Coração.*[11] These appearances not only garnered publicity and performance invitations, they were also extremely profitable in terms of monetary compensation.

The "actuality of neighborhood" as it coheres in and around the Forum Romeira is related to RFA's good standing within the municipal government. Even temporary possession of the *sede* at Forum Romeira translates into increased visibility, as the *Câmara* often includes RFA in other Forum events. In this way, RFA's relationship to and role within the neighborhood is reproduced and even augmented by its association with the built environment of Alenquer's governing center. Eviction from this municipally owned space would signal a loss not only of material support but also official status and the localist networking that is possible from the town center. RFA's home place not only provides a space for internal activities essential to the group's survival as a performance troupe, but helps forge a situated relationship between RFA members, local publics, and local government. RFA's home place legitimates and shelters its web of cultural kin.

Ranchos Folclóricos and Cultural Kinship

Ranchos folclóricos forge relationships with one another following a model of familial kinship. *Ranchos* often represent themselves as the offspring or "legacies" of groups from previous decades. RFA, for example, invokes its association to two historic Alenquerian *ranchos* by describing itself as *"o fiel continuador dos Ranchos Folclóricos do Cacho Dourado e dos Malmequeres"* (the faithful successor of the *Cacho Dourado* and the *Malmequeres Ranchos Folclóricos*) (RFA n.d.). The *Rancho dos Malmequeres,* in existence from 1945 to 1959, disbanded the year RFA was formed. RFA inherited several dancers from this group, as well as their *ensaiador,* António Dionísio.[12]

The second group associated with RFA, the *Cacho Dourado,* was founded in Alenquer in 1937 and terminated in 1939. Although RFA never inherited any of the *Cacho* performers, this venerated *rancho* did bequeath RFA one of its signature dances, "Verde Gaio de Alenquer," (see appendix). The *Cacho Dourado* was one of Portugal's first international folklore groups, and was founded in tandem with the French folklore group *Rancho da Borgonha.*

> The *Cacho Dourado rancho* was associated with celebrations surrounding the harvesting of grapes and production of wine. They performed in Lisbon and then in France . . . But after 1939 . . . World War I . . . they stopped having these congresses—they used to be called congresses. [The *Cacho Dourado*] was the fifth international *rancho* founded in the world . . . Because war broke out, they stopped having these congresses . . . then the Portuguese *rancho* disbanded. (Luís 1996)

Cacho Dourado's notoriety as one of the first Portuguese *ranchos* to perform internationally was passed on to RFA like a material inheritance. RFA capitalizes on this impressive "familial" history whenever possible. In performance, for example, the *apresentador* (emcee or announcer) always narrates the tie between *Cacho Dourado, Malmequeres,* and RFA as evidence of the group's authenticity and historic lineage. In fund-raising letters to local politicians or private businesses, RFA invokes this association as evidence of its longevity and durability—that is, RFA is a sound investment due to its impressive local pedigree and its potential for endurance. RFA, as "the faithful legacy" of two landmark groups, firmly entrenches itself within a long line of Alenquerians dedicated to the performance of local tradition. RFA attributes its success to hard work and commitment, but also to the good fortune of having high-quality *rancho* "bloodlines."

In addition to links with historical *ranchos,* RFA also maintains family ties to extant groups. According to José Hermínio Carvalho, RFA's president and head accordionist, the vast majority of *ranchos* in Portugal have *padrinhos* (godparents) and several *afilhados* (godchildren). Carvalho (1996) explains: "The *Milharado Rancho,* which is in the Bucelas zone, is our godchild . . . For example, if I am going to baptize a baby, as the godfather—I'm the godfather, I was the one who named the baby. The formation of *ranchos* was done similarly. In order to form, they would invite an established *rancho* to act as the godfather. We're the godparents of many *ranchos.*" The tradition of choosing *rancho* godparents derives, as José Hermínio implies, from the Catholic baptismal practice of choosing two people (the *madrinha* and the *padrinho*) to name a newborn child and oversee its religious education, should the parents die. The *padrinho rancho* assists the *afilhado* by contributing to its budding repertoire and by offering the new *rancho* several of its signature *modas.* The *padrinho rancho* also attends and supervises the first several rehearsals, teaching members of the *afilhado* choreography and music typical of its region. The *padrinho rancho,* in effect, blesses the *afilhado* through offering the sacred gifts of repertoire and expertise.

These inter-*rancho* alliances, however, can also become strained and confused when dealing with issues of repertoire. In specific situations the sharing or giving of performance material is condoned (as is the case, for example, when a *padrinho rancho* baptizes its *afilhado,* or when a local *rancho* decides to disband just as another group is created, bequeathing its entire repertoire to the fledgling *rancho*). GFB acquired its current repertoire according to the latter scenario, for example. However, repertoire raiding or unauthorized borrowing of performance material is a common practice which fractures intergroup relationships.[13] Repertoire raiding is particularly destructive to those groups, like RFA, striving to maintain a discrete, autonomous musical and choreographic identity, differentiating themselves from the sometimes fifteen to twenty *ranchos* within the same locality. Creating and maintaining a singular identity or, better yet, a signature style and unique repertoire guarantees a greater volume of festival invitations and moneymaking performance engagements. Although older, respected *ranchos* like RFA are expected to turn a blind, paternalistic eye to a certain amount of repertoire imitation by younger area *ranchos,* RFA performers nonetheless become angered by blatant transgressions.

Local citizens can also serve as *rancho* godparents. When RFA was founded, the daughter of a prominent Alenquerian family, the Gões family, became *madrinha de rancho.* The Gões family played an important role in RFA's initial period of development. A clan of wealthy engineers and agriculturists, the Gõeses hosted an extravagant party every year on their farm near Ota in honor of RFA's anniversary. This event commenced in the morning and continued well into the night. Over the course of the day, RFA and other local residents shared meals, RFA performed, and at dusk the men participated in a *garraiada.*[14] These parties not only helped concretize the bond between RFA and godparents, but also publicized this auspicious local coalition through public festivity.

According to José Hermínio Carvalho (1996), RFA and the Gões family have since fallen out of contact. In theory, if the *madrinha* is a local resident, her responsibility is to "make sure that the *rancho* doesn't disband, in order to respect those that came before them. It's a project that has to continue, it can't stop." In practice, however, José Hermínio admits that it is difficult to maintain such a relationship, particularly against the backdrop of dramatic social and political changes. José Hermínio linked the cooling of the relationship between RFA and the Gões family to the 1974 fall of fascism in Portugal: *"Não só mudaram as mentalidades, em termos de política, como as pessoas passaram a ser outras também"* (Not only did political attitudes change, but people also changed) (Carvalho 1996).

The charged political period between 1974 and the early 1980s not only disrupted RFA's relationship to the Gões family, it also caused tremendous conflict within the *rancho* itself. RFA has responded, however, by strengthening membership bonds and forging new relationships with local businesses and prominent individuals. Since the process of privatizing Portugal's economy began in the mid-1980s, several Alenquer businesses have experienced robust growth. One of these businesses, Calbrita, a building materials manufacturer that employs several RFA dancers, has, for all intents and purposes, assumed the role of RFA godparent. At the time of my fieldwork, Ricardo Pereira, proprietor of Calbrita, issued several large checks to RFA every year. This decidedly post-revolutionary coalition, however, is less one of cultural and spiritual support and more a relationship of explicit economic patronage. Calbrita serves as RFA's corporate sponsor.

Calbrita's charitable donations to RFA serve several functions. By supporting RFA, Pereira is able to give something back to the locality from which he extracts both raw materials and human resources. Giving to RFA, a group dedicated to preserving and disseminating Alenquer's local traditions, Pereira contributes indirectly to the production of locality through performance. This gesture is also more explicitly self-serving. By supporting the leisure activities of his employees, he improves employer-employee relations. He also builds a positive reputation for himself among the Alenquer locals—locals who not only supply his workforce, but also comprise part of the consumer market for his products.

During the *Estado Novo,* the state provided the forum for these sorts of local coalitions. Through *casas do povo,* defined as "employer-employee institutes for rural workers" (Wheeler 1993, 70), the state mediated social relations between classes and helped promote harmony in the workplace. The state sometimes functioned, as the Most Portuguese Village Contest demonstrated, as a kind of uber-*padrinho.* Today, however, employer and employee negotiate these relationships directly. The state no longer performs the role of intermediary. Further, today's *padrinho/afilhado* coalitions between prominent citizens and local *ranchos* derive more from mutual economic "back-scratching" than from a social catholicist sense of moral obligation.

RFA Families and Membership

In her "Essay on Representation in Portuguese Ethnography," anthropologist Caroline Brettell examines "master ethnographic texts" written by foreign and domestic anthropologists of Portuguese society. She argues that "several words or themes emerge in the construction of the Portuguese other. Portugal is [represented as] a peasant society, with strains of communalism and . . . matriarchal tendencies" (1993a, 243). Critiquing the work of Jan Brogger for its exoticized portrayal of the Nazaré fishing community as a "pre-modern Communal family," Brettell identifies a cluster of analytical constructs which "deeply influence the structure of later ethnographies and which . . . affect the way the world views the [Portuguese] people" (1993a, 243). In addition to the prevalent construction of Portuguese rural society as communal and matriarchal, Brettell also identifies themes of village isolation, self-containment, egalitarianism, harmony, homogeneity, and community solidarity propagated throughout anthropological studies of Portugal.

In analyzing the social dynamics of RFA, both as a bounded collectivity and in relation to other local populations, I invoke the trope of the family, not the "pre-modern Communal family" Brettell compellingly critiques, but a family whose history includes contention, transience, revolution, and even

Figure 13. Four young *mascote*s from the *Rancho Folclórico de Alenquer* preparing for performance. Alenquer, Portugal, 1996. *Photograph by author.*

murder. Group coherence and communality are, unsurprisingly, tempered by conflict, and it is primarily through the disruption of *rancho* harmony that Portugal's recent social and political changes are made visible and negotiated.[15] RFA serves members by providing an ongoing forum for processing, acting out, and producing locality through the rehearsal of new local relationships and the contrasting performance of turn-of-the-century social roles.

In August 1996, RFA had thirty-one performers, comprised of the *cante* (vocalists), the *tocata* (instrumentalists), and the *dançarinos* or *dançadores* (dancers).[16] Compared to other groups whose membership base is drawn primarily from young single performers in their teens and twenties like GFB, RFA is a relatively mature group. Age range is distributed evenly from the youngest member who is eleven years old to the oldest who is seventy-four.[17] The age distribution is also indicative of the large quantity of extended families (up to three generations) who perform together in RFA. All RFA members have or had at least one family member perform in RFA. Within the Rodrigues family, for example, six members performed in RFA in 1996—in order of membership: Fernando; his brother, Armindo; his daughter, Glória; his sister-in-law, Fátima; his niece, Lucília; and his brother's father-in-law, Alexandre.[18] The vast majority of RFA members also have family members who perform or performed in other neighboring groups. These statistics indicate the extremely high incidence of *rancho* participation among extended families. As RFA performers often declare, "folklore stays in families."

Other family members also participate in RFA as *mascotes* (mascots) or *acompanhantes* (companions). In 1996, RFA had five regular mascots, ranging in age from four to ten years old (see fig. 13). Mascots, the young children of *rancho* dancers, do not rehearse with the group, but are fully costumed during performances and usually participate in the "Marcha de Entrada" (Entrance March) by holding flags, signs, or agricultural props. RFA's devoted group of *acompanhantes* participates in performance preparation, upkeep of the *rancho sede*, and costume repair and attends most rehearsals and performances. The majority of *rancho acompanhantes* are women, all of whom are related through family to *rancho* performers. In addition to providing moral support during performances, the *acompanhantes* also care for the *rancho* children (*mascotes* and non-*mascotes*) while their parents perform.

The matrix of family interrelationship among RFA performers exists, according to RFA members, due partially to traditions of child rearing and pragmatism. Many women, like Fátima Rodrigues, take a one- or two-year hiatus from the group during pregnancy and while their children are very young, reentering later with the children in tow. Upon entering the group with their mothers, these children either become *mascotes* or part of the group cared for by the *acompanhantes*. As the children grow older, many become official *rancho* performers, as is the case with Fátima's daughter, Lucília. Fátima's nine-year-old twin sons, although not yet members in 1996 attended all the rehearsals and performances.[19] Fátima Rodrigues (1996) explains: "I didn't join earlier because Acácio and Fernando were very young. So I didn't have to have someone else look after them during the long [performance] trips, I didn't join. I only joined when they were a little older, so they could stay with me—and so that someone else wouldn't have to care for them." As Fátima suggests, mothers who participate in RFA almost always bring their children with them to rehearsals and performances. Hiring babysitters from outside the family is virtually unheard of among RFA mothers. A primary reason for this is economic circumstance. The majority of RFA performers work as skilled laborers at just above minimum wage, and many report living hand to mouth (see table 3.1).[20] RFA's working mothers often leave their children with older relatives during the workweek. Thus asking family to baby-sit during the weekends is often not a viable alternative. Finally, because the majority of RFA women work up to sixty hours a week, they report not wanting to spend their weekends performing folklore to the exclusion of spending time with their children. Child rearing is, therefore,

Table 3.1. Income Level of RFA Performers in 1996

Minimum Wage or Below 45,000–52,000	10%
53,000–100,000	54%
101,000–200,000	32%
201,000 and Up	4%

Note: Table shows monthly income of all full-time wage-earning RFA members. Amounts are presented in Portuguese escudos. In 1996, 1,000 escudos were roughly equivalent to $6.50 U.S.

integrated into all RFA activities out of pragmatism and a desire to combine motherhood with leisure-time activities. It is not surprising, therefore, that many children of *rancho* members, who are literally raised on folklore, become *rancho* performers as young adults.

Another reason RFA members cite for the prevalence of extended families in their *rancho* is that folklore interest as well as talent gets passed down from generation to generation. As Manuel Anacleto (1996), a twenty-year RFA veteran whose two daughters also perform, states, "*Como se diz cá em Portugal, 'filho de peixe sabe nadar'*" (As we say here in Portugal, "the child of a fish knows how to swim"). The predisposition for being able to dance folklore is often described as *jeito* (knack). Fernando Rodrigues (1996), RFA's treasurer and folklore dancer, his daughter, Glória, a dancer, and his wife, an *acompanhante,* describe the way their entire family joined as a kind of involuntary chain reaction.

> Fernando: I was a part [of the *rancho*], I liked it and my brother always went along with me to the *bailaricos* and parties . . . I was part of the *rancho* [he said], "I'll go too." And it was like that: Armindo came along almost as his brother's hitched trailer.
> Glória: And I was the hitched trailer of my father and my uncle.
> Fernando: I was like that and Armindo was influenced.
> Maria do Carmo: They used to dance together at home.[21]

The "hitched trailer" metaphor describes how a "contagious" interest in folklore was sparked, but *jeito* describes how the family was able to actualize this interest through performance.

In the Rodrigues family everyone was easily integrated into the *rancho,* due to their demonstrated talent as dancers. However, some members of RFA families have been gently phased out due to the administration's perception that they lack the physical ability to learn the dances or simply *não têm jeito* (don't have the knack). Usually members who are not accepted as dancers are either given another role to play within the group, such as playing percussion or becoming an *acompanhante,* or are offered such limited performing opportunity that they quit the group altogether.

Ana Luís, for example, whose father, Vítor, and sister, Claudia, both perform, quit RFA rehearsal after several months of frustration. Ana describes the process as painful, but feels that she caused the group to waste a lot of time in rehearsal when Armindo worked with her to the exclusion of others. Ana's partner, Tiago, who was also learning to dance and whose father, Joaquim, plays percussion, has also quit the *rancho.* According to Ana's mother, Fátima, the pair did not dance well together. Ana has since become an *acompanhante.* The same happened with Ana Costa Pereira, who had hoped to join as her husband António Luís's dancing partner. After three rehearsals she was asked not to continue. Ana has some hard feelings about the process and told me, "I don't know what happened. One day António Luís told me not to come to rehearsal. I never stay in the house, though. Oh, no. I go everywhere with the *rancho.* I go on the bus to performances; I watch rehearsals. I won't stay home while he goes out with the *rancho*" (Holton n.d.). She is now an *acompanhante.*

As Ana intimates, joining a *rancho,* particularly when one spouse performs and the other does not, is often stressful on the nuclear families of *rancho* members. Strategies for negotiating these difficulties differ greatly according to gender. For married RFA women, virtually the only way to negotiate the responsibilities of nuclear family and *rancho* family is to ensure the membership of one's husband. All the married women in RFA have husbands who are also members. And those who are dancers all dance with their husbands. On the other hand, in 1996 there were seven married men who performed in the *rancho* without their wives. Some RFA women have told me that it would be close to impossible to perform in a *rancho* without the company of their husbands—"*Nem pensar! Não dava*" (Don't even think about it! It wouldn't work).

It follows that the primary cause of permanent membership termination among RFA women is marriage. Joaquim, the *reco-reco* player, told me about his daughter who used to dance in the *rancho.* I asked why she no longer performed. He laughed and told me that after she got married she became "*forte—que não dá para dançar*" (stocky—which is no good for dancing). RFA's female vocalist, Margarida, quit in 1994, citing her new marriage as the primary reason for resigning. Vina, an RFA dancer, has an older sister who danced in RFA for many years but also quit after getting married. Claudia, a young, talented RFA dancer, told me that after her wedding to Mário, the man to whom she was engaged in 1996, she must quit RFA. In a revealing exchange, Mário, Claudia, Claudia's mother, Fátima, and I discuss her ensuing departure:

Kim: Why don't you like folklore?
Mário: I don't know, maybe because it takes up a lot of our time . . .
Fátima: There aren't many young people in our *rancho* . . .
Kim: And you aren't jealous that she dances with someone else?
Mário: No.
Claudia: Dancing with someone else, no, but dancing in the *rancho*, yes. Because of him, I already quit once last year. (Claudia Luís 1996)

In RFA, all married women whose spouses did not join the *rancho* have terminated their membership. Some single women have negotiated these gender politics by choosing a mate from within the *rancho.* As João Luís Murteira (1996), a dancer, says, "*há muitos casamentos feitos no rancho*" (there have been many marriages made in the *rancho*). Lourdes and João Mendes, for example, courted and married in their first years as *rancho* dancers. Another strategy among soon-to-be-married women whose fiancés dance in other *ranchos* is to have the men transfer their memberships to RFA, as was the case with Lídia and Luís Ventura, and Fátima and Luís Santos Carvalho. Just as weddings have terminated the *rancho* membership of newly married women, the *rancho* has also benefited from the addition of male dancers who wish to join their new wives in RFA. The gendered double standard which exists among married couples in RFA, however, serves to create a specific type of collective family—one where married female dancers must be chaperoned by and partnered with their husbands in rehearsal and performance. In addition, when conflict arises, the stakes are immediately increased. RFA must negotiate the often united positions of entire familial units. And should the conflict go unresolved, the risk of alienating an entire family to the point of resignation could seriously jeopardize RFA's integrity as a performance troupe.

Contrary to the frequent representation of Portuguese rural families as matriarchal (Brettell 1993b), RFA demonstrates marked patriarchal characteristics. With one short-lived exception, male performers have always occupied RFA's three leadership positions: *ensaiador, presidente,* and *apresentador.*[22] This male-dominated leadership structure was challenged in the early 1990s by Olinda Pereira's twelve-month tenure as *ensaiadora,* with disruptive effects upon RFA's membership and social harmony. Olinda Pereira, an exemplary dancer and RFA veteran, assumed the position shortly after the death of RFA president Joaquim Pires.[23] Olinda was to work in conjunction with RFA founder, Crispim Luís, as co-*ensaiador,* but due to Crispim's physical frailty, Olinda assumed the position alone. Olinda (1996) described her tenure as *ensaiadora* as a period of marked improvement in RFA performance, particularly in terms of choreographic precision. She described her-

Figure 14. *Rancho Folclórico de Alenquer* performing in celebration of *25 de Abril.* Olinda Pereira dances in the foreground with her husband, Carlos. Camarnal, Portugal, 1996. *Photograph by Tim Raphael.*

self as an exacting *ensaiadora* with great attention to detail. She reported working particularly on the varying positions of the arm (see figs. 14 and 15)—something which other *ensaiadores* had ignored because folklore dances typical of the Estremaduran and Ribatejanan regions are oriented toward the feet. She also conceived of a performance strategy for demarcating the identities of RFA's onstage personae. Each dancer wears a unique costume, most differing according to turn-of-the-century occupation. RFA, for example, features a variety of "characters" from rural bride and groom to farmhand to grape harvester. Olinda suggested the dancers carry props indicative of their identities—cisterns, horse crops, sieves, etc. This idea was popular among *rancho* members, and Olinda felt it enlivened RFA's onstage appearance.

Given the positive changes Olinda made, it is perhaps surprising that her tenure as *ensaiadora* was so short-lived. One RFA leader attributes Olinda's

Figure 15. *Rancho Folclórico de Alenquer* performing in the *Feira da Ascensão*. Alenquer, Portugal, 1996. Note the careful positioning of the arms. *Photograph by author.*

failure to her inability to direct people in a gentle manner: "She always commanded people. It was never a request." The opposite failing, however, was also offered as reason for Olinda's resignation: "People weren't sure what she wanted. She was never very clear." In the end, Olinda, her husband, Carlos, and another couple—Olinda's close friends—quit RFA over a dispute involving costume changing etiquette. Olinda proposed creating separate changing spaces for men and women during touring performances. She stated that several husbands were uncomfortable with their wives changing in front of other RFA men. Most *rancho* members fought against this proposed reform, stating that it was impractical and that the only man ruffled by RFA's unisex changing traditions was Olinda's husband, Carlos. According to Olinda and her supporters, the reform was meant to deter extramarital indiscretions which at that point in RFA history threatened the very survival of the group. One female dancer believed that the alleged adulterous activity was simply malicious rumor furthered (and perhaps originated) by Olinda's proposed reform. After a hostile exchange between the Pereiras, their compadres, and the rest of the *rancho*, eight dancers resigned, including Olinda and Carlos. Olinda and Carlos's resignation lasted thirteen months. Their resignation, absence, and subsequent reentry—contingent on Olinda and Carlos's apology to RFA leaders—was extremely difficult for the entire *rancho.*

In attempting to process differing accounts of these events, I asked Olinda's most fervent critics if perhaps part of the problem had less to do with Olinda's reforms and directorial style and more to do with gender politics. One male performer stated that women's position in Portuguese society had changed dramatically over the last decade, but that most men still had trouble taking orders from women, particularly in public. Olinda, a capable woman with a strong personality, assumed the role of *ensaiadora* at a time of dramatic social change. Today, Portuguese women are playing new roles within their families and within society in general. Thirty years ago women comprised just 15 percent of the Portuguese workforce, while today they account for over 50 percent (primarily in areas of health and education) (Barreto 1996a, 27–28). Female students now comprise 50 percent of those enrolled in high school and well over half of those pursuing university degrees. Concomitant with these changes have been changes in the complexion of Portuguese families: the median number of children per family has decreased, rates of divorce have skyrocketed, and Portugal's birth rate has plummeted, making it one of the lowest in Europe (Barreto 1996a, 27–28). When viewed against the backdrop of Salazarist ideals for female circumscription within the domestic sphere and unquestioned obedience to household patriarchs, such changes occurring over a short period of time have a dramatic impact on Portuguese families and on RFA specifically.

Backlashes to these changes manifest themselves in *rancho* culture. When I asked various RFA performers to describe their region, several older male performers said, "You will always know a Ribatejanan man. He only cares about three things: women, *fado,* and *vacadas* [bullfights]. Deep down, that describes us too." This historic regional archetype of Ribatejo's horseman not only informs RFA's "revival" of folkloric characters on stage, but also informs many male performers' contemporary *self*-identification. However, in a world where women have increased control over their potential life choices—to marry, to divorce, to work, to bear children—the stereotype of the philandering horseman free to pursue and control women at his fancy now seems oddly out of place.

In light of Portugal's changing gender roles, RFA's debate regarding the act of changing costumes—or changing spaces while changing costumes—takes on marked symbolism. Many families throughout Portugal are in the midst of radical role changes. Perhaps Olinda's proposed reform was an attempt to protect feminist gains from the threat of backlash. Or perhaps (and I suspect this might be more the case) Olinda's attempt to segregate the sexes so as to avoid adulterous behavior expresses an anxiety toward change. Manufacturing regulations regarding gendered behavior after society has stripped away these regulations serves a conservative function, ensuring that the sexes literally "stay in their places" amidst widespread flux and uncertainty.

Olinda's tenure as RFA's first female leader was a profoundly complex and charged experience and must be framed within a larger societal context of change and reprisal regarding gender roles and the institution of the family. Only through focusing on this moment of upheaval does the diachronicity of examining folklore performance during a period of intense change pay off. National statistics concerning women's changing role within society become situated within local families. RFA, from this point of view, could never be characterized as "timeless," "homogenous," or "isolated," as traditional representations of Portuguese society in nonurban settings insist, according to Brettell's analysis. RFA, a heterogeneous family of local residents, possesses a dynamic history that reflects and refracts the macro trends of late twentieth-century Portugal. Framing these issues within the study of performance adds another dimension to the examination of social roles. RFA members negotiate changing gender roles in the midst of folkloric *role playing*. RFA performers dance together as swaggering horsemen and blushing brides at a time when the symbolism of these local characters is in direct tension with Portugal's contemporary social relationships.

It is not only this sociohistorical incongruity which makes performing folklore in late twentieth-century Portugal sometimes difficult to grasp. *Rancho* membership also strains many of its nuclear families in other ways. Fátima Santos Carvalho (1996), a farm laborer, supplements her discussion of the interpersonal costs of *rancho* membership with details of her family's financial sacrifice:

> I've had difficulties in my life. My husband was not working the job he is now. He worked for the *Câmara* in a low-paying job. But the moment they [the *rancho*] needed me, I would always take off work, my husband would also always take off work . . . We were one of the pairs who never missed rehearsals. I would come from the fields . . . late at night, I didn't eat, just took a bath, to go to rehearsal.

Against the backdrop of increased financial hardship, increased conflict within nuclear families, and the abrasive sociohistorical incongruity involved in organizing a performance of the past, what explains RFA's forty-year endurance? What function does the RFA family provide its members in twentieth-century Portugal? João Luís Murteira (1996) believes the RFA collective endures due to what he terms their "extraordinary camaraderie": "All this [camaraderie] motivates you to continue, and in our local slang to 'turn intestines into heart,' to endure—to ask your boss for time off—so that the *rancho* can be together. But as long as you have harmony among the members, we try to overcome all the monetary problems this can bring—always brings." Fátima Santos Carvalho (1996), who has belonged to four *ranchos* throughout her twelve years as a performer, also remarks on this camaraderie by comparing RFA to the *Rancho Folclórico de Canados,* where she last danced:

> The Alenquer *rancho* is a family. I feel a friendship so great for them . . . [In the Canados *rancho* people] are a bit independent . . . they form cliques and sometimes this makes you feel kind of bad. I had a group of friends there, but not that kind of friendship that really grips me . . . We got along with a few couples but the others were independent. People in a *rancho* or in something folkloric with tons of couples, we must feel good when we dance . . . [if we are in cliques] we're always inhibited; we don't get into it, because we don't care about it. That kind of independence doesn't work.

In individual interviews many RFA performers echo João Luís and Fátima's sentiments by invoking the uniquely Portuguese concept of *convivência* to describe their personal commitment to RFA.[24] Historian Douglas Wheeler attempts to define the term, "*Convivência* is a word which our language cannot match for its succinct expressiveness . . . My dictionary defines this word inadequately, so I offer here my personal definition: '*peaceably living together to mutual benefit*' " (1994, 4). If RFA members underscore their peaceable life together, it is with the implicit knowledge that *convivência* is an inherently fragile social achievement which, when realized, helps individuals through the vicissitudes of personal hardship by providing a familial collective for discussion, problem solving, and friendship.

RFA performers strive toward *convivência* with vigilance and determination because their performance collective—their folklore family—helps to process, act out, and produce a rapidly changing sense of locality. Localist pride and solidarity are explicitly linked to the contingencies of performance. It is through the slings and arrows of group conflict that RFA members role-play their way into an understanding of local history and gendered change over time. RFA also serves as a site for testing new local relationships of patronage, competition, and friendship. RFA looks to local business leaders, municipal government officials, and folklore enthusiasts for funding, moral support, and donations to *rancho* repertoire and the ethnographic museum. RFA, in turn, provides post-revolutionary *rancho* "godchildren" with training, *modas,* and prestige, conferred through the establishment of folklore bloodlines. RFA provides homegrown audiences with a performative incarnation of Alenquer history, responsibly researched and restored, for the creation of a distinctly local sphere of identification built upon sedimented layers of local memory and recollection. The webbing characteristic of these multilayered kinship systems, according to RFA members, has kept the *rancho* vital and purposeful, even in post-revolutionary times of strain and uncertainty.

For RFA members, locality, a "property of social life," is not given, but rather "ephemeral unless hard and regular work is undertaken to produce and maintain its materiality" (Appadurai 1996, 180–81). And when *convivência* cannot be achieved, then membership turns over, the complexion of the folklore family changes, and expelled performers go in search of new locality building projects staged in different venues. The only constant in this tangle of variables is that folklore performance produces community, and folklore performers serve as locality builders. RFA's bonds of cultural kinship are not born of passive communing, but of continuous rehearsal.

4

Festival Hospitality: New Paradigms of Travel and Exchange

Como Se Estivesse na Sua Casa!

Some anthropological studies (Herzfeld 1987, 1980) have posited hospitality as a better vehicle for theorizing cultural commonality among Mediterranean countries than the classic gatekeeping concept of "honor and shame" developed in the 1960s (Peristiany 1965). Such debates have given rise to the reexamination of honor and shame in specific Mediterranean localities (Gilmore 1987) and have led to the call for increased anthropological study of hospitality, perceived by some as a neglected topic. Although many of the seminal anthropological studies of twentieth-century Portugal pay careful attention to social dynamics which comprise and link rural "households" (Cutileiro 1971; Cabral 1986; Brettell 1986; O'Neill 1991; Cole 1991), and to the ethno-architectural composition of "the Portuguese house" (Peixoto [1904] 1967; Leal 2000), Portuguese hospitality has only recently claimed the attention of anthropologists as they reflect upon their own initial receptions within fieldwork sites as an entrée into the topic (J. Cabral 1991a; Almeida 1996).

Herzfeld argues that anthropology, in particular, should engage the concept of hospitality as a point of analytical departure, due to its applicability at various levels of sociocultural contact and its direct imbrication in ethnographic methodology:

> Hospitality can be studied not only at the level of village ethnography, but also at that of its national and regional transformations—as, for example, in the stereotyping of national attitudes to tourists ("our traditional hospitality" and the like) . . . [Also] since the anthropologist is a guest in both the local and national senses, this expansion of the focus of interest forces us to consider our

> own part in the construction of the ethnographic generalizations on which all comparison necessarily rests. (1987, 75–76)

Hospitality is an especially timely topic in Portugal at the national level Herzfeld mentions—not only with regard to tourists, but also to scores of newly arrived immigrants. Historically a country of sustained out-migration, Portugal has become the destination for hundreds of thousands of Angolan, Mozambican, Cape Verdean, Guinean, and Brazilian immigrants, Portuguese *retornados* from the ex-colonies, Eastern Europeans, as well as a steady stream of northern European vacationers and real estate investors. As of 2001, Portugal had a total of 350,000 legal foreign residents and 50,000 Luso-African Portuguese citizens (Machado 2002). A country once characterized by its ethnic homogeneity (Santos 1993b), cordoned off during most of the twentieth century by the strictures of fascist emigration and trade policies, has recently absorbed a diverse coterie of international refugees and migrants, prompting some to deem Lisbon "Little Africa" (Rocha et al. 1993).

The shift from a country historically known as a sending context to one now also characterized as a receiving context (Baganha and Góis 1998) has pushed issues such as citizenship, xenophobia, postcolonialism, and a re-evaluation of old notions of "racial democracy"[1] onto the front page of Portugal's newspapers and into the forefront of national consciousness. Debates over visa requirements, resident status, government assistance, and immigration control contribute to arguments concerning the social laws and cultural rites which govern hospitality in the Portuguese context.

The demographic shake-up catalyzed by the Revolution has also affected *ranchos folclóricos*. *Ranchos* in and around Lisbon grapple with an influx of immigrants of different races and ethnicities, some of whom have participated in the re-creation of late nineteenth-century Portuguese peasant traditions.[2] The prospect of including immigrants from lusophone Africa, for example, in a Portuguese *rancho* performance—known under Salazar as the expressive "emblem of the nation"—tests the boundaries of Portugal's postcolonial inclusivity, and the limits of the mythic lusophone "racial democracy." During the *Estado Novo,* Salazar coined the African colonies "overseas provinces," euphemized terminology to describe colonial appendages forced against their will to connect up to the body of the Portuguese nation. But this rhetoric was predicated on geographical and social distance. How does such a formulation hold up when Portugal's old colonial limbs migrate to the interior trunk of the nation?

In the case of the *Rancho Folclórico de Alenquer,* the *Rancho Infantil* now has one young Cape Verdean performer who joined the group in 2002 as her family sought the benefits of *rancho* participation—physical exercise, structured recreation, positive role models, and public recognition. Anxieties over authenticity expressed in chapter 2 that forbade *rancho* performers to "chew gum, wear glasses, or use makeup" due to the historical inaccuracy of maintaining such contemporary practices while impersonating nineteenth-century peasants have been suspended with the participation of Luso-Africans—a move akin to color-blind casting. This is not to say that such mixing—at both the theatrical and social level—is not without conflict.

In the spring of 2002, I attended a rehearsal of the new *Rancho Infantil de Alenquer.* Nine pairs of children ranging in age from four to fifteen formed a neat circle in the middle of the rehearsal space. I recognized many of the small performers—children of adult dancers who were *mascotes* during my initial fieldwork from 1994 to 1996. In his characteristically serious tone, Armindo, the *ensaiador,* shouted out the name of the *moda* the children would rehearse as the usual clusters of family members sat at tables along the outskirts of the dance floor, watching and chatting. During the rehearsal, several mothers and grandmothers of the performers told me how *bem recebido* (well received) the children's group had been since its inception in 1999. The *Rancho Infantil* was the pride of Alenquer, one mom boasted, invited to many prestigious national events and even to perform *no estrangeiro* (abroad). Ostensibly, in the same way that the *Rancho Infantil* had been well received both nationally and internationally, RFAs leaders and parents welcomed the new Cape Verdean performer into their midst. In the rehearsal, Lara, the pretty seven-year-old girl with coffee-colored skin and hair piled on top of her head, was paired with a local Portuguese boy. Throughout the rehearsal when she and other younger initiates had trouble with the choreography, older girls would rush to their sides, hooking elbows with maternal reassurance while gently correcting uncertain footwork. Lara's mother was seated at one of the tables watching the rehearsal and chatting with other mothers. From all appearances, the new performer and her family had indeed been *bem recebido,* as is the custom in Portugal, a country known for its Mediterranean hospitality and its long colonial history of mixing freely with African populations.

Later on in the private homes of RFA leaders, however, the subject of the new *rancho* members gave rise to a heated discussion of race. Derogatory remarks about African construction workers in Lisbon and racially charged jokes were balanced by claims that the Portuguese are generally tolerant of outsiders. Armindo, a low-level manager at a local plastics factory, said that he was used to dealing with foreigners, as he had traveled to Germany several times with his boss on company business and had no problem relating

Figure 16. Graffiti scrawled across a wall in the Rotunda subway station. Lisbon 2004. *Photograph by António Joel.*

to people from different cultures. "That's why I have no problem dealing with you, Kim!" he says with a mischievous grin. "Haven't I welcomed you into my home? A stranger from America?" This rhetorical question meant to prove his open-mindedness through the demonstration of hospitality toward a North American ethnographer. Indeed, Armindo's family and many of the other families had shown me remarkable generosity over ten years of research and prolonged visits—often feeding me and lodging me on their children's beds and pull-out sofas. But hospitality, as Derrida (2000) argues, always begins with a question, "the foreigner question" as he terms it, destined to produce information about the identity and geographical provenance of the stranger desiring welcome. The answers to these questions condition my reception as a light-skinned North American, sometimes scrutinized due to the stigma associated with Luso-American emigrants, just as they condition the reception of Lara, a mulatta immigrant from one of Portugal's ex-colonies.

Although Armindo underscores his openness to foreigners and RFA members have made a public display of welcoming the young Cape Verdean performer, private discussions of race turn much less hospitable. I observed a written manifestation of this often "private" intolerance in the form of anonymous subway graffiti in Lisbon's Rotunda station. Figure 16 shows the statement scrawled in large letters, "*Negro, volta pro teu mato!*" (Black man, go back to your jungle!). And the counterpoint response reads, "*Trouxeram-*

nos do mato, agora aguentem!" (You brought us from the jungle, now deal with it!). The barbed graffiti dialogue provides a striking contrast to the active amiability I had witnessed at the rehearsal.[3] This clash between humane actions and hostile words constitutes the inverse of what I've often experienced in the United States, where the pressures of political correctness result in canned scripts of tolerance which only sometimes permeate social behavior.[4] Can the clash between action and attitude be explained by the pressures which govern Portuguese hospitality—social behavior measured more often by gestures (an offer of food and shelter) than by words?

Anthropologist Robin Sheriff documents a similar gulf between discourse and behavior among white middle-class Brazilians. One informant in her study stated, "There were families of the middle class, of the upper-middle class [that had] this discourse of racist people, but it wasn't ideological. [The members of this black family] were well received in most houses, I mean it was neither an ideology nor a disposition! On the contrary, it was just joking around" (Sheriff 2000, 119). Sheriff theorizes this incongruence as the concerted cultural "silencing" of racial conflict within discursive realms of contact in present-day Brazil. It is interesting to note that the informant uses the example of the black family's hospitable reception as evidence that racism is "not ideological." My reading of this statement, however, viewed from the vantage point of my experience in Portugal, is that hospitality's moral obligation trumps racial dis-ease and antagonism during face-to-face contact, where the roles of host and guest take precedence over other potential dynamics.

This chapter explores issues of hospitality and travel as manifested against the backdrop of post–*25 de Abril* festivity. The influx of immigrants, Portugal's entrance into the European Union, the increase in personal freedom and mobility, and the rise in localist movements all contribute to a new engagement with and performance of hospitality. It is not only the addition of foreign performers to *ranchos folclóricos,* but also the performance practices spawned by post-revolutionary freedom which have catalyzed new paradigms of welcome and exchange. With "sociability paralyzed" (Ó 1992) under Salazar, what traveling *ranchos* did during the *Estado Novo* unfolded under circumstances which discouraged interaction and exchange among groups from different regions. As one RFA performer described it, under Salazar, "it was just get off the bus, perform, and go home without a word to anyone." In the eighties and nineties, however, the rapid proliferation of post-revolutionary *ranchos* accompanied a paradigm shift in *rancho* performance practice from a competition-based model employed during the *Estado Novo* to a post-revolutionary model emphasizing travel, regional promotion, and social interactivity.

This change has been sparked, in part, by the wide-scale proliferation of anniversary festivals celebrating *rancho* founding dates, where *rancho* guests and hosts gather en masse for weekends of community building and interregional discovery. Such a shift demands a new form of engagement with hospitality practices and performances. The final section of this chapter examines RFA's anniversary celebration as a case study for assessing how postrevolutionary freedom and mobility are expressed in new manifestations of *rancho* hospitality and local cooperation.

Open Doors and Open Windows

As Derrida (2000) argues, hospitality begins with an open portal into the home—doors and windows that serve as material signs of openness or closure, communicating the "receptivity" of the host. I began my foray into issues of hospitality in Alenquer accidentally when asking RFA performers to interpret an incident involving an open window which had left me bewildered. When I first moved to Lisbon in the late eighties to teach at a language school, I rented a room from an elderly Portuguese widow, the friend of a friend of my aunt Dottie who lives in the north of Portugal. I moved in, put away my things in the tiny bureau, and opened the heavy drapes, the gossamer curtains, the *persianas* (rolled slats of heavy plastic hung on the exterior of the window for a hermetic seal when completely unrolled), and finally the screenless windows in order to air out the musty third-floor room which faced the street in a lower-middle-class neighborhood. Everyday when I got home from work, the drapes, curtains, *persianas,* and windows would all be shut, and I would begin my ritual of opening them again, for fresh air, Lisbon's dazzling sunlight, and the late autumn warmth. As my first week progressed, not only did the elderly woman continue shutting my bedroom window during the day, but she would come in and shut it at night while I was sleeping. She also began covering my water glasses with cardboard "hats" so as to keep the dust out, she explained. As the elderly woman and I continued our dance of opening and closing windows and glasses, my aunt suddenly appeared from Beira Alta (a five-hour drive from Lisbon) to give me slippers and an umbrella, because she had heard that I was not properly "covering myself up!" Finally, things came to a boiling point when my aunt called and told me that I must keep the windows closed if I wanted to stay on in the apartment. As an asthmatic, in need of a constant supply of fresh air and sunlight to kill molds, I decided to bid my tearful companion farewell and rent an apartment of my own.

Upon relating this story to select RFA friends and asking for their interpretation, they offered many variations upon the same theme. After determining the ritual window closings were not due to excessive heat, cold, noise, or insect problems, several RFA members explained that it is not right for a young single girl living in the city to have her window wide open during the day and certainly not at night. This would be, at best, an act of immodesty and, at worst, a sign of promiscuity, and would set the neighbors—especially if it was a "popular" neighborhood—to gossiping. Secondly, an open window, particularly in the city, is an affront to the privacy of the house or apartment; it is an invitation inside, where nosy neighbors gain visual and auditory entry into the home. Having windows closed, my RFA friends explained, helped neighbors mind their own business. Lastly, a few RFA members suggested that keeping windows closed, particularly in Lisbon, is a historical habit, left over from the days of Salazar when people worried about conversations being overheard and the penetrability of domestic space by the secret police and their army of civilian spies.[5]

Varying explanations of my open window dilemma speak to threshold rituals involving "different types of dirt," according to Mary Douglas's (1995 [1966]) analysis of pollution taboo. My need to dissipate the molds and mustiness of an old woman's extra room transgressed rules for the management of sexual availability, social intrusion, and political surveillance. The dirt I attempted to "air out" led to the entrance of other genres of dirt. And these varying and sometimes competing registers of social, sexual, and political transgression necessarily inflect an examination of hospitality—a practice concerned with entry into orifices of the home and potentially dangerous movement over liminal zones of domestic vulnerability.

Even though my previous experience in Lisbon sensitized me to the culturally coded beliefs which condition entrance into domestic space, I arrived in Alenquer having read ethnographies of Tras-os-Montes, where doors were routinely left open at dinner time to receive guests (O'Neill 1991), and expected similar dynamics among RFA performers. During my longest period of fieldwork, from 1994 to 1996, however, members of the *Rancho Folclórico de Alenquer* generally did not spend much time at each others' private homes. Performers who did see each other socially outside of rehearsal and performances were often related, either blood relations or *compadres* (people who are related as "spiritual kin," in Cutileiro's terms [1971]—those who are the godparents of each others' children). Olinda, Manuel, Lídia, and Luís, related through spiritual kinship, did spend time together in each others' homes, particularly at Lídia and Luís' home. Olinda and Carlos live in a small, well-kept apartment in the town of Alenquer and preferred to visit Lídia and her family, who live in a small row house on the property of a large rural estate. (Lídia is a domestic laborer in the "big house" and Luís works on site as a horse trainer.) Armindo's family sometimes went to Fátima and

Claudia's house, for example, because Armindo and Fátima are cousins. They get together particularly during celebrations of harvesting rites due to the fact that Fátima and her husband have a small hobby farm with a few pigs, chickens, and a grape arbor, and often invite family over to press grapes and for an annual *matança do porco* (pig killing). Outside of those who were related, only extremely close friends visited one another in private residences. Zé Hermínio, for example, occasionally stopped by Armindo's house for a drink, but this was often under the pretext of *rancho* business.

I asked RFA members why there wasn't more socializing within domestic space, and the most common explanation was, "nowadays life is too busy to receive many guests at home." Within the vast majority of RFA families, both husband and wife work, at least one parent often arriving home after 7 P.M. Many RFA children also have multiple extracurricular activities which require parents' attendance or assistance. Glória, for example, participates in a theater group at her high school in addition to being a *rancho* dancer. Lucília takes accordion lessons, competes on a gymnastics team, and dances folklore. Acácio and Fernando both play on a hockey team and perform folklore.

In addition to the overscheduling characteristic of RFA performers' lives, there is also the consciousness of emerging class differences that inhibits socializing within private homes. Although, as illustrated in chapter 3, most RFA performers are either skilled laborers or low-level service industry employees, some members have managed to achieve a higher socioeconomic status—defined primarily through multiple car ownership, private home ownership (as opposed to apartment living), and occasional family vacations. Although no adult RFA performer holds a university degree, a few men such as Armindo have worked their way toward higher salaries and have significantly greater wealth compared to other performers, some of whom struggle to maintain stable housing and put food on the table. These changes in earning potential are the product not only of individual ambition and achievement, but also due more generally to the economic invigoration of the Vale do Tejo region—an area now linked to Lisbon via new highways and public transportation lines.

Because RFA has been together for so long, with a core nucleus of members literally growing up together in the group, these changes in socioeconomic circumstance present the potential for conflict, as some families have benefited from the region's economic development and others have not. In his ethnography of a poor rural community in Minho, João de Pina Cabral documents an "obsession with equality," where wealthier families "go to great pains to play down their affluence" (1986, 150). In Alenquer, the strategy for smoothing over socioeconomic differences includes localizing RFA gatherings away from private residences. The home of one pair of veteran RFA dancers, for example, was described as a place that very few people had ever visited because it was in shambles ("a cair"), messy, and in no condition ("sem condições") to receive guests. When I was trying to arrange an interview with another family, Fátima, the wife, said that she would love to do the interview at her home but was ashamed ("tenho vergonha") of the location of her house on the edge of a quarry where, after a full day of excavating and bulldozing, her belongings were covered in blankets of dust. Fátima's husband, Luís, worked at the quarry owned by Calbrita, and the house was lent to them, rent-free, until their financial situation stabilized. Both of these examples cloaked class-based anxieties over the size, condition, and location of private residences in language describing transgressions in housekeeping standards—an acceptable, albeit gendered, reason to keep visitors at bay. This "matter out of place" (Douglas 1995 [1966])—ceilings falling in, invasions of quarry dust—constitutes dirt associated with the feminized lower strata of social hierarchies, "grotesque" bodies and spaces (Bakhtin 1968; Stallybrass and White 1986) best kept hidden in an environment of increasingly disparate levels of socioeconomic advancement. As people move out of their traditional socioeconomic places, there is greater anxiety about controlling the place of "matter."

In the face of relatively closed domestic spheres, communal spaces take on greater importance in the life of RFA, particularly during the annual festival. This dynamic differs from the rural Transmontanan community researched by Brian O'Neill, where "the intimacy of the house—its fireplace, benches, kitchen, bedrooms and furniture—are also projected out into the exterior during select moments of the year. During family or religious festivals, doors will be opened to specific people, 'opening' the house a bit to the collective space of the surrounding neighborhood" (1991, 157).[6] RFA, on the other hand, keeps domestic and communal spaces rigorously separate. Constituting the *rancho sede* as "home place," as I've analyzed in chapter 3, obviates the need for trafficking within the private homes of *rancho* members. RFA's annual anniversary festival, held each year in early May, sparks the proliferation of hospitable encounters in communal haunts throughout Alenquer—the *rancho sede,* the ethnographic museum, the firehouse, the open-air arena, and the corner café.

Feira da Ascensão: Frameworks for Festive Reorientation

Many *ranchos folclóricos* throughout Portugal have begun celebrating the anniversaries of their inception dates. These celebrations have spawned a new class of folklore events where old Salazarist folklore competitions have given rise to festivals designed for the non-agonistic display of inter-regional riches. Such events also provide the opportunity for extensive travel throughout the whole of Portugal, as well as the occasion for forming new inter-regional alliances and socializing with strangers.

As the host *rancho* of an anniversary festival, many folklore groups have tied the celebration of an internal marker event (founding date) with larger regional holidays or *festas,* in order to garner greater public support and participate in cross-promotional arrangements with local businesses and nonprofit organizations. In the case of Alenquer, RFA changed the month of its anniversary celebration, which had taken place in August for several years in the early eighties, to May in order to dovetail with Alenquer's largest local festival, *Feira da Ascensão*—an event that draws tens of thousands of spectators from all over Portugal's Vale do Tejo region. By combining the *rancho*'s anniversary celebration with the large-scale display of local industry, arts, agriculture, and heritage sites, the folklore group situates itself within a dynamic matrix of local promotion and development, where scores of community insiders and outsiders come to enjoy Alenquer's specific brand of municipal hospitality. RFA in turn invites guest *ranchos,* ideally one from each of four separate provinces, to perform in the anniversary festival, treating up to three hundred guests to a four-course meal and tour of Alenquer before the evening performance. The success of the folklore event is measured not only in numbers of spectators and onstage finesse, but also in how "well received" the *rancho* guests have been. A positive evaluation of *rancho* hospitality reflects well on the *rancho* administration and artistic leadership, the largesse of the municipality, and the dynamism of the region. It can also cement a reciprocal invitation, which in turn guarantees a performance date for RFA in another region, translating into local prestige and an opportunity for the *rancho* performers, their extended families, and friends to travel together to distant locations they might not have otherwise had the occasion to visit. Effective *rancho* hospitality within the post-revolutionary anniversary circuit constitutes a crucial element in a group's success and mobility at both local and national levels. *Rancho* guests and hosts enliven local initiatives for economic development while concretizing webs of social and commercial networks.

Alenquer's annual *Feira da Ascensão* begins forty days after Easter, in celebration of the municipal holiday *Quinta-Feira da Espiga* (literally, Wheat Stalk Thursday). Four and a half days in length, the *feira* attracts over 20,000 visitors annually, drawn from Alenquer and surrounding areas in the Estremadura and Ribatejo regions (Rema 2002). The president of the *Câmara Municipal de Alenquer* and a team of local councilman created the *Feira da*

Ascensão in 1981 to enliven and promote their *concelho,* following "a dark period" of several decades from 1950 to 1980 when local fairs had dried up due to public apathy. Luís Rema, the Alenquer cultural councilman responsible for the fair's yearly organization, describes the *Feira da Ascensão* as replacing the *Feira de Gado* (Cattle Fair), a local event which disappeared in the early fifties.

> The Cattle Fair started in the beginning of the twentieth century . . . and ended around the early 1950s due to the disinterest of the people. And also the problem was, politically, many times these things during the period of the *Estado Novo* weren't pleasant. Because people got together . . . and because, as you know, there weren't a lot of people talking, there was the possibility that people would be there speaking badly—people speaking to one another, developing a critical consciousness, and so these things were never looked upon favorably [by the government]. (2002, my insert)

In the minds of Luís Rema and other organizers, the *Feira da Ascensão* provides a corrective to the political circumscription of the *Feira de Gado* under the *Estado Novo.* Restrained sociability and the dangerous potential for "bad talk" has been transformed into what organizers describe as a robust demonstration of local identity, commerce, and culture, where the diversity of offerings and free entertainment encourages widespread public participation.

Indeed, initiating, renewing, and sustaining social contact with friends, relatives, and citizens from neighboring towns constitutes an avowed objective of the *feira.* As Álvaro Pedro, president of the *Câmara Municipal de Alenquer,* states, "we hope to have many visitors . . . it is the perfect time for the sons and daughters of Alenquer to return to their origins and spend time with family and friends. [Our *feira*] also serves as a point of encounter for many citizens who embrace this land as their own" (Pedro 2002). Implicit in the language of Pedro's statement is the rhetorical framework of hospitality. Just as Pedro hopes regional newcomers to the *feira* will embrace Alenquer "as their own land," or *como estivesse na sua casa* (as if in your own house), he also urges Alenquer's sons and daughters to "return to their origins," or to return home.

The apex of Alenquer's hospitable outreach occurs on the closing Saturday night of the festival. At midnight, Alenquer hosts the *Noite do Visitante* (Night of the Visitor), where in four select locations throughout the center of town, thousands of guests are treated to grilled sardines, loaves of crusty bread, and casks of locally produced wine. The supply of food and drink seem limitless, and guests sometimes stay until sunrise. As Luís Rema (2002) explains,

> Wine and bread freely available, this is a very characteristic festival of people from Ribatejo and Estremadura . . . and there are thousands of people this night . . . during this one night four or five thousand come . . . it's craziness . . . so this night that we call Visitor's Night is genuinely characteristic of the Portuguese people, which really [shows] their kindness, their way of being, their extroverted side during moments where the wine also helps people become more joyful. So, the night of the sardine is certainly the highest point of the *feira*—when we receive the people.

According to Rema's testimony the *Feira da Ascensão,* in existence since the 1980s, showcases typical regional and national characteristics—kindness and joyful outreach—brought out by the sharing of bread, wine, and sardines. Visitor's Night is staged after midnight, in open air locales with crowds populating the streets; these are the time/place conditions described by anthropologists of ritual performance across Africa and Latin America, where "anti-structure" (Turner 1969, 1974) or carnivalesque freedom from normative social comportment (DaMatta 1992) can open social spaces for the experience of *communitas* and inversion. The *feira*'s open agenda of hospitable outreach, attracting masses of local families and strangers, salves the wounds of *Estado Novo desconfiança* (mistrust), setting the stage for a new paradigm of festive interchange, one tied up with post-revolutionary ideologies of personal and social freedoms.[7]

Indeed, throughout the several *Noites do Visitante* that I have attended, guests from all over the *concelho* along with groups of people from neighboring *concelhos* spill out into the streets, beyond the designated feasting areas. At the 2002 *Noite do Visitante,* groups of teenagers from an Alenquer high school clustered in tents of laughter and conversation. Alenquer mothers and grandmothers fixed sardine sandwiches for their own children and children of friends and neighbors. Alenquer men gathered around large charcoal grills, drinking, telling jokes, and distributing hundreds of silvery sardines atop hunks of thick white bread. People driving home in passing cars, some of them friends, some strangers, were flagged down and urged to join the feasting. Some rowdy teenagers lay down in the road, acting as human obstacles impeding the departure of people they wanted to stay. The overall mood was one of festive reunion that verged, at times, on delirium. At about 2:30 A.M. when I was getting tired, several RFA performers asked me repeatedly, "Do you like this? Are you having fun? You can't go home now—we're just getting started!"

The primary circle of *Feira* sociability is bounded by Alenquer's *concelho* limits. This is particularly visible during the *Noite do Visitante,* where kinship ties and social ties forged by a common workplace, neighborhood, school, or recreational association help organize clusters of feasting and sociability. There is also, however, a decidedly outward orientation on this night. Revealed particularly after the first round of wine has been consumed, Alenquerians reach out toward strangers and passersby. Asked if they would like a sandwich or a plastic cup of wine, some passersby accept and are folded into the celebration. *Feira* hospitality organized and financed by the municipal government serves to renew social ties throughout the whole of the locality, cementing a sociocultural identity which adheres to *concelho* limits. The large number of spectators characteristic of Saturday night and the commercial tenor of the *feira,* directed toward finding a far-reaching market for local products, conspire to orient the *Noite do Visitante* outward as well, beyond the boundaries of Alenquer. This outward, inclusive focus is evident in the mission statements of festival organizers and the social dynamics characteristic of the revelrous midnight barbecue, where *as pessoas andam mais alegres e abertas* (people are happier and more open) (Rema 2002).

The dynamics of the local economy also increasingly inflect post-revolutionary festivity in Alenquer. Due to its proximity to Portugal's capital and the new EEC-funded highways that pass alongside Alenquer heading north to Torres Vedras and south to Lisbon, Alenquer possesses a privileged and strategic position with regard to the industrial reordering of the metropolitan area of Lisbon (Russo and Martinho 1994). The *concelho* of Alenquer, which encompasses 302 square kilometers and approximately 35,000 residents, is a hybrid site marked by a history of agricultural dynamism, particularly in the areas of viticulture, as well as an increasingly robust industrial sector. As is the case with many areas of Portugal, primary sector activity is diminishing; in Alenquer, agriculture is becoming a "part-time or free-time" endeavor ("Plano Director" 1991). The tendency toward industrial growth is substantial, particularly in the southeastern zone of the *concelho* near Carregado, which constitutes an *area de recepção* (receiving area) for industries migrating to the north from Lisbon. This zone, already characterized by "a significant volume of industrial units, has great potential for the installation of new industry and services, principally those linked to transportation or large scale merchandise storage" ("Plano Director" 1991).

Alenquer's municipal government recognizes the need to encourage industrial development within the *concelho* but is anxious to retain an agricultural identity and preserve its rural landscapes—strategies thought to be healthy for tourism and residential real estate investment by Lisbon professionals seeking weekend homes outside of the city ("Plano Director" 1991). The *Feira da Ascensão* plays to both parts of Alenquer's agricultural-industrial duality. Throughout large rectangular fairgrounds in the center of Alenquer proper, local farm equipment businesses line up shiny orange tractors

Figure 17. Local business leaders, politicians, and RFA performers at the opening ceremonies of the *Feira da Ascensão*. Alenquer, Portugal, 1996. *Photograph by author.*

for display. Local wine producers offer samples of ruby red table wine. Alongside these exhibitions stand booths dedicated to the showcasing of metal products produced at local plants and various types of stones excavated from Alenquer quarries. Although the majority of the exhibitors represent small- to medium-sized businesses, larger factories and even multinational corporations participate in the *Feira* through donations of products to local *ranchos folclóricos* in celebration of their anniversaries and through advertisement in the *Feira* magazine and posters.

While several RFA members are currently or were once employed by local factories, *ranchos folclóricos* are thought to represent Alenquer's agricultural way of life—not only in their onstage representation of turn-of-the-century peasant traditions but also in their contemporary "real" lives. Luís Rema (2002) states, "Folklore is a tradition that is born in the countryside, its ethnography is based on the values of the countryside, the values of country people, the values of the land . . . wine is born from the land, is worked by many people who participate in folklore, the small producers of wine are people who love folklore." In this way *ranchos folclóricos* are unifying agents at the *Feira da Ascensão,* bringing together two disparate sectors of Alenquer's local economy in logistical and dramaturgical webs of support and reinforcement. RFA brings together, for example, Ricardo Pereira, owner of a local quarry, as RFA's de facto *padrinho,* along with upper managers at Saclene Lda., the plastics factory which employs RFA performers Armindo and António Luís and which donates material for RFA's anniversary posters and banners, in opening ceremonies where industrial leaders embrace performers dressed in peasant costumes (see fig. 17). Both vectors of socioeconomic activity are represented in the *Feira*'s *rancho* performances, one onstage, one behind the scenes, spinning festive narratives of cooperation between commerce, industry, and agriculture—sectors which in reality exist at cross-purposes within the *concelho* of Alenquer.[8]

Displays of local goods and services, heritage sites, and *rancho* performances showcase the region's cultural and economic potential. In addition to being wined and dined during the *Noite do Visitante*, *Feira* guests are also welcomed in a more commercial register. Implicit in the central fairground displays is the invitation to invest—either at an individual level by purchasing a bottle of Alenquer wine, a tractor, or a country villa, or at the corporate level by financing the migration of industrial factories into the *concelho*. By conducting a diachronic analysis of the *Feira* magazine and other brochures and programs, one can easily glean the increasing emphasis placed on the commercial benefits of festive hospitality. In the 2000 *Feira* program, organizers apologize for not having enough exhibition space open to local merchants. In the 2002 *Feira* magazine, the organizers describe a new plan for expanding the space available to commercial exhibitors, publishing a list of the 102 Alenquer businesses, corporations, and nonprofits that set up display stands throughout the enlarged exhibition grounds.[9] In his welcome statement, *Câmara* president Álvaro Pedro stated,

> What is unquestionable for us, what is most valuable in the context of the Twenty-First *Feira da Ascensão* is the business presence at the exhibition—in the central pavilion and the first floor of the Forum Romeira, demonstrating the far-reaching diversity of products on display which in some way or another relate to our reality . . . Happily, the commercial fabric [of our *concelho*] has expanded in recent years. (2002, my insert)

Anthropologists of Portuguese festivity have documented the increase in commercial activity which accompanies local festivals and religious celebrations at individual, neighborhood, and parish levels of consumption (Brito 1991; Leal 1991). In his investigation of a *taberna* ledger in a Trás-os-Montes village, for example, Joaquim Pais de Brito notes a dramatic spike in the purchase of shoes and socks during the month of June in preparation for the *Festa de Nossa Senhora de Fátima* (1991, 179). In a study of the *Espírito Santo* celebrations in a São Jorge *freguеisa*, João Leal documents a pronounced increase in the purchase of perishables and other ingredients needed to support the collective feasting and widespread donations of bread and milk that mark Easter festivities (1991, 33). The increase in economic activity in the Trás-os-Montes and São Jorge examples, however, constitutes the incidental product of celebrations devoted specifically to religious and social purposes.

The *Feira da Ascensão*, on the other hand, has been designed with the stated purpose of showcasing local businesses and invigorating the local economy. What is also striking in the Alenquer example is the absence of a link between increased consumption and religiosity, despite *Quinta-Feira da Ascensão*'s *concelho*-wide importance as the "holiest day of the year" (Melo et al. 1989).

Alenquer's post-revolutionary *Feira da Ascensão* is a decidedly secular event. Nowhere in the programming (which includes the performances of twelve local *ranchos folclóricos* and their guest *ranchos*, gymnastic and acrobatic tournaments, pop music concerts, *fado* concerts, hip hop and samba dance routines, youth orchestras, swimming competitions, ballet recitals, and taekwondo matches) do any religious processions or observances figure into the official events. *Dia de Ascensão* is commonly invoked according to its more profane identity as *Quinta-Feira da Espiga*, where secondary schools throughout the *concelho* teach children how to mark the holiday by making traditional bouquets of wheat stalks, poppies, olive branches, daisies, and vines. These bouquets are then placed by the door of family homes as talismans guaranteeing the bountiful presence of bread, olive oil, joy, and money throughout the year. Some RFA members remembered making these bouquets in school, but very few currently celebrate the holiday by going to church.

When I asked RFA members what *Quinta-Feira da Espiga* meant to them, many of the male RFA leaders laughed, launching into jokes about this special Thursday's opportunities for sexual coupling in the fields while picking poppies and wheat stalks—recast as phallic symbols. Zé Hermínio joked, "*É a única vez durante o ano que as filhas dizem a verdade às mães. Dizem que apanharam o espigão!*" (It's the only time during the year that daughters tell the truth to their mothers. They say they got the big wheat stalk!) Through laughter the female performers told me to ignore Zé Hermínio, but agreed that this was a common spin on the holiday. *Quinta-Feira da Espiga*, then, has a popular identity associated with vestiges of spring fertility rites, sexual dynamism, and social invigoration. For the local government leaders, *Quinta-Feira da Espiga/Ascensão* is a time to strengthen social ties among *concelho* residents, concretize *concelho* identity, offer hospitality to surrounding regions as potential "markets," and, most important, showcase and capitalize upon economic potential, particularly in the commercial and industrial sectors. Loosely combining traditional agricultural rites associated with spring fertility with other secular celebrations, the *Feira da Ascensão* in its early twenty-first-century incarnation is a robust demonstration of localism, civic pride, entrepreneurial drive, and spirited post-revolutionary sociability.

Performative Receptions

I have attended the annual *Feira da Ascensão* three times (1996, 2001, and 2002). In these years I have seen it grow and take on a greater importance within the municipality and in the life of the *Rancho Folclórico de Alenquer.* Preparations for the festival demand the constant reunion of *rancho* members. This intense period of contact is described by many RFA performers as their favorite time of year, despite the long hours and hard work entailed. Preparations for RFA's anniversary festival and its culminating performance on Saturday night engage almost every member of the *rancho.* The *rancho* must clean and rearrange the *sede* and the ethnographic museum located above the dance floor and administrative offices; the week of the *Feira da Ascensão* is the only time that the RFA Ethnographic Museum is open to the public. RFA must also make sure that the performers' costumes are in optimal condition, which means repairing soles of shoes, pants, and socks. Posters and programs are created to facilitate promotion and marketing. Each guest *rancho* receives several *lembranças,* or small gifts, such as bottles of local wine, flags and ribbons, metal plaques, and sometimes T-shirts and other favors which RFA leaders design and order. The four guest *ranchos* must also be contacted with formal invitations and directions on where and when to assemble for the festivities. Finally, the largest and, by many accounts, most enjoyable task is preparing the Saturday night dinner for guest *rancho* performers and their traveling companions as well as local dignitaries and other RFA supporters—a group often numbering over three hundred people.

For the last several years RFA's anniversary dinner has been held at the fire station, which sits atop a steep hill overlooking Alenquer's downtown. In May, fuchsia bougainvillea spills over stucco archways into the narrow street which winds around the hill leading to the fire station. During the days before the guest *ranchos* arrive, RFA performers drive or walk up the hill to help prepare the dinner. One of the first tasks is to assemble fifteen to twenty long folding tables end to end to make room for all of the guests (see fig. 18). RFA performers carefully set each place with a full set of flatware, soup bowls, plates, glasses, coffee cups, and napkins. Throughout most of the nineties, RFA spent a hefty portion of their festival budget on table, silverware, and plate rental. By 2000, the *rancho* had purchased three hundred place settings, to save on future rental costs. The pristine uniformity of the tables, especially now that the dinnerware is owned by the *rancho,* is an object of great pride, and one of the first prerequisites for receiving guests *como deve ser* (as it should be).

Figure 18. RFA banquet tables set up at the fire station in anticipation of many guests. Alenquer, Portugal, 1996. *Photograph by author.*

The food preparation takes place over several days. After the menu is decided upon in consultation with a local cook hired for the occasion, RFA leaders order the ingredients from local vendors. In 1996 the total RFA festival budget was 315,372 escudos (roughly $1,892 U.S.), with the majority of the expenses related to the dinner (RFA 1996). Some local restaurants, cafés, and beverage companies donated supplies, and the rest of the food and drinks were purchased, if possible, from establishments linked to RFA performers. The fish, for example, was always purchased from Dulce Anacleto's small *peixaria* (fish store) in town, before she had to close the shop in the late 1990s. Dulce used to dance in the *rancho,* and her husband, Manuel, and both daughters are all RFA performers.

On the Friday and Saturday before the dinner, RFA performers gather to prepare the food. The men usually congregate around the open fire, helping the chef with the hot soup and the main course. Men usually cut and season the meat and devein the shellfish. Most of the women deal with the fresh produce. In 1996, when I first helped with these preparations, I noticed that all of the women gathered together around a large table to peel and chop vegetables. Chatting in one large group was a relatively unusual occurrence. The tensions described in chapter 3 regarding leadership positions usually caused the women to fracture into two groups during rehearsals and performance trips, sticking to one side of the divide or the other. Festival preparations seemed to "suspend" these historical tensions, as everyone united to work toward a common end—the attentive and lavish reception of *rancho* guests.

As I joined the group and began helping prepare the potatoes, several of the women began to chuckle at my clumsy peeling skills. I told them that I was accustomed to using peelers and not paring knives, which sparked a huge debate about which utensil I should use. A couple of women wanted me to take their knives because sharper knives would make it easier for me, while several others disagreed, fearing I would cut myself! This discussion gave way to several adroit demonstrations of peeling a potato, even with a dull knife, in one impossibly long continuous scroll. I told them that I would not even attempt such a virtuoso performance, but took their advice and tried to improve my peeling by digging farther inside of the potato and flicking my thumb to the outside.

Throughout the rest of the day and during subsequent years of festival preparations, various RFA members would give me encouragement or comment on the state of my progress in learning various domestic skills deemed essential for the effective running of a home and the successful receiving of guests. The lesson I had learned in peeling potatoes was part of a larger exhibition in the artistry of hosting guests. Hospitality grants the opportunity to "perform" these skills, and such an exhibition necessarily carries an instructive charge due to the reciprocity implied in the arrangement. "Welcome those as you would like to be welcomed" is an adage which undergirds festival preparations. Along these lines, the summer performance season inevitably includes comparisons of other *rancho* dinners, engaging RFA members in common threads of discourse, "The north is a hospitable region—see how well they served us?" Or "This soup is *fraca* [weak or poorly made]; these folks better dance better than they cook!"

Negative assessments of *rancho* hospitality can be chalked up to all sorts of deficiencies and problems. Once in 1996 I traveled to an anniversary festival with RFA in the Beira Alta region. Instead of having a meal in a large hall like Alenquer offers, guest *ranchos* were treated to dinner in a local restaurant. Many RFA members looked negatively on this arrangement and surmised that the host *rancho* had no *sede* in which to receive guests, which could in turn point to a lack of local governmental or commercial support for the *rancho.* Intimate settings where *rancho* performers cook, serve, and wash dishes mirror domestic hospitality—an arrangement thought to confer more respect to the guest, and thus more prestige to the host.

Many RFA women took great pride in their housekeeping and food preparation talents and men in their barbecuing acumen. The anniversary festival granted RFA members the opportunity to showcase these skills not only in front of one another, but also for wider audiences of local leaders and guest *rancho* performers from other regions. Treating municipal councilmen and business leaders—individuals RFA depends upon financially—to a four-course meal is not only a gesture of thanks and a display of skill, but also an act of inversion, facilitating the "moral and conceptual subordination of the guest to the host ... [whereby] hospitality ... becomes a means of expressing and reversing a pattern of domination at one and the same time" (Herzfeld 1987, 77, my insert). An act of hospitality can never engage host and guest as equals, as this would invite rivalry (Pitt-Rivers 1968, 21). Therefore, in agreeing to travel to Alenquer and consuming the feast prepared by RFA performers, local leaders and *rancho* guests comprise the "captive" audience at RFA's dinner and subsequent onstage performance.

Pitt-Rivers's seminal essay "The Stranger, the Guest and the Hostile Host" examines the social dynamics implied by the etymological root of the Latin *hostis*, meaning both guest and enemy. Transforming the stranger/enemy into a stranger/guest presupposes the suspension of hostility and can constitute a "rite of incorporation." Rites of incorporation contain a territorial element, whereby "a host is host only on the territory over which on a particular occasion he claims authority" (Pitt-Rivers 1968, 26). In the case of RFA's anniversary festival and dinner, municipal councilmen and local business leaders give over control to *rancho* leaders, the ceremonial masters, whose territorial dominance articulates itself situationally in a cultural, as opposed to a political or commercial, register. Later during the folklore performance guests are brought onstage in the arms of RFA performers playfully duplicating dance steps from Alenquer's peasant past. Drinking local wines, dining on barbecued meats seasoned with secret recipes of RFA families, and miming the dance traditions RFA members collected from elderly neighbors, festival guests from near and far are transformed from potentially hostile strangers into local community members for the night.

It is through the ritual consumption of local culinary specialties and the performative embodiment of local dance and music traditions that *rancho* guests from distant provinces become folded into local processes of community building and inter-regional exchange. The hope is that these relationships will continue into the future and that the invitation to perform at the Alenquer festival will be reciprocated in upcoming years. Indeed, many of RFA's younger members have kept up pen pal arrangements with folklore performers from other regions, met while performing in anniversary festivals. Lucília, for example, met a young folklore performer from the Algarve in the early nineties and still keeps in touch with her today, sometimes traveling alone to the Algarve to visit during holidays. These types of folklore-generated relationships and exchanges are distinctly post-revolutionary phenomena facilitated by *rancho* anniversary festivals, which not only stipulate the formulaic participation of five *ranchos* from differing regions, but include increasingly lavish displays of local hospitality designed to provide entertainment, enrichment, and ultimately yield reciprocal exchange.

An internal memo to all RFA performers, particularly those selected as festival *guias*, or guides, reveals the careful dramaturgy involved in receiving guest *ranchos* and programming their experience of Alenquer:

> 2: Guides, along with available RFA directors, should proceed to the local municipal market to await the arrival of the guest *ranchos folclóricos* . . .
>
> 5: Guides should accompany their groups during a visit to the *feira* and, if possible, should conduct a visit to sites of interest throughout our *concelho*
>
> 6: At 6:30 guides should get in the buses of their guest *ranchos* and lead them to the hall of the Volunteer Firefighters of Alenquer for dinner at 7:00
>
> 7: After dinner, the guest *ranchos* proceed to the Vila [of Alenquer] where groups can make small tours of the Vila keeping in mind that they should be fully costumed and back at the *sede* at 8:45
>
> 8: From there a small procession will begin of all the *ranchos* through the *feira* grounds and up to the main stage . . .
>
> 9: Guides, together with invited dignitaries, should proceed to the stage for the offering of small gifts to their respective *ranchos.*
>
> **NOTE:**
>
> **—Guides, together with other designated members, should serve the dinner to their respective ranchos . . .**
>
> **—Guides should give as much attention as possible to their guest ranchos, so that they want for nothing, in as much as is possible**
>
> **DON'T FORGET THAT SERVING WELL IS ONE OF OUR VIRTUES**
>
> (RFA 2001, bold and capitals in original)

RFA guides are usually younger members of the troupe and are organized in pairs—two to each visiting *rancho.* In addition to leading tours of the *Feira da Ascensão,* the historic sites of the *concelho,* and the town shops, RFA guides act as waiters and waitresses during the dinner, running back and forth from the kitchen area to the long tables, serving a four-course meal to as many as fifty people each. The memo makes explicit RFA's expectations of the guides. They should make certain that their guests want for nothing—this means addressing all needs throughout the day, from bathroom breaks for small children to procuring first aid kits for guests with bee stings and asthma attacks. Young guides take busloads of *rancho* performers from distant provinces on tours of local schools, libraries, castle ruins, and for picnics at the Montejunto peak. The directive at the bottom of the memo underscores the way in which successful hospitality and local identity are inextricably intertwined. Recognizing that "good service" is an Alenquerian "virtue," RFA guides feel pressure to conform to local expectations. Representing Alenquer according to local conceptions of autochthonous identity means serving well—this should not be construed as "customer service" because, as Mauss (1990 [1950]) argues, gift exchange must not be viewed as commerce or trade, but service associated with the incorporative rites meant to bond guests to hosts. Providing good service by being a cheerful and attentive host, offering boxes full of gifts, and feeding *rancho* guests and their traveling companions a bountiful feast of local specialties is an activity which showcases the social and geographical landscape of Alenquer in its best light, satisfying the objectives of RFA directors, local business leaders, *Feira* organizers, and the municipal government.

Travel, Leisure, and Exchange

Alenquer *ranchos* that hold their anniversary festivals during the *Feira da Ascensão* must balance an intense local focus with exterior outreach. RFA leaders, for example, carefully select four guest *ranchos* to participate in the Saturday night performance according to several criteria. First, guest *ranchos* should represent four differing provinces drawn from northern, central, and southern zones. To show maximum geographical representation, guest *ranchos* should represent provinces that do not border one another. If financially and logistically possible, the inclusion of one foreign troupe confers added prestige upon the host *rancho.*[10]

In addition to geographical considerations, *ranchos* are selected according to the quality of their repertoire, costumes, performers, and leadership. RFA, for example, would never consider inviting a group to perform in the festival that was not an FFP affiliate, as quality is also assessed according to levels of officially legitimated "authenticity." In order to evaluate *rancho* quality, RFA leaders scout other *ranchos* during their performance season while also relying on word of mouth and general reputation. It is widely known among folklore performers that *ranchos* go through varying epochs of vitality. Making certain that qualitative evaluations of folklore groups remain current avoids embarrassing performances by *ranchos* that have passed their prime.

The demands of reciprocity also figure into the selection of guest *ranchos.* Throughout the year, RFA accepts invitations for all types of performances. The *Câmara Municipal de Alenquer,* for example, invites RFA to perform at several locations throughout the *concelho* every *25 de Abril* to commemorate the Revolution. RFA is also often invited to perform in towns throughout Estremadura and Ribatejo as the entertainment for small local *feiras* and religious *festas.* For these *feira/festa* engagements, RFA receives payment which comprises a portion of the group's annual budget. Generally, paid performances do not have to be reciprocated. Anniversary festivals celebrating the founding date of a *rancho,* on the other hand, form a different class of unpaid performance events that often imply reciprocal arrangements.

Although not measured in monetary compensation, *rancho* performers enjoy many rewards from a festival invitation. In addition to the prestige implied by any performance request, anniversary invitations afford *rancho* members the opportunity to travel. Due to the geographical criteria which orient the selection of guest *ranchos,* an invitation to perform at an anniversary festival often implies travel to distant parts of the country. In the case of RFA, most families do not take holidays far from home due to financial constraints. Many performers view these anniversary performance trips as mini holidays, replete with the company of friends and family and the experience of new people, cuisines, musics, and landscapes.

In 1996, RFA traveled to the Algarve to perform in an anniversary festival. Not understanding the dual nature of these performance trips, I was totally unprepared for the touristic activities that were to unfold. When we first arrived at the coastal town, RFA performers dug through the back of the bus to unpack umbrellas, swimsuits, sunscreen, and elaborate picnic lunches. Not having a swimsuit, I swam in my clothes—to the disbelief of my companions! Most of the younger performers spent the entire afternoon swimming and tanning along the water's edge. Some older men sat at seaside bars enjoying cold beer and snacks as other couples, arm in arm, explored the souvenir stands along the boardwalk, buying towels, T-shirts, and postcards to show friends at home. It was not until the sun began to set that RFA returned to the bus for the ceremonial dinner hosted by the Algarvian *rancho* and the outdoor performance scheduled for 9:30 P.M. That beautiful Sunday afternoon at an Algarve resort beach amounted to an experience of leisure enjoyed by people who, in general, were not members of "the leisure class" (MacCannell 1976). Except for the costs of souvenirs, beer, and popsicles, RFA performers were able to enjoy a holiday without incurring expenses. The *Câmara* financed the bus rental; RFA paid the driver; the host *rancho* treated RFA performers to an elaborate dinner and tour of the town, and other meals had been brought from home.

For RFA dancer António Luís Pereira, folklore performance serves many important functions in his life—the two most important being traveling and making new friends:

> For me [folklore] is a pastime, because I played soccer for 12 years. Later I had a knee operation, and I had to quit playing. So I had to find something to take

> away stress, to burn off some energy. So I go there [RFA rehearsals] on Wednesday. We entertain ourselves, we travel. I always say, "I got to know the district of Lisbon playing soccer . . . now I am getting to know Portugal through folklore." There are two things. The trip—always visiting new places—and making new friends. (1996, my inserts)

António Luís's testimony underscores the benefits of *rancho* membership and the way in which the discovery of new places and people enriches this pastime beyond simply "burning off energy."

The experience of travel for many RFA women offers benefits in addition to the pleasures of tourism. A surprising number of RFA women do not drive. Fátima Rodrigues, for example, relies on her husband and daughter to shuttle her into town for errands. When they are not available, Fátima hitchhikes. On several occasions I hitchhiked with her, standing in front of her house at the edge of a curve in the road overlooking fields and several other small stuccoed houses. While we were waiting for passing motorists, I asked her if she considered this practice dangerous. Fátima chuckled and said that she would never get into the car of a stranger. She only flags down people from Alenquer that she knows and trusts. Other women who do not drive are more circumscribed. Ana Pereira, an attractive woman in her thirties who currently stays home to care for her young daughter, for example, waits for her husband to come home for lunch or return at the end of the day so that he can take her out on errands. Ana views this arrangement as a way of making António Luís more responsible and attentive to her needs. Other women who don't drive either rely on public transportation or walk many miles to work.

When I asked RFA women who drive to explain this phenomenon, they matter-of-factly stated that some men don't want their wives to drive because it gives them too much freedom. The implication was that limiting women's physical mobility served as a means of moral control, reducing the risk of sexual misconduct or other illicit wanderings. The social isolation caused by the lack of self-directed travel among women has been exacerbated by traditions of segregated recreation, where after work men often gather in local bars and taverns to socialize, leaving their wives at home. In her study of northern Portuguese rural couples who immigrated to France, Caroline Brettell (1995) documents a shift in segregated recreation, where immigrant couples tended to spend more free time together following exposure to the cultural habits of French couples. Folklore travel has a similar expansive effect on folklore families, serving as a vehicle for integrated recreation, where husbands and wives spend time together during long bus rides and tours of new towns and provinces. Several female RFA performers and *acompanhantes* spoke of folklore as an antidote to domestic confinement—

a way to keep the family together and marriages healthy. Weekend trips to anniversary festivals throughout the summer months constituted coveted opportunities to get out of the house/workplace and "see the world" without rupturing gendered norms of socio-spatial comportment.

By traveling to *rancho* anniversary festivals, RFA members experience parts of the country they might not otherwise visit and engage in touristic activities without incurring personal expenses. RFA performers get to know other folklore enthusiasts from around the country, sometimes forging long-term friendships and social networks. RFA women, particularly those who do not drive, step out of confining domestic and *concelho* spheres, while married couples break with traditions of segregated leisure time to spend more free time together. It is considered an honor and a pleasure to receive an invitation to perform at an anniversary festival, outreach which is generally reciprocated by an invitation to Alenquer in subsequent years.[11]

Hospitality and Improvisation

During the preparation period which preceded RFA's 1996 anniversary festival, I kept asking performers a question which I had posed periodically throughout my fieldwork, without much of a response. This question was particularly relevant during festival time due to the hours and hours of unpaid labor required for event planning and execution. I tried to understand the Herculean level of commitment that *ranchos folclóricos* make to what is essentially a hobby by asking RFA members why they performed folklore. This question was always met with such uniform bewilderment, that I thought perhaps my Portuguese phrasing of the query was confusing. I tried several different syntactical variations: Why is folklore so important to *rancho* performers? Why do you spend all your free time performing folklore? What motivates you to continue performing folklore, despite the personal hardships it sometimes causes? Why do you perform folklore when you are not paid for it? The more I pushed for answers to this basic question, the more frustrated I became. RFA performers said they couldn't understand what I wanted to know. Or that it should already be evident. Or that I was being an *Americanazinha* by implying that folklore performers should be paid to make it worth their while. Or that weren't all those discussions of *convivência* enough of an answer?

The weekend before the festival, RFA gathered at the Ethnographic Museum to clean. As several of us were down on our hands and knees wiping thick salmon-colored wax on the dry floor boards, Fátima said, "Hey Kim! *This* is why we perform folklore!" Everyone laughed heartily, a few throwing their dust rags into the air. The next day as we were chopping barrels of vegetables with dull knives in preparation for the banquet dinner, someone else said, "No, *this* is why we perform folklore!" Again, laughter.

The following weekend, four busloads of *rancho* performers from all over the country arrived at the door of Alenquer's *sede*. Many carried black plastic bags protecting carefully ironed costumes. Others carried infants and toddlers who had fallen asleep during the ride. Others carried accordions, banners, flags, and drums. After a half an hour of what seemed like general mayhem—hundreds of people trying to find bathrooms, cups of water, storage areas, telephones—an older man in a brown leather hat started playing the accordion. A few other players from varying groups fought their way through the crowd to join him. Soon the growing circle of instrumentalists began improvising a *fadinho*, with others throughout the crowd shouting out alternating verses. People toward the edge of the circle began clapping. In a matter of minutes the room was filled with song. Performers from the arid central plains, the coastal towns of the Algarve, and the mountainous northern region—strangers—came together side by side to sing *ao desafio* in call-and-response, improvised verses which built upon one another, rising to a playful crescendo. The musical dialogue energized the cacophonous crowd, as multiple circles of dancers hooked arms and swung each other in revelrous dips and twirls. I was caught in the action, off to one side, cursing the fact that my video camera was in a bag at the far end of the room. Just as I was about to start battling my way toward the bag, Armindo tapped me on the shoulder, leaned over, and whispered, "*This* is folklore. This is why."

I have thought of this moment often, not only as the most satisfying answer to my question, "Why perform folklore?" but also as an important example of the affective evolution of festive hospitality post–*25 de Abril.* In a sense, improvised moments such as these constitute the fruits of festival preparation, the reward for diligent "service" and attentive welcome. Such chance interchange is as much the targeted end of RFA's festival as is the culminating Saturday night performance. The scheduled performances are indeed impressive. The long lines of folklore performers snaking their way through the evening fairground to an enormous wooden stage set atop risers creates a magnificent sight. Local radio personalities emcee the folklore production, introducing each song with deep resonant voices and professional aplomb. The rich differences between regional costumes and repertoire can be appreciated due to the festival performance format where each group performs for twenty minutes, following one another in a serial continuum without intermission. And, of course, certain dances, such as the Ribatejanan *fandango,* where virtuoso dancers execute quick, choppy footwork while balancing clay jugs on their heads, and the Algarvian *baile mandado,* where couples twirl round and round for minutes on end in time to rapid-fire accordion riffs, are enormous crowd pleasers, often sparking audiences into ovations.

Although these elements of the onstage spectacle indicate a successful event, the improvised comingling of people and music which emerged out of the chaotic coming together of guests and hosts constituted the festival highlight that RFA performers most often talked about afterward. Standard hospitality scripts—the stringent expectations of the *guias*, the lavish banquet, the tours and preparations, if done well, open a space for unscripted dialogue, in both musical and social registers. Impromptu "call-and-response" communicates the guest's comfort in alien territory and the host's willing reception. This dance of increasing social proximity is the felicitous outcome of post-revolutionary shifts in festive modes of engagement, where the articulation of localism features an exterior reach, and strangers come together in the name of folklore to enact rites of trans-regional incorporation.

Alenquer's *Feira da Ascensão* presents a compelling portrait of the way in which folklore performance participates in a *concelho*'s attempt to reimagine itself in the decades following *25 de Abril. Feira* organizers combine a celebration of local arts and education with the display of local industry, agriculture, and commerce. The commercial aspect has become an increasingly important feature of the *Feira*, as organizers aim to create new markets for Alenquer products, inspire investment in real estate and industrial projects, and concretize Alenquer's participation in the economic revitalization of the Vale do Tejo region. Folklore groups take advantage of commercial largesse during this period to secure donations in goods, services, and cash for their anniversary festival and annual budget. *Rancho* performers also act as unifying agents within Alenquer's agricultural/industrial divide; onstage celebrations of late nineteenth-century agrarian culture and lifestyle complement the perception that folklore performers possess "real life" affection for farming and wine making—and indeed, many RFA members have hobby farms replete with livestock, small crops, and grape presses. Many RFA members, however, also work in local factories and quarries. Positive personal relationships with employers have catalyzed networks of support and patronage among local business, industry, and the RFA. These alliances are strengthened and dramatized during festival preparations and official ceremonies of gift exchange, friendship, and gratitude.

Feira da Ascensão's *Noite do Visitante* and RFA's enormous festival banquet catalyze new post-revolutionary modalities of sociability, where guests from near and far participate in collective feasting and, through the sharing of food, drink, and hospitality, renew existing social bonds while forming new relationships across regional borders. This experience, according to both RFA performers and *Feira* organizers, marks a break with Alenquer's festival traditions under the *Estado Novo,* often characterized by public *desconfiança* and *disinteresse* (apathy), where *rancho* members would "get off the bus, perform, and go back home, without a word to anyone." RFA's anniversary festival, and the *Feira da Ascensão* more generally, represent the transfer of communal life from fugitive gatherings nurtured in domestic spaces under Salazar to the reestablishment of unfettered sociability in public spaces. Such a move is facilitated by an increase in *rancho* travel and mobility, by ritualized encounters between hosts and guests in town halls and municipal fire stations, and by unscripted moments of expressive interchange.

Changes in the tone and structure of *rancho* performance outlets—dominated by an ethos of competition under the *Estado Novo* and by hospitality and exchange post–*25 de Abril*—have been complemented by FFP cultural reforms. Urged to conduct ethnographic research in order to re-create locally specific songs and dances from the turn of the century and to banish patriotic costumes favored under Salazar, *ranchos* reconnect with local communities and history, disseminating this knowledge at anniversary festivals throughout the country and sometimes abroad. The dual spatial orientation exhibited in these practices—a reentrenchment in local spheres of commerce, sociability, and festivity and an exterior outreach toward national and international spheres of interchange and discovery—epitomizes the "local/global nexus" theorized by scholars of globalism. RFA, in its desire to host hundreds of strangers in Alenquer and its role as guest in foreign territories, puts local identity and history into a robust circulation, along an axis of ever-increasing orbit beyond the borders of the *concelho.* From one vantage point, anniversary festivals which value and accentuate regional *difference* and *variety* stand as a bulwark against the homogenizing forces of globalization. As the following chapter explores, newly reformed *ranchos* showcasing the micro-contours of local identity have resisted transformation and "jazzing up" to conform to conceptions of Europeanness. Chafing against pressures from Portugal's cultural elite to transform themselves for inclusion in official national festivals like Lisbon 94, Europália 91, and EXPO 98, many *ranchos folclóricos* have struck out on their own. Forging alliances with foreign and domestic folklore groups, *ranchos folclóricos* enmesh themselves in networks of exchange, where the laws of hospitable reciprocity ensure the proliferation of border crossings and the emergence of an alternative sphere of cosmopolitanism.

5 

"We Will Not Be Jazzed Up!": Lisbon 94 and *Ranchos'* Festival Absence

"We Will Not Be Jazzed Up!"

Acting on information I received in 1993 from an acquaintance working in Lisbon 94's promotion department who had said that festival programming would include folklore performance, I planned my initial research on *ranchos folclóricos* around Lisbon's tenure as the Cultural Capital of Europe. In late August of 1993, I received a package from the Portuguese Tourist Office in New York containing preliminary schedules and descriptions of Lisbon 94 events. I scoured the material for the calendar of folkloric productions. Although I found none, I assumed this material was still in process and that I would be able to obtain more complete programming information upon my arrival in Lisbon. On September 1, 1994, I stood in a long line at Lisbon 94's ticket booth in Rossio, eagerly awaiting a copy of the official program for the fall and winter events. After two hours in line, I received armfuls of beautifully produced pamphlets, brochures, maps, playbills, and posters. Again, I scoured the material for folkloric productions. Other than an exhibit on regional costumes at the Museu de Traje, there seemed to be no other live events featuring Portuguese folkloric music or dance.[1] Puzzled by the absence of *ranchos folclóricos* at this international celebration of Portuguese cultural identity, I began to investigate why folkloric production had been omitted.

In a lengthy interview, Augusto Gomes dos Santos (1994), president of the *Federação do Folclore Português,* explained the exclusion of *ranchos folclóricos:*

> Unfortunately, our country's leaders are ashamed to present the customs and habits of the Portuguese people. They feel inferior. They say that this is not cul-

ture, it is pathetic and shabby. For them culture is that which takes place in Vienna, that which takes place in Paris, that which takes place in London, for them this is culture. It's a concert in Paris, in New York, in Washington, in Rio de Janeiro, this is what culture is. What comes from the Portuguese people, for them, is only culture when it is convenient. But in contact with the elite spheres of other countries, folklore is hidden.[2]

In his statement, Santos critiques the marginalization of folklore performance as compared to "high art" forms favored and promoted by the ruling elite during the 1990s. He theorizes the hegemonic definition of culture not according to the qualitative merits of cultural form but according to the *location* of cultural event. According to Santos, the elite believe "culture" worthy of public presentation can only be found in major urban centers across northern Europe and America, but not within Portugal. He portrays Portuguese leaders as Janus faced, respecting folklore performance and publics within the bounded national context while "hiding" Portuguese folklore from the critical gaze of international sophisticates. As Santos implies later in the interview, the promotion or exclusion of specific cultural forms is not only context driven but context generative. In other words, folklore performance is evicted from Lisbon 94 due in part to the international reach of the event and the fact that, according to Santos, festival organizers are intent on "hiding" folkloric tradition from such prestigious venues.

Popular response to this exclusion has also been context generative—throughout the nineties *ranchos folclóricos* have organized their own international festivals, creating a performance sphere or "performanscape" that is alternative to the high-priced, official events sponsored by the Portuguese government and the European Union. Santos (1994) explains:

Europália[3] . . . an eight-month festival that takes place periodically in Brussels where every year a different country is chosen, and three years ago Portugal was chosen . . . cost the Portuguese government around 2.5 million *contos* . . . Money is later given to Portugal by the European Union for the development of Portuguese culture . . . But the money that the EU gives for this purpose never reaches the cultures at the bottom. It stays in certain cultural strata—it goes to theater houses, the ballet, etc. At the time I was approached, who was organizing the show in Brussels? A Belgian couple, they were not Portuguese. So they brought in Filipe La Féria[4] to go to Brussels with a show . . . [makes a big theatrical gesture with hands and flashes a toothy smile]. The Belgian couple was making the selections—and came here to talk to me. They chose two *ranchos* or so. I don't know what kind of performance they put on, I only know that the Portuguese emigrants living in Belgium were disgusted by the weak demonstration of Portuguese folklore staged in the center of Belgium. Even the Belgians asked, "So *this* is your folklore?" They brought in a few little *ranchitos*, but the

> show was by no means a tour de force. So, afterward, they asked me to come to Brussels for a month and organize a folklore festival . . . sponsored by our emigrants. Our festival took place in the Grande Place, in the heart of Belgium. The Belgian government agreed, yes sir, our ambassador was there, and he said, "This, yes! *This* is a festival of the Portuguese people! This is a festival of Portuguese traditions! . . . At the Grande Place there were so many people, so many people, there was a world of people . . . all *running* to the Grande Place, they didn't want to leave. Ah, what a grand show!"

As Santos compellingly illustrates, the Portuguese emigrants living in Belgium responded to the official marginalization of folklore performance by generating an alternative performance sphere. Initially, I mistakenly conceived of this sphere in strictly spatial terms—*ranchos folclóricos* expressed distinctly local histories and identities and must, therefore, adhere to these spaces for legitimacy, public support, and performance forums. I had aligned folklore performance with the local in contrast to more "global" highbrow forms such as opera featured throughout Lisbon 94. As Santos reveals, however, *ranchos folclóricos'* alternative performance sphere is *not* delimited by local or regional borders. Hundreds of Portuguese *ranchos* maintain rigorous international performance schedules, traveling not only to Spain, Germany, and France, but to places far more distant in geographic and cultural terms, such as Egypt, Japan, and Russia. Although *ranchos folclóricos* were explicitly excluded from Lisbon 94, this does not mean they have been confined to the isolated nooks and crannies of Portuguese rurality. It just means that due to the classifying operations producing and resulting from differences in taste, *ranchos folclóricos* were shut out of Portugal's "official cultural sphere" throughout the 1990s.[5]

The difference between the publics, performers, and producers of this official cultural sphere and folklore's alternative performance sphere can be broken down along the lines of taste, as Bourdieu conceives of it. Dividing a population into classes is an operation which produces and interprets signifying distinctions and belongs to the order of the symbolic (Bourdieu 1984, 172). Taste, "a symbolic expression of class position . . . is the generative formula of life-style, a unitary set of distinctive practices" found in all the objects and practices with which people surround themselves—houses, furniture, paintings, books, cars, clothes, and entertainments (Bourdieu 1984, 173–75). Folklore performance could certainly be classified as a form of "entertainment" for which people either have a taste or do not. However, folklore performance adds another dimension to Bourdieu's theory as it also embodies "life-style" on stage.

Lifestyles are sign systems "socially qualified (as 'distinguished', 'vulgar' etc.) . . . transform[ing] the distribution of capital . . . into . . . perceived differences, distinctive properties, that is, a distribution of symbolic capital" (1984, 172). *Ranchos folclóricos* frame and enact this symbolic capital through revivalist folklore performance. They perform in clothes typical of farmhands, fishmongers, shoemakers, and shepherds—the garb of working-class lifestyle. They perform courtship dances and sing melodic street vendors' calls—the gestures and sounds of lifestyle. They carry pitchforks, cisterns, laundry baskets, and walking sticks—the material props of lifestyle. Bourdieu maintains that taste, particularly for the working classes, operates at a semiconscious level and is the product of a kind of unknowing internalization of the structure of social space—transforming "necessity into a virtue by inducing 'choices' which correspond to the condition of which it is the product" (Bourdieu 1984, 175). This feature of subliminality, which, according to Bourdieu, guides class-driven preferences for objects, people, places, and practices, erupts into the realm of the conscious when *ranchos folclóricos* deliberately frame and perform working-class lifestyle on the proscenium stage.

Therefore, when the cultural and political elite endeavor to "hide" the "habits and customs" of the Portuguese "people" by excluding *ranchos folclóricos* from official events, they are not only exercising a class-driven aesthetic censor (i.e., we do not want to include *ranchos* because the music is monotonous, the singers unpolished, or the costumes drab), but are expressing "shame" and "embarrassment" toward the lifestyles many of these working-class dancers not only perform but live. *Ranchos folclóricos'* role in sparking such an attitude, of course, is not just a contemporary phenomenon. It is important to recall the 1955 letter written to SNI by a Portuguese man expressing disgust for the *rancho* performers he came across in the London train station—sitting on the floor, dirty and unkempt, surrounded by empty wine jugs and grimy packages.[6] The SNI letter reveals disdain, not necessarily for the onstage practices of *ranchos folclóricos* geared toward recreating the past, but for the "real" people and contemporary lifestyles such practices employ and represent. This example resonates into the 1990s and explains the emigrants' outrage in Brussels at Europália's weak folkloric presentation. The emigrants in Brussels did not only protest the Europália Festival because it was a missed opportunity for recalling their youthful days of dancing and singing. They likely also perceived the paltry presentation of Portuguese folklore, selected and staged by outsiders, as a personal affront, a direct comment not only on their native homes and histories but on their lives in the present.

In Portugal, as in other southern European countries, modernization is not only a recent but an incomplete process, allowing oxcarts and computers to exist side by side, signifying the incongruous coupling of agrarian past and technological present. As cultural anthropologist Nadia Seremetakis argues in her analysis of the effects of European unification on Greece,

> the uneven historical development of European peripheries . . . is characterized by the incomplete and disjunctive articulation of the pre-modern, different phases within modernity, and the postmodern . . . The notions of authenticity and inauthenticity are symbiotic concepts that equally repress and silence non-contemporaneous and discordant cultural experiences and sensibilities. Thus the modernist critic would look at Greek society and dismiss any residues and incongruities emanating from the pre-modern as both romantic and invented . . . Static impositions of the polarity authentic/inauthentic [lead] to the dismissal of important cultural systems and sensibilities that have been repositioned within the modern as non-synchronous elements. (1994a, 17)

Seremetakis's reading of contemporary cultural dynamics within Greece also applies to Portugal and Portuguese immigrant communities throughout Europe and the Americas. Due to uneven economic development and modernization, Portugal's modernizing project is indeed suffused with the "residues and incongruities emanating from the pre-modern." Folkloric *revivalism* is a bit of a misnomer when one compares the quotidian lives of many folklore performers to the fin de siècle lives they portray on stage. There exists a distinct intermingling of past and present, of pre-modernity and postmodernity in contemporary Portuguese life, which in the context of "revivalist" folklore performance sometimes makes action indiscernible from en-action.

Action and reenactment are distinguished following Richard Schechner's theory of restored behavior in which performance is defined as "twice-behaved behavior" (1985, 36). The intermingling of past and present and of action and en-action was demonstrated time and again by the folklore groups I followed. Several members of the *Rancho Folclórico de Ceifeiras e Campinos de Azambuja*, for example, showed me a series of black-and-white wedding photographs hung in their rehearsal hall display case. The bride and groom were dressed in what I thought were *rancho* costumes, flanked by musicians also in "costume," carrying accordions and percussion instruments commonly used by *rancho* instrumentalists in the Ribatejo region. I asked if the wedding shot was a publicity photo. Jorge, one of the group's leaders, laughed heartily and said, "no, of course not, this is a *real* wedding!" The couple pictured in the photo explained that they had met and courted during their first months as new *rancho* members, but that their wedding had nothing to do with performance. They were wearing wedding clothes, family heirlooms, which had been passed down to them by grandmothers and great uncles. The musicians in the photo were close friends hired to play at the wedding reception, and also happened to be *rancho* instrumentalists. The photo was in the display case because it documented the personal and sociological history of the *rancho,* not because it documented the *rancho*'s *performance* history. In other words, I mistook the photo for a "non-synchronous," "fabricated," or "restored" artifact characterized in Schechner's terms by "twiceness," when really it documented a contemporary "real life" wedding —a wedding featuring "residues and incongruities" from the past. Given this dynamic characterized by chronological and mimetic pileups, it may be more appropriate to analyze revivalist folklore performance not so much as invented tradition (Hobsbawm and Ranger 1983), but as a dialogic encounter between "mythic past" and modernizing present. This idea directly opposes much of the most recent thinking on heritage. David Brett, for example, states that "the appeal of heritage is based more than anything else upon . . . freedom from real concrete time because to be held within heritage is . . . to be preserved from real time" (1996, 158). But *ranchos* engage both the past and "real" time. If staged performances of *ranchos folclóricos* are viewed in this way, the absence of *ranchos* from official festivals becomes not simply a matter of aesthetic taste or social exclusivity, but a disavowal of the ragged past-present trajectory folklore performance represents.

According to Santos, the integration of folklore performance into Lisbon 94 could only occur if *ranchos* agreed to be "jazzed up"—literally and figuratively. In Bourdieu's terms, this would mean grafting the symbolic markers of taste associated with one group onto another. In Santos's (1994) words, this is tantamount to "assassinating the habits and customs of the Portuguese people." Refusing to participate in this "jazzing up," Santos rejected Lisbon 94's plan to produce an evening of folklore performance contingent on significant alterations to *rancho* personnel, repertoire, musical arrangement, and instrumentation. Santos (1994) explains,

> I was contacted via telephone by someone who wanted *ranchos* to perform in Lisbon 94. But the person spoke in this way, a command: "Mr so-and-so, we want you to choose some *ranchos* to participate, but we don't want more than x number of people for each *rancho,* we don't want more that twenty to twenty five people." What's more, the person said, "the *ranchos* will only dance. I'll decide on the music." He wanted a rock band, a modern group, to rehearse the music—this group would play, they'd bring in a vocalist to sing, and the *ranchos* would dance. No sir, not a chance! Bringing in artists to sing, professional musicians to play—organ, piano, saxophone, and whatever—and the *ranchos* to dance? Oh, no! The *ranchos* have their own instrumentalists, they have their own singers, they have their own dancers, and either the entire *rancho* goes with their own musicians and singers—the authentic representation of the people—or else I'll have nothing to do with it. The federation is totally against this. This

is the assassination of the customs and habits of the people. They want to wrap up a smart, pretty package, something very clever for the foreigners to see. Oh, no! It's either popular culture exactly as it is, or no—like this? No. Like this? No, no, I won't accept it. So, my friends, you can keep your own culture, and we'll keep ours.

Santos's spirited commentary illustrates the evolution of a kind of cultural tribalism spawned in part by the increasingly global component to Portuguese cultural production in the 1990s. According to Santos, *ranchos* needed to be "jazzed up" by the addition of piano, saxophone, and professional vocalists, not for the sake of seasoned folklore publics, but for "foreigners to see." It is important to point out that the "foreigners" Lisbon 94 sought to accommodate were undoubtedly distinct from the "world of people" which had packed the Grande Place in Brussels. Again, these differing publics are defined not in terms of local/global or domestic/foreign dichotomies, but by cultural taste and social class—which resonate *across* national, lingual, and ethnic borders. Thus, Lisbon 94 organizers intuited the type of "pretty package" which would have a generic appeal to concertgoers in Paris, Washington, Rio de Janeiro, or Venice.

The idea of "wrapping up a pretty package" by stripping away certain *rancho* instruments, melodies, and performers offended Santos, but not because he holds a bias against change. *Ranchos folclóricos* make all sorts of alterations to tradition according to contemporary needs and limitations. They often substitute amplified music for acoustic, machine-sewn costumes for handmade period originals, accordions for concertinas. It was not so much the alteration of tradition as it was the substituted elements which Santos objected to. Substituting piano and saxophone, instruments associated with Western symphonic music and North American jazz, for traditional folkloric instruments such as the *reco-reco* and the *bilha;* professionally trained vocalists for *rancho* amateurs; slick rock and roll musicians for neighborhood instrumentalists; and smartly arranged folkloric medleys for popularly constructed songs and dances meant symbolically "assassinating" the identity of the *povo* by imposing the cultural sign system of the dominant.

The only components of the *rancho folclórico* performance constellation Lisbon 94 proposed remain were the dancers. The easy explanation for this is that the costumed bodies of *rancho* dancers are emblematic of folklore performance itself. It is never the musicians or vocalists who are featured on official *rancho* letterhead, magazine articles, or tourist brochures; it is instead colorful, exoticized representations of *rancho* dancers (see fig. 19). These dancerly bodies are called upon time and again to signify and "sell" the totality of folkloric revivalism. *Rancho* costumes independent of the

Figure 19. Photograph of folklore performers in a coffee table book with text in French, German, and English, designed to appeal to Western tourists. *Reprinted from* Portugal *by Otto Siegner, n.d. Munich: Verlag Ludwig Simon, 182.*

dancers who animate them, however, also serve as prized tourist commodities in and of themselves. Strolling along the Avenida de Liberdade, Lisbon's central artery and home to several posh hotels, one passes the display windows of upscale tourist shops featuring Portuguese ceramics, hand-sewn linens, and red wool folklore costumes ornamented with gold piping and bright blue and black embroidery. The fact that these costumes are explicitly positioned not only as onstage spectacle but also as commodities indicates Lisbon 94's focus on *turismo de qualidade* (quality tourism). These costumes, infinitely reproducible and marketed as artifacts of the past, also allow tourists to see the "twiceness" in folkloric performance. Situated in Lisbon, framed within posh retail stores where sophisticated Portuguese clerks dressed in Calvin Klein beige and Italian heels cater to an international clientele, folklore costumes exude artifice, the representation of days most certainly gone by. In this context the material trappings of folkloric tradition present themselves etically not emically. The promiscuous coupling of past and present, the dangerous proximity of folklore costume to contemporary dress, as in the Azambuja wedding photo, is rendered invisible within the high-rent tourist shops and onstage alongside slick Portuguese pop stars. Proposing folklore dancers perform in a show "jazzed up" by professional vocalists and rock artists, Lisbon 94 organizers employ a performance strategy whereby theatricality calls attention to itself through the use of stylistic contrast, bricolage, and generic syncretism. This postmodern performative strategy was intended to disrupt the prevalent image of Portugal as a "traditional," "backward" nation by employing the aesthetic languages not only of "high art" but also of the modernist avant garde.[7]

In his preface to the English edition of *Distinction,* Bourdieu argues that the relevance of his research extends far beyond the confines of France where the study took place. He argues that it is particularly easy to demonstrate the universality of his study in regard to the social elite whose "cultural products are . . . international" (1984, xii). This notion that elite cultural production flows easily across national and continental borders involving an interchangeable circuit of global audiences and artists exists in contradistinction to classic anthropological portrayals of folkloric culture as remaining spatially fixed within the ghetto of the local, the product of a hermetically sealed provincialism.

The internationality of Portuguese *ranchos folclóricos,* as demonstrated by Santos's emigrant festival in Brussels' Grande Place, disrupts this dichotomy. Portugal's EEC membership and the concomitant increase in international forums for the showcasing of domestic culture has spawned a shift in what the nation endorses as representative of Portugal and the Portuguese. Folklore no longer serves the nation as it once did. At this particular juncture in Portuguese history, the elite are not searching for the roots of national identity in the vernacular architecture, traditional dress, and popular songs and dances of its rural peasantry. Portuguese political and economic aspirations of the 1990s demand a different kind of cultural production based not upon preservation but renovation. Within this new project folklore becomes stigmatized as an extension of that which must be revised, covered up, dressed up, and/or jazzed up. The stigmatization of folklore at the national level, as exemplified by Lisbon 94's exclusion of *ranchos,* has been answered by the creation of an alternative performance sphere which simultaneously retreats into the local for monetary support and ethnological data and expands into the global for new, "unofficial" performance venues, legitimation, and international coalition building along pathways often first blazed by Portuguese emigrants.

What follows in the remaining sections of this chapter is an examination of the dramaturgy informing Portugal's cultural renovation as enacted in 1994 during Lisbon's tenure as the Cultural Capital of Europe. The official *presence* made explicit in Lisbon's festival costume is always implicitly ghosted, in my view, by the charged *absence* of *rancho folclórico* performers.

Portugal's New Course

Addressing an international audience of distinguished scholars and politicians in May 1987, Portuguese president Mário Soares trumpeted his country's rapid transformation: after forty-eight years under the repressive policies of Europe's longest authoritarian regime, Portugal had secured a promising future as an official member state of the European Economic Community (EEC). "Portugal was a country gagged, isolated and suspended in time . . . [but] Portugal now knows what it wants, where it is going and what it has to do to get there. It is a country that has rediscovered its course" (1990, 2–5). This change of course, however, necessitated a change in image —a costume change, and in 1994, following the wide-scale transformation of public space, Lisbon donned her *traje de gala* (ceremonial gown) to perform center stage as the European Capital of Culture. According to the world-systems theory, Portugal currently occupies a "semiperipheral" position relative to the northern European core, due to its intermediate level of economic development and its role as intermediary link between first world and third (Wallerstein 1974; Arrighi 1985). Since its inception in the twelfth century, however, the Portuguese nation-state has continuously attempted to "become part of the center" (Gaspar 1990). Soares articulates this centripetal ambition in his speech by employing the rhetoric of Portugal's sixteenth-century navigational triumphs to describe his country's "rediscovered course" toward Europe. The rhetorical juncture of glorious past with semiperipheral present illustrates an element of the Portuguese social imaginary Boaventura de Sousa Santos terms *"imaginação do centro"* (imagining the center) (Santos 1993a, 20).

In 1987, the same year Soares delivered his speech, the collective imagining of European centrality gave rise to plans for the transformation of Lisbon's urban costume and the performative expression of Portugal's new status as EEC member state. Riding the wave of widespread enthusiasm over Portugal's 1986 European integration, Portuguese delegates to the EEC secured Lisbon's title as "European Cultural Capital" for 1994.[8] Eager to participate in the newly inaugurated European City of Culture Programme, Portuguese delegates lobbied for 1994 so that Lisbon's honorary title would dovetail with the twentieth anniversary of Portugal's 1974 Revolution. "Lisbon 94" (L94) marked an important coming together of national and international agendas, commemorating the Revolution while marking Portugal's cultural debut within the European Community. Hence, L94 celebrated both the 1974 reduction of Portugal's borders following colonial liberation and the 1986 expansion of Portugal's socio-spatial boundaries following

EEC membership. This negotiation between the conflicting forces of reduction and expansion, and between national liberty and European integration, was compellingly reflected in L94 publicity and urban renewal.

In the wake of an unprecedented proliferation of large-scale anniversaries, memorials, and commemorations around the globe, many cultural theorists have turned their attention toward the analysis of national festivals (see Turner 1982; Falassi 1987; Davis 1986; Handelman 1990; Ozouf 1988; Bennett et al. 1992; Gillis 1994; Kirshenblatt-Gimblett 1995; Ley and Olds 1988; Wallis 1994; and Myerscough 1994). In an era where new communication technology and the globalization of capital along with burgeoning localisms have threatened the importance and sovereignty of the nation-state, the national cultural festival represents a new, "very particular repackaging" of national imagery (Wallis 1994, 267).

Scholarship concerning the ideology of national festivals often focuses on material artifact and performative event. Here, however, I respond to the recent call of critical theorists for politicized, interdisciplinary readings of space (Soja 1989; Lefebvre 1991; Certeau 1984; Harvey 1989; Rodman 1992) by examining the transformation of Lisbon's urban space in preparation for its debut as the European Capital of Culture. In an attempt to unmask the "relations of power . . . inscribed into the apparently innocent spatiality of social life" (Soja 1989, 6), I analyze the spatial rhetoric of L94's outdoor ad campaigns and urban restoration and examine the performative production and utilization of these spaces.[9]

This analysis is framed by my own experience as a four-year resident of Lisbon, a Luso-American ethnographer of Portuguese folklore performance, an L94 audience member, and, as Roland Barthes deploys the term in all of its etymological resonance, an "*amateur* of cities, one who loves the city" (1988, 191). Using press releases, playbills, exhibition catalogs, promotional documents, foreign and Portuguese newspaper articles, and interviews with L94 artists and administrators, I examine the official discourse produced by the organizers of Lisbon 94 to answer the following questions. How did Lisbon 94 organizers "dress up" the city's built environs in order to revamp Portugal's cultural image? How are the co-articulated themes of national liberty and European integration spatially produced? I am also concerned with the ways in which this hegemonic spatial production is "talked back to." Throughout 1994, socioeconomic conditions within the city and preexisting characteristics of Lisbon's built environment provided a dialogic counterpoint contesting L94's spatial rhetoric. When considered in concert, this amalgam of spatial production creates a richly nuanced depiction of Portugal's late twentieth-century identity, one that lays bare the ambiguities and contingencies of existence in the semiperiphery.

I have conceptualized L94's "dressing up" of urban space using costume as a central metaphor not only because the rhetoric of clothing is repeatedly invoked in L94 newspaper reviews and press releases, but also because the act of costuming is a transformative and signifying practice. In Western dramatic tradition, costume is that which is deliberately added to or subtracted from the actor's body in order to alter his or her image or persona. This is precisely the way L94 organizers conceived of and personified Lisbon's infrastructural metamorphosis. On the eve of February 26, Lisbon took "off her braces and glasses" (Provan 1994, 30), proudly displaying her elegant *traje de gala* (ceremonial gown) (Antunes 1994a; Guardiola 1994), and with an eastern rotation of her *cara lavada* (clean face) (Ruela 1993a), invited the rest of Europe to witness her spectacular urban makeover.

Lisbon as European Capital

The European City of Culture (ECC) Programme originated in November 1983 during the first meeting of the European Community's culture ministers. The original objective of the program, which would designate a different European municipality the "City of Culture" each year, was "to help bring the peoples of the Member States closer together" (*Official Journal of the European Communities* 1985). Conceived as a vehicle for emphasizing common European elements across national cultures, the ECC also endeavored to celebrate the "richness born out of diversity" (*Official Journal of the European Communities* 1985).

Because Lisbon had initially been slotted as the 1996 City of Culture, Portuguese delegates, endeavoring to combine the twenty-year anniversary of the 1974 Revolution with the ECC title, orchestrated a last-minute exchange with Copenhagen.[10] Portuguese authorities thus faced foreshortened preparation time further exacerbated by a flawed organizational strategy. In 1990 the national Portuguese government and the local authorities of Lisbon (*Câmara Municipal de Lisboa* [CML]) each established separate study teams to prepare for Lisbon 94. Political rivalry, however, compromised the productivity of this bifurcated team. In an attempt to unify the fractured groups, state and local authorities combined forces in 1992 to form the *Sociedade de Lisboa 94* (SL94), where each governing body appointed half the board members.[11] SL94, headed by Vítor Constâncio, then separated into smaller subdivisions by cultural area: Animation, Cinema and Video, Classical Music and Opera, Exhibitions, Literature and Thought, Popular Music, Publishing, Theater and Dance, and Urban Intervention. Many leaders of these subgroups, drawn from the cultural, political, and academic elite, also held other high-profile cultural posts. The funding for L94 was provided by the national government (43 percent), the municipal government (43 percent), private investors (12 percent), and the EEC (2 percent) (Myerscough 1994, 46).

SL94 agreed on a four-part objective: Lisbon 94 should (1) extend and improve cultural venues, (2) fully utilize existing capacity of cultural venues, (3) raise visibility for the cultural sector, and (4) stimulate the cultural market by creating new publics (Myerscough 1994, 189). In a comparative analysis of all European Cities of Culture from Athens in 1985 to Lisbon in 1994, John Myerscough catalogs the differing foci of each city using three taxonomies: infrastructure, festival programs, and artistic concepts. Myerscough identifies Lisbon as being primarily concerned with infrastructure, "seeking to upgrade venues and run a full season of activity in order to raise the status of the sector and stimulate markets" (1994, 9).

SL94's objectives cannot, however, be analyzed in isolation. Lisboa 94 is situated along a continuum of international events showcasing Portugal throughout the nineties. In 1991 Portugal took center stage in Brussels for the Europália Festival. In 1992 Portugal held the presidency of the EU, hosting European politicians and diplomats. And in 1998 Lisbon hosted EXPO 98. The relentless seriality of Portugal's commitment to international cultural events has necessitated the intermingling of ongoing infrastructural restoration with cultural festivity. This seriality has also produced a dynamic of interperformativity akin to intertextuality, where each event builds upon and borrows from others in the continuum. Lisbon's overhaul throughout the nineties was continually in process, the unveiling of restored edifices piecemeal, and the spectacle of new architecture cumulative. Portugal's cultural identity, like Lisbon's infrastructure, was an improvisatory work in progress.

Shrouded in Shadow: L94's Failed Promotional Campaign

Publicis/Ciesa (PC), a French advertising firm, was initially awarded the contract for publicizing L94 and launched its 1993 pre-festival ad campaign with a series of evocative photographic images (see fig. 20). Single chairs of all shapes and sizes, some shrouded in white fabric, loomed large in the foreground of photographs shot in a variety of Lisbon's picturesque locales. As the "basic visual element," the chair was to suggest PC's key conception of "Lisbon as an immense stage" ("Lisboa 94 Já Tem Campanha de Imagem" 1993, 39). The chairs occupied empty plateaus of space devoid of people, at the river's edge, at the bottom of cobbled steps, beside ornate columns, and inside a theater. The text on the images read *"Estar em toda a parte"* (To be

Figure 20. Advertising image of a chair from the failed L94 publicity campaign.

everywhere), "*Estar à altura*" (To measure up), "*Estar em maré alta*" (literally, To be at high tide, but idiomatically connoting popularity or plenitude), "*Estar por dentro*" (To have an inside track, To be an insider), and "*Estar muito ocupada*" (To be very busy).

The Lisbon public responded to PC's ads with indifference and bewilderment. According to an L94 employee quoted in the Portuguese press, "We were inundated with telephone calls asking what those chairs meant, and why they had their backs to the river" ("Lisboa, Que Futuro" 1994, 11). In contrast to the campaign's textual rhetoric, which invoked a variety of heightened corporeal states, the photographic image suggested stasis, solitude, even desolation. Dramatic, high-contrast lighting cast deep shadows on and around the chairs haunting the empty spaces. The PC campaign drew upon visual cues invoking the mythic melancholy of Portugal, a nostalgia for the past viewed from the shade of a semiperipheral present. Portugal, however, had spent years of forced isolation on the continent's edge, and an empty chair placed in the middle of a shadowy void was not the type of image makeover SL94 organizers had hoped for.

Gaston Bachelard's description of the shadow suggests some of the problems with the campaign: "[The shadow] has lost its 'being there' . . . one that has so declined as to fall from *the being of its shade* and mingle with the rumors of being, in the form of meaningless noise, of a confused hum that *cannot be located.* It once was" (1994, 217, italics in original). When applied to the iconography of the PC image, Bachelard's synesthetic description of shadow as an *unlocatable* "confused hum" contradicts L94's objective of centering Lisbon as an audible presence on the "cultural map of Europe" ("Lisboa 94" 1994, 10). By employing the representative imagery of the shadow, PC inadvertently obstructed Portugal's symbolic emergence from the shade of the periphery. By calling attention to the stark contrast between Portugal's sixteenth-century "glory days" and its current global status, the campaign failed to promote a fresh image for the country. Portugal is haunted by the heroic figures of its past.[12] As Portuguese historian Xavier Pitafo describes, historical memory plagues the Portuguese social imaginary: "Our specialty is in the invocation of shadows . . . the same old film playing The Lost Empire . . . We have never recovered and are unable to forget it . . . If you switch off the light in a room, you see . . . its afterimage on the retina. That is our situation with the lost colonial empire" (quoted in Enzensberger 1989, 159–60).[13]

In addition to the burden of historical memory, Boaventura de Sousa Santos analyzes Portugal's fixation with the past as the product of a literary "mythic excess" generated by a closed coterie of cultural elites who, historically isolated from the decision-making machinery of the political strata, created, reproduced, and amassed vast quantities of interpretive myths concerning Portugal and the Portuguese. According to Santos, the cultural elite were never forced to compare, apply, or verify their ideas, or to bring them to bear on reality. Santos draws an analogy between the blindness of the literati and the subsequent invisibility of the country (1993b, 30–31). It is precisely this mythic excess SL94 sought to combat by firing PC and replacing them with another French advertising firm, EuroRSCG (ER). PC's ethereal, melancholy photos were replaced by pictorial representations of industry, innovation, action, and verve. ER strategized a straightforward, readable image for Portugal, one which was not fixated on the past but oriented toward the future, one which represented at the same time it invented Portugal's "new course" of international visibility as a member of the European Union.

"Lisbon Never Stops": L94s Replacement Ad Strategy

Bold red letters punctuating black billboards promised pedestrians that "Lisbon Never Stops!" PC's realistic photos featuring moody lighting and three-dimensional space were replaced by clean, two-dimensional images where bright colors, crisp lines, and broad, energetic symbols emphasized themes of activity and cosmopolitanism. Strategically placed at various

Figure 21. Outdoor L94 billboard at Praça da Espanha. Lisbon 1994. *Photograph by author.*

entry points into the city, the billboards welcomed L94 tourists arriving by boat, train, plane, and car. ER's "Lisbon Never Stops" campaign was meant to "surround . . . those whose passive attitude ha[d] to be altered, giving a festive air to the city" (EuroRSCG n.d.).

At Praça de Espanha an impressive network of motorized wheels which literally "never stopped" decorated a large billboard set upon two stately black columns (see fig. 21). Seven spoked wheels turned round and round, mirroring Praça de Espanha's vehicular rotary, which guides multiple lanes of traffic in and out of the city. The smooth, seductive motion of interdependent cogs circulating ad infinitum, however, waxed ironic in this particular spot in the city, as traffic frequently congeals into the bottleneck at Praça de Espanha, part of the mounting traffic problem created by the very modernization Lisbon 94 celebrated. Traffic problems were noted in several L94 reviews as impeding public access to cultural events or at least making their experience less enjoyable (*Público* 1994, 28). In a 1994 interview with Portuguese author and 1998 Nobel Prize winner José Saramago entitled "My Lisbon No Longer Exists," "noise," "pollution," and "hellish traffic" are cited as new, contemptible elements in a changing Lisbon he neither likes nor recognizes (Arias 1994, 2).

In addition to representing physical motility, the billboard at Praça da Espanha also alluded to industry and progress. Gold wheels of varying dimensions staggered horizontally across a black surface, however, suggest the toil and grime of nineteenth-century labor, not late twentieth-century computer-age technology. This symbolism is particularly resonant when viewed in concert with Portugal's economic development vis-à-vis the rest of Europe. Portuguese industrialization did not occur until the mid-1950s, almost a century behind most of northern Europe and fifty years behind other countries on the periphery of Europe, such as Sweden and Russia (Neves 1994, 48–49).[14] Portugal's industrial growth, therefore, has occurred over a foreshortened period of time where certain phases of development were sped up. Further, Portugal's industrial modernization is characterized in socioeconomic terms by unevenness and fragmentation. Sociologist Augusto Santos Silva underscores the regional inconsistency of Portugal's socioeconomic development. Rather than following a pattern of linear progress, Portugal's recent development has been characterized by "complex dynamics of coexistences, adaptations, dissolutions, reemergences, restructuring, and intersections" (1994, 149). If we consider these dynamics of "coexistence" in analyzing L94 publicity, then the billboard at Praça da Espanha no longer appears anachronistic. Visual symbols conjuring nineteenth-century industry coexist with other L94 outdoor ad-space featuring, for example, Jenny Holtzeresque digital messages. In this sense the "Lisboa Não Pára" campaign represents a variety of coordinates on the map of Portuguese industrial development and modernization, coordinates which exist simultaneously in the present while remaining oriented toward Portugal's European future.

Looming large outside the Alcântara Mar train station, an L94 billboard ran a nonstop digital message across its facade. The message read, "In Lisbon liberty is much more than an avenue. It is the entire city. We are in the middle of a stage measuring 807937 hectares. Lisbon is in rehearsal. Lisbon is in exhibition . . . Listen and look . . . but don't stop. In Lisbon there are no intermissions." This scarlet digital pronouncement beamed across the sleek black billboard stood out in the midst of Alcântara Mar, one of Lisbon's older riverside neighborhoods, where clotheslines of drying laundry decorate traditionally tiled houses with terracotta roofs. The billboard's message, packed with tropes describing Lisbon's continuing metamorphosis, provided a dizzying array of conceptual metaphors with which to process the city's new identity. The city as stage, the city as avenue, the city as liberty, the city in rehearsal, the city on exhibition. This digital message laid bare the promotional strategist's brainstorming, where meta-labels were tried on, discarded, and tried on again. The Alcântara billboard displayed the fruits of L94's promotional think tank, where the processual, unfinished, and open-to-revision nature of Lisbon's late twentieth-century makeover remained open for public scrutiny. As if ER couldn't decide which gown Lisbon should wear on

Figure 22. Communist mural expressing anti-EU sentiments. "National Referendum! European Union, Get Out of Portugal!" Lisbon 1994. *Photograph by author.*

opening night, they opted for a layered effect, piling dress upon dress upon dress until the urban mannequin became heavy with representational overload.

The billboard's message seemed both a precise summary of the frenetic pace with which Lisbon has been transformed and a prescient foreshadowing of things to come. Indeed, there have been very few intermissions in the last decade as the EEC pooled funds with the Portuguese government and private investors to construct the first superhighway connecting Portugal's two largest cities, Lisbon and Porto, to renovate Lisbon's subways, and to build cultural mega-centers, *hipermercados* (wholesale supermarkets), and posh apartment high-rises–cum–shopping malls. During this process Lisbon has indeed been "in rehearsal" for a position of global consequence within the European Union. Boaventura de Sousa Santos reports, however, that the Portuguese have been given little opportunity to "Listen" or "Look," much less "Stop" and ponder the radical transformation of their country since EEC integration. According to Santos, the government negotiated Portugal's EEC membership "without consulting . . . any of the different social interest groups. Various investigations . . . revealed [the public's] almost complete ignorance of the economic, political and social consequences of joining the EEC" (1993a, 50). Throughout the application process a vocal minority associated with Portugal's communist party tried to sensitize Portuguese citizens to the perils of EEC membership (see fig. 22). Santos warns of a future where short-term excitement over Portugal's infrastructural overhaul leads to long-term disappointment, where Europe becomes more competitive within the global marketplace at the expense of its own (Portuguese) periphery (1993a, 53).

In proclaiming that "liberty is much more than an avenue," the Alcântara Mar billboard invokes one of Lisbon's most powerful national symbols. In 1919, renowned Portuguese poet Fernando Pessoa described the Avenida da Liberdade (Liberty Avenue), constructed in 1882, as "the finest artery in Lisbon":

> It is 90 meters wide and 1500 meters long, full of trees from beginning to end, and includes small gardens, ponds, fountains, cascades and statues . . . The garden plots . . . are closed by four marble statues representing Europe, Africa, Asia, and Oceania. In the Avenida da Liberdade there are two theaters, four cinemas, and several cafés and confectioners; it contains also some palatial residences. During the summer months, some of the cafés spread their service up into the central garden-plots which are profusely lit; this open air service, with the music added to it, enlivens the whole Avenida on summer evenings. (1992, 48)

Pessoa's description of the Avenida, an idealized portrayal, formed part of his patriotic project to fight against what he termed Portugal's "demotion" from European and civilized status (Lopes 1992, 18). Decades after Pessoa's description, the Avenida became the object of a different patriotic plan. According to Eduarda Dionísio, the Avenida served as "Lisbon's urban theme" (1993, 38) shortly after the 1974 Revolution, as architect Vieira de Almeida constructed an ambitious plan for its conservation. The Avenida, a potent symbol of Portugal's hard-won liberty in 1974 and an artery which should therefore serve "a collective purpose," was at grave risk of falling into decay or being monopolized by socially irresponsible developers (Almeida 1974).

Almeida's plan never came to fruition, and the development of the Avenida continued piecemeal, arriving at its current state, where sleek, modern office space abuts decaying, abandoned buildings. In preparation for Lisbon 94 and Expo 98, however, city planners and politicians revisited the theme of the Avenida, generating ideas for a new conservation plan. The on-again, off-again "Avenida Plan," according to Dionísio, is like "a dialogic allegory, the stones on the sidewalk in conversation with urban buildings, while real estate deals continue to be made" (1993, 38). This inability to agree upon a "collective purpose" has allowed Lisbon's "finest artery" to become a schizophrenic potpourri of modern high-rises, ornate historic properties smartly preserved, degraded older buildings spray-painted with "Earth

Figure 23. Earth Party graffiti along Avenida da Liberdade, "Say No to the Avenida Demolitions!" Lisbon 1994. *Photograph by author.*

Party" graffiti, and gaping holes exposing the foundations of buildings recently demolished (see fig. 23).[15]

Referred to by name in the L94 ad campaign, the Avenida and its current physical state begs the questions: how does this powerful urban symbol articulate the ideals of liberty? And how in turn does this reflect upon L94's commemoration of twenty years of liberation? Dionísio compares the Avenida's commingling of disparate architectural styles and uneven states of disrepair or preservation to current Portuguese television programs where folk singers, opera divas, and rock bands perform back-to-back within the same hour-long slot (1993, 38). This mixing of the old with the new, the traditional with the modern, the Baroque with the minimalist, whether viewed as a product of poor, tasteless, or innovative planning, is precisely what L94 organizers opted for. SL94 aimed to strike a "just balance in a programme that [was], by deliberate choice, neither elitist, nor self consciously populist" (Myerscough 1994, 196). Vítor Constâncio defined L94 as a "vast exercise in the democratization of Culture" (Antunes 1994b).[16] Though the Avenida da Liberdade was not "dressed up" for L94 as were other urban spaces, and though it exists for many as sad testimony to failed revolutionary follow-through, the Avenida stands as a fitting symbol of L94 ideology.

ER also placed an L94 billboard featuring rows of colorful clocks on the riverside edge of Praça do Comércio and Terreiro do Paço. The clocks, each set to a different time zone, suggest a cosmopolitan Lisbon, where international visitors enter the city by sea, their first sight the majestic Praça do Comércio. This famous square, one of the largest in Europe, "is where Lisbon originates, maritime city par excellence, inviting the visitor to ascend the shallow steps from the river to dry land and enter its domains" (Coimbra 1990, 76). The rose-colored government buildings which line Praça do Comércio have been called "the pink embrace," greeting "all men of good will" (Coimbra 1990, 76). The eroticized description of Praça do Comércio positions Lisbon as seductress. Barthes theorizes an erotics of the city where the urban center, a sexually charged meeting ground, is "the site of our encounter with the other" (1988, 199). During L94, Lisbon, the "grand dame, the Tejo at her feet," summoning "all her powers of seduction" (Kaplan 1991, 282) and poised on the banks of the Praça do Comércio, newly coiffed and costumed, awaited the opportunity to "give a very agreeable impression to the most exacting of tourists" (Pessoa 1992, 40).

Indeed, luxury tourist liners often hover about the docks at Terreiro do Paço, tourists disembarking nearby and stepping into Lisbon's "pink embrace." Portugal's tourist industry, up 6 percent in 1994, has been courting the international traveler with renewed vigor as tourist-related business becomes an increasingly important component of Portugal's economy. Some theorists suggest that Europe's southern perimeter will become a strictly leisure-oriented space for industrialized Europe. Henri Lefebvre envisions countries such as Portugal as a kind of " 'non-work' space . . . set aside not just for vacations but also for convalescence, rest, retirement, and so on" (1991, 58)

Though this may be Portugal's fast-approaching future, particularly along the coastal regions, Lisbon is busy negotiating new urban dilemmas focused on accommodating the movements of vast flows of people—both resident workers and seasonal vacationers—in and around the city. Praça do Comércio emblematizes such a dilemma. Throughout the 1980s and early 1990s, this historic gateway into the city, designed to enrapture tourists with its "pink embrace," was obscured by hundreds of parked cars and a colorful assortment of "heroin parkers."[17] Although the city government discussed legislation in 1994 designed to clear the square of cars and restore it to its former dignity, Lisbon's acute shortage of parking facilities and exploding rates of car ownership complicates such matters of aesthetic pride.[18]

The "exacting tourists" Pessoa describes must now cope not only with a sea of parked cars but with the thousands of daily commuters who are ferried in and out of Lisbon at Praça do Comércio from their homes across the Tagus. Though not the travelers targeted by ER's L94 ad campaign, many of

Figure 24. Outdoor L94 billboard at Terreiro do Paço. Lisbon 1994. *Photograph by author.*

these commuters of varied ethnicity are among Lisbon's newly arrived and represent the changing face of Portugal's workforce. Lisbon's African population has grown steadily since the end of the colonial wars in 1974. Lisbon is one of the European cities with the greatest number of African residents (Rivas 1994a). Portugal's drastic transformation from being "the only uniethnic nation-state in Europe" (Santos 1993b, 22) to a mini–melting pot of African and Asian immigrants is reflected in Lisbon's "nonofficial" cultural life, though largely ignored by the international mega-events of the 1990s.[19] L94's official title, "Lisbon: A Meeting Point of Cultures," was obscured by more-immediate concerns, such as the Europeanization of Portugal's image. Victor Constâncio articulates L94's primary goal: "Portugal has always been a part of European culture . . . [and] we seek now to restate our presence and to claim greater recognition" (1994, 3). He also asserts that Lisbon 94's "mission will be accomplished if . . . the city is projected into the European context" (Antunes 1994b). SL94 minimized Portugal's relationship to Africa throughout L94 promotion and programming (only a few major program events featured cultural production from the ex-colonies).[20] The "meeting point of cultures" theme, intended to evoke Portugal's postcolonial ties to lusophone Africa and Asia and Lisbon's own identity as "a major African city" (Rivas 1994a) rang resoundingly hollow; Portugal set its sights on European integration by emphasizing a distinctly Western commonality.

In much the same way Anderson posits the newspaper as the materiality out of which emerges *national* consciousness (1991), the clock billboard at Praça do Comércio provided an object for the public contemplation of *international* belonging, a belonging, however, privileging European cohesion over other global associations (see fig. 24). The L94 billboard, where clocks from varied time zones shared the same ten-foot space, not only invoked a false semiotics of nonhierarchal globalism (where all the world's time zones existed on the same two-dimensional plane and were given equal visual weight), it also subverted itself; none of the clocks actually kept time! A promotional campaign centered around incessant cultural activity and an urban society that "never stops" displayed a strange hermeneutic paradox by erecting clocks whose hands were literally tied.

Is the viewer to assume an image of Portugal where time is stopped—Lefebvre's backwater vacationland? An anthropological treasure to be left undisturbed in its timeless present? Does the billboard forecast Portugal's role as intermediary between first and third worlds, where time is halted and history's wounds are negotiated and healed? Or perhaps most immediately, does the billboard represent a municipal community which has stopped time to prepare for a decade of mega-events which supersede and to some degree preclude the spontaneous cultural production of everyday? Eduarda Dionísio describes Portuguese culture today as occupying a stagnant liminal space between official closings and openings, with "no space [or time] for the present" (1993, 112, my insert). Portuguese culture in the nineties was instead harnessed to the all-consuming project of costuming municipal space in the name of national image production.

Dressed for Success: Lisbon's New Cultural Venues

Measured in tourist dollars, budget allotments, and percentage points, Portuguese culture functioned in the 1990s as a specialized branch of the economy where the viability of cultural venues was constantly in flux and "the criteria of profitability is present in the disappearance of traditional cultural spaces and the utilization of others for similar ends" (Dionísio 1993, 93–94). L94 objectives focused not only on filling cultural venues to capacity through the stimulation of new markets, but also on the creation and restoration of cultural spaces designed to rival those of other Western capitals.[21]

Although L94 commissioned and paid for the renovation of several buildings, among them the Coliseu dos Recreios, the Museu de Arte Antiga, the Tivoli, and the Museu de Chiado, several other new constructions, most notably the colossal Centro Cultural de Belém (CCB) and the Caixa Geral dos Depósitos (CGD), were showcased for the first time in 1994 and considered part of Lisbon 94's grand unveiling.[22] The CCB and the CGD are both enormous modernist structures financed primarily by the state at a combined cost of roughly $520 million U.S. Both structures serve an array of functions—providing cutting-edge banking facilities, large-scale conference rooms, upscale restaurants, coffee stands, gift shops, museums, and concert halls, promulgating, in Dionísio's view, "confusion between state and private initiative . . . between money and culture . . . with the primary objective of propaganda and ostentation" (1993, 104). Both the CCB and the CGD are described by several Portuguese journalists as "monuments to the nineties" (Dionísio 1993, 105; Pomar 1994c, 24) due not only to their enormous physical presence within the city but also because they exist as ideological synecdoches for the political government that created them. In 1994, the PSD government proudly claimed responsibility for the creation of these monuments to Portugal's modern identity. The success of these structures constituted a bright spot in an otherwise fraught political environment. "The period 1992–93 was the darkest year of the PSD government's rule . . . Rising unemployment, bankruptcies, unpaid wages, accusations of high level corruption, deep controversies over education, health and agricultural policies all reduced the credibility of the PSD government" (Nataf 1995, 192).

The completion of the CCB and CGD, massive high-tech structures, cultural centers for the highbrow expenditure of leisure time, reflected well upon the Portuguese government. As performance historian Marvin Carlson asserts, the monumental theater, a distinctly northern European phenomenon originating with the advent of "regularized," "rational," or "Cartesian" city planning, provided "an example of good government in action that would induce and inspire good behavior in people" (1989, 72–73). In addition to these spaces lending government credibility, ruling powers also began to recognize the potential of public theaters to produce a city of confident and dutiful subjects (Carlson 1989, 72–73). Drawing on Carlson's correlation between the theater-as-monument and the desire of the ruling class to control its urban subjects, the symbolism of the monument resides not only in the defining physical characteristics of the edifice, but also in the amalgam of activities housed within it. In the case of the CCB and CGD, each ATM cash withdrawal, each opera ticket sale, each gift shop purchase, and each coffee imbibed contribute to the symbolic memorializing of official Portuguese culture in the nineties. The ostentation and propaganda suggested by Dionísio as the external qualities of the theater-as-monument are also performed interiorly by the cultural consumers who inhabit these spaces. In this sense L94 organizers sought not only to raise Portugal's sub-standard cultural venues to a northern European level, but also to train Portuguese citizens to become dutiful cultural consumers.

Such training was echoed in the promotional mantras published by ER on L94 "D Day" to celebrate the February 26 festival opening. A message entitled "New Year's Resolutions" was widely published throughout the print media and aired on television:

> Starting today I will see theater and dance, I will be diligent about going to the cinema, and I'll never miss an art exhibit. Starting today I will go to the opera, I will discover jazz, I will attend concerts and mega-concerts. Starting today I will explore the city day and night, I will record the past and interrogate the future. Starting today I will go to Lisbon 94. (EuroRSCG n.d.)

The conflation of self-improvement with cultural consumption took the form of a New Year's resolution where L94 promotional rhetoric exhorted the targeted market of Portuguese citizens to internalize its ad copy through recitation (it is phrased in the first person), and then do as the ad instructs. The CCB and CGB not only provided elegant grounds for consumer training, they were also living monuments to such a process, monuments to house and produce the new cultural citizens of the Euro-center.

From Rags to Miniskirts: The Coliseu's Restoration

Among L94's restorations of preexisting cultural venues, the Coliseu dos Recreios, a space perceived as "an authentic emblem of the city" (Silva 1993, 38), was deemed the "ex-libris of Lisbon 94" (Pomar and Portas 1994, 46).[23] The Coliseu, first built in 1890, stands majestically over the cobbled streets of Portas de Santo Antão, a block from the Avenida da Liberdade. Portugal's largest covered concert hall, the Coliseu, boasts more than a century of eclectic cultural fare, from opera to circuses, from boxing matches to Ice Capades, from political rallies to ballet, from Portuguese *fado* concerts to fashion shows, and "holds within its walls some of the most important moments of Lisbon's cultural life" (Silva 1993, 38). In the last several decades, however, the Coliseu's physical environs, programming, and clientele plummeted to an all-time low. Its lobby was used for local bingo games; the bar on the upper floors began offering peep shows, strip tease, and exotic dancing. The seating and interior of the building deteriorated to a general state of shabbiness. As one journalist wrote, "the specter of decadence hovered (over the Coliseu) forecasting a shady future" (Silva 1993). The Coliseu was hence ripe for inclusion in L94's ambitious plans for upgrading significant cultural spaces representative of Lisbon's rich architectural history.

David Lowenthal explains the importance of maintaining historical buildings: "Architectural and other material manifestations of heritage augment identity and community self-esteem . . . A rich and representative patrimony is held to promote citizenship, to catalyze creativity, to attract foreign sympathy and to enhance all aspects of national life" (1994, 45). L94 launched an architectural competition to save Lisbon's mythic cultural space from the clutches of degradation. Winning architect Maurício de Vasconcellos's primary goal was to "improve the qualities of the space, providing greater comfort for the public" (Ruela 1994, 83). Vasconcellos also wanted "to avoid taking away any of the memories, but instead to actualize them. I wanted to design a new Coliseu without destroying the old one" (Ruela 1994, 83).

The Coliseu closed its doors for over a year to complete Vasconcellos's renovations, at a cost of more than 1 million *contos.* Although Vasconcellos's stated intention was to build on the Coliseu's existing foundation of memories, many critics emphasized the theater's radical transformation. The stage was rebuilt, the audio and lighting systems modernized, the seating structure reorganized, the main entrance and lobby redesigned, the peep-show bar destroyed, the dressing rooms augmented and improved, and there were general additions of more bathrooms, emergency exits, a new fire detection system, an upscale music, video, and bookstore, a large conference hall, a VIP room, and a press lounge. Journalist Rosa Ruela described the Coliseu's metamorphosis in terms of costume: "The Coliseu used to be a very old lady with rags for clothes . . . Suddenly she becomes a woman in a miniskirt. She is another" (1994, 83). The woman clad in a miniskirt exuded the sleek, sexy modernity targeted by SL94 for Lisbon's image makeover. The eroticism of Praça do Comércio's "pink embrace" spills over into the gendered space of the Coliseu. The peep-show harlot becomes a fashionable modern woman, not dissimilar in appearance and costume to the new market of cultural patrons L94 sought to "stimulate."

Vasconcellos himself acknowledged that the Coliseu's visual impact was "completely changed" (Ruela 1994, 83). Dominated by silver, charcoal gray, black, and white, Vasconcellos's new cooler palette existed in stark contrast to the old Coliseu, decorated in warm shades of wine red and chocolate brown. "Crisp, clean and with a vague likeness to the Centro Cultural de Belém . . . the Coliseu is colder. Functional and comfortable, the concert hall disappoints by not being cozy" (Ruela 1994, 83). A warm, quaint coziness, however, was clearly neither the architect's nor SL94's desired effect. Like CCB and CGD, the Coliseu's cutting-edge design scheme reflected the sharp, impersonal space of technology, not the softer intimacy of the home.

Physical intimacy among patrons was also precluded by the new seating arrangements. Formerly, the Coliseu's *geral* (general seating section) was marked by long rows of shallow wooden benches crowded together over a raked platform. The placement of the benches made for an extremely claustrophobic audience experience. The *geral* section, often oversold, cramping bodies side by side, also featured rows so condensed that giving and receiving "legendary kicks in the back" (Martins 1994a, 16) proved unavoidable. Vasconcellos ameliorated these conditions by separating the *geral* seating so that each audience member occupied his or her own numbered discrete chair, measuring fifty centimeters in width.

Though some journalists characterized the *geral* seating change as Vasconcellos's "most agreeable surprise" (Silva 1993, 36), others felt *geral* audience members would find the new individuated seats "peculiar" (Ruela 1994, 83). Certainly, as a regular *geral* audience member both before and after the Coliseu's makeover, I can attest to the added physical comfort of the cushioned chairs, increased lateral space, and legroom. The old cramped *geral* seating, however, was often populated by younger, less affluent ticket holders and became known as the domain of transgressive behavior and vocalized cultural critique. Due to close physical proximity and the common experience of less-than-ideal viewing conditions, members of the *geral* often shared an experience of what anthropologist Victor Turner defines as *communitas* (1969, 97) In the Coliseu's former *geral,* cigarettes were often shared, flasks of alcohol passed, coats borrowed and lent, and dialogue exchanged. If during the course of the evening, a performer became unfavorably regarded, *geral* audience members often intoned their dissatisfaction by booing, heckling, or most frequently by stomping their feet, an action amplified by the former *geral's* wooden floorboards.

Through the physical partitioning off of bodies, individuated seating hindered the spatial "immediacy" characteristic of *communitas.* Material enclosure in the form of high seat backs and armrests encouraged private interchange between companions, not widespread public dialogue among strangers. The rowdy, uncontrollable behavior of the *geral* became contained through seating design and spatial suggestion. This architectural alteration clearly implies behavioral modification, where Lisbon's audience members are once again subject to cultural training. As Ruela so colorfully describes, "One thing is certain. Gone are the days of foot stomping reverberating through the Coliseu. Reconstructed in concrete, the 'ex-*geral*' is now a very well behaved young lady" (1994, 84).

Ruela employs the female body to personify spatial change and to characterize through metaphor the "personality" of the new general seating section. The female figure invoked above is not one who smokes, drinks, shouts, and stomps her feet, but one who is "very well behaved." The renovation of the female body was also at play in the decision to demolish "Bar 25."

In demolishing the stripper bar, Vasconcellos and SL94 cleaned up the Coliseu's image by evicting the naked female body. The replacement of exotic dancers with smartly packaged videos, books, and CDs was accompanied by a dramatic reconception of the Coliseu's programming throughout 1994. SL94 orchestrated the replacement of circuses, wrestling contests, acrobatics, boxing matches, magic shows, and other *variedades* (variety shows) by "more erudite" events (Ruela 1994, 84). In 1994 the Coliseu hosted sold-out performances by many of the world's greatest orchestras and offered operas such as *La Traviata, Elektra,* and *Carmen.*

Combining new "erudite" programming with architectural renovation and the "cleaning up" of the Coliseu's corollary businesses, SL94 profoundly changed Lisbon's emblematic cultural space. Such changes did not "actualize" the Coliseu's long history of memory as Vasconcellos had hoped, but instead reconditioned memory. This reconditioning of collective memory, part and parcel of a move toward the Euro-center, also necessitated "concerted forgettings" (Gillis 1994, 7). The Coliseu's patrons were asked during 1994 to forget a history of eclectic and sometimes lowbrow programming; they were asked to forget the naked female bodies employed by Bar 25, and the old woman in rags who haunted the space. The *geral* patrons were asked to forget the history of vocalizing spontaneous public opinion during performances by sitting in dignified, individuated seats and "behaving." The renovated Coliseu buried layers of memory under fresh coats of cultural paint, primed for Portugal's revival on the European stage.

Tempted by the promise that "Lisbon Never Stops," more than 1.5 million people, primarily domestic tourists, consumed L94's cultural fare, demonstrating, according to one observer, "that the Portuguese are hungry for culture" (Braga 1994, 2). Gallery and museum attendance rose dramatically with a public of 685,000. Thirty popular music events were attended by 323,000 spectators (Braga 1994, 2). The program of Great World Orchestras consistently sold out. Newly restored cultural venues regularly filled to capacity. According to an L94 public relations employee, "the public far surpassed what we could have imagined" (Braga 1994, 2). Lisbon 94 also succeeded in meeting each of its four objectives: it created new publics, filled existing cultural venues to capacity, restored cultural venues, and raised the cultural sector's visibility. SL94 achieved all its goals without exceeding the allotted budget of 8 million *contos* (Artur 1994).

The bipartisan team of SL94 and the municipal and federal governments cloaked themselves in Lisbon 94's public success. A few journalists, however, tempered enthusiasm with queries as to the sustainability of Lisbon's cultural animation. Still others, such as Alexandre Pomar, Miguel Portas, and Eduarda Dionísio, viewed the event with greater pessimism still. Dionísio states, "It is much more difficult to discern a true enemy these days, one of flesh and bone . . . You need to think a lot harder to dislike Cavaco, the European Economic Community, and the *Centro Cultural de Belém*" (1993, 32).[24] Dionísio ponders the way in which large-scale national spectacle masks hegemony, where within buildings such as the CCB, power remains elusive and unlocatable, and where the EEC and former Prime Minister Cavaco Silva dress up and obscure political agenda in the festive garb of culture. Pomar and Portas argue that the spectacle of architectural improvement and the "accumulation of [cultural] events" disguises Portugal's status as a "capital still condemned to a peripheral condition" (1994, 45).

Despite SL94's efforts to the contrary, Portugal's "peripheral condition" revealed itself in the urban spaces where Lisbon's party gown had come undone—a zipper broken, a seam split, a hem unraveled. These spaces clearly exposed the cleavage separating projected festival image and late twentieth-century reality. Journalists from virtually every major Portuguese paper obsessed over the unfinished or in-process state of Lisbon's overhaul on the eve of its grand unveiling (Ferreira and Braga 1994; Cruz 1994; Lopes and Garcia 1994; Antunes 1994a, among others). Readily apparent to any pedestrian traversing the streets, Lisbon was a city *em obras,* or under construction. Mammoth cranes and cement trucks scarred the urban skyline. The incessant drumming of jackhammers and industrial drills rose above quotidian urban din. Renovation, restoration, new construction, and demolition dominated Lisbon's landscape, taking as its object residential homes, office space, subway stations, museums, movie theaters, fountains, government buildings, city squares, palaces, ports, historic monuments, retail centers, parks, and highways.

L94 commissioned artists to decorate large placards to cloak and "dignify" (Ruela 1993b) some of the more prominent construction sites (see fig. 25). These placards covered Lisbon as she dressed herself, attempting to conceal the physical labor necessary to construct her costume. The decorative shrouding of public work sites throughout Lisbon is significant for several reasons. In terms of the European pecking order Portugal remains stalled in the "catching up phase" (Mateus et al. 1995). Construction sites act as physical reminders of Portugal's underdeveloped status, and like a fig leaf over genitals, decorative panels over hammers and drills signal unease at occupying the bottom of Europe's socioeconomic barrel.[25] By concealing the body of the worker as well as the tools he or she wields, L94 organizers obscured the tremendous physical and financial cost of upgrading Lisbon to northern European standards.[26]

Figure 25. Placards decorating construction site in the heart of Rossio. Lisbon 1994. *Photograph by author.*

In the throes of dramatic spatial, socioeconomic, and political change brought forth by the 1974 Revolution and 1986 EEC membership, Portuguese scholars have debated the extent to which Portugal suffers from a crisis of identity (Lourenço 1994, 1992; Santos 1993a, 1993b; Cruz 1992; Macedo 1990; Herr and Polt 1989; Barreto 1992; Sapega 1995; and Almeida 1991). Responding implicitly to these debates, SL94 set about manufacturing a new image for Lisbon and by extension for Portugal. The machinery responsible for such image production—including the rough drafts, the discarded ideas, and the finished products—revealed itself in Lisbon's "readable" spaces: PC's failed "chair" campaign, ER's "Lisbon Never Stops" replacement strategy, new cultural mega-centers such as the CGD and CCB, and renovated cultural venues such as the Coliseu.

By examining SL94's spatial production we begin to understand how the dominant class strategized Portugal's European inclusion. According to L94's ad campaign, Portugal was a country no longer confined to cultural isolation along the continent's edge. Through verve, industriousness, and tenacity that "never stops," Portugal would pull itself up by its bootstraps to join a unified Europe from its center. Cultural venues such as the CGD, CCB, and the Coliseu exposed a will to refinement, and provided dignified environs on par with the rest of Europe for the training of cultural consumers and the rehearsal of mannerly cultural consumption.

But L94's readable spaces overlapped, abutted, and dissected a palimpsest of social space that "talked back" to Lisbon's festival costuming. The traffic at Praça de Espanha, the green graffiti along the Avenida da Liberdade, the immigrant commuters who board the ferry at Terreiro do Paço, the parked cars and drug addicts at Praça do Comércio, the Coliseu's displaced exotic dancers and *geral* audience members, and the decorated construction sites when viewed against the backdrop of L94 initiatives revealed "socio-political contradictions . . . spatially realized" (Lefebvre 1991, 365). Exposing the costs of modernity, the tenuousness of liberty, and the scars of underdevelopment, these contradictions prohibit a reductive formulation of Portugal's cultural image and political position within a unified Europe.

The dialogue between official and unofficial culture during L94 reveals the animating tensions that define the production and representation of Portuguese national identity. "Portugal, unlike the other peoples of Europe, must look in two mirrors to see itself, the mirror of Prospero and the mirror of Caliban, knowing that its true face lies somewhere in between" (Santos 1993a, 33). Portugal is a quixotic mixture of colonized and colonizer, a nation of immigrants and emigrants, a country that is at once nowhere and everywhere. SL94 chose to promote the Prospero component of Portugal's hybrid identity, confining Caliban—the *ranchos folclóricos* rehearsing turn-of-the century popular culture in old factories, butcher shops, basements, and town squares—to alternative performance spheres hidden from the official framing of Portugal's European inclusion.

6 

Dancing along the In-between: Folklore Performance and Transmigration in Newark, New Jersey

Twentieth-century Portugal has witnessed many governmental strategies for promoting nationalist ties among lusophone communities in far-flung continents. During the *Estado Novo,* dictator António Salazar drew a unifying rhetorical frame around distant colonies, defining them as interior to the body of the nation despite their severed geographic circumstance—Angola and Mozambique were not, for example, colonies but rather domestic appendages, "overseas *províncias.*" This rhetorical formulation pointed not only to Salazar's imperialist ambitions, but also to the desire for an inclusive nation-state, one which viewed overseas and domestic citizens as working parts in the same rambling collective. Following World War II, the Portuguese state actively cultivated ties to Portuguese emigrants living in North America and northern Europe; emigrant remittances contributed greatly to the health of the Portuguese economy, particularly in times of great expenditure such as the colonial wars of the 1960s and 1970s (Brettell 1993b, 1995, 2003). Since the collapse of the *Estado Novo* dictatorship in 1974 and the end of the colonial empire, Portuguese emigrant communities around the world have been the object of increased governmental attention and funding. Maria Baganha (2001) has suggested that the state transferred the object of its traditionally exterior focus from the overseas colonies to emigrants in diaspora.[1] Feldman-Bianco (1992) argues that this post-1974 shift points to a reconceptualizing of the nation as defined by people as opposed to places.

Revivalist folklore performance figures prominently in the intensification of the relationship between emigrants and the Portuguese state in the late twentieth century. Both private and public institutions in Portugal strategize emigrant preservation of national customs throughout the world as an essential tool for increasing Portugal's geopolitical visibility and maintaining ties between Portuguese migrants and their native homeland. As I will argue in this chapter, the existence of emigrant *ranchos folclóricos* ensures a constant traffic of goods and services, performers and publics between Portugal and Portuguese communities in diaspora. Revivalist folklore is both a vehicle for the economic and emotional linking of emigrants to Portugal and a tool for achieving what Rumbaut and Portes (2001a, 2001b) term "selective acculturation" within the United States.

Selective acculturation among immigrant groups, as Rumbaut and Portes define it, is marked by a "paced learning of the host culture along with retention of significant elements of the culture of origin" (2001a, 309). In their extensive anthology analyzing fourth-wave experience of "segmented assimilation" across an array of U.S. immigrant groups, scant mention is made of the role of expressive culture in processes of adaptation to new national contexts. I would argue, however, that in the Portuguese-American community of northern New Jersey, selective acculturation cannot be understood without considering the way in which it is communicated and reinforced through folkloric performance.

Folklore performance supports both Portuguese and U.S. im/emigration policies by invigorating Portuguese language use, moral values, and endogamy while celebrating Luso-American commercial success and rising political visibility in New Jersey. Portuguese folklore performers enact a "back and forth" dynamic between Portugal and the United States, where home and host society become "a single area of social action" (Margolis 1994, 29). New Jersey folklore groups depend upon transnational media and transmigrants, "those who claim and are claimed by two or more nation states" (Glick-Schiller 1999, 96), for their survival. Many New Jersey *rancho* members return from Iberian holidays armed with costumes, videotapes of folklore performances, and "gifts" of new songs and dances donated by childhood friends from hometown *ranchos*—the material with which groups in diaspora update and strengthen performance repertoires (Cardoso 2003).

New Jersey *ranchos folclóricos* dance along the transmigratory in-between, reinforcing core Portuguese values while performing ethnic traditions on American soil—an expression of difference accepted and often celebrated within the multicultural context of Newark, New Jersey, and its surrounding areas. Newark, a city which has struggled for decades to recover from the devastating effects of the 1967 riots, has turned a history of racial strife into a platform for image overhaul, where tropes of peaceability between diverse ethnic groups form the foundation of a new post-riot identity. Newark's growing arts scene reflects this diversity, and the city's renaissance has been tied to the development of large-scale arts infrastructure (Strom 2002, forthcoming) as well as the proliferation of smaller-scale ethnic festivals and parades (Holton 2003). The annual Portugal Day parade and its display of *ranchos folclóricos* figures prominently in Newark's arts-driven revival. The fact that Portuguese folklore has been able to thrive in Newark and accompany Luso-American commercial success and political empowerment serves as a testament to Newark's transformation. *Ranchos* forward an image of Newark as a city that welcomes diversity and allows varied immigrant groups to maintain autochthonous traditions within northern New Jersey's hearty regional embrace.

New Jersey folklore performance radiates out toward both sides of the Atlantic, imbricated simultaneously in processes of U.S. adaptation and the maintenance of ties to Portugal. In constant dialogue between sending and receiving contexts, emigrant performers both live and enact transnationalism. This chapter examines the struggles within the Portuguese community of northern New Jersey over issues of assimilation, the state policies and pressures which catalyze selective acculturation's dynamic of national duality, and the ways in which folklore performance affirms and makes visible this transmigratory dialectic.

Rumbaut and Portes argue that today's era of mass immigration—"now overwhelmingly non-European in composition . . . [raises] serious questions about the applicability of explanatory models developed in connection with the experience of European ethnics [earlier in this century]" (2001b, 5). It is evident here that Rumbaut and Portes view European migration as a phenomenon of the past. This is not, however, the case with Portuguese migration to the United States—particularly to the state of New Jersey—which saw a surge in the 1960s and 1970s due to a variety of factors, from the colonial wars and political instability in Portugal to the U.S. repeal of the quota system in 1965. The Portuguese have been called an "invisible minority" in the United States, due to low levels of civic engagement and political participation. The Portuguese remain an invisible minority, I would argue, also due to scholarly inattention to these communities. In a modest attempt toward visibility, this chapter examines Portuguese immigrant communities as part and parcel of the fourth-wave migration to the United States.

This chapter is based on three years of ethnographic fieldwork (2000–2003) in the Portuguese-American communities of northern New Jersey. In addition to participant observation of numerous New Jersey *rancho* rehearsals and performances, I have conducted ethnographic interviews with folklore dancers, musicians, directors, and festival organizers primarily from the *Sonhos de Portugal rancho* of Kearny, New Jersey, and the *Danças e Cantares de Portugal rancho* of Elizabeth, New Jersey.[2] This chapter is also informed by research at the Rutgers–Newark archive of the Ironbound Oral History Project (IOHP), a store of primary audio, visual, and textual documents containing over one hundred interview transcripts with Portuguese-speaking immigrants of northern New Jersey, and the Newark archives of the *Luso-Americano* biweekly newspaper.

Assimilation Debates

Folklore performance figures prominently in recent debates within the Portuguese community concerning the extent to which Luso-Americans should become integrated into mainstream U.S. society and culture. The New Jersey Network documentary entitled *Ironbound Ties to Portugal* (1999) illustrates several vectors of this discourse, situating folklore performance on one side of what the film portrays as the assimilation/anti-assimilation binary. Midway through the film, the camera focuses in on a large dinner table filled with *bacalhau* (codfish) and *vinho verde* (sparkling "green" wine). Seated at the table in the midst of an intense debate are Luso-American community leaders Linda Rodrigues, a university professor, Armando Fontoura, Essex County sheriff, and Licínio (Lee) Cruz, a local judge and co-owner of Cruz Construction Company. At issue is the move by some Portuguese families out of the Ironbound—Newark's "Little Portugal" neighborhood (see fig. 26).

> "Why do our people leave the Ironbound?" asks Professor Rodrigues, who still lives in the neighborhood.
> "For the American dream," Sheriff Fontoura says with a smile.
> "And I don't have it?" Rodrigues asks in disbelief.
> "You have it. You left the Ironbound too, may I remind you, my dear. You went to graduate school. . . ."
> "But I came back," Rodrigues asserts. "My parents stayed here."
> "As soon as they could, my parents left," Judge Cruz says. "My father saw a better future for his family in the suburbs."
> "When Lee's father left, the Ironbound was still good," says Fontoura.
> "It's still good. It's still good, here, okay, Armando?" Rodrigues asserts over the rising din.
> "Look," Fontoura says, "let me ask you something. What's wrong with our people here in America—this is the melting pot—marrying within the American society, ours sons and daughters marrying Jewish Americans, Italian Americans, Irish Americans? That's the American way, that's what we do, that's the way it's supposed to be."

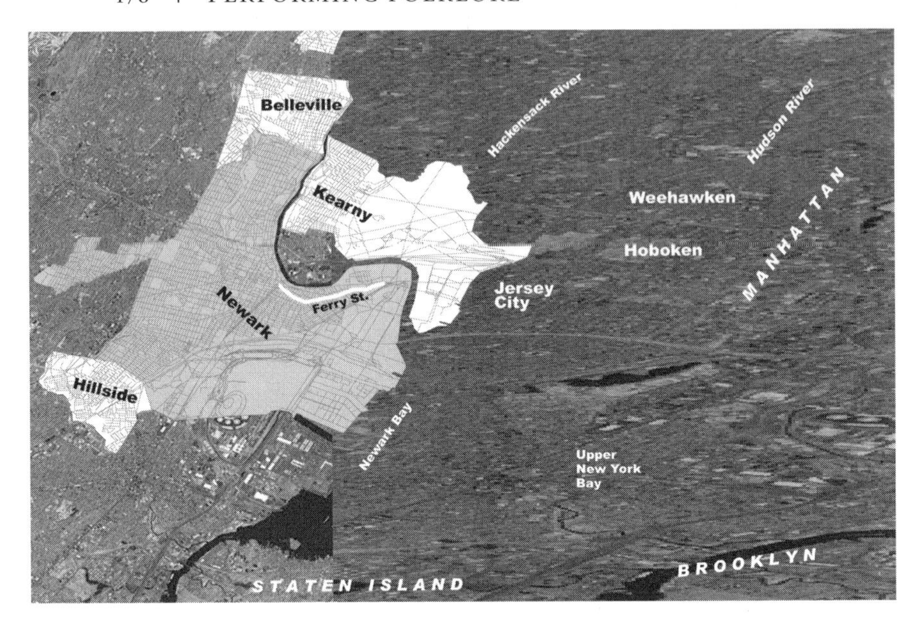

Figure 26. Map of Newark and surrounding areas. Ferry Street, also known as "Portugal Avenue," marks the heart of the Ironbound. Neighboring towns of Kearny, Hillside, and Belleville are also outposts of Portuguese immigration. US Geological Survey, 1999/09/23, Landsat ETM + Scene, WRS-2 Path 014 Row 032, Level: Orthorectified (sourced through Global Land Cover Facility, University of Maryland) (contrast stretching and detail processing: Martin M. Elbl); US Census Bureau, TIGER Line 2002 (overlay extraction: Martin M. Elbl).

The conversation continues with Luís Nogueira, then-director of Newark's *Sport Club Português,* wondering aloud if intermarriage will result in the loss of the Portuguese language and culture, causing Newark's Luso-Americans to be "phased out."

As if in answer to anxiety over the dilution of Portuguese ethnicity, the film quickly cuts from the dinner table to a clip of an enormous feast sponsored by the *Sport Club Português* in Newark. *Sardinhas* and *leitão* (sardines and suckling pig) rotate from large spits as hundreds of people gather at picnic tables, speaking in Portuguese. The camera pans from the barbecue to a heated soccer game, where two players are arguing over a foul the referee never called. Then the camera switches to a folklore performance going on beside the barbecue where a large, well-rehearsed *rancho folclórico* begins a whirling dance for a cheering public. This segment of the film ends with the *Sport Club* director speaking into the camera: "We put everything together in one event, we play soccer, dance folklore, we do the barbecue . . . For a change, we have a different kind of unity. A lot of people remember the feasts and the parties from back home in Portugal . . . It's in our blood, it's part of our culture."

As the documentary suggests, Portuguese identity in diaspora not only involves tension over demographic changes within the Portuguese enclave in the Ironbound, but also over the more generalized process of assimilation and its effects on ethnic identity, solidarity, and sociability. In the film, the expressive markers of Portuguese ethnicity—soccer, religious devotion to Fátima, *fado,* and folklore—are all spliced together in an amalgamated portrayal of ethnic purity, anathema to Sheriff Fontoura and others' call for assimilation. From the perspective of the film's producers, performing folklore is a means to fight *against* integration and ethnic dissolution. As I will argue in the last section of this chapter, the reality of folklore's role with regard to assimilation is more nuanced and dialectical, contributing to both sides of the film's binary formulation.

Assimilation has been a hot topic of debate among anthropologists and sociologists who study America's post-1965 fourth wave of immigration—widely acknowledged as the United States' most profound demographic transformation in a century (Rumbaut and Portes 2001b, 7). Traditional Chicago School models of linear assimilation which theorize the seamless loss or absorption of ethnicity into white mainstream society over the course of three generations of socioeconomic ascent have recently been challenged by scholars who present a more complex and varied portrait of ethnic adaptation (Rumbaut and Portes 2001a, 2001b). Assessing issues of bilingualism, patterns of sociability, and the dynamics of co-ethnic communities, Rumbaut and Portes argue that the second generation of fourth-wave migrants undergo what they term "segmented assimilation," where "outcomes vary across immigrant minorities" and where "rapid integration and acceptance into the American mainstream represent just one possible alternative" (2001b, 6). Based on studies of thousands of second-generation immigrants from diverse ethnicities, Rumbaut and Portes demarcate an array of coordinates along the trajectory, ranging from complete assimilation to oppositional ethnic plurality.

The Portuguese immigrant community of northern New Jersey, I would argue, falls in the middle of this trajectory, practicing a form of selective acculturation which is "commonly associated with fluent bilingualism in the second generation . . . [and] absorption by second generation youths of key values and normative expectations from their original culture and concomitant respect for them" (Rumbaut and Portes 2001a, 309). In the case of Portuguese Newark, the dynamic of selective acculturation has also been impacted by such factors as a condensed urban settlement pattern,[3] a tightly knit, relatively homogenous co-ethnic community, and Portuguese and U.S. im/emigration policies.

State Policies, Language Use, and Selective Acculturation

As Bela Feldman-Bianco (1992) argues, Luso-Americans have experienced shifting pressures from both the U.S. and Portuguese governments with regard to assimilation. In the 1920s and 1930s Portuguese migrants "were subjected to restrictive immigration laws and second class citizen status in both the United States and Portugal" (Feldman-Bianco 1992, 146). Conflicting national ideologies also left immigrants torn: the U.S. "melting pot" formulation, which guided immigrants into an ideal of swift and total assimilation, versus a doctrine of racial pride and superiority proffered by the Portuguese government, which encouraged the "exclusive maintenance of Portuguese culture and language" (Feldman-Bianco 1992, 146).[4]

Starting in the 1970s, however, both countries changed their official stance vis-à-vis Portuguese migration. The United States repealed the 1924 National Origins Quota Act in 1965, dissolving strict limitations on immigration according to country of origin. Cultural pluralism, an ideology which encouraged the maintenance of diverse ethnic traditions and values within the North American polity, came to dominate the U.S. approach. This ideology also dominates Newark's city government rhetoric today. In describing Newark's ongoing revitalization, Mayor Sharpe James (2004) states, for example, "Our greatest strength lies not in bricks and mortar, but in our rainbow of peoples and cultures whose diversity and energy have fueled our rebirth and growth. Sample our restaurants, visit our cultural attractions, meet our diverse people." The Portuguese Ironbound section of the city is often singled out for its active participation in Newark's renaissance (James 2002). Boasting low crime rates, carefully maintained residential buildings, and a booming commercial district replete with ethnic restaurants and shops, the Ironbound's "Little Portugal" figures prominently in Newark's narrative of urban renewal and multicultural acceptance (Rae-Turner and Koles 2001, 153–54; Grogan and Proscio 2001, 137–38).[5]

The postcolonial Portuguese state also enlarged its concept of nation in recent decades, passing a law in 1981 which permits dual nationality and allows Portuguese emigrants who had lost their native citizenship to regain it. As Irene Bloemraad points out, nowadays it is almost impossible for a Portuguese emigrant to claim singular non-Portuguese citizenship: "if a Portuguese swears the [U.S.] oath of allegiance today, the state of Portugal will continue to consider that person a Portuguese national. Many immigrants therefore find themselves in a situation of *de facto* dual citizenship" (Bloemraad 2002, 205, my insert). The change in both U.S. and Portuguese ideology toward Portuguese emigrants residing in the United States encourages selective acculturation. It is in the interest of both countries, according to current policies, for Portuguese-Americans to recognize an allegiance to both sending and receiving contexts.

The Portuguese government has not confined its overseas focus solely to issues of emigrant citizenship. In 1996, it also created a special consultative council, the *Conselho das Comunidades Portuguesas* (CCP [Council for Portuguese Communities]), comprised of one hundred elected representatives from various international hubs of Portuguese emigration who gather regularly to communicate their concerns directly to Lisbon.[6] The Portuguese government also began giving increased cultural support to Portuguese in diaspora following the Revolution of 1974. In several well-publicized visits to Newark in the 1990s, for example, Portugal's prime minister, António Guterres, and secretary of the Portuguese communities, José Lello, gave speeches suggesting that the immigrant community both maintain Portuguese customs and traditional values abroad while simultaneously committing to their current geographical locale through increased assimilation, U.S. citizenship procurement, and political participation. Speaking at the inauguration of the new Portuguese Consulate of Newark in 1998, Guterres promised, "We [the Portuguese government] will do our best to be present here, but you [Luso-Americans] must strongly participate in the civic and political life of the United States" (*Ironbound Ties to Portugal* 1999, my inserts). Five years later, the minister of foreign commerce and Portuguese communities, António Martins da Cruz, reiterated this very same message in a 2003 address to Luso-Americans in Danbury, Connecticut. Reporting on the event, Henrique Mano writes, "Martins da Cruz asked the Portuguese to integrate themselves into their adopted homeland, but also encouraged them to keep the umbilical cord tied to their country of origin" (2003, 8). Cruz elaborates by suggesting that "the best way not to forget Portugal is to teach your children and grandchildren, the new generation, Portuguese culture and language. The best way to keep the nation of Portugal always present here is to speak Portuguese, to have *ranchos folclóricos,* and to have groups which prolong our culture here" (Mano 2003, 8). In this statement, Martins da Cruz singles out folklore performance as an important vehicle for conjuring the nation of Portugal on American soil and keeping Portuguese culture alive while integrating into U.S. society.

This official stance urging emigrants to both stay connected to Portuguese culture while becoming assimilated agents in their adopted homeland is accompanied by an aggressive campaign by the *Instituto Camões* to solidify Portuguese language acquisition in emigrant communities abroad —particularly among second- and third-generation immigrants. The *Insti-*

Table 6.1. Portuguese Emigration to the United States by Decade (1901–2000)

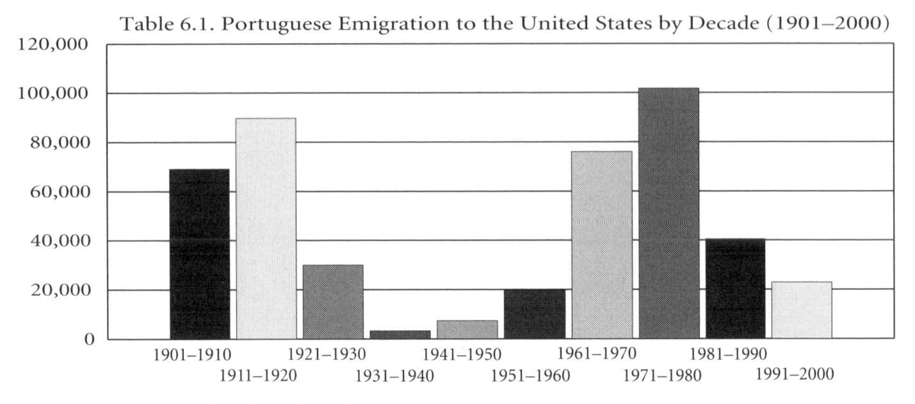

Source: Immigration and Naturalization Service, 2002.

tuto Camões plan, which involves supporting community language schools and university Portuguese studies programs and the founding of Portuguese language centers around the globe, aims to increase the number of Portuguese speakers throughout the world, so that Portuguese, currently the sixth most-spoken international language, can become a vital communicative vehicle in the world of business, international trade, and foreign relations. According to this plan, emigrant communities act as both linguistic incubators of future Portuguese language vitality and intermediaries between Portugal and newly adopted homelands.[7]

The change in U.S. and Portuguese policy toward im/emigrants occurs concomitant with a surge in Portuguese migration to the United States. Emigration from Portugal to the United States rose dramatically between 1965 and 1980 (see table 6.1). This surge is due to a variety of exogenous and endogenous factors, including Portuguese economic hardship, political instability, and colonial war, the U.S. repeal of the 1924 National Origins Quota Act in the 1965, and a softening of the 1974 northern European labor market, which resulted in the redirection of Portuguese emigrants previously destined for France, Germany, and Belgium.[8]

During the period between 1960 and 1980, many Portuguese destined for the United States settled in New Jersey. According to the 1990 census, New Jersey boasts the fourth largest population of Portuguese, behind California, Massachusetts, and Rhode Island, in that order (see table 6.2). However, New Jersey distinguishes itself by having the highest proportion of continental Portuguese and an extremely high concentration of recently arrived Portuguese emigrants (see table 6.3). The 1980 census numbers for New Jersey reveal that 83 percent of the population of foreign-born Portuguese arrived between 1965 and 1980.[9] Another indicator of New Jersey's relatively newly arrived Portuguese population is the large percentage of Portuguese

Table 6.2. Number of Luso-Americans and Portuguese Language Use by State, 1990

	General Population	Luso-American Population	Portuguese Lang. Use*
California	29,760,021	275,492	78,232
Massachusetts	6,016,425	241,173	133,373
Rhode Island	1,003,464	76,773	39,947
New Jersey	7,730,188	56,928	55,285
Hawaii	1,108,229	39,748	1,110

Source: 1990 U.S. Census of Population, Detailed Population Characteristics, adapted from Vicente 1999.

* This category indicates the number of Luso-Americans who still speak Portuguese at home.

Table 6.3. Citizenship and Year of Immigration for New Jersey's Foreign-Born Persons by Country of Birth, 1980

Place of Origin	Foreign-Born Pop. of N.J.	1975–80	1970–74	1965–69	1960–64	1950–59	Before 1950
Azores	219	15	84	50	16	25	29
Continental Portugal	28,234	7,520	9,788	6,021	1,886	1,126	1,893

Source: 1980 U.S. Census of Population, Detailed Population Characteristics.

families that speak Portuguese in the home. According to the 1990 U.S. census data illustrated in table 6.2, out of a population of 56,928 Portuguese in New Jersey (first ascendancy only), 55,285 people aged five or older speak Portuguese in the home (Vicente 1999, 61–66). This shows a much greater proportion of Luso-Americans who have retained native language use relative to the Portuguese communities in Massachusetts, Rhode Island, and California—native language use, of course, being an essential component of selective acculturation.

The cultural and lingual vibrancy of northern New Jersey's Portuguese population is also evident in the built environment. Throughout Newark's East Ward Ironbound section and interspersed throughout the downtown areas of the neighboring towns of Kearny, Hillside, Bellville, Perth Amboy, and Elizabeth, Portuguese-owned businesses announce themselves through bilingual signs, often incorporating the colors of the Portuguese flag and other emblems of national identity such as the sixteenth-century caravel and the one-eyed portrait of Luís de Camões. Many apartment buildings in these areas feature ceramic tiles of Fátima and the three shepherd children, red clay roofs, elaborate urban gardens with fig trees and grape arbors, and abutting stone mosaic sidewalks reminiscent of urban Portugal. In the business districts of Newark, Kearny, and Elizabeth, many retail shops, banks, and professional offices post signs announcing *"Fala-se Português"* ("Portuguese Spoken Here"). The local ATM machines have a Portuguese-language option, and the Portuguese community has its own lusophone yellow pages.

The concentration of Portuguese-American residents in Newark—one of the city's largest ethnic groups according to the 1990 census (Vicente 1999)—has allowed for a staggering number of Portuguese businesses to flourish.[10] This robust commercial presence has a double effect of serving the monolingual foreign-born population while obligating the second- and third-generation Portuguese and ethnic outsiders to become conversant in the language/culture in order to navigate the area as consumers and fellow merchants. This in turn feeds the educational programs funded by the *Instituto Camões* by populating them with students who feel they must know Portuguese to break into the northern New Jersey job market. The multicontextual and quotidian use of Portuguese in northern New Jersey, as a language of commerce, religion, and domestic life, has created a structure of mutually reinforcing linguistic joists which facilitates the maintenance of the language into the second and third generation. This feature of New Jersey's Portuguese-American community is directly attributable to both state policies and ideologies with regard to late twentieth-century emigration.

In conclusion, the post-1974 Portuguese government has asserted a two-pronged policy of cultural preservation and U.S. assimilation, while the United States has welcomed Portuguese emigrants by repealing the 1924 National Origins Quota Act in 1965 and forwarding a post–civil rights era agenda of multiculturalism.[11] These state policies have created a hospitable environment for the "retention of significant elements of the culture of origin," "fluent bilingualism in the second generation," and the perseverance of "key values and normative expectations from the original culture"—the primary components of selective acculturation, according to Rumbaut and Portes's definition. The ethos of transnational hybridity is reflected in the built environment of northern New Jersey and the large quantity of Portuguese-owned businesses that thrive throughout the region. The transmigratory dynamic of living between two national contexts, where home and host society commingle in a "single arena of social action," is also facilitated by the predominance of newly arrived emigrants within the community, the high density of Portuguese in northern New Jersey, and their settlement in urban enclaves.[12]

Dancing along the In-between

Portuguese emigrants in northern New Jersey gain social and cultural capital by "keeping their feet" in two national contexts. The adroit navigation between Portugal and the United States has resulted in commercial success and political empowerment, which, in turn, requires making visible one's commitment to both originary and adopted homelands. This is where revivalist folklore performance becomes a vital part of transmigration, imbricated as it is in the commercial and political life of northern New Jersey's Portuguese community and in national emigration ideologies.

Performative manifestations of ethnic identity within the New Jersey Luso-American community are an index of how selective acculturation works and a vital resource for achieving it. When Foreign Commerce Minister Martins da Cruz singled out *ranchos folclóricos* in his appeal to Luso-Americans to "keep the umbilical cord tied to Portugal" while integrating into the United States, he points to the ways in which folklore performance invigorates Portuguese language use and cultural values while simultaneously celebrating Luso-American commercial success and political empowerment. Folklore groups depend upon transmigrants and transnational media for the creation and periodic renewal of their performance repertoire and costumes, the restoration of musical instruments and historical props, the recruitment of performers and publics, and the exchange of ideas and advice among folklore groups throughout the Portuguese diaspora. Northern New Jersey's thriving folklore scene is both an expressive symbol of and a practical means toward the achievement of selective acculturation.

Rancho performance in diaspora differs from *rancho* performance within the bounded space of Portugal. As outlined in chapters 2 and 3 post-revolutionary Portuguese *ranchos* have fought social stigma due to folklore's association with the *Estado Novo.* Following the Revolution, Portuguese *ranchos* overhauled costumes, musical repertoire, and choreography to rid folklore of its ties to fascist cultural policy. Shedding fascist spectacle that had turned folklore dancers into whirling national flags, reformed *ranchos* now, in theory at least, research turn-of-the-century tradition using ethnographic methodologies. Reformed *ranchos* in Portugal perform historically reconstructed dances drawn from the locality in which performers live. FFP reforms aim to transform revivalist folklore in Portugal into an act of scholarship as well as a performative articulation of local identity.

The hundreds of *ranchos folclóricos* that exist in Portuguese immigrant communities of northern Europe, Brazil, South Africa, Southeast Asia, Canada, and the United States, however, have not for the most part experienced fascist stigma nor undergone post-revolutionary cultural reform. *Ranchos* in diaspora generally do not conduct ethnographic research but rather recreate dances from books, videos, television programs, or in consultation with other folklore groups in Portugal. Some perform the nation not the locality, using amalgamated costumes and repertoire sampled from all of Portugal's twelve regions, as is the case with select *ranchos* in Germany (Klimt 1992, 2000a). Other *ranchos* combine Portuguese folklore with performance traditions from their current cultural environment, as is the case in Malaysia's Portuguese settlement (Sarkissian 2000). Still other *ranchos* select one region to represent, as is the case with many *ranchos* in New Jersey, and this region, Minho, acts as a synecdoche for the nation as a whole.[13] Although at first glance they appear similar to Portugal's fascist troupes of the 1950s in their patriotic celebration of the nation, *ranchos* in diaspora construct "Portuguese" identities to differing political and social ends.

There are currently sixteen active *ranchos* in northern New Jersey.[14] New Jersey *ranchos,* like their Portuguese counterparts, are comprised of amateur musicians and dancers who perform reconstructions of traditional songs and dances from the late nineteenth century. Typically composed of thirty to thirty-five members, New Jersey *ranchos folclóricos* feature eight to ten pairs of dancers, a section of instrumentalists called the *tocata,* and several vocalists. The dancers are typically the youngest members of the group—ranging in age from five to thirty and are often second-generation Luso-Americans. The musicians, usually first-generation immigrant men in their forties and fifties, play instruments such as the accordion, concertina, clarinet, and various forms of guitars and percussion, depending on the regional repertoire. The vocalists perform alone or in pairs. *Ranchos* in New Jersey, like those in Portugal, often operate under the auspices of larger cultural associations or social organizations.

New Jersey *ranchos* typically rehearse weekly throughout the fall and winter and perform regularly during the spring and summer months at festivals and religious and civic celebrations. *Ranchos folclóricos* are often hired to mark the observance of *both* American and Portuguese holidays, such as Father's Day, Mother's Day, the Fourth of July, *São Martinho, 25 de Abril,* and Fátima celebrations. Many New Jersey *ranchos* also perform in secondary schools throughout the state, at Newark's colleges and universities, and at international folklore festivals throughout the country. New Jersey *ranchos* occasionally travel to Portugal to perform or to other Portuguese emigrant communities in Europe, South Africa, and the Americas. The most important date on the New Jersey *rancho* performance calendar, however, is Newark's enormous Portugal Day festival, which takes place during the week of June 10th. Most *ranchos* appear in the cacophonous weekend parade alongside their own floats, while also performing in other festival programming throughout the week.

One of the ways New Jersey's community of 72,196 Portuguese immigrants maintains transnational links between Portugal and the United States is through what Appadurai (1996) calls "global mediascapes." Folklore dancing is just one expression of globalized associationism that ties in to other media-driven activities such as reading Portuguese immigrant newspapers (*LusoAmericano, 24 Horas,* or *Mundo Português*), watching Portuguese cable channels (SPT-TV or RTPi), and listening to Portuguese radio programs. This lusophone mediascape not only furthers the goals of *Instituto Camões*'s linguistic ambitions, it also creates "communities of sentiment," where through the collective cultural consumption of videos, TV, audio cassettes, and newspapers, groups of people "begin to imagine and feel things together" (Appadurai 1996, 8). Through lusophone mediascapes, *ranchos folclóricos* maintain contact with their homeland and with other Portuguese immigrant communities around the globe. This mediascape becomes an essential tool for both *rancho* repertoire building and *rancho* promotion; immigrant *ranchos* learn new songs and dances from watching TV and gain visibility from appearing on Portuguese cable and advertising their performances in *LusoAmericano.*

Virtual travel between Portugal and the United States is also complemented by real trips home. Although the Luso-American population is considered more permanently situated in the United States compared to Portuguese communities in northern Europe, who describe their emigrant lives as "temporary" (Klimt 1992), many of New Jersey's Portuguese return regularly to their birthplace and dream of Iberian retirements. Over one-third of the Luso-Americans interviewed for the Ironbound Oral History Project reported visiting Portugal annually. Many in this group still maintained family homes or newly purchased apartments in Portugal. *Retornados*—those who had settled in lusophone Africa and were forced to return to Portugal after *25 de Abril,* later moving to the United States—comprised the population that returned to Portugal least frequently. Among the second-generation Luso-Americans, all had been to Portugal at least once and some returned annually with their parents or alone to visit grandparents.[15]

According to the *rancho* performers I interviewed, returning to Portugal contributes significantly to the health and maintenance of the folklore group. As Joe Cerqueira (2003) describes, "The costumes of all of New Jersey's *ranchos* come from Portugal; all of the *ranchos* that exist today got their costumes in Portugal. The only *rancho* that didn't buy their clothes there was *Barcuense* in 1977—but the *ranchos* today—all clothes, all pieces of the costumes, as well as the musical instruments came from Portugal." In addition to the regular purchase and restoration of costumes, props, and musical instruments, *rancho* members also report returning to Portugal for repertoire acquisition. Tony Cardoso (2003), director of *Sonhos de Portugal,* describes how they acquired the song "Vida de Emigrante" (Emigrant's Life).

> Tony: One of the musicians we had in our group is now back in Portugal for good. But before he moved back he brought us that music . . . it's been one of our favorite dances.
>
> Kim: So he wrote the music?
>
> Tony: He didn't write the music. He used to perform with a group in Portugal and it was one of the people in that group that taught him the music. The dance was also given to us too by, Toto was his name. It was very difficult in the beginning to learn it, but we picked it up.

The fact that Cardoso's Luso-American *rancho* was given a song about emigration by a folklore troupe in Portugal shows how transnational interchange truly dominates the experience of most *ranchos* in northern New Jersey and the way in which sending and receiving contexts become "a single arena of social action" (Margolis 1994, 29). Portuguese *ranchos* sing about emigration and American *ranchos* sing about Portugal. The dialectic of "double utopia" analyzed by Feldman-Bianco and Huse (1998), where Portuguese emigrants in America dream about returning home and those left in Portugal dream about emigrating, resonates in this example.

Folklore dance in New Jersey is also a way for Portuguese-born parents to instill distinctly Portuguese moral values in their second- and third-generation "American" children and grandchildren. Parents who arrange for their children to join a *rancho* are seen as responsible caregivers who go out of their way to promote children's physical safety and cultural education. Generally, parents whose children dance folklore receive positive reinforcement from the immigrant community for helping to preserve Portuguese culture and for raising responsible, respectful children. On the other hand, parents whose children do not participate in folklore performance may incur critique. Daisy Currais, a second-generation Ironbound resident whose parents both danced in *ranchos,* explained that her "mother got a lot of shit from other mothers" for not forcing her daughters to dance folklore and allowing them to leave the Ironbound for high school and college (Currais 2004). She states

> We were rebellious teenagers. We refused. No, actually, I remember when we were little asking Mom why she never [forced us to join]. 'Cause all of our friends were forced into *rancho.* Like their moms and dads were like, "You must dance *rancho.* You must be part of this Portuguese thing." And [my] mom and

> dad met in a *rancho*! When they were teenagers, that's all they knew. . . . I think people who dance *rancho* now are forced, almost like "it will keep you off the streets. Dance *rancho*!" (Currais 2004, my inserts)

As this statement implies, *rancho* dancing is thought to have tangible social value—a way to keep Portuguese immigrant children, exposed to Newark's liberal urban environment, off the streets and out of trouble. *Rancho* dancing is widely perceived to keep kids on the straight and narrow by encouraging conservative moral values such as monogamy, respect for authority, and celebration of an agrarian lifestyle abandoned by immigrants who moved from Portuguese rurality to U.S. industrial urbanism throughout the 1960s, 1970s, and 1980s.[16]

Paired dancers in New Jersey *ranchos* tend to be second-generation immigrants chosen by the directors of the *rancho* in consideration of uniform height, skill, and age. However, another factor, not often verbalized, influences the constitution of pairs, that is, many dancer pairs court one another (Carvalho 1990, 30). Public courtship in Portuguese immigrant families is a charged issue. Many second-generation Luso-Americans interviewed for the IOHP describe being subject to strict parenting[17] and disciplined guidelines for dating: children should ideally choose a Portuguese-American partner. Once a partner is chosen and courtship becomes public, children should stay with this partner, preferably until marriage.[18]

Luso-American college-age students also describe strict parental monitoring of courtship, especially for daughters. Dating in the presence of adult family members, acquaintances, or at the very least other peers is preferable to going out on a date alone. Given these guidelines, participation as a dancer in *ranchos folclóricos* increases the chances of finding a Portuguese mate (Carvalho 1990). Jessica Moreira (2003), a nineteen-year-old dancer in the *Danças e Cantares de Portugal rancho,* describes the courtship of couples in her group and the familial pressures she feels to find a Portuguese mate:

> Jessica: Well actually one of them, the girl, was dancing and then I guess they started going out and she brought her boyfriend to the group so they could stay as partners. And then another couple, they've been [*rancho*] partners since they were five. They started in the *Rancho Infantil* and they've been partners for ten years now. She's twenty and he's eighteen, and they started going out about a year ago.
>
> Kim: Would you say it's important to your parents that you date a Portuguese guy?
>
> Jessica: Yes.
>
> Kim: Why?

Jessica: I don't know, my father thinks the Portuguese are better than everything else, he just regards us as way up there, I guess cuz he's in . . . construction, the Portuguese just kind of strive a little more and he sees *os outros* [the others] as *perguisosos* [lazy].
Kim: Do you think the *rancho* is a way to ensure that you . . .
Jessica: Even if he doesn't say it directly, I know he wants me to go out with a Portuguese guy . . . The *rancho* is to keep myself involved, to keep myself going, keep the culture going. (Moreira 2003, my inserts)

While Jessica's father's rationale for preferring a Portuguese husband for his daughter is due to a belief in Portuguese industriousness, some other second-generation teenagers cite language as the primary reason for wanting a Portuguese mate. Sónia DaCosta (2001), interviewed for the IOHP, states that marrying outside the Portuguese community would cause problems in her extended family. "I want my husband to be able to talk to my parents and grandparents," she says. Folklore performance not only "keeps the culture going" among younger generations through the rehearsal of Portuguese songs and dances, it also "keeps the culture going" by fostering Luso-American friendships and endogamous pairing. Dancing folklore also facilitates adult supervision of public courtship and exerts social pressure on couples to maintain their relationships and work toward marriage.

Ranchos folclóricos also instill in second-generation dancers a respect for their rural heritage and the traditional gender roles that come with it. *Ranchos* both in the United States and in Portugal reconstitute popular songs and dances ostensibly created by a nameless, faceless collective of rural peasants at the end of the nineteenth century. Rurality, seen from the vantage point of Portuguese immigrants living in northeastern U.S. cities, becomes a utopian space (Feldman-Bianco and Huse 1998). Many *rancho* songs and dances hearken back to a static, fictionalized past, where social hierarchies are unquestioned and rural life is stripped of the backbreaking labor and economic impoverishment that often characterized the quotidian life of agrarian workers. *Rancho* dancers carry onto the stage agricultural tools long obsolete in a material celebration of peasant lifestyle. These are "objects of ethnography" in Barbara Kirshenblatt-Gimblett's (1991) sense of the term, stripped of their utility, framed as aesthetic mementos or theatrical props. Through song lyrics that remember bucolic courtship, camaraderie, and choreography that has dancers, arms akimbo, whirling around in dizzying reveries, *ranchos folclóricos* invoke rural life in its most idealized form.

Many New Jersey *rancho* members come from families of Portugal's rural north (Carvalho 1990, 12), and *rancho* dancing promotes an embodied, albeit "invented" (Hobsbawm and Ranger 1983), celebration of this ancestral past. Jessica Moreira, for example, describes a float that members of her Portuguese youth group—many of them second-generation *rancho* dancers—constructed for the Portugal Day parade.

> We had Minho represented with the brick stove. We had the smoke machine inside so it was smoking the *chouriços* [smoked sausage], it looked so pretty . . . And of course for Minho we had the girl and the guy dressed in *rancho* outfits. And then we had Trás-os-Montes represented with a *carro de mão* [wheelbarrow] made out of wood with hay on it . . . and we had Nazaré with a fish net with dried fish . . . and we had a girl with the *sete saias* [seven skirts] and a *peixeiro* [fisherman]. Do you know the story of the *sete saias*? I'm such a dork, I know all this stuff. Well, the *peixeiras* [fishmongers] in Nazaré have *sete saias* because the *peixeiros*—their husbands—used to go out to sea for seven months and every month they used to take off a *saia* and then when they were at their last *saia*, they know their husbands are coming home. (2003, my inserts)

In the float, Portugal's regions were each represented by a pair of Luso-American teenagers dressed as Portuguese peasant archetypes. These couples were further described by the props characteristic of rural life according to region—a cart of hay, a brick stove, a fishing net. This Portuguese youth group float celebrates rural peasant life in all of its regional diversity while also embodying idealized patterns of conservative sociability. The story of the *sete saias* is a powerful illustration of this—the wife waiting patiently (and chastely) for her husband, shedding one skirt at a time, invoking her body as a calendar to mark the husband's return. According to the *sete saias* sequencing, it is only the husband who will enjoy the *peixeira*'s full state of undress.

"Não É para Ti" (It Is Not for You), a dance frequently performed by *Sonhos de Portugal,* playfully exhibits female chastity. Throughout the choreography, young male dancers try to kiss their female partners and are snubbed with the dramatic wag of an index finger and a kerchiefed shooing. Dressed in long skirts, aprons, and scarves, female *rancho* dancers role-play traditional constructs of rural femininity.[19] Male dancers, typically dressed in long pants and vests, adroitly guide their female partners through *viras,* strong hands placed firmly on the small of their partners' backs in a symbolic display of masculine power and leadership. In many *viras* the men and women dance in pairs in a single broad circle. Individuals occasionally break off and dance with other partners or form smaller foursomes of men and women circling rapidly in quadrants of autonomous unpaired movements. These dancerly breeches, however, are always followed by the resumption of male/female pairing and a return to the permanent partnerships where boyfriends and girlfriends end up in the proper premarital embrace. *Rancho* costumes and choreography present an anachronistic portrait of traditional gender roles, flying in the face of the high incidence of female industrial labor and increasing rates of university study among Portuguese immigrant women living in the United States.[20] In contrast to the urban relocation and concomitant liberalizing forces faced by many Portuguese immigrants living in the northeastern United States, *rancho* dancing provides a performative model for the maintenance of conservative moral values, traditional gender roles, and the celebration of rural ancestry.

In addition to catalyzing ties to Portugal and solidifying Portuguese ethnic identity, *rancho* dancing also becomes a vehicle to demonstrate assimilation and social prestige within the United States. Many immigrants experience a double-edged lack of prestige. In the northeastern United States, Portuguese immigrants often start out as blue-collar workers, sometimes enduring classist maltreatment from dominant nonimmigrant communities (see Ribeiro 2000). In Portugal, emigrants who return home for summer vacation or retirement are often ostracized as uncultured nouveaux riches who return from years of U.S. labor speaking neither Portuguese nor English well, with a bent toward conspicuous consumption (see Cole 1991 and Brettell 2003). According to New Jersey *rancho* members, performing folklore helps mitigate this stereotype of Portuguese emigrants, boosting their status, both within the Luso-American community and in Portugal. As one dancer explained, "We are not rude people who went away only to make money, as most people might think; we are able to cultivate forms of traditional music and dance even better than *ranchos* in Portugal. *Ranchos folclóricos* are evidence that migrants have culture" (quoted in Carvalho 1990).

Dancing in a Portuguese *rancho,* according to Rutgers–Newark college student Brian Santos, raised his social standing within a New Jersey public high school. Brian, who dances in the *rancho Sonhos de Portugal,* recalls a performance that took place in Kearny, New Jersey:

> My friends in high school were always really interested in it. There's an international festival every year at the high school and when I was a student there, we performed. Basically, it is one day dedicated to all the different cultures represented in the school, and there are different performances from different cultures and the Portuguese is always one of the most popular. We always got standing ovations, everyone loved it, the teachers, the students, they would always call us on stage and ask us lots of questions. (B. Santos 2002)

Brian's testimony shows the effects of the 1974 Ethnic Heritage Act, which encourages multicultural celebration, even at the high school level where, particularly in a diverse region like northern New Jersey, children of emigrants raise their social capital by performing ethnic difference in a public context. Brian explains that, contrary to some of the kids in Portugal who get teased by their peers for performing in *ranchos,* dancing folklore is seen as "cool" by many of his New Jersey friends, Portuguese and non-Portuguese alike. His family is also very supportive of his participation in folklore because "It shows that I am involved in our culture" (B. Santos 2002). Brian, then, receives concentric circles of social kudos by dancing folklore, starting with the most intimate social context, that of the nuclear family, radiating out into larger rings of friends, neighbors, classmates, teachers, and administrators. Brian even articulates the stature of his *rancho* within a national framework, "We actually are considered professionals, we're in the Hudson County Book of Professional Entertainers, so anyone who is looking for a certain musical group can find us there. You know we're also in the Library of Congress, in Washington, D.C. We're documented in there!" (B. Santos 2002). *Rancho* director Tony Cardoso echoes this story of broad recognition and visibility: "We've danced at the Statue of Liberty . . . we were even invited to perform at Giants Stadium . . . We've also been on Portuguese TV and even the American FOX channel, you know FOX 5? . . . it was really something for the kids to be on a major channel, to be on national TV" (Cardoso 2003).

Folklore performance, as it exists within a well-developed system of cultural consumption and reproduction, is an ideal vehicle for maintaining ties to Portugal and the Portuguese diaspora, while asserting a political and cultural voice in the United States—the twin goals of the Portuguese state policy post-1974. In addition to celebrating ethnic difference and catalyzing social prestige and visibility, *rancho* performance is also intimately linked to Luso-American commercial success and emergent political power in northern New Jersey. Many *ranchos* are officially tied to cultural organizations. *Sonhos do Portugal* and *Os Sonhos Continuam,* for example, are affiliated with the Portuguese Cultural Association in Kearny, New Jersey. *Danças e Cantares de Portugal* is affiliated with the Portuguese Instructive Social Club in Elizabeth, New Jersey. The *Rancho Folclórico da Casa do Minho* is affiliated with the *Casa do Minho* in Newark. Some groups, however, are also officially or unofficially linked to prominent Luso-American merchants and entrepreneurs. The *Rancho Folclórico 'A Eira',* for example, is linked to Bernardino Coutinho, owner of the Coutinho Bakery chain and founder of the Portugal Day parade. *Sonhos de Portugal* and *Os Sonhos Continuam* are linked to Licínio Cruz, a district judge and president of the successful Cruz Construction Corporation.

Links to prominent community leaders can mean a variety of advantages for *ranchos* in northern New Jersey. Tony Cardoso emphasizes the financial and logistical support his *rancho* has received from Cruz Construction:

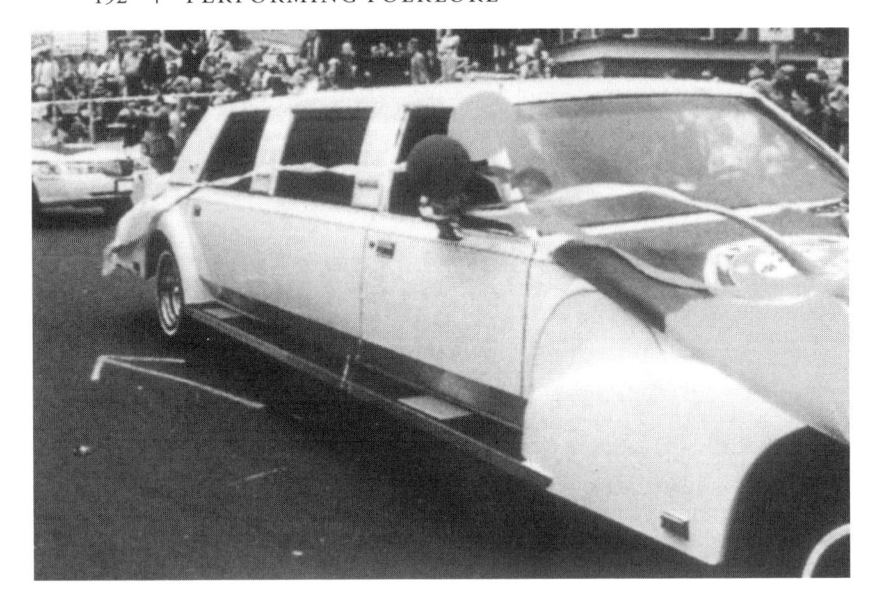

Figure 27. Photograph from the Portugal Day parade. Newark 2001. *Courtesy of the Bernardino Coutinho Foundation.*

> Cruz over the years has supported the group with money and outfits at times... Every year they make a contribution when it comes to Portugal Day in Newark. They not only give the truck trailer to the group, they also supply the wood every single year ... to build it, to supply the wood, which is a couple thousand dollars, and another couple thousand for other materials. [The float] takes about three days to assemble. (Cardoso 2003, my insert)

The bond between Cruz Construction and *Sonhos de Portugal* is fortified and made visible not only during the enormous Portugal Day parade,[21] but also through annual performances at the company picnic and other business functions sponsored by Cruz Construction. Similar to the commercial *padrinhos* Portuguese *ranchos* cultivate, New Jersey *ranchos* often share personnel with their corporate sponsor. Tony Cardoso, for example, has worked for Cruz Construction for decades. He sees his role in the *rancho* and in the company as symbiotic and mutually constitutive. Cruz Construction not only lends *Sonhos de Portugal* financial assistance, but also social cachet that comes with being linked to a successful Portuguese-American business. *Sonhos de Portugal,* in turn, symbolically enacts the company's commitment to Portugal and to its Luso-American employees through the performance of nineteenth-century popular traditions—traditions that help an emigrant workforce cohere overseas while advertising the company's services and ethnic provenance.

Figure 28. *Rancho folclórico* dancers preparing for a Portugal Day parade performance. Newark 2001. *Courtesy of the Bernardino Coutinho Foundation.*

Ranchos in an emigrant context encourage both mnemonic recall and erasure. Evoking memories of summer *festas* in Portugal (Cerqueira 2002), *ranchos* help a community in diaspora, caught up in the liminal moment of performance, forget their current geographic circumstance by traveling back in time and space, as if reversing emigration. Bonds between Luso-American entrepreneurship and folklore performance, however, add a charged, symbolic layer to collective memory. *Rancho* performers, barefoot on stage, holding hoes and pitchforks, exist in marked contrast to their corporate *padrinhos*, successful navigators of America's industrial northeast and exemplary portraits of the American dream attained. *Ranchos* in this context become a measuring stick for the success of the emigration project—an initiative often fueled by the desire to leave an impoverished agrarian plight for a place that promises industrial opportunity and social mobility. The staged celebration of rural life, a misty unreality, exists in metonymic tension with the figure of New Jersey's Luso-American entrepreneur, men dressed in three-piece suits driving expensive cars, their economic rise often the product of successful urban businesses. The symbolic tension created by the relationship between *ranchos folclóricos* and their commercial sponsors is nowhere better illustrated than the Portugal Day parade, where barefoot dancers in peasant garb march alongside sleek white limousines (see figs. 27 and 28), marking both experiential distance and emotional proximity between rural past and urban present in a complex homage to two national contexts.

In addition to intimate ties to emigrant entrepreneurship, *rancho* performance has been a consistent presence at celebrations of Luso-Americans' rise to political power in New Jersey. There has been much ink spilled in an attempt to document and theorize the historic lack of political participation among the Portuguese in the United States (Almeida 1999; Barrow 2002; Marinho and Cornwall 1992; Moniz 1979). Casual debates on the topic often arrive at the same conclusion: voting is not part of the Portuguese culture due to the fascist government which stifled political agency from 1926 to 1974. However, as Onésimo Almeida (1999) points out, lack of political participation throughout Portuguese emigrant communities predates the installation of the *Estado Novo.* As recently as 1996, the authors of a proposed documentary entitled "Newark's Silent Majority: Citizens without a Voice" describe the situation in the Ironbound:

> More than fifty years ago they started coming, drawn by the hope of a promising future in a bountiful country. Today they find themselves possessing the material things the country offered, but missing the joy and power of a people who govern themselves. Newark's Portuguese-Americans don't vote . . . They have turned the Ironbound into an inner city paradise, but have never elected one of their own to the City Council. And they are bitter about it. The Ironbound is a dumping ground and its people whipping boys for cynical politicians who revel in Luso-American political impotence, never failing to ignore it. (Lancellotti and Gardner, quoted in Almeida 1999)

Lancellotti and Gardner's depiction of Newark's Portuguese in 1996, however, no longer reflects the reality of the community in 2004. Since the late 1990s much has changed. The Portuguese government installed a new and improved Portuguese Consulate in a prestigious building on the outskirts of the Ironbound in 1998. Official ribbon-cuttings attended by the Portuguese prime minister and Luso-American leaders became the forum for a revitalized campaign aimed at increasing political participation among Luso-Americans. In November 1998, Augusto Amador became the first Portuguese-American councilman elected to office in the history of Newark. And in May 2002, with the election of Governor James McGreevey, Dina Matos McGreevy, a Portuguese-American, became New Jersey's first lady. The Portuguese government itself acknowledged this change during the 2003 Seminar on Participation and Citizenship in Lisbon, citing the increase in Luso-Americans elected to political office as a model upswing in civic engagement ("Martins da Cruz Quer Luso-Descendentes" 2003).

Since the late 1990s, as Newark's Luso-Americans have raised their political visibility and received increased attention from the Portuguese government (Pocinho 2003), *ranchos folclóricos* have served as the expressive exemplar of this new civic engagement. Many of New Jersey's *ranchos* have performed at voter drives, election parties, and alongside campaign speeches. In fact, in May 2002, newly elected New Jersey governor James McGreevey hosted a party on the lawn of the governor's mansion in celebration of Portugal Day marked by the performances of three Newark *ranchos*. Reviews and color photographs of these *rancho* performances made their way into the mainstream local press as well as the lusophone mediascape, announcing, in the words of several journalists, the political arrival of the Portuguese.[22] In 2003 Portugal Day was again celebrated at the governor's mansion—this time *ranchos Sonhos de Portugal* and *Os Sonhos Continuam* comprised the featured entertainment. In addition to the rapid-fire footwork of the *rancho* dancers which commanded rapt attention from the large crowd of Portuguese-Americans, there was an additional costumed dancer who captured the public's fancy. Teetering on the edge of the performance space, dressed from head to toe in a tiny embroidered *rancho* costume the color of the Portuguese flag, was two-year-old Jacqueline McGreevey, the daughter of New Jersey's Irish-American governor and his Portuguese-American wife. As the diminutive figure clapped her hands in time to the accordion's animated melody, raising her arms in emulation of the other second-generation dancers, expressive culture embodied political ideology. As the Portuguese government reminds any Luso-descendent who will listen, "[politics] and the preservation of cultural roots are not incompatible" ("Martins da Cruz Quer Luso-Descendentes" 2003).

In summary, *rancho* dancing enculturates a new generation of Portuguese-Americans according to the moral values of their parents' homeland. Second-generation Luso-Americans perform romanticized choreographies of rural life, where their parents' experience of backbreaking agricultural labor and poverty in northern Portugal is obscured by the festive presentation of ethnic heritage in an adopted homeland. Through the execution of paired dance steps, the vocalization of popular song lyrics, and the adherence to contemporary rehearsal practices, folklore dancing models conservative behavior such as the maintenance of traditional gender roles, respect for authority, and monogamy. Folklore dancing also provides children of emigrants with a pool of endogamous courtship possibilities, while affording them informal adult supervision of weekend social activities. Second-generation Luso-American dancers make a visible commitment to their ethnic heritage through folklore performance, which in turn grants them positive social reinforcement in family, school, and neighborhood contexts.

Revivalist folklore performance ties into U.S. immigration ideologies. As a result of legislation such as the 1965 repeal of the National Origins Quota Act, the passage of the 1974 Ethnic Heritage Act, and the general valorization of post–civil rights era multiculturalism, the United States has witnessed the proliferation of "ethnic celebrations, a zeal for genealogy, increased travel to ancestral homelands, and greater interest in ethnic artifacts, cuisine, music, literature and, of course, language" (Halter 2000, 5). *Rancho* dancing participates in this trend, revealing New Jersey's Portuguese population as "exotics at home, hidden in plain sight" (di Leonardo 1998), a part of the state's ethnic diversity which local officials work to promote. Through the celebration of its ethnic neighborhoods and multicultural arts programming in municipal parks and the New Jersey Performing Arts Center, Newark has pinned much of its hopes for urban revitalization on the "marketing of ethnic heritage," a late-twentieth-century U.S. phenomenon that anthropologists are increasingly theorizing as part and parcel of American modernity (di Leonardo 1998; Halter 2000). Portuguese *rancho* performance, a consistent presence at "Diversity Day" festivals on New Jersey college and school campuses, Newark's Portugal Day parade, and other U.S. folklore festivals, plays into both municipal and federal ideologies celebrating ethnic difference and inclusivity.

Changes in Portuguese state emigration ideology also undergird the development of *ranchos folclóricos* in diaspora. Once seen as traitors to their homeland, Portuguese emigrants are now the object of increasing state support and attention. In numerous high-profile visits to Newark in the past ten years, Portugal's political leaders have urged Luso-Americans to fortify ties to their homeland while becoming actively engaged in America's political and civic life. Both private and public institutions in Portugal have sponsored initiatives that aim to affect this hybrid policy; U.S. naturalization campaigns are funded alongside Portuguese language schools throughout emigrant communities in the United States. Northern New Jersey's second-generation Luso-Americans have been marked by this two-pronged policy, practicing what Rumbaut and Portes term "selective acculturation." Along the lines of Rumbaut and Portes's definition, Luso-Americans in Newark exhibit a high rate of bilingualism in the second generation, balancing assimilation into mainstream American society with the retention of core values and cultural practices from their parents' native context. Given New Jersey *ranchos'* relationship to Luso-American entrepreneurs and campaigns for U.S. political participation, revivalist folklore in diaspora reflects Portugal's emigration ideology. *Rancho* performers enact a commitment to their ancestral home through the restoration and dissemination of Portuguese tradition in diaspora while basking in the success of the emigration project through association with Luso-American business leaders and their growing political clout within New Jersey.

Rancho dancing participates in a chain link of lusophone media production and consumption which strengthens and perpetuates the vitality of the Portuguese language and of Portuguese expressive culture, catalyzing communities of sentiment around the globe that can imagine themselves as an ethnic collective, despite geographical separation. New Jersey *rancho* members make use of new televisual, communications, and information technologies in order to amass repertoires, research fellow *ranchos,* and promote their own performance agendas across national and continental borders. Seeking to repair instruments, purchase costumes, and videotape live performances, New Jersey *rancho* scouts and enthusiasts travel to Portugal regularly, ensuring a constant transatlantic traffic in goods, services, and people related to the thriving revivalist folklore industry. Folklore performance links Portugal and the United States on myriad levels, offering transmigrants a way to process national, lingual, and cultural plurality through the lens of expressive tradition.

Conclusion

This project began with a simple question. Why did the number of revivalist folklore groups in Portugal rise exponentially after the Revolution of 1974? Given the dominant role folklore played within *Estado Novo* cultural policy and the burgeoning corporatist infrastructure which evolved around folklore performance, one might assume that once such political scaffolding dissolved, so too would *ranchos folclóricos.* As this study documents, however, just the opposite has occurred. Branco, Neves, and Lima (2001) identify post–*25 de Abril* as a "boom" period for the foundation of *ranchos folclóricos,* According to this research, 81 percent of Portugal's "traditional musical groups" were founded after 1974. What, then, explains *ranchos folclóricos'* surprising post-revolutionary vitality?

Some explain the increase in amateur musical groups as part of a general unleashing of cultural dynamism following *25 de Abril,* as music played an increased role in the dissemination of feelings and ideas within Portugal's revolutionary climate (Cardoso 1986, 47). From this point of view the post–*25 de Abril* rise of nationally acclaimed musical groups such as *Brigada Vítor Jara, Banda do Casaco,* and *Almanaque* fomented new appetites for popular music and folkloric traditions, in a distinctly post-revolutionary political register. The "revolutionary fervor" argument, however, cannot explain the sustained growth of *ranchos folclóricos* in Portugal *and* the Portuguese diaspora over the course of the last thirty years. Examining *ranchos'* rise against the backdrop of the dramatic liberalization of Portuguese society, the loss of the colonial empire, the joining of the European Union, and Portugal's 1965–80 wave of im/emigration, we can being to piece together a broader analysis of *ranchos folcloricos'* post-revolutionary adaptation, one which underscores the importance of expressive culture to identity-building projects within emigrant communities, and to localist projects spawned by Portugal's new European alignment. António Salazar's formulation of *Estado Novo* ideology, "all for the nation, the nation for all," seems oddly out of place today, considering how contemporary *ranchos folclóricos* bypass the nation in favor of localist projects of tradition gathering, imbricated in festive plans for regional promotion and economic development, and how *ranchos* in diaspora use folklore to balance competing allegiances to originary and adopted homelands. Revivalist folklore does not serve the nation in the ways it once did. Once the face of the nation, *ranchos folclóricos* now operate behind the scenes, on the margins of the nation—in the nooks and crannies of regional festivals inaugurated after *25 de Abril* to boost local economies and solidify networks of cultural kinship within Portuguese municipalities, and in the social clubs and urban parades of Portuguese emigrant communities celebrating ethnic identity within new multicultural contexts.

Ranchos folclóricos protean adaptation following *25 de Abril* illustrates how the transition to a democratic and increasingly cosmopolitan Portugal reflects both continuity and rupture with Portugal's fascist past. The *Estado Novo* regime (1926–74) co-opted revivalist folklore performance as nationalist propaganda. Contrary to the current democratic regime's seeming indifference to folklore performance, dictator António Salazar employed *ranchos folclóricos* as the ex libris of his cultural policies. *Ranchos folclóricos* emblematized the corporatist ideal for a humble, hermetic society rallied around conservative, rural values and Salazar's famous catholicist formulation of "God, family, and nation." Wrapped up in the escapist pleasures of collective festivity, *rancho* performers were meant to spend their leisure time dancing and singing, not fomenting political opinion. By forcing *ranchos* to register all rehearsals and performances, *Estado Novo* censors were also able to keep a watchful eye on disparate communities throughout the country. *Ranchos folclóricos* aided and abetted the Salazarist panopticon while creating a positive image for the country and instilling in the Portuguese a "cult of tradition."

The *Estado Novo*'s corporatist structure also advanced a nuanced sociospatial policy, one which was furthered by the performance practices of *ranchos folclóricos*. Corporatism pulverized the country into isolated micro-units of social space as a way of defusing the potential mass mobilization of political insurrection. *Ranchos* remained tied to these micro communities through affiliation with local *casas do povo*. Many *ranchos*, however, expressed cultural difference in *broad* strokes, representing a vague likeness to generalized ideas of regional differentiation. At the same time *ranchos* operated within the pulverized space of the local, they also unified these disparate local cells through the performative amalgamation of national tradition. Most *rancho* performers throughout the country dressed alike, donning infinitely reproducible folklore uniforms—the women in short skirts the color of the national flag, the men in black pants and vests. Many *rancho* repertoires also featured a generous sampling of regional songs and dances, providing a polyphonic composite of Portugal's folkloric nation.

Given the importance of *ranchos folclóricos* to Salazarist policy, many contemporary folklore troupes fight stigmatization as conservative legacies of fascism. After periods of intense nation building such as the *Estado Novo* era, very few untainted cultural forms remain for new leadership attempting to redefine the nation within a different ideological framework. Portugal's cultural patrimony has been depleted by fascism's politics of the spirit. Folklore performance has been labeled tainted goods. Portugal's democratic regime must, therefore, either "dress up" fascist-tainted popular culture, such as *fado* and folklore performance, and/or begin to reclaim wayward artists who have found fame and fortune elsewhere in order to develop an archive of expressive practices for the purposes of fashioning a new cultural image. So, where does this leave *ranchos folclóricos* in post-revolutionary Portugal? What, if any, ideological work do *ranchos folclóricos* accomplish within democratic Portugal?

Ranchos folclóricos' relative absence from the official Portuguese festivals of the 1990s illustrates the changed relationship between folklore and the nation. In the case of Lisbon 94, Portugal's national identity was strategized according to new modalities of European commonality. Becoming European in the late twentieth century meant re-staking claims to a European history, while "dressing up" infrastructure and culture so that material and expressive representations of Portuguese Europeanness were readily apparent to national and foreign publics alike. The massive renovation of the city's built environment involved battles over representation and image politics. Portugal's macrocephalic concentration of national and EEC funds for Lisbon's 1994 overhaul also had as its objective the creation of a northern European space equipped with Western-style hotel accommodations—fax hookups, parking garages, conference facilities, opera houses, retail centers—for the convenience and comfort of the discerning vacationer, multinational CEO, foreign investor, and European diplomat. In this sense, Lisbon's dressing up can be seen as an attempt to diversify Portugal's spatial offerings; highly "developed" urban space on par with industrialized Europe provides the wealthy traveler with "all the comforts of home," while Portugal's rural interior, largely unmarred by the "scars of industrialization" (Ferrão 1996), offers the traveler a window into the exotic, nineteenth-century agrarian past. Many economic analysts pin Portugal's hopes for future economic growth on the development of the service sector, particularly the area of tourism. In the past, Portugal has been characterized by the promiscuous overlapping of socio-spatial activities—industry and agriculture existing side by side, luxury housing and *bairros da lata* (communities of makeshift shacks constructed from aluminum and cardboard) abutting one another. Lisbon's attempt to upgrade its built environment can also be seen as an act of socio-spatial cleansing through segregation—achieving a tourist niche market within a unified Europe by separating the spaces of modernity from the "primitive" spaces of pre-modernity.

It follows that this process of spatial purification must include not only the built environment, but also the cultural activities that take place within the capital. As a prerequisite for festival inclusion, L94 organizers, for example, proposed that *ranchos folclóricos* "jazz up" their musical arrangements, instrumentation, and personnel according to newly Europeanized standards of cultural sophistication and emergent domestic identity. National *rancho* administrators refused to comply with such demands, leaving *ranchos* unmarked by this official articulation of Portuguese Europeanness. By upgrading the capital's cultural venues, developing urban infrastructure, and training a new class of cultural consumers, Lisbon dressed herself in the garb of European centrality while ousting *ranchos folclóricos* and their "poor theater" aesthetics from official programming.[1]

During the 1990s, as Portugal dashed from one international showcase to the next, *ranchos folclóricos* were forced to create an alternative performance sphere, what I term a "performanscape." This sphere is not circumscribed by strictly local borders in response to official culture's globalist drive—the predictable local lowbrow/international highbrow dichotomy. Instead, it draws on a transnational network of lusophone immigrants to create what Arjun Appadurai calls "communities of sentiment" (1996, 8), communities comprised of individuals across disparate locations who "begin to imagine and feel things together." This community of sentiment provides emotional purpose, cultural venues, and funding opportunities for *ranchos* to travel and perform in various hubs of lusophone immigrant settlement. Contrary to the EEC's one-time events, such as the City of Culture Programme and the Europália Festival, *ranchos'* transnational performances are created by people, often lower-middle-class immigrants, with the driving desire to build and maintain social and cultural ties across national borders.[2] The EEC's official cultural initiatives of the nineties did not mark *ranchos* in terms of aesthetic transformation, but rather accompanied the solidification of an alternative performance sphere "outside" of the one bogged down by the weighty task of strategizing Portugal's European commonality and "dressing up" its domestic image.[3] By comparing the specific contours of the official cultural "inside" that claims to celebrate the twin achievements of liberation and Europeanization with the ghosted folkloric "outside," we develop a clearer understanding of the new ideological frameworks and spatial dislocations that exert pressure on expressive culture in contemporary Portugal.

Portuguese *ranchos folclóricos* increasingly organize their own international presence, performing in hubs of Portuguese emigration such as Paris, Bordeaux, London, Frankfurt, Vienna, Brussels, Newark, New Jersey, and Fall River, Massachusetts. *Rancho Folclórico de Alenquer* recently traveled to southern France to appear in an international folklore festival staged outdoors in a national park. It was their first performance outside of Portugal. RFA members showed me the video of the trip—hours of footage documenting the bus ride through Portugal, Spain, and France, impromptu interviews with French hosts and audience members, and conversations of RFA performers and families, many of whom had never been out of the country. The one comment that RFA members kept repeating in describing what was, for many, the highlight of their folklore careers, was "*a gente foi muito bem recebida*" (we were very well received). RFA's experience of hospitable welcome paved the way for uninhibited sociability and cultural exchange, dynamics which increasingly characterize Portuguese folklore performance following *25 de Abril.* Although the French festival organizers, who had contacted RFA through INATEL and a municipal councilman in Alenquer, tried to find Portuguese-speaking emigrants to host RFA performers during their stay in France, many hosts were native French. Lucília Rodrigues and her mother, Fátima, told stories of communicating through gestures and facial expressions. Others described the feasts they were served in private homes of busy people who took the time to talk and try to understand more about Portuguese culture. After the trip, Armindo and Zé Hermínio spoke of trying to arrange a visit for a French troupe to perform in Alenquer's annual festival and trying to secure future engagements for RFA in France and Germany.

Although this is not the type of European communing the EU ministers envisioned when planning the European City of Culture initiative, RFA's visit to France prompted intense conversations about continental commonality and difference. Packed in borrowed municipal buses full of performers, their families, and friends, *ranchos* tour Europe not as official ambassadors of national culture, as they would have been under Salazar, but as global citizens caught up in the "critical cosmopolitanism" that inflects cultural practices in an age where transnational "routes" (Clifford 1997) and roving "ethnoscapes" (Appadurai 1996) upstage the nation as the primary arbiter of imagined communities (Anderson 1991) and where the notion of "cosmopolitics" theorizes a dynamic of belonging constituted by "(re)attachment, multiple attachments, or attachment at a distance" (Robbins 1998, 3). Free, albeit through targeted exclusion, from the master frame of Portugal's official European image, folklore troupes perform for foreign audiences who house *rancho* members in their private residences overnight, forming "attachments" which will be maintained at a distance through pen pal correspondence and annual festival exchanges. Portugal's *ranchos* have charted their own European circuit following in the footsteps of emigrants who traversed the continent in search of new economic horizons and who now form the base for folklore's alternative performance sphere. No longer the visualist face of the nation, having been shorn of fascist *bonitinho* and having resisted post-revolutionary pressures to "jazz up," *ranchos folclóricos* operate behind the scenes on the stages of foreign parks and the occasional Grande Place, sometimes engaging, in the words of Augusto Gomes dos Santos, differing "worlds of people."

When traveling within or beyond Portugal's borders, *ranchos folclóricos'* onstage offerings have changed since *25 de Abril.* Instead of the nationalist spectacles favored under Salazar, *ranchos* now pursue new standards of authenticity to legitimate historical recreations of distinctly local traditions. Since its official formation in 1977, the *Federação de Folclore Português* (FFP) has sought to authenticate *rancho folclórico* repertoire, costume, instrumentation, musical arrangement, and choreography by wiping clean the traces of fascist ornamentation. FFP administrators encourage *ranchos* to research local tradition through ethnographic investigation, attendance at academic conferences, and sometimes library study. This emphasis on research acts as a corrective for Salazar's neglect of formal education, where many working-class populations were kept illiterate as a means to maintain social control. At another level, FFP's authenticity campaign reflects the modernist project of collecting, classifying, and displaying rural tradition. FFP places an increased emphasis on material artifact as opposed to expressive culture as a way to insure against reinscribing the fascist abuse of the performative.

FFP administrators link ideas of authenticity to strict notions of regional differentiation. Ironically, however, the regional divisions enforced by the FFP adhere to old fascist categories of sociocultural cohesion, categories that have endured a long history of flux and instability, and which many Portuguese fault for not reflecting "true" constellations of sociocultural coherence. Over a very short period of time, Portugal has gone from an overwhelmingly agrarian economy to one concentrated in the service sector. In 1960, for example, 45 percent of the active population held jobs in the agricultural sector. By 1995 this number dropped to 10 percent, while those holding jobs in the service sector jumped to 55 percent.[4] Concomitant with these changes has been domestic migration from rural to urban areas, and continued out-migration from rural Portuguese areas to northern European and North American cities. In addition to the demographic flux caused by domestic migration away from rural regions, post-revolutionary and post-colonial Portugal has also seen a tremendous influx of Portuguese soldiers and civilians returning from Africa following the colonial wars in the 1960s, and hundreds of thousands of Africans immigrating to Portugal starting in the 1970s to escape civil unrest and poor economic conditions. Additionally, in the 1960s Portugal began developing its tourist industry, so that "in a very short span of time Portugal went from a virtually unknown country to one visited annually by millions of Europeans" (Barreto 1996b, 36). Post-revolutionary Portuguese society has been "on the move, after many decades of immobility" (Barreto 1996b, 36).

It follows that in the midst of widespread migration, European reintegration, and the establishment of a free market economy, Portuguese culture has also been newly bombarded by a host of foreign influences—Brazilian *telenovelas,* Hollywood films, Cape Verdean music, Indian cuisine, Parisian fashion, Tudor architecture, and so forth. The FFP reform of Portuguese rural tradition must be seen as a last ditch attempt to "get it right," to record an authentic agrarian past, before it is swallowed up in the vortex of Portugal's post-revolutionary shake-up. Regional and local compartmentalizing of tradition not only reveals the scientific seriousness of this undertaking (as opposed to the drive to create *fantasia* and *bonitinho* which inflected fascist folkloric invention), it also guarantees interested publics. As António Barreto points out, the fact that more and more Portuguese emigrants are settling in northern Europe insures the ability of emigrants to return home often and maintain meaningful ties to their regions of origin (Barreto 1996b).[5] Attachment to local place looms large in emigrants' drive to return home annually, and many, particularly working-class emigrants, prefer to return to an unchanged agrarian countryside reminiscent of their youth (Klimt 1992). The summer performances of *ranchos folclóricos* are integral components of immigrants' annual pilgrimages home (Santos 1994).

Carefully researched revivalist folklore performance which accentuates cultural difference at the local level also satisfies the goals of *turismo em espaço rural* (Moreira 1994), a category of rural tourism offering diversified cultural fare designed to encourage extended "tours" of the Portuguese countryside. In addition to visiting Portugal's variegated landscapes—the arid plains of the Alentejo, the majestic coastline of the Algarve, the lush, verdant hills of Trás-os-Montes—tourists can also view the distinctly heterogeneous traditions performed, classified, labeled, and displayed by reformed *ranchos folclóricos.* In anthropologist Micaela di Leonardo's (1998) terms, *ranchos folclóricos* are indeed "exotics at home," performing not national identity as was the case during fascism, but a highly complex subset of socio-spatial localisms. These domestic exotics not only serve the growing tourist industry by providing rustic tourism with various cultural niche markets, but also serve the extensive emigrant community by solidifying ties to natal home through stabilizing and affirming spatial memory.[6]

Ranchos folclóricos' cultural significance depends on the vital relationship between performance and memory which Joseph Roach (1996) theorizes as a dynamic of surrogation. When "death or other forms of departure," such as emigration, revolution, or social change, create "cavities" in the fabric of community, then culture both reproduces and recreates itself through a process of substitution (1996, 2). Surrogation, according to Roach, undergirds the very definition of performance, an activity which offers a substitute for something else that preexists it, "hence flourish the abiding yet vexed affinities between performance and memory, out of which blossom the most florid nostalgias for authenticity and origin" (1996, 3–4). *Ranchos folclóricos'* post-revolutionary adaptation to new social and political circumstance—through repertoire and costume reform, through folklore's increasing role within local processes of social bonding and economic development and transnational processes of acculturation and identity building—involves both concerted forgetting and strategized remembering. The transformation of folklore performance emerges not simply as backlash to the *Estado Novo*'s invention of tradition, but as a process of substitution which fills the "cavities" created by Portugal's social liberalization, wide-scale im/emigration, and transnational realignment. Revivalist folklore has survived and flourished because, in the way that theatrical expression makes possible, *rancho* performers have stepped into new social and performative roles throughout countless Portuguese localities and outposts of Portuguese migration around the globe.

A recent celebration of Portugal Day at New Jersey governor James McGreevey's mansion illustrates the role of *rancho* performers as cultural surrogates in the production of local origins and transnational belonging for a diasporic audience of Portuguese emigrants. The June 6th, 2004, program featured performances by Newark's *Rancho Folclórico 'A Eira'* as well as *fado* performances by local Luso-American musicians. The celebration's grand finale, however, was reserved for a *rancho folclórico* that had flown in from Portugal especially for the event. As the emcee made clear, this troupe, the *Grupo Folclórico e Etnográfico da Vimieira,* had been chosen in honor of Mrs. Dina Matos McGreevey, the first lady of New Jersey, whose family had emigrated from the Vimieira region. After twenty minutes of performance and a round of hearty applause, the troupe's director approached the microphone with a basketful of gifts. Dina Matos McGreevey left her perch beside political dignitaries and uniformed members of the Portuguese American Police Association to receive the gifts—municipal flags, a brass plaque, local delicacies—mementos from her originary home across the sea. Dressed in peasant garb, the *rancho* director beamed at the audience, relating stories of Mrs.

McGreevey's largesse in donating funds for public works projects in the Vimieira region. "We are so proud of Dina," the *rancho* director said within a "hometown girl makes good" narrative, as the elegant first lady bowed her head to receive the compliment, giving the *rancho* performer heartfelt *beijinhos*—small kisses on either cheek. The visit of the Portuguese *rancho* was a homecoming of sorts—the symbolic integration of local Portuguese origins and new emigrant horizons, brokered and enacted by thirty adults and children performing the songs and dances of nineteenth-century peasants.

APPENDIX

Musical Notation of Select *Modas* from the Repertoire of the *Rancho Folclórico de Alenquer*

Bico e Tacão

♩. = 120
Vocalist
accordion doubles voice and chords
Accordion
Cana
Bilha
Reco-reco
3
D
A
A7
Voc.
Bi - co e ta - cão com o pé no chão bi - co e ta - cão com o
Acc.
Cana
Bilha
(scrape)
Reco-reco
(scrape)

D
A
Voc.
pé no ar
bi - co e ta - cão mas que
lin - da mo - da,
Acc.
Cana
Bilha
(scrape)
Reco-reco
A7
D
A
Voc.
bi - co e ta - cão pa - ra
eu bai - lar.
Vá
lá não custa es - ta
é no bi cooe ta -
Acc.
Cana
Bilha
(scrape)
(scrape)
Reco-reco

13
D
A
1.
Voc.
mo - da, não vi - ra nem ro - da mas me - lhor não há Só
cão, e pre - cis - so alen - cão na po - si - cão do pé
Acc.
Cana
Bilha
Reco-reco
(scrape)
(scrape)
2. 16
D
repeat form 3 times
D
A7
D

Carreirinhas Marcadas
♩. 120
C
Accordion
Cana
Bilha
Reco-reco
G7
C
Accord.
(scrape)
G7
C
(scrape)
(scrape)

G7
C
Accord.
Cana
Bilha
Reco-reco
(scrape)
(scrape)
G7
C
Accord.
Cana
Bilha
Reco-reco
(scrape)
(scrape)
G7
C
Accord.
Cana
Bilha
Reco-reco
(scrape)
(scrape)

G7
C
Accord.
Cana
Bilha
Reco-reco
(scrape)
(scrape)
G7
C G7 C
Accord.
play 3x
Cana
Bilha
Reco-reco
(scrape)

Carreirinhas Valseadas

Contradança
Accordion
C
G7
C
Acc.
G9
C
G7
Acc.
C G7
G7
C G7 C
Acc.
C G7
C
G7
Acc.
1.
C
2, 3.
G7 C
G7
C G7 C
from first repeat 3 times

Corridinho Serrano

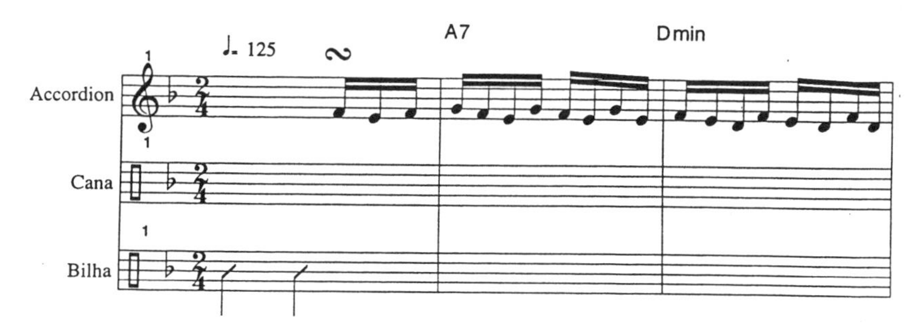

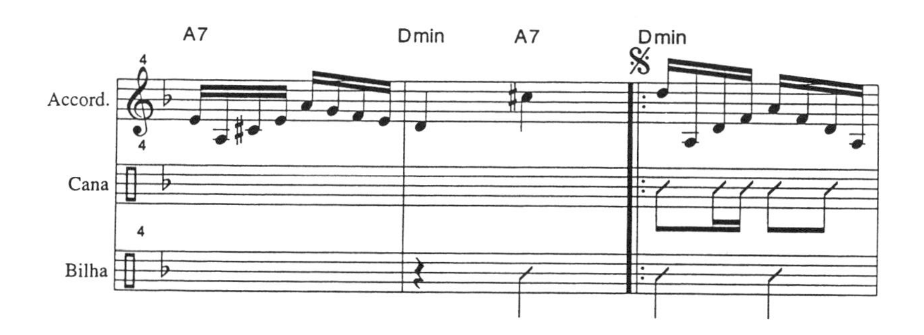

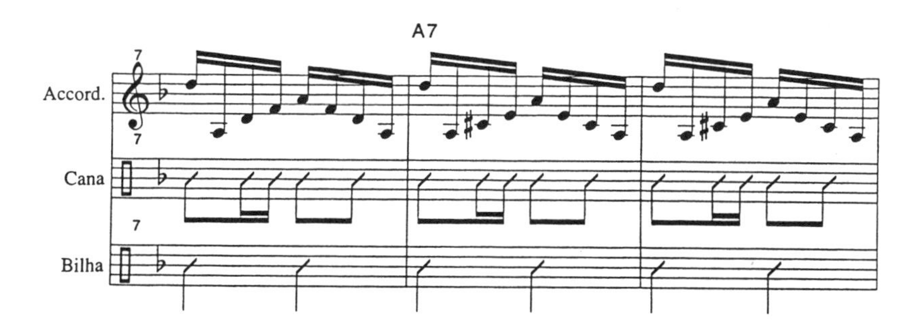

Dmin
10
Accord.
10
Cana
10
Bilha

A7
1.
Dmin
12
Accord.
12
Cana
12
Bilha

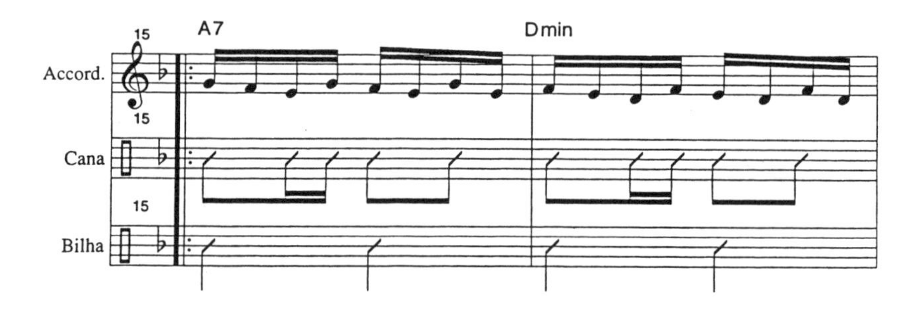
15
A7
Dmin
Accord.
15
Cana
15
Bilha

17
A7
1.
Dmin
Accord.
Cana
Bilha

19
2.
Accord.
Cana
Bilha

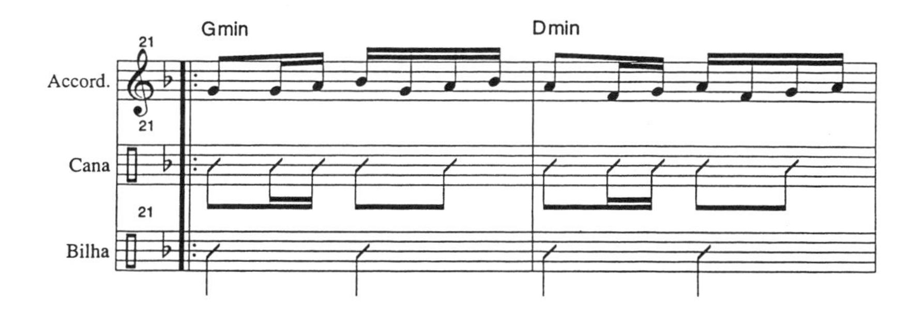
21
Gmin
Dmin
Accord.
Cana
Bilha

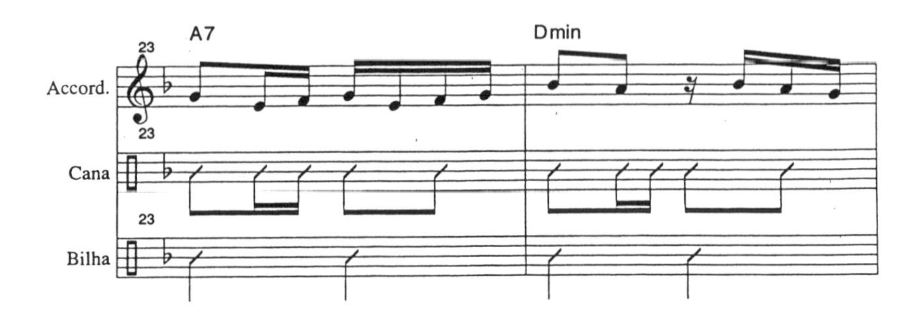
A7
Dmin
23
Accord.
23
Cana
23
Bilha

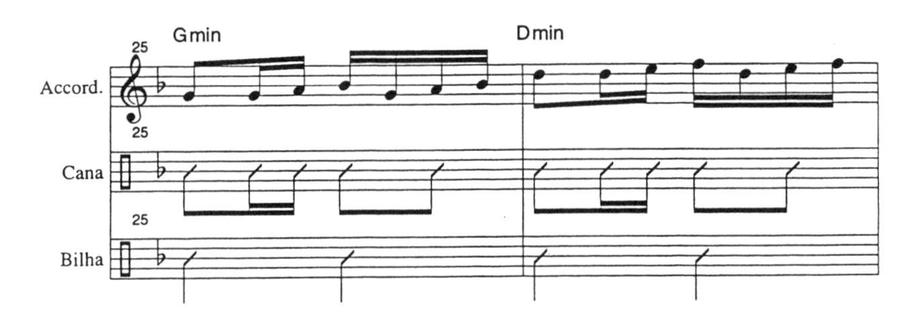
Gmin
Dmin
25
Accord.
25
Cana
25
Bilha

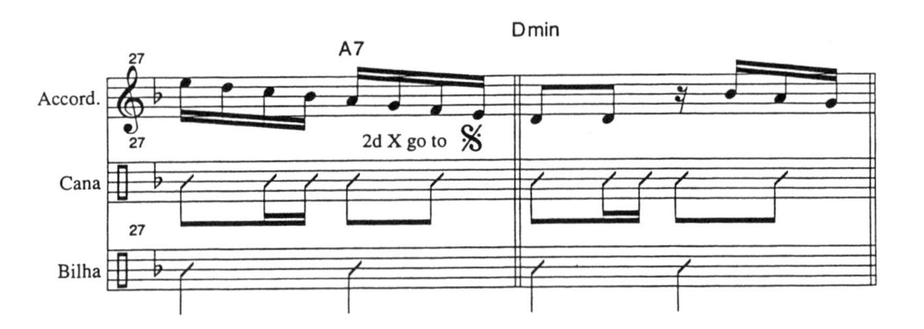
Dmin
A7
27
Accord.
27
2d X go to
Cana
27
Bilha

29
Accord.
29
Cana
29
Bilha

A7
31
Accord.
31
Cana
31
Bilha

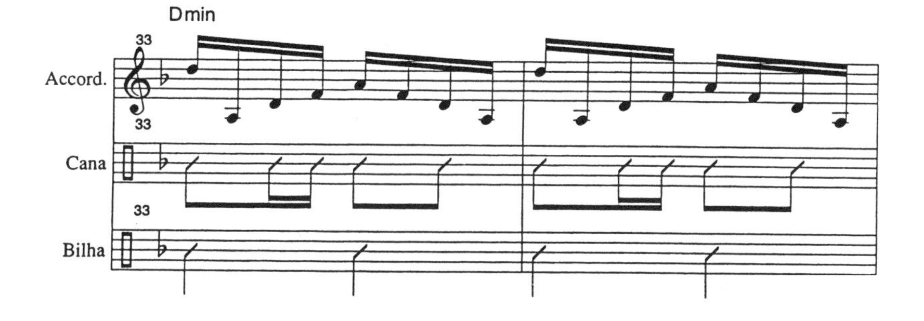
Dmin
33
Accord.
33
Cana
33
Bilha

A7
Key Change
35
Accord.
35
Cana
35
Bilha

Fmin
37
Accord.
37
faster
Cana
37
Bilha

C7
39
Accord.
39
Cana
39
Bilha

Fmin
41
Accord.
41
Cana
41
Bilha

C7
43
Accord.
43
Cana
43
Bilha

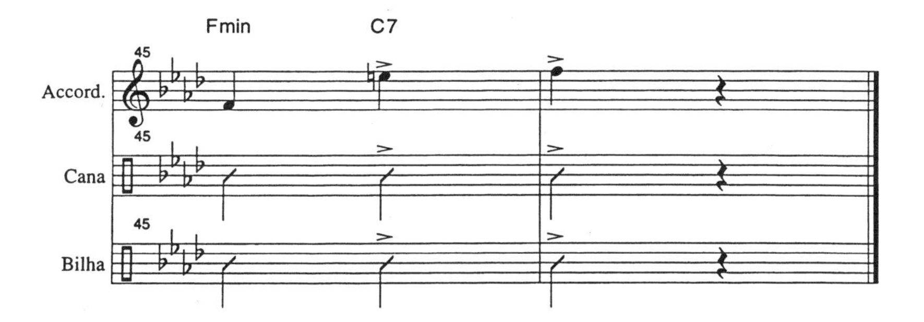
Fmin
C7
45
Accord.
45
Cana
45
Bilha

Moda a Dois Passos

Moda do Caçador
♩.. = 85
Vocalist
Accordion
D
Emin
D
A7
(Accordion embellishes melody with rhythmic chording and arpeggios)
Voc.
Acc.
D
Ai se ou - vires as - so - bi -
A7
D
ar, ai, não julguesque é ca - ça - dores,
1.
2.
A7
D
ai, an - da agora mui - to em mo - da,
A7
D
as - so - biar aos a- mores.
Ai, que for -

2.
Ai, tia Anica venha cá,
ai, desça abaixo ao seu jardim,
ai, venha ver o caçador,
que está só a olhar para mim.

Chorus

3.
Ai, caçador que vai a caça,
ai, não vai só pelas perdizes,
ai, mata coelhos e lebres,
tambem mata codernizes.

Chorus

Ó Ai ó Linda
♩.= 140
Vocalist
Accordion
Ó aí ó
Voc.
Acc.
lin - da a mo- da do bai - la - ri - co, foi na quar - ta e veio na
lin - da eu con- he - ço o meu a - mor,— pelos ca - di - lhos da
(v. 2)
quin -ta, foi na quar- ta e veio na quin - ta. Ó ai ó cin - ta. A mo -
cin- ta, pelos ca - di - lhos da
1.
da do bai- la - ri - co, não tem na- da que sa-ber, É an- dar com um pé no ar, e out-ro
no chão a ba- ter A mo - no chão a ba- ter Ó ai ó
2.

3.
15
Voc.
no chão a ba - ter.
15
Acc.

Paródia
♩. = 120
Cmin
G7
Cmin
tr
Accordion
G7
Cmin
Acc.
G7
Cmin
Acc.
Cmin
G7
1.
Cmin
Acc.
2.
Acc.
play 4x from 𝄋

Tanto Vira que Revira
Accordion
Accordion embellishes melody with chords and rhythmic tags
Voc.
Acc.
Dancers
D
A7
CHORUS
O nosso vira a vi - rar não vir - a como ou - tro vi - ra.
De - pois de bem re - vi - ra - do, o vi - ra tor - na a vi - rar.
Vi - ra se - mpre a re - vi - rar, tan - to vi - ra que re vi - ra par. Ai
Pró vi - ra ser bem dan - ça - do, tem de se ter um bom

3.
Não há dança portuguesa,
com mais cor de regional.
Que tenha tanta beleza,
como o vira em Portugal.

4.
Tudo vira, tudo vira,
no vira, vira quem quer,
mas para virar melhor,
só o Rancho de Alenquer.

Chorus

Verde Gaio de Alenquer
135
Vocalist
Accordion
Cana
Bilha
accordion doubles voice and chords
D
A7
Al- en -
quer tem lin - das vi - nhas nas en - cos - tas que há por lá. Al - en - quer tem lin-das vi - nhas nas en-
cos - tas que há por lá.
Pode ha - ver te - rras rai
Voc.
Acc.

2.
Há beleza sem igual,
nas tuas hortas e pomares.
(repeat)
Não há terra em Portugal,
que te chegue aos calcanhares.
(repeat)

3.
Agua das tuas ribeiras,
fazem da terra um tesouro.
(repeat)
Onde o sol encontra leiras,
cheinhas de trigo louro.
(repeat)

4.
Agua, fruta, pão e vinho,
são teus dotes naturais.
(repeat)
Alenquer dos meus carinhos
tu es bem melhor que as mais.
(repeat)

NOTES

Introduction

1. In his book *Modernity at Large,* Arjun Appadurai uses five terms—"ethnoscape," "mediascape," "financescape," "technoscape," and "ideoscape"—to describe global cultural flows. He employs the suffix "-scape" to emphasize the "the fluid, irregular shapes of these landscapes" and to indicate that these terms "are not objectively given relations that look the same from every angle, but rather that they are deeply perspectival constructs, inflected by the historical, linguistic, and political situatedness of different sorts of actors" (1996, 33). Conceived as the building blocks of "imagined worlds" (extending Benedict Anderson), Appadurai describes these locales as the spaces within which it is possible to "contest and sometimes even subvert the imagined worlds of the official mind and of the entrepreneurial mentality that surround them" (1996, 33).

2. Unless otherwise stated, all translations are my own.

3. In her writing on the global economy, Saskia Sassen states, "The question for me is how globalization is constituted, not just as a narrative, but in terms of concrete, often place-bound operations. Thus the narrative about globalization that is centered on the information economy and telematics is, in my analysis, a very partial and distorted representation because it leaves out a variety of elements that are part of globalization; secondly, what it leaves out tends to be overwhelmingly that which lacks power" (1996, 138).

4. The 1974 coup was directly followed by a period of revolutionary change (1974–76) where the Communist and Socialist Parties were in power. Democracy followed in fits and starts during the 1980s as revolutionary legislation was ultimately reversed.

5. Many of the nation's most promising artists, musicians, and performers, such as Helena Vieira da Silva, Emanuel Nunes, Maria de Medeiros, Paula Rego, and Joaquim de Almeida, among many others, left the country during the *Estado Novo* in search of freedom of expression and advanced training.

6. Many popular musicians, most notably *fado* diva Amália Rodrigues, experienced a "silencing" of their creative work for several months following the 1974 coup. In her autobiography, Amália states, "How did [the revolutionaries] know I was against them when the revolution occurred? They don't know anything! [After the 25th of April] People took over the newspapers and not a word was written about me. People took over the radio and my records were never played. People took over the television and I couldn't appear. But they couldn't turn the public against me . . . The public never abandoned me. But why did this happen? Why all of this hatred? I was never the Minister of anything. I've never given an order in my life" (in Santos 1987, 182).

7. *Fado,* a popular urban ballad form, provides the analysis of post-revolutionary folklore performance with an important comparative case. After 1974, an entirely new generation of *fado* vocalists has emerged, creating an international stir.

Novo Fado (new *fado*) performers such as Mísia, Teresa Salgueiro, Mafalda Arnauth, and Mariza have injected an old form with new repertoire, in some cases a new politics, and a new set of musical and lyrical stylistics.

8. I write about a similar dynamic within the flamenco performanscape (Holton 1998b).

9. Unlike Portuguese residents of northern Europe, many of whom view their immigrant status as temporary, U.S. emigrants tend not to return as regularly to Portugal and commit more permanently to life in their adopted homeland. For a detailed analysis of this dynamic, see Brettell 1986; Klimt 1992; and Baganha 1998.

10. Appadurai argues that in the last several decades diaspora has begun to "bring the force of the imagination, as both memory and desire, into the lives of many ordinary people, into mythographies different from the disciplines of myth and ritual of the classic sort. The key difference here is that these new mythographies are characters for new social projects, and not just a counterpoint to the certainties of daily life . . . For migrants, both the politics of adaptation to new environments and the stimulus to move or return are deeply affected by a mass-mediated imaginary that frequently transcends national space" (1996, 6).

11. This situation is changing, however. Ethnomusicologist Salwa El-Shawan Castelo Branco, who founded and heads the ethnomusicology master's program at the Universidade Nova de Lisboa, has encouraged her graduate students to research previously neglected topics such as urban musics and revivalist traditions. She and co-editor Jorge Freitas Branco (2003) have put together a groundbreaking collection *Vozes do Povo: Folclorização em Portugal* (Voices of the People: Folklorization in Portugal). Castelo Branco is also in the midst of an extensive research project with Maria João Lima and José Soares Neves funded by a national grant to analyze questionnaire responses from all of Portugal's thousands of *ranchos*.

12. Independent of the activities of revivalist folklore troupes, Dias also found folklore suspect as a scholarly discipline: "The sentimental and aestheticist attitude of many amateur folklorists has created throughout the world an unfavorable atmosphere in relation to folklore . . . In many fields the folklorist is considered a mere collector, never a man of science" (1990 [1955], 74–75).

13. There are countless examples of this stereotype within the Portuguese media, scholarly journals, and literary texts. One of the most colorful incarnations is the recent cover story of *Expresso*'s "Vidas," comparing the Luso-American sheriff of Newark, Armando Fontoura, with the rough-and-tumble mobster Tony Soprano of the hit HBO series *The Sopranos*. The article, which balances a short life history of Sheriff Fontura with a portrait of Newark, New Jersey, and a depiction of how Fontoura refuses to let *The Sopranos* film in Essex County, begins like this: "It is ironic that Armando Fontoura speaks, at times, like the bandits he so dislikes. 'So, [Fontoura says], I called the mayor and asked him 'what kind of shit are they up to? We catch them shooting people, exploding cars, beating up people. Mafia land—is this how you want to be known? It's crazy, fuck it" (Jenkins 2001). The author's (rather inaccurate) portrayal of Fontoura in this opening paragraph as successful but crude and uncultured constitutes an example par excellence of the Portuguese emigrant stereotype.

14. Onésimo Almeida (2001) has written several *crónicas* which document in pleasing detail the way Luso-American cultural adaptations "play" in Portugal.

15. Augusto Gomes dos Santos of the *Federação de Folclore Português* and Henrique Rabaço of the *Instituto Nacional para o Aproveitamento dos Tempos Livres dos Trabalhadores* (INATEL) had initially recommended these six groups to me due to their reputation as "serious, quality groups," their active performance schedules, FFP affiliation, and because they were widely viewed as the most "representative" of the Estremadura and Ribatejo regions.

16. The married couple I did not interview during this round of interviews had temporarily dropped out of RFA in the early summer of 1996 due to financial problems. The single man I did not interview was ill during this period.

17. The Rutgers–Newark Ironbound Oral History Project was founded by the author in 2001 as a means to document the Portuguese-speaking population of northern New Jersey, a community which has received little scholarly attention. To date, 72 student researchers have conducted and transcribed over 150 oral history interviews with lusophone immigrants residing in northern New Jersey. These semi-structured interviews, typically 1–2 hours in duration, contain information as to the date and reasons for migration, strategies for adaptation, plans for return migration, expressive manifestations of ethnic and cultural identity in the United States, and conflict and collaboration within the Portuguese-speaking community of New Jersey, among other topics. The collection is in the process of being digitized for public access online as part of the New Jersey Digital Highway grant administered by Dana Library at Rutgers–Newark.

1. Choreographing the Spirit

1. Starting in 1881, the Ford Motor Corporation employed the theories of Frederick Taylor to create an integrated plan for worker leisure time in order to increase productivity and harmony in the workplace. These pioneering initiatives created ripples of influence throughout Europe in the early twentieth century (Valente 1999, 16).

2. José Carlos Valente (1999, 15–40) presents a detailed account of the international Joy in Work movement, and much of this paragraph draws from his historical study.

3. In 1944 the *Secretariado de Propaganda Nacional* (SPN [Secretariate of National Propaganda]) was renamed the *Secretariado Nacional de Informação* (SNI [National Secretariate of Information]). Cultural historian Heloisa Paulo asserts that "the new name [SNI] camouflages the development of an apparatus of propaganda, which became significantly more repressive and sophisticated than the modest SPN" (1994, 79). Throughout this chapter, both the terms "SPN" and "SNI" are used according to the period under discussion.

4. Heloisa Paulo employs this terminology—the "intellectual" and the "popular"—to distinguish between the SPN-sponsored museum exhibits, national ballet performances, classical music concerts, and modernist poetry soirees designed for the urban elite, and the local festivals promoting wide-scale participation in traditional music and dance geared toward Portugal's lower classes (1994, 82). In terms

of priority, however, the SPN gave more attention to the diversion and manipulation of the working classes through the restoration of tradition than to the development of modernist high culture (Pinto 1995, 195).

5. In her book *Exposicões do Estado Novo 1934–1940,* Margarida Acciaiuoli states that even before taking power, Salazar had conceived of a plan to reconstitute national architecture of symbolic importance in order to "exorcise the instituted disorder, social and economic chaos and the loss of a cohesive identity" which, in his view, characterized early twentieth-century Portugal (1998, 11).

6. In a rigorous exploration of Salazarist discourse, Daniel Melo identifies a primary discursive vector pitting the country against the city in binary opposition. Salazar conceived the city as a site of potential moral corruption, political volatility, and cultural contamination through contact with foreign products and ideas. Due to its infrastructural intertwining with industry and industrial labor, a necessary evil in the mind of economist Salazar, the city was also conceived as a site of potential dehumanization and suffering—social dynamics which could lead to the implantation of communist ideas and mobilization (2001).

7. Salwa Castelo Branco and Jorge Freitas Branco define folklorization as "The process of constructing and institutionalizing traditional performative practices constituted from fragments of generally rural popular culture with the objective of representing the traditions of a locality, region, or nation" (2003, 1).

8. In a detailed analysis of the processes of political demobilization, António Costa Pinto (1995, 171–204) outlines how corporatist structures were designed to create a society without conflict. The *Estado Novo*'s singular political party, the National Union, legitimated "the new regime and its 'exclusion' of activist candidates [and] was important as an instrument for the 'political channeling' of local notables rather than the masses . . . [It] was a state agency responsible both for the 'integration' of local elites and broad political 'demobilization' " (Pinto 1995, 191–92).

9. I have used my own translations of the Portuguese edition of Ferro's book (1982) when I found the English translation (1939) lacking.

10. The rooster is one of Portugal's national symbols.

11. The following villages were selected as semifinalists in the 1938 Most Portuguese Village Contest: Vila Chã and Bucos from the Minho province; Alturas do Barroso and Lamas do Olo from Trás-os-Montes e Alto Douro; Boassas and Merujal from Douro Litoral; Almalaguez and Colmeal from Beira Litoral; S. Julião de Cambra and Manhouce from Beira Alta; Paul and Monsanto from Beira Baixa; Aljubarrota and Oleiros from Estremadura; Azinhaga and Pego from Ribatejo; N.S. da Orada and S. Bartolomeu do Outreiro from Alto Alentejo; Peroguarda and Salvada from Baixo Alentejo; and Alte and Odeceixe from Algarve.

12. Daniel Melo assigns a strategic and symbolic importance to the jury's choice of Monsanto, arguing that the village's geographic proximity to Spain and its history as a "vigilant sentinel for Portugal" make it a natural choice; for, "behind the official appeal to nationalist sentiment" on the part of the judges "resides the need to fortify [national] cohesion within an environment of instability brought on by the Spanish Civil War" (2001, 222–23).

13. For more on the importance of reviving the handicrafts movement as an alternative to industrial labor structures, see Melo 2001, 176–86.

14. For a detailed account of the collection of painters, sculptors, and designers who created a unique visual style for the large-scale initiatives organized by Ferro, see Acciaiuoli 1998.

15. The inaugural ceremony of the 1940s World Exhibition in Lisbon featured live performances by "a *rancho* from the Minho province, older hooded performers from Monsanto, choral groups from Baixa-Alentejo, cowboys on horseback, and a marching band" (Acciaiuoli 1998, 171).

16. Due to FNAT indexing systems which sometimes conflate the categories of "*Grupos folclóricos*" and "*Casas do Povo*" in their records, it is difficult to determine the exact number of folklore troupes affiliated with FNAT between 1943 and 1949. Valente (1999, 140) suggests combining the two categories, given that FNAT "sources don't always distinguish between the two." Adding six registered folklore troupes to nineteen registered *Casas do Povo* brings the possible total to twenty-five.

17. For a detailed account of Minho's mythic identification in nineteenth- and twentieth-century discourse of various generic persuasions, see Medeiros 1995.

18. In 1954, the year of the *Feira*'s consolidation, only three local *ranchos* existed: Vila Chã de Ourique (founded in 1936 in preparation for the Most Portuguese Village Contest), the *rancho* in Coruche (1944), and the *rancho* in Azinhaga (1948). Over the course of the next three years, the *Feira do Ribatejo,* which promised to highlight the public folklore competition, inspired the formation of eight more *ranchos*—several of which were created in short order at the behest of a *Feira* organizer (Ferrão 1991, 1–2).

19. Viana believed that "pure invention" was only justified in those regions which "lack history and links to regional tradition"—namely urban centers like Lisbon (1954, 12).

20. For a case study documenting the *Rancho Folclórico do Porto*'s transposition of turn-of-the-century music into higher keys, see Melo 1990.

21. Many *ranchos folclóricos* list competitive festival first and second place awards on official group stationary. Other material vestiges of *Estado Novo* folklore competitions still constitute onstage features of post-revolutionary *rancho* identity. During the "Marcha da Entrada" (Entrance March), where *ranchos* approach the stage in a long procession, the first performer often carries a long pole decorated with multicolored ribbons. Ribbon color signified competitive placement (first place, second place, etc.) during the *Estado Novo.* Today ribbons are given to all *ranchos* who participate in varying performance venues, and the ribbon pole functions more as a marker of *rancho* longevity than competitive value.

22. The only exception is the province of Minho, which Ribas breaks down into four subgroups. Minho is known as the "capital of Portuguese folklore" and as such has received a disproportionate amount of scholarly attention. Intense ethnomusicological and dance research of Minhotan traditions over the last century has produced an impressive amount of scholarly documentation, thus explaining these sub-categories.

23. Armindo Rodrigues and José Hermínio Carvalho, who together decide upon the selection and sequence of performance material, speak of this process in terms of narrative, plot, and pace. Diversity of choreography, meter, melody, *recolha* date, and region all inform repertoire selection.

24. Even though RFA ostensibly represented the *concelho* of Alenquer and the *província* of Estremadura, the group drew its performance repertoire freely from other regions throughout Portugal. This trans-regional amalgamating of folkloric tradition also occurs in many *ranchos* comprised of Portuguese migrants residing abroad whose purpose is not to recover the specificity of region but, rather, the entirety of nation. See, for example, Andrea Klimt's (1992) doctoral dissertation on Portuguese migrants living in Germany. For an example of this dynamic in the Mexican context, see Olga Ramírez's (1989) discussion of folklore performance in the 1920s and 1930s. She states, "In building a Mexican national identity, caution had to be exercised not to alienate the various ethnic groups and sectors of society. Therefore, an emphasis was placed on acknowledging diversity within the Mexican nation through some of its regional folk practices . . . Folk dance offered one means through which various ethnic groups could be superficially recognized and thus incorporated into the dominant Mexican hegemonic order" (1989, 19).

25. Salwa Castelo Branco and Jorge Freitas Branco outline the history of Minho's *traje à vianesa* (Viana peasant woman costume), fashionable in the 1920s among Portugal's upper classes and worn during occasions such as masked balls. In subsequent decades the costume gained in popularity, acquiring the status of "national representation, particularly abroad" (Branco and Branco 2003, 5). The Viana folklore costume, splashed across the pages of countless tourist brochures, emblematizes the colorful festivity targeted by Salazar's propagandistic initiatives. When I first approached José Hermínio Carvalho about working with his group, he chuckled and asked in disbelief, "*Mas porquê o nosso grupo tão pobrezito? É melhor estudar os grupos do Norte, do Minho onde há folclore riquíssimo!*" (But why our poor little group? It would be better for you if you study the groups from the North, from Minho where there is incredibly rich folklore!) José Hermínio employs the word rich in all its multivalence—northern folklore is rich in terms of ethnographic resources, local monetary support, and in terms of symbolic opulence as manifest in the women's lush red and gold archetypal costumes. Further, Elisabeth Cabral, director of the Museum of Popular Art, states, "The women located [in regions] . . . closest to the sea polychromize and complicate their wardrobe. There the blend of colors is perfect, alive in hue and animated with a play of tones. And among all the coastal zones the richest [costume] exists . . . in the region of Viana do Castelo" (1991, xv). The keywords—rich, alive, color, animated, and play—extracted from Cabral's and Hermínio's testimony also relate to Salazar's cultural policy, which promoted folklore performance as the festive spectacle designed to offset an austere quotidian existence. The *traje à Vianesa*, featuring mostly bright red, royal blue, and gold with decorative embroidery and *barras*, or stripes, bordering the skirts, has been reproduced and sold in tourist shops throughout Portugal and abroad. The appealing design has come to emblematize Portuguese folklore and was widely "cited" in *rancho folclórico* costumes throughout the country during the *Estado Novo*.

26. See Daniel Melo's historical study of Lisbon's *marchas populares* (2003).

27. Daniel Melo's historical study affirms the link between *marchas* and *rancho* formation during the *Estado Novo* (2001, 193).

28. On November 8, 1997, I attended the Conference on Portuguese Culture and the Portuguese-American Experience at the University of Massachusetts–Dartmouth. This conference was attended by many local Luso-American residents, business professionals, secondary school teachers, retirees, and high school students. One panel of Luso-American politicians launched an acerbic verbal attack on the Luso-American community (particularly those in New Bedford who represent a sizable ethnic majority) for not voting. Following the panel presentations, a heated debate ensued among spectators, where recently immigrated Luso-Americans reminded the panelists (all of whom were second or third generation) of the devastating effects of living under fascism. An older Luso-American language teacher from New York State said, "I vote, but I do not begrudge those immigrants who cannot. We were brainwashed for forty-eight years, we were not allowed to speak, we were not allowed to write, we were not allowed to cast a vote. We are the victims of oppression and need to be re-educated." The language teacher sat down amid vigorous applause. A Massachusetts representative responded, "This is no excuse. We Portuguese were lucky to have such a benevolent dictator. Think of the Nazis. Now that's oppression." I believe the gulf in their respective views can be chalked up to differences in experiential levels of processing authoritarianism. These differences also affect one's comfort level when participating in or discussing organized politics. Even voting, an ostensibly anonymous gesture in the United States, is a charged activity and one which, according to the conference panel, many Luso-Americans avoid.

29. According to Armindo Rodrigues (1996a, 1996b), after the Revolution, the *rancho* split into two political camps: those who supported the *Partido Social Democrático* (PSD) and those who supported the *Partido Comunista Português* (PCP). Both political parties had constituents in leadership positions within the *rancho;* Zé Maria, a member of the Communist Party, was rehearsal master at the time of the conflict, and Sr. Rodrigues, Armindo's father and a member of the PSD, was *rancho* president. Political disagreements rapidly turned into personal conflict and caused the resignation or temporary absence of several performers.

30. Although Alenquer performers reported no overt censorship, they did describe pervasive feelings of suspicion toward local acquaintances and even fellow *rancho* members. José Hermínio Carvalho (1996) stated that following the 1974 Revolution, as the identities of PIDE (the *Estado Novo*'s secret police) spies were revealed, the *rancho* discovered that a close friend of many performers had been a PIDE informant for decades. The local spy, who José Hermínio did not name, had been an enthusiastic supporter of the *rancho* and had attended countless performances and social functions. Perhaps this covert method of "keeping tabs" on the activities of *ranchos folclóricos* satisfied the *Estado Novo*'s need for information and control; strong-arm censorship tactics were thus deemed unnecessary. Alenquer's folklore spy was subsequently run out of town following the disclosure of his link to PIDE.

31. Other *ranchos* relied on historical or ethnomusicological texts to recreate local performance traditions (Melo 1990; Branco 1992). Still other groups, such as

the *Grupo Folclórico de Belas,* "inherited" their repertoires from local groups who had disbanded and passed along their portfolios of songs, dances, and costumes.

32. For a compelling account of the suspicion aroused by ethnographer Michel Giacometti as he traveled throughout the Portuguese countryside recording oral traditions, see Branco and Branco 2003

33. As he introduces RFA's songs and dances in performance, Crispim Luís often says "these were the *modas* your grandparents and great-grandparents danced throughout Alenquer's *casas das brincadeiras.*" Crispim Luís (1996) defines these "houses of games" as places (private residences, wine cellars, sheds, etc.) where people would gather to "have fun"—tell jokes, play cards, dance, and sing.

34. Manuel, Dulce, and others spoke often of pre-revolutionary dance training as occurring during *bailes.* These local dances attracted people of all ages and featured traditional (turn-of-the-century) choreography and music played by one or more accordionists. Sometimes events such as *valsas a prémios* (literally, "waltzes for prizes") included competition.

35. *Dançar ao desafio* is when pairs take turns presenting their best, most rapid steps. It is akin to a "dance argument."

36. For an in-depth analysis of the relationship between notions of surveillance and spectacle, see Jay's (1993) chapter "From the Empire of the Gaze to the Society of the Spectacle."

2. Battling the *Bonitinho*

1. On *25 de Abril* (April 25th), 1974, a military coup brought an end to the *Estado Novo.* Many Portuguese scholars use the date *"25 de Abril"* to refer to the Revolution. Incidentally, there is disagreement among some social scientists regarding whether *25 de Abril* can be rightly defined as a revolution. This is a lengthy and complicated debate. Generally, those who do not favor the term "revolution" conceive as the period between 1974–75 as a "revolutionary period" and define *25 de Abril* as a military "coup." Because most of the sources I draw from use both *"25 de Abril"* and "Revolution" interchangeably, this is the terminology I have adopted as well.

2. Although Portugal applied for admission to the European Economic Community in May of 1977, the EEC would not consider its application until the country had stabilized its democratic institutions. Following the reversal of the revolutionary legislature and the consolidation of a European-style parliamentary democracy, Portugal signed the Treaty of Accession into the European Community on June 12, 1985. "Democracy, a freer economy, and a European orientation were to go hand in hand" (Herr 1992, 15).

3. See, for example, Amália Rodrigues's account of this period in Santos 1987.

4. Due to the Revolution and a precipitous rise in the college-age population, October 1974 witnessed tens of thousands of incoming university students "com um vazio de um ano pelo frente" (with an empty year ahead of them) (Branco and Oliveira 1993, 9).

5. These objects later formed the foundation of the Museu do Trabalho (Labor Museum) in Setúbal.

6. This paragraph draws from the excellent two-volume study of Giacometti's *Missão*, written by Jorge Freitas Branco and Luísa Tiago de Oliveira (1993, 1994).

7. Santos formed the precursor of the FFP, *Amigos de Gaia*, in 1959. Due to the *Estado Novo*'s "unfavorable environment," however, *Amigos de Gaia* was only able to make modest gains in the guidance of folklore research and performance (Santos 1986b).

8. This tradition is still performed throughout the *concelho* of Alenquer. For a detailed discussion of the "Reis" iconography and songs in Alenquer, see Melo et al. 1991.

9. Many *ranchos* in the area surrounding the FFP *sede* (the town of Arcozelo, just south of Porto) have begun to revive regional agricultural rituals and festivals. The FFP organized a festival in Arcozelo, where *ranchos* from around the country could display not only the traditional songs, dances, and costumes of their regions (the typical fare of folkloric festivals), but also regional crafts, culinary dishes, legends, jokes, games, etc. For more on this festival, see Barbosa 1996.

10. Margarida Seromenho (2003) asserts that the FFP exerted a far greater influence in the north of Portugal due in part to the location of FFP headquarters in Vila Nova de Gaia, south of Porto. My research in Alenquer and various *concelhos* throughout Estremadura and Ribatejo, however, showed FFP to have a great degree of impact in these regions as well. Even the *ranchos* in Alenquer that did not seek or never succeeded in gaining FFP federation were keenly aware of new standards of authenticity and, with varying degrees of rigor, implemented changes in costume and repertoire.

11. INATEL's *VIII Estágio de Formação e Reciclagem de Directores e Ensaiadores de Grupos e Ranchos Folclóricos* was directed toward *rancho ensaiadores* and *directores* throughout the Distrito de Lisboa (in the province of Estremadura) and the Distrito de Setúbal (in the province of Ribatejo). There were twenty-three *rancho* leaders from both districts who attended, and another four *ranchos* (among them RFA) who participated by performing *modas* most typical of their respective *concelhos*. The program boasts two full days of classes (theoretical, historical, and practical) by academic specialists in ethnomusicology, museology, material culture, and dance anthropology. The academic classes offered were Crafts, Ethnographic Aspects of the Saloian Region, Collections and Ethnographic Museums, Conservations and Restoration of Period Dress, Creation and Organization of Folklore Groups, The Cult of the Holy Spirit in Estremadura, Popular Portuguese Dances, Popular Dances from Estremadura, Popular Dances from Ribatejo, Directing Folklore Groups, Folklore Groups and Their Social Function, Introduction to Folklore and Ethnography, The Conservation of Expressive Heritage: Games and Rounds, Popular Portuguese Literature, Comparative Ethnographic Music, Traditional Music from Estremadura, Traditional Music from Ribatejo, Research and Ethnographic Data Collection, Research and Musical Collection, Portugal: Man and Country, Popular Portuguese Theater, Tradition, Habits, and Costumes, and Popular Dress in Estremedura. The practical colloquia were Folkloric Instruction for Children, Folkloric Festivals and Shows, Folklore and Tourism, Integration of Song within Dance Spectacle, and A New Dynamic for Folklore Groups (INATEL 1992).

12. Poor economic conditions and the colonial wars in Africa sparked a new wave of Portuguese emigration in the 1960s and 1970s. Salazar maintained an ambivalent attitude toward emigration—erecting strict literacy regulations designed to limit peasant leave-taking, while simultaneously turning a blind eye to the thousands of people who left clandestinely (Brettell 1993b). Some scholars explain this ambivalence as part of a plan to stimulate remittance: "by making it difficult for women to emigrate . . . and by . . . [ignoring] the clandestine emigration of men, the state fostered familial separation and thereby ensured the flow of money back to Portugal" (Brettell 1993b, 55). Since Portugal's entrance into the EEC, there has been a clearer, more positive stance regarding emigrants. The state has focused on Portuguese emigrants living throughout the Americas, Africa, and Europe as vital to the country's semiperipheral position as global intermediary. The FFP has been instrumental in unifying emigrants around the globe in the common pursuit of folkloric revivalism (see, for example, Santos 1986a). These topics will be further elaborated in chapter 6.

13. The word *farda* (translated literally as "military uniform") is now used as a derogatory term referring to the spectacular folklore costumes worn during the *Estado Novo.* The word *traje* is used to signify the more dignified and authentic period costumes worn by "reformed" *ranchos.*

14. Taussig, following George Frazer, engages the law of similarity and the law of contact or contagion to examine the notion of the copy, in magical practice, and the ways in which it affects "the original to such a degree that the representation shares in or acquires the properties of the represented" (1993, 47–48).

15. According to Coelho's assessment of the *moda* as a *corridinho,* the title "Carreirinha" is inaccurate. *Carreirinha* is a song and dance form characteristic of the Estremadura (Ribas 1982).

16. The family of RFA president and head accordionist José Hermínio Carvalho, in fact, migrated from southern Alentejo to Alenquer in the late nineteenth century to find work. He reports that many other families from surrounding villages also moved to Alenquer during this time.

17. RFA has no record of the pre-FFP version of the "Morna" (it was not recorded on their album and no one has video footage of the *moda* performed or rehearsed). Therefore, it is difficult to judge whether this *moda* approximated the Cape Verdean *morna* in anything but title. Coelho does not volunteer an opinion on this matter in his report. He, in fact, never mentions Cape Verde in the written critique, although RFA members state that the FFP gave oral instruction on the inauthenticity of RFA's *morna* based on its association with the ex-colony. The *morna,* a popular song form known for its melancholy, garnered international interest with singer Cesária Évora's rise to the top of the world music charts in the 1990s.

18. António Reis has had a troubled past with RFA. One of the oldest members (he joined as a young boy in 1964) and widely known as the best dancer in RFA history, António Reis quit the *rancho* after a dispute with Armindo's father, who was then RFA president. A while later António was called upon to serve in the colonial wars where he was injured. After a six-year absence from RFA, several of the members invited him to return, initially as the *reco* player and then as the *cana* player. It is unclear to me why he was not invited to join again as a dancer. António is extremely

displeased with his current status as a RFA percussionist—a position traditionally given to older members who lack the vitality to dance and the skill to play accordion.

19. Chapter 4 offers a detailed examination of RFA's annual festival, which takes place during Alenquer's *Feira da Ascensão.*

20. For example, in a festival near Fátima, RFA was listed in the program and on the official poster as representing the Ribatejo, when in fact Alenquer is located within the Estremadura region. The festival organizers most likely fudged RFA's geographic description because there was already another group from Estremedura performing in the festival.

21. RFA dancers have also expressed their heightened desire during *festas* to dance as perfectly as possible, due not only to the fact that they are being paid, but also because dancers respect Dionísio's choreography.

22. For a history of cartographic revision and its effect on folklore performance, see Holton 1999. See also Girão 1933a; 1933b and Santos 1985.

23. See Gaspar's description and analysis of new regional divisions created by NUTE II (*Nomenclatura de Unidade Territorial para Fins Estatisticos*—Nomenclature of Territorial Units for Statistical Ends), which call for an amalgamation of southern Estremadura and Ribatejo in a territorial unit called "Lisboa e Vale do Tejo" (Lisbon and the Tagus Valley). This amalgamation positions Lisbon as the unifying force behind the social and economic formation of this area (1993a, 108–39). According to NUTE II's cartographic division of space, both Alenquer and Azumbuja are included in a subregion called Vale do Tejo.

3. From Intestines into Heart

1. The proliferation of *rancho* "anniversary" celebrations, which catalyze important local coalitions between business, industry, folklore groups, and local consumers, is a phenomenon addressed in chapter 4.

2. An exception to this is the democratic government's handling of abortion rights. Lisboa (2002) presents a detailed account of this national debate.

3. Caroline Brettell (1995) analyzes the way in which Portuguese immigration to France changes marital dynamics with regard to gendered segregation of leisure activities. Her research shows that couples who immigrated to France during the late 1960s ended up spending more time together, a change that many women viewed as positive. In Portugal, Brettell's study shows, men tended to spend leisure time together outside of the home, while women spent their time in the domestic space, alone or with other women.

4. The RFA *sede,* like many other *rancho sedes,* has moved from place to place throughout the group's thirty-five years of existence. In 1959, RFA first rehearsed at the *Arcada* located in the *Igreja do Epirito Santo* (Church of the Holy Spirit) alongside the river. It then moved to a space in the old school of Areal where, according to RFA dancer, João Luís Murteira (1996), *"o tecto a querer cair em cima de nós e o chão a querer cair para baixo"* (the ceiling was about to cave in on top of us and the floor fall from beneath us). In 1987, RFA moved to the town *matadouro* (slaughterhouse). In the early 1990s, after plans were announced to turn the slaughterhouse into Alen-

quer's municipal library, the *Câmara Municipal de Alenquer* (Alenquer's Mayoral Office) leased RFA their current *sede* at Forum Romeira, an old textile factory. These last two locales, though both owned by the *Câmara,* have been less provisional and more like "permanent homes," according to many *rancho* members. In both the *matadouro* and the Forum Romeira, RFA spent portions of the *rancho* budget and weeks of *rancho* labor on renovations. RFA has not paid rent for either *sede,* but is responsible for financing the utilities and maintenance of the space. Many *rancho* members report feeling proud of the space in Forum Romeira, due to its geographical centrality, the building's official association to local culture, the aesthetic history of the building, and the physical dimension and design of the *rancho sede.*

5. The Forum Romeira, built in 1872 by French engineer Phillippe Linder for Portuguese industrial baron Francisco José Lopes, is classified as an *Imóvel de Interesse Público,* or Property of Public Interest, the rough equivalent of the North American Historic Register. Refering to Forum Romeira's stature and beauty, the authors of *O Concelho de Alenquer* state, "The architectural conception of the building and its annexes impress us still today" (Melo et al. 1989, 195).

6. Appadurai defines "neighborhood" as "the actually existing social forms in which locality, as a dimension or value, is variably realized. Neighborhoods, in this usage, are situated communities characterized by their actuality, whether spatial or virtual, and their potential for social reproduction" (1996, 179).

7. This term, *amor à camisola,* literally means "for the love of the shirt." It is a phrase many RFA members use to describe their commitment to folklore performance, especially in view of the fact that this work is unpaid. Crispim Luís (1996), RFA's *apresentador,* or "announcer," explained the derivation of term: "We work in the *ranchos* for the love of the shirt, we don't earn anything, like before when soccer players didn't earn anything. Today they earn heaps of money . . . but in the olden days they also earned nothing, that's why you say, 'we will play soccer for the love of the shirt.' "

8. The first time I visited GFB's Ethnographic Museum, located on the second floor above the rehearsal space, I was told I could not use the flash on my camera, safeguarding against the potential damage to delicate antique fabrics, prints, and photographs displayed throughout the museum's impressive collection. When we got to the part of the museum where the old kitchen pottery was displayed, my guide, Sr. Constâncio, pointed out several plates and urns that had been chipped or completely shattered by the roof that had recently caved in. We both laughed at the irony of maintaining rigid rules regarding cameras in an environment which possessed far more immediate and widespread danger to the museum's collection.

9. Each *concelho* is broken down into smaller subdivisions called *freguesias.* In the *concelho* of Alenquer, for example, there are sixteen *freguesias.* RFA operates from within the *Freguesia de Triana.*

10. In descending order according to amount, RFA's 1996 budget comprised donations from the *Câmara* (specifically the *Comissão da Feira,* which organizes the *Feira da Ascensão*), donations from INATEL, donations from the *Freguesia de Triana,* donations from local businesses (particularly the construction material firm Cal-brita), proceeds from paid performances, and proceeds from the *sede* bar (RFA 1996a, 1996b).

11. I attended RFA's taping of *Música no Coração.* Following the performance, Marco Paulo, a popular music celebrity and TV personality, approached the *rancho* members and talked about local cafés, schoolteachers, and theater directors he knew during his youth in Alenquer. RFA dancer Lídia Ventura used to live next door to Marco Paulo's mother and proudly informed everyone that Marco used to baby-sit for her. These types of auspicious alliances based on localist commonality, Armindo later confided, will keep RFA thriving for many years to come. For more on Marco Paulo's career and life history, see Caseiro 1995.

12. António Dionísio was one of RFA's three founders, along with Crispim Luís (the RFA *apresentador* in 1996) and Renato Lourenço, who was the owner of Alenquer's local newspaper, *A Verdade.* António Dionísio, Renato Lourenço, and Crispim Luís have since died.

13. Incidentally, such fracturing most often occurs among neighboring groups operating from within the same *freguesia* or *concelho* due to the similarity and to some extent interchangeability of their music and dance traditions.

14. A *garraiada,* described to me as the opposite of a bullfight, is a small, informal game featuring a young bull in a ring where the bull chases the men into hiding.

15. The first year I worked with RFA, tales of group harmony and cohesion were underscored, and live evidence of conflict kept to a minimum in my presence. During the last segment of my research, however, other types of stories were offered and contention was openly expressed. I point out this sequence not because I believe one mode of representing the collectivity to be "true" and the other "false." RFA's longevity attests to the collective valuation of problem solving and accommodation, which results in a certain level of functional harmony, easily demonstrable during the initial phases of research and relationship building. Personal and political conflict, experiential elements with the potential to disrupt group durability, carry the burden of consequence and so are less readily revealed.

16. During the two years I spent with RFA, the group lost two female vocalists, gained a pair of dancers (a married couple), lost a triangle player, lost a single male dancer, and gained a young female vocalist. One female dancer was also *assistindo* (auditing) rehearsals in hopes of joining as a performer in the winter of 1997.

17. In 1996, the age range of RFA members was distributed fairly evenly from adolescents through middle age. Twenty-three percent of RFA members were between ten and twenty years old, another 23 percent were between twenty-one and thirty years old, and another 23 percent were between thirty-one and forty years old. Twenty percent of RFA members were between forty-one and fifty years old and 10 percent were fifty-one years old and above (percentage points were rounded off to the nearest whole number).

18. When viewing the entire history of the Rodrigues's RFA membership, the statistics become even more impressive. Fernando's father was RFA president in the 1970s. His mother was a dancer and his wife a dancer. His twin nephews, who performed in a neighboring *rancho,* were waiting to join RFA in 1996.

19. Fátima's twin sons, Fernando and Acácio, age nine in 1996, danced in the *Rancho Folclórico Infantil de Carregado.* At this time, RFA already had fourteen pairs of dancers. This is the limit in terms of space for dancing on stage. There were also no suitable female partners (in terms of height) for the twins in RFA. So, in the interim,

the boys performed in a neighboring group, waiting for membership turnover in Alenquer. This is a common practice among RFA families. The daughters of Fátima and Luís Santos Carvalho, Ana and Joana, also danced in a neighboring children's *rancho* in hopes of someday joining Alenquer. It is worth noting that since 1996, RFA created its own *Rancho Infantil* to accommodate all of the adult performers' children who wanted to dance, as well as a growing number of local youth seeking extracurricular activities.

20. Most RFA adults are employed as skilled laborers or in low-level service industry positions. In 1996, 20 percent of RFA members were employed as metal workers (blacksmiths, welders), 20 percent as full-time students, 13 percent as drivers (bus, truck, limousine), 10 percent as masons, 10 percent as food workers (domestic servant, cook, waiter), 7 percent as agricultural laborers, 7 percent as homemakers, one person as a merchant, and one person as a lower-level factory manager. These percentages include only those RFA members who were employed full-time in spring of 1996. One homemaker was also a part-time retail clerk, and one driver was also a part-time firefighter. At the time of this survey, one unemployed RFA member had been recently laid off as a factory assembly line worker and was actively seeking work.

As for formal education, in 1996, 82 percent of RFA members had a sixth grade education or below. Eighteen percent stayed in school beyond seventh grade. As of 1996, no one had earned a college degree, although two female high school students spoke of concrete plans to begin university study, contingent on passing the national entrance exams.

21. Although many RFA members become folklore performers due to prior familial participation, others are sought out. It is more common for single male dancers to be directly recruited due to the continual surplus of single female dancers in need of partners. António Luís Pereira (1996), who joined three years ago, had been dancing at a local wine harvesting party when he was approached by Armindo, his colleague at work. "I had a certain gift for dancing and he invited me—'Hey, come dance with us.' 'No way.' 'Yeah!' And he kept bugging me, so I went."

22. This situation changed in 2001 with the addition of Lucília Rodrigues as a member of the *rancho* administration.

23. Pires's death caused a great deal of anguish to RFA members, not only because he was a longtime friend of many performers, but also because his death was a suspected homicide. Local police investigated the case, and one of the primary murder suspects was an RFA accordionist who quit the group a year after the investigation began. Several RFA performers were called into court to testify. The case is still unsolved.

24. This term was also used by amateur choir members in Lisbon, "The word *convivência* was the term most frequently invoked when singers were asked to give a one word definition of their choir" (Cardoso 1986, 49).

4. Festival Hospitality

1. The ideology of "racial democracy" came to constitute a set of beliefs and discourses elaborated by sociologist Gilberto Freire to describe twentieth-century

Brazil as relatively free from racial prejudice (1986 [1946]). Based on assertions that Portuguese slave-owners mixed more readily with native Africans and in so doing displayed a more benign form of colonizing dominance compared to European slaveholders in North America (Harris 1964; Skidmore 1993 [1974]), this ideology also enters Portuguese discourse on race.

2. Some immigrant populations such as Lisbon's Goan community have formed their own folklore groups, performing traditions brought from their original national context (see Sardo 2003).

3. For recent studies of immigration and reception in the Portuguese context, see Vala, Brito, and Lopes 1999, Vala 1999, and Gustavo Santos 1996.

4. I have witnessed this dynamic repeatedly in Portugal. In the early nineties when I was living in Lisbon and working in a language school which taught English as a Foreign Language to employees of large companies, I often had classes comprised of adult Portuguese and Luso-African students. Initially, I was amazed at the harmony in the classroom. People of different races pairing up for dialogue practice, helping one another with writing assignments, and buying each other coffees during class breaks. One time an African woman had her car broken into during class, and six or seven Portuguese students—men and women—raced to the sidewalk to see what they could do to help. I remember thinking to myself, this is so different from the northeastern United States where I had grown up. Race really doesn't seem to be an issue here. During the subsequent years that I worked in this school, though, I came to a more nuanced understanding of the dynamics. Talking to students after class and in different social contexts, I was privy to earfuls of racist comments concerning Lisbon's newly arrived African community. Again, compared to the consistent warmth and camaraderie across race I witnessed in the classroom, this commentary seemed incongruent, revealing a gulf between attitude and comportment.

5. This *Estado Novo* interpretation was also how my Portuguese grandmother responded to my story. Although raised mostly in the United States, my grandmother would visit her Aunt Laura Rego in Lisbon annually throughout the fifties and sixties. She remembers parties in her aunt's living room, filled thick with cigarette and cigar smoke, because "no one wanted to open the windows back then."

6. In this essay, O'Neill (1991) differentiates between peasant houses, which tend to open into communal spaces, and middle-class homes, which tend to be cordoned off.

7. The trope of *desconfiança* is ubiquitous in discussions among Alenquer folklore performers and festival organizers as to the *Estado Novo*'s local legacy. For example, when Luís Rema (2002) recounted the process of trying to create the *Feira da Ascensão* in the early eighties, he stated, "The festival started timidly, I'd say, like many projects in Portugal at that time, with some mistrust . . . on the part of many people. But what is certain is that you quickly felt that a festival of this nature in present-day Portugal is fertile in many *concelhos*."

8. In Jorge Russo and Paulo Martinho's geographic analysis of Alenquer, they point to clashes between industrial enterprises, which compromise the environmental health of the landscape without providing local jobs sufficient to compensate for the "scars" left by cavernous excavation sites and riverside factories (1994).

9. The exhibitors at the 2002 *Feira da Ascensão* were divided into different categories according to types of goods and services offered. The largest number of exhibitors sold vehicles and agricultural equipment. Second were exhibitors selling construction materials or services, furniture, and decoration consultancy. Third were exhibitors selling food, beverages, and wine. Several exhibitors also represented metalwork factories, transport companies, refrigeration plants, storage facilities, gas and electricity plants, and local schools and gyms ("Expositores Presentes" 2002).

10. RFA has only recently begun to travel outside Portugal to perform and has never invited a foreign *rancho* to its anniversary festival. Armindo explains the absence of foreign invitations as resulting from several factors. When FFP president Augusto Gomes dos Santos's influence was at its peak in the 1990s, many of his favored groups throughout Portugal received foreign invitations. Because RFA's affiliation process was somewhat contentious, it became clear that RFA could not count on FFP networking to extend their horizons beyond national borders. The second reason Armindo gave centered on issues of geographical "bad luck." The fact that Alenquer is located on the border between the Estremadura and Ribatejo provinces and has also been the recipient of various nineteenth- and early-twentieth-century waves of emigration from the north and south means that Alenquerian expressive traditions reflect a hodgepodge of cultural influences. This demographic and expressive mixing is seen to taint Alenquer's regional representativity, which, Armindo believes, negatively impacts their chances at foreign invitations.

11. In cases where RFA performs at the anniversary festival of a *rancho* considered to be of inferior quality, RFA leaders do not feel compelled to invite this *rancho* to perform at the *Feira da Ascensão.*

5. "We Will Not Be Jazzed Up!"

1. Lisbon 94 did, however, sponsor several compact discs which featured traditional Portuguese music: Salwa Castelo Branco's excellent compilation *Musical Traditions of Portugal* (1994), which included recordings of *ranchos folclóricos;* an innovative CD organized by Rubem de Carvalho, which featured contemporary pop musicians performing the music of Zeca Alfonso, the "voice of the Revolution," known for his enchanting renditions of rural and urban folk music; and finally, *As Músicas do Fado,* a compact disc featuring twenty-four *fados* from varying time periods performed by many different musicians.

2. This notion of shame relates to Rui Aragão's (1985) discussion of a national "inferiority complex" in his book *Portugal: O Desafio Nacionalista:Psicologia e Identidade Nacionais*—a book which, according to its dust jacket, was "silenced" by Portuguese intellectuals due to its "bothersome and disturbing analysis of contemporary Portugal, coincident neither with the political discourse of the party in power nor with the opposition." Aragão analyzes salient features of what he views as Portugal's "collective national character," arguing that Portugal's inferior status vis à-vis other countries is due to the loss of the colonial empire and concomitant decline in the areas of art, literature, science, industry, and technology. Augusto Gomes dos Santos differs from Aragão in that he draws a distinction between the

povo (people), who take pride in Portuguese tradition, and the ruling class, who seem "ashamed" of popular culture when operating within an international context.

3. For an analysis of Portugal's modern dance movement, *Nova Dança Portugal,* as exhibited during the Europália Festival, see Lepecki 2001.

4. Filipe La Féria is a Portuguese director of musical revues—perhaps best compared to Bob Fosse in North America—known for his extravagant use of spectacle and flashy presentational choreographies.

5. Although a detailed analysis of Lisbon's 1998 International Exhibition (EXPO 98) is beyond the purview of this chapter, recent scholarship confirms the marginalization of *rancho* performance throughout its festival programming. Tim Sieber argues that

> except for rare appearances . . . folkloric music and dancing was . . . largely excluded from the Expo program, as it is associated for many with images of Portuguese backwardness and countered Expo's efforts to constitute Portugal in modern terms . . . Lisbon's *ranchos folclóricos* . . . were only added to the Expo program late in the summer, in response to consistent pressure and popular demand. (2002, 171–72)

When viewed together, *Europália* 91, Lisbon 94, and EXPO 98, international festivals dedicated to the display of Portuguese culture, all muted *rancho* performance for the purposes of highlighting Portugal's modernizing transformation.

6. See chapter 2, page 64.

7. Although the Lisbon 94 folklore production never came to fruition, *fado,* Portugal's most famous popular music, was combined with other avant-garde or high art music and dance components to similar targeted effect. In Lisbon 94's production of *AmarAmalia,* a balletic homage to world-renown *fadista* Amália Rodrigues, traditional *fado* ballads featuring acoustic guitar were interspersed with music by contemporary composer Pierre Boulez. The raw, throaty vocals of Amália, an important icon for the urban poor even after her rags to riches climb, were framed by a backdrop of sleek, metal scaffolding and sinewy dancers performing the modern dance vocabularies of Martha Graham. For an analysis of the L94 museum exhibit dedicated to *fado* at the Museu Nacional de Etnologia, see Holton 2002a.

8. By the time Portugal's application to the EEC was accepted, the majority of Portuguese were in favor of European integration. A very vocal Communist minority, however, felt the "objective of EEC integration [was] . . . an instrument for the destruction of the conquests of the Revolution" (Nataf 1995, 159).

9. In his book *The Production of Space* (1991), Henri Lefebvre outlines the general limitations of semiology as an analytical tool applied to space. Semiology, he argues, reduces space to symbolic "markings" and "traces," not taking into account that space simultaneously produces and is produced, replete with "jumbled," "multifarious," "self-contradictory," and "overlapping" instructions. He argues, however, that certain spaces are created to be "deliberately readable" and are therefore decoded as signs (1991, 140–47). I contend that SL94 produced spaces—outdoor ads, urban interventions, and the construction and restoration of cultural venues—which were "deliberately readable" for the purposes of presenting an easily dis-

cernible cultural image for Portugal. My analysis, however, also heeds Lefebvre's warning. Employing the performance paradigm, I position L94's "readable space" against the backdrop of an animated urban environment, and foreground the embodied processes of using and producing space—processes informed by the "instructions" of architectural form as well as other forces, objects, and beings.

10. Although the process of designating Cities of Culture changed in 1996, adding a competitive component to the application process, initially cities were appointed according to who volunteered and were intended to follow one another in alphabetical order (*Official Journal of the European Communities* 1985). The alphabetically ordered designation process was soon abandoned, however, as member states lobbied to combine their EEC designation with national commemorations and other international events.

11. Although forming SL94 ameliorated some of the problems between local and national officials, the process of organizing and executing L94 was fraught with partisan strife. A major bone of contention was the firing of the original French advertising firm Publicis/Ciesa (a firm with connections to rightist politics in France) and the hiring of the firm EuroRSCG (a French firm with connections to the Left). This move, to be further discussed in the present chapter, coincides with the loss of power by the PSD (Portuguese center rightist party) within SL94.

12. Teresa Rita Lopes, for example, describes Lisbon as a "haunted city" where renowned poet Fernando Pessoa "doesn't fit, not by a long shot, into the Pantheon where he is visited and glorified. We are continually greeted in the happenstance of the streets, by his welcoming shadow" (1992, 29).

13. Ironically, even Portugal's dictator António Salazar, who held tightly to possession of his colonies in an attempt to preserve long after such a practice was vehemently denounced the "Portuguese Empire" by the UN, states,

> Our country's past is full of glory, full of heroism, but what we've needed, and especially in the last hundred years has been less brilliance and more staying power, something less showy but with more perspective . . . [memories of] our pages of glorious past [make us] burn ourselves up in flames and then just relapse into melancholy fatalism . . . That's the cause for our being a sad people; we're removed from the realities of life because we're given to living in a sham heroism. (Quoted in Ferro 1939, 248)

14. Economist João César das Neves states that Portuguese economic performance, though not stagnant, was much less dynamic than that of the rest of Europe in the late nineteenth century, partially explaining the country's late industrial development. According to Neves, Portugal could not industrialize during the early twentieth century due to the world wars that ravaged Europe. Neves draws on the theories of Jaime Reis, who cites Portugal's lack of "openness," international interdependence, and exportable resources during the last half of the nineteenth century as primary components hindering Portugal's industrial development (1994, 49).

15. Portugal's Earth Party has marked many decaying buildings along the Avenida with green graffiti stating, "*Isto é um crime*" (This is a crime). According to several vendors I spoke with who operate in front of the graffiti, these messages have

decorated the Avenida for years. Many of the vendors sympathized with the Earth Party's anger at the degraded state of the Avenida, wondering why these historic buildings have been left to crumble.

16. SL94 attempted not only to democratize Lisbon's urban space and cultural offerings. According to EuroRSCG's "Estratégia de Comunicação" (Communication Strategy) handbook, the principal commercial objective for L94 publicity was to "democratize distribution" (EuroRSCG, n.d.). Augusto Gomes dos Santos, FFP president who lamented the barbed absence of folklore performance, however, would argue that L94 did not succeed in offering a democratic array of cultural fare.

17. "Heroin parkers" was the term used by my teenage neighbors in the Alfama to describe the scores of drug addicts who work amid Lisbon's impromptu parking areas. Because petty crime is on the rise in Lisbon, many new car owners fear for the safety of their automobiles. They fall prey, therefore, to a type of vehicular blackmail perpetrated by Lisbon's burgeoning class of *tóxico-dependentes* (drug addicts), who forcefully volunteer to help you maneuver into a parking space for a small fee (usually 50 to 100 escudos in 1996—roughly 60 to 75 cents). Payment of this fee also "guarantees" that your car will remain safe until you return. Implicit in this deal is that if you do not pay, you risk incurring the anger of the parkers and subsequent damage to your car.

18. Since my ethnographic research in the mid-nineties, Praça do Comércio has been cleared of cars and become the site of several high-profile sculptural exhibits and other cultural initiatives.

19. As described in Manuel Rivas's essay "África, Capital Lisboa" (1994a), Angolan and Mozambican authors, particularly Mia Couto, Pepetela, Manuel Lima, and Germano de Almeida, are widely read throughout Lisbon. Lisbon publishers edit several periodicals solely dedicated to African culture. Lisbon also boasts over twenty African discotheques and a thriving African music industry. The authors of *Lisboa Africana* describe Lisbon as the destination of countless African "immigrants, students [and] political exiles . . . who follow that Atlantic path the other way, the path which for centuries brought the Portuguese to Africa" (Rocha et al. 1993, 7).

20. Two of the most widely publicized events pertaining to Africa were the Museu Nacional de Etnologia's exhibition, entitled Escultura Angolana (Angolan Sculpture), and Paulo Ribeiro and Clara Andermatt's collaborative dance piece, *Dançar Cabo Verde.*

21. This explicit comparison of Lisbon to other Western cities was sharply reflected in an ER publicity campaign, which ran the following double-page ads throughout Portugal's print media: "London is the place for watching the changing of the guards. For good theater, change your place to Lisbon." Or, "In Paris you will find the great names in fashion, in Lisbon the great names of concerts." Or, "To get to know actors, there is no place like Los Angeles. But to get to know cinema, Lisbon is better" (EuroRSCG n.d.).

22. The construction of both these buildings ran over budget and consistently behind schedule. The buildings were initially planned to open in 1992, but instead opened in smaller phases starting in mid-1993. L94 was consequently the forum for their complete unveiling as fully functioning cultural mega-centers.

23. The Museu de Chiado, French architect Jean-Michele Wilmotte's restoration of the old Museu Nacional de Arte Contemporânea, also received ample media attention and very favorable reviews.

24. Aníbal Cavaco Silva of the center rightist party, PSD, served as Portugal's prime minister during the conception, organization, and execution of L94.

25. In two essays entitled "A Vergonha" and "Para Nossa Vergonha," Rogério Martins (1993) catalogs a variety of economic and social indicators to underscore Portugal's "shameful" underdevelopment vis-à-vis the rest of Europe.

26. The erasure of workers' bodies is even more ironic in light of Portugal's high incidence of work-related deaths, one per every business day in 1995, according to official statistics ("Acidentes de Trabalho" 1995). Several construction workers literally gave their lives to Lisbon's renovation.

6. Dancing along the In-between

1. This shift is also reflected in the official language used to describe new governmental departments post-1974. What used to be called the Secretary of the State of Emigration (Secretaria de Estado da Emigração) was changed to the Secretary of the State of Portuguese Communities (overseas) (Secretaria de Estado das Comunidades) (Baganha 2001; Feldman-Bianco 1992).

2. As in Portugal, many New Jersey folklore performers move from *rancho* to *rancho* throughout the course of their performance careers. Reasons for leaving a *rancho* can include personality conflicts with fellow performers or *rancho* directors, a desire to join friends, spouses, or other family members in a neighboring *rancho,* or geographical relocation. Several of the performers I interviewed had been members of other groups, including the *Rancho Folclórico Roca-á-Norte* of Newark, New Jersey, and the *Rancho Folclórico Barcuense* of Newark, New Jersey, before joining their current *rancho.* It is also important to note that the Portuguese Ironbound neighborhood located in Newark's East Ward acts as a central nucleus for the Luso-American community of northern New Jersey as a whole. Many families who moved from Newark to neighboring towns of Kearny, Harrison, Belleville, and Elizabeth regularly return to the Ironbound to buy groceries, go to church, do their banking, or patronize cafés and restaurants. For now, Newark's Ironbound remains the heart of northern New Jersey's Portuguese community, even as residence fans out into wider swathes of the city's Metropolitan Statistical Area.

3. For an excellent study on the settlement patterns and social dynamics of the Portuguese community in Canada, see Teixeira 1999.

4. Feldman-Bianco argues that during the 1920s and 1930s the Portuguese state viewed emigrants as "second class citizens" and traitors to their country for having left (1992, 146–47). Other scholars document widespread social stigmatization of Portuguese emigrants upon returning home throughout the twentieth century (Brettell 2003; Cole 1991). Although the economic success of the emigrants in mid- to late twentieth century made the state dependant on the remittances of the Portuguese abroad, this symbiosis did little to lessen the migrants' difficult reentry into Portugal for holidays or retirement: "they are still pejoratively called 'French,' 'Canadian,' 'Brazilians,' 'Americans' " (Feldman-Bianco 1992, 150).

5. For more on the history of Newark and the evolution of the Ironbound section, see Rae-Turner and Koles 2001 and Cunningham 1988.

6. There is a feeling among many CCP representatives that the Portuguese government has not used the emigrant think tank to its fullest potential. Hoping to augment the visibility and political influence of Portuguese communities in diaspora, select CCP members have even proposed the creation of the *Partido do Emigrante* (Emigrant Party) in order to secure elected seats for emigrants in the Portuguese Parliament. See, for example, Fernando Santos 2002a and "Conselho das Comunidades Portuguesas," *Luso-Americano* 2003. For more on CCP's history, see "Com Onze Tarefas para Cumprir," *Luso-Americano* 1997.

7. Portuguese-American communities are particularly important elements in this plan because unlike Portuguese communities in France and Germany, whose migratory leave-taking is consistently framed as "temporary" (Klimt 1992), Portuguese immigrants in the United States tend to reside permanently in their host country. For a comparative analysis of European state involvement among their emigrant populations, see Vicente 1999.

8. Maria Baganha and Pedro Góis argue that northern Europe basically reversed its "open door" policy with regard to immigrant laborers in the mid-1970s, "promoting the integration of previously-arrived immigrants while discouraging the arrival of new immigrant labor. In other words—permitting family reunification and prohibiting economic emigration" (1998, 235).

9. Of course, the numbers in tables 6.1, 6.2, and 6.3 do not include the large proportion of emigrants who left the country clandestinely and settled in the United States as undocumented aliens. Although there have been no systematic studies of illegal Portuguese immigration, Maria Baganha has estimated, for example, that illegal immigration to France and Germany between 1950 and 1988 comprised at least 36 percent of total immigration to those countries (Baganha 1998, 192). If we extrapolate to a U.S. context, adding data from the Ironbound Oral History Project, where close to half of the interviewees arrived in New Jersey illegally, it is clear that these official numbers do not accurately quantify the number of Portuguese living in the region.

10. Maria do Carmo Pereira (1996) has conducted an exhaustive study on the history of Portuguese business and commerce in northern New Jersey. According to her research, during the 1970s, 360 new Portuguese businesses were created, among them 56 restaurants, 37 construction companies, 40 automobile service stations, and 12 import/export retail establishments. From 1981 to 1990 there were close to double the amount of new Portuguese businesses established. Out of 691, 148 were construction companies, 44 automobile service stations, 30 restaurants, and 18 travel agencies (1996, 52–59).

11. Obviously, the extent to which the United States is a hospitable receiving context depends not only on the historical moment, but also varies according to country of origin. These variances are fully explored in the studies which comprise Rumbaut and Portes's edited volume. The attacks of September 11th and the legislation these events provoked, of course, also mitigate the ideology of multicultural pluralism, sparking a new and yet unfolding phase in the United States' approach to immigration.

12. Another factor which contributes to the dynamic of selective acculturation is the tightly knit, co-ethnic community of the Ironbound, which has a history of intergroup support and assistance. This relatively homogenous community is overwhelmingly continental (see table 6.3, for example), with a strong regional orientation toward the north of Portugal.

13. The vast majority of New Jersey *ranchos* identify themselves with the northern province of Minho. António Medeiros (1995) argues that beginning in the last half of the nineteenth century the region of Minho is imbued with mythic characteristics of primordialism, acting as a synecdoche for the nation and regional repository of national memory.

14. These *ranchos* include *Rancho Folclórico 'A Eira'* (*adulto* and *infantil*), *Rancho Folclórico Roca-ó-Norte, Rancho Infantil Aldeia Velha do Sport Club Português, Rancho Folclórico Os Camponeses do Minho do Sport Club Português, Rancho Folclórico da Casa do Minho, Rancho Infantil 'O Futuro' da Casa do Minho, Danças e Cantares de Portugal, Os Sonhos Continuam, Sonhos de Portugal, Rancho Folclórico Barcuense, Grupo Folclórico Belas Ilhas, Rancho Folclórico Raízes de Portugal, Recordações de Portugal, Rancho Infantil de Union, Rancho Folclórico da Casa do Ribatejo.*

15. Two of the second-generation interviewees had even moved back to Portugal for middle school due to their parents' fears of violence in Newark area schools, only to return to the United States later after the parents had changed their minds.

16. João Carvalho suggests that *rancho* song texts "express the patterns of behavior the community wishes to perpetuate. These are childraising, obedience to parents, courtship strategies" (1990, 39). I wish to argue that, in addition, the embodied *process* of performing in a *rancho* ensures cultural reproduction of Portuguese moral values.

17. Many interviewees described a curious duality in the discipline their parents employed. In the U.S. household, rules for socializing were much more restrictive than they were when the families traveled to Portugal for the summer. Second-generation interviewees explained that their parents were more relaxed in Portugal, because in the context of small hometown communities everyone knew each other and parents could count on neighbors to report any wrongdoing.

18. Public courtship can mean bringing the boyfriend/girlfriend to family functions and being seen with this partner in "public" (within the Portuguese community).

19. This practice cites a fictional "pseudo past," an idealized construct; for, as many anthropologists note, nineteenth- and twentieth-century women, particularly in the north of Portugal, often performed heavy agrarian labor, while men went off to war or in search of work (Brettell 1986).

20. Many historians of Portuguese immigration to the United States document high rates of female industrial labor (Taft 1969 [1923]). A recent study of immigration between 1960 and 1980 documents a trend, where university attendance is higher for Luso-American women than it is for Luso-American men (Mulcahy 2001).

21. The Portugal Day parade in Newark, organized each year by Bernardino Coutinho and his family, has exploded in popularity. What started on June 10, 1980, as a one-day event to "unify the Portuguese community" on the anniversary of Luís de Camões's death has ballooned into a week-long event with an operating budget

of $600,000 and a total spectatorship of well over half a million people (Coutinho and Coutinho 2002).

22. See, for example, "A Drumthwacket Foi Sábado 'Uma Casa Portuguesa, Com Certeza'" 2002.

Conclusion

1. The term "poor theater" was coined by Jerzy Grotowski (2002 [1968]), an experimental Polish theater director who advocated stripping performance of its ornamentation down to the bare essentials in order to release the energy of both performer and spectator.

2. As I argue elsewhere, Appadurai's notion of communities of sentiment underplays the purposefulness of these transnational coalitions. It is not through the magical effects of globalized media that distant people stumble into community. It is not by mere coincidence that these *rancho* performers and audiences read the same books and watch the same videos, but rather through deliberate and determined action (Holton 1998b).

3. In his paper "Democracy as Hatred: Accumulation, Affect, and the Rituals of State Formation in Central America," Gareth Williams states that "the question of the present, is how to address what Adorno called the 'nature of essential change in the relation between culture and organized power.'" Williams argues that this question triggers the dilemma of "how to think the present negatively, that is to say against it, when the idea of 'outside' is constantly under erasure within contemporary order" (1998, n.p.). Theorizing *ranchos'* performance sphere as existing "outside" of official EEC initiatives presupposes a "by invitation only" inside, where cultural forms are either celebrated, transformed, or silenced by the machinations of festival programming.

4. This paragraph draws heavily on statistics published in António Barreto's essay "Três Décadas de Mudança Social" (1996b).

5. In her study of Portuguese-born immigrants living in Germany, Andrea Klimt states, for example, "during the time of my fieldwork, the adamant commitment to remaining Portuguese and to returning 'home' and the resolute disdain for 'becoming German' were the means by which migrants maintained a sense of self worth in contexts of considerable denigration" (1992, 281).

6. Maintaining ties to the emigrant community also serves the Portuguese economy by aiding in the continuation of Portuguese patterns of remittance. Emigrant remittance has significantly buoyed the Portuguese economy throughout the mid- to late twentieth century (Brettell 1993b; Barreto 1996b).

WORKS CITED

"A Drumthwacket Foi Sábado 'Uma Casa Portuguesa, Com Certeza.'" 2002. *Luso-Americano,* June 5, 8.

Abu-Lughod, Lila. 1988. "Fieldwork of a Dutiful Daughter." In *Arab Women in the Field,* edited by S. Altorki and C. Fawzi El-Solh, 139–61. Syracuse, N.Y.: Syracuse University Press.

Acciaiuoli, Margarida. 1998. *Exposições do Estado Novo 1934, 1940.* Lisbon: Livros Horizonte.

"Acidentes de Trabalho Fazem 202 Mortes no Primeiro Semestre." 1995. *Luso-Americano,* October 25, 8.

Almeida, Miguel Vale de. 1996. *The Hegemonic Male: Masculinity in a Portuguese Town.* Providence, R.I.: Berghan Books.

Almeida, Onésimo Teotónio. 1991. "A Questão da Identidade Nacional na Escrita Portuguesa Contemporânea." *Hispánia* 74: 492–500.

———. 1999. "The Portuguese-American Communities and Politics: A Look at the Cultural Roots of a Distant Relationship." *Gávea-Brown* 19/20: 229–43.

———. 2001. *Viagens Na Minha Era: Dia-Crónicas.* Lisbon: Temas e Debates.

Almeida, Pedro Vieira de. 1994. "A Cor de Lisboa." *Jornal de Letras,* March 29, 9.

Almeida, Vieira de. 1974. "A Conservação e Transformação da Avenida da Liberdade." *Diário de Notícias,* December 19, 5.

Alves, Vera Marques. 1997. "Os Etnógrafos Locais e o Secretariado da Propaganda Nacional: Um Estudo de Caso." *Etnográfica* 1 (2): 237–57.

———. 2003. "O SNI e os Ranchos Folclóricos." In *Vozes do Povo: A Folclorização em Portugal,* ed. Salwa Castelo Branco and Jorge Freitas Branco, 191–205. Oeiras, Portugal: Celta.

Anacleto, Dulce. 1996. Interview by author. Audio recording. Carregado, Portugal, June 16.

Anacleto, Manuel. 1996. Interview by author. Audio recording. Carregado, Portugal, June 16.

Anderson, Benedict. 1991. *Imagined Communities: Reflections on the Origin and Spread of Nationalism.* Rev. ed. London: Verso.

Antunes, Fernando. 1994a. "Lisboa 94 (Sem Torre de Belém) 'Mete Água' na Patriarcal." *Jornal de Notícias,* February 4, 10.

———. 1994b. "Lisboa Capital da Cultura em Fevereiro." *Jornal de Notícias,* February 4, 10.

Appadurai, Arjun. 1990. "Topographies of the Self: Praise and Emotion in Hindu India." In *Language and the Politics of Emotion,* ed. Catherine A. Lutz and Lila Abu-Lughod. Cambridge, U.K.: Cambridge University Press.

———. 1996. *Modernity at Large: Cultural Dimensions of Globalization.* Minneapolis: University of Minnesota Press.

Aragão, Rui. 1985. *Portugal: O Desafio Nacionalista: Psicologia e Identidade Nacionais.* Lisbon: Teorema.

Arias, Juan. 1994. "Mi Lisboa ya no Existe." *El País,* January 15, 2–3.

Arrighi, Giovanni, ed. 1985. *Semiperipheral Development: The Politics of Southern Europe in the Twentieth Century.* Beverly Hills, Calif.: Sage.

Artur, Faria. 1994. "Lisboa 94: A Despedida em Grande." *Diário de Notícias,* December 3, 31.

Augé, Marc. 1995. *Non-places: An Introduction to an Anthropology of Supermodernity.* London: Verso.

Bachelard, Gaston. 1994. *The Poetics of Space: The Classic Look at How We Experience Intimate Places.* Trans. Maria Jolas. Boston: Beacon Press.

Baganha, Maria Ioannis B. 1990. *Portuguese Emigration to the United States, 1820–1930.* New York: Garland Publishing.

———. 1998. "Portuguese Emigration after World War II." In *Modern Portugal,* ed. António Costa Pinto, 189–205. Palo Alto, Calif.: Society for the Promotion of Science and Scholarship.

———. 2001. Keynote address. Given at Race, Culture, Nation: Arguments across the Portuguese-Speaking World, conference at Brown University and University of Massachusetts–Dartmouth, March.

Baganha, Maria Ioannis B., and Pedro Góis. 1998. "Migrações Internacionais de e para Portugal: O Que Sabemos e Para Onde Vamos." *Revista Crítica de Ciências Sociais* 52/53 (November 1998/February 1999): 229–80.

Bakhtin, M. M. 1968. *Rabelais and His World.* Trans. H. Iswolsky. Cambridge, Mass.: MIT Press.

Barbosa, Rafael. 1996. "Feira Rural em Arcozelo Juntou 'Aldeias' de Todo o País." *Jornal de Notícias,* May 27, 15.

Barish, Jonas. 1981. *The Anti-theatrical Prejudice.* Berkeley and Los Angeles: University of California Press.

Barreto, António. 1992. *Os Silêncios do Regime: Ensaios.* Lisbon: Editorial Estampa.

———. 1996a. "O Panorama das Gentes e Sociedades." *Semanário Económico,* April 19, 27–33.

———. 1996b. "Três Décadas da Mudança Social." In *A Situação Social em Portugal, 1960–1995,* ed. António Barreto, 35–60. Lisbon: Instituto de Ciências Sociais, Universidade de Lisboa.

Barreto, António, and Clara Valadas Preto. 1996. "Indicadores da Evolução Social." In *A Situação Social em Portugal, 1960–1995,* ed. António Barreto, 61–162. Lisbon: Instituto de Ciências Sociais, Universidade de Lisboa.

Barrow, Clyde W., ed. 2002. *Portuguese-Americans and Contemporary Civic Culture in Massachusetts.* Dartmouth, Mass.: Center for Portuguese Studies, University of Massachusetts–Dartmouth.

Barthes, Roland. 1988. *The Semiotic Challenge.* Trans. Richard Howard. New York: Hill and Wang.

Behar, Ruth. 1995. "Introduction: Out of Exile." In *Women Writing Culture,* ed. Ruth Behar and Deborah A. Gordon, 1–29. Berkeley and Los Angeles: University of California Press.

Behar, Ruth, and Deborah A. Gordon, eds. 1995. *Women Writing Culture.* Berkeley and Los Angeles: University of California Press.

Ben-Amos, Dan. 1994. Foreword to *Folklore and Fascism: The Reich Institute for German Volkskunde,* by Hannjost Lixfled, ix–x. Bloomington: Indiana University Press.

Bennett, Tony, Pat Buckridge, David Carter, and Colin Mercer, eds. 1992. *Celebrating the Nation: A Critical Study of Australia's Bicentenary.* St. Leonards, Australia: Allen and Unwin.

Bloemraad, Irene. 2002. "The North American Naturalization Gap: An Institutional Approach to Citizenship Acquisition in the United States and Canada." *International Migration Review* 36 (1): 193–228.

Boal, Augusto. 1985. *Theatre of the Oppressed.* Trans. Charles A. and Maria-Odilia Leal McBride. New York: Theater Communications Group.

Bourdieu, Pierre. 1977. *Outline of a Theory of Practice.* Trans. Richard Nice. Cambridge, U.K.: Cambridge University Press.

———. 1984. *Distinction: A Social Critique of the Judgement of Taste.* Trans. Richard Nice. Cambridge, Mass.: Harvard University Press.

Braga, Isabel. 1994. "A Grande Surpresa Foi o Público." *Público,* December 14, 2–3.

Branco, Jorge Freitas. 2003a. "Carlos M. Santos (1893–1955): Folclorizador num Tempo Madeirense." In *Vozes do Povo: A Folclorização em Portugal,* ed. Salwa Castelo Branco and Jorge Freitas Branco, 447–51. Oeiras, Portugal: Celta Editora.

———. 2003b. "Uma Cartilha Portuguesa: Entre Militância Cultural e Doutrinação Política." In *Vozes do Povo: A Folclorização em Portugal,* ed. Salwa Castelo Branco and Jorge Freitas Branco, 233–43. Oeiras, Portugal: Celta Editora.

Branco, Jorge Freitas, and Luísa Tiago de Oliveira. 1993. *Ao Encontro do Povo I: A Missão.* Oeiras, Portugal: Celta Editora.

———. 1994. *Ao Encontro do Povo II: A Colecção.* Oeiras, Portugal: Celta Editora.

Branco, Salwa El-Shawan Castelo. 1989. "A Etnomusicologia, a Política e Acções Culturais na Música Tradicional em Portugal." In *Estudos em Homenagem a Ernesto Veiga de Oliveira, 85–100.* Lisbon: Instituto Nacional de Investigação Científica.

———. 1991. "Cultural Policy and Traditional Music in Portugal since 1974." In *Music in the Dialogue of Cultures: Traditional Music and Cultural Policy,* ed. Max Peter Bauman, 95–107. Wilhelmshaven, Germany: Florian Noetzel Verlag.

———. 1992. "Safeguarding Traditional Music in Contemporary Portugal." In *World Music: Musics of the World: Aspects of Documentation, Mass Media and Acculturation,* ed. Max Peter Baumann, 177–90. Wilhelmshaven, Germany: Florian Noetzel Verlag.

———. 1994. Liner notes. *Musical Traditions of Portugal,* 3–76. Smithsonian Folkways SF40435.

———. 2000. *Voces de Portugal.* Madrid: Akal, Músicas del Mundo.

Branco, Salwa El-Shawan Castelo, and Jorge Freitas Branco, eds. 2003. *Vozes do Povo: Folclorização de Portugal.* Oeiras, Portugal: Celta Editora.

Branco, Salwa El-Shawan Castelo, José Soares Neves, and Maria João Lima. 2001. "Representações da Memória: Primeiros Resultados do Inquérito aos Grupos de Música Tradicional em Portugal." *OBS, Publicação Periódica do Observatório das Actividades Culturais* 10 (December): 11–22.

Branco, Salwa El-Shawan Castelo, and Maria Manuela Toscano. 1988. "'In Search of a Lost World': An Overview of Documentation and Research on the Traditional Music of Portugal." *Yearbook for Traditional Music* 20: 158–92.

Brett, David. 1996. *The Construction of Heritage.* Cork: Cork University Press.

Brettell, Caroline B. 1986. *Men Who Migrate, Women Who Wait: Population and History in a Portuguese Parish.* Princeton, N.J.: Princeton University Press.

———. 1993a. "An Essay on Representation in Portuguese Ethnography." In *Portuguese Studies in International Perspective,* ed. E. de Sousa Ferreira and M. Villaverde Cabral, 242–65. Lisbon: CEDEP.

———. 1993b. "The Immigrant, the Nation, and the State in Nineteenth- and Twentieth-Century Portugal: An Anthropological Approach." *Portuguese Studies Review* 2 (2): 51–65.

———. 1995. *We Have Already Cried Many Tears: The Stories of Three Portuguese Migrant Women.* Prospect Heights, Ill.: Waveland Press.

———. 2003. *Anthropology and Migration: Essays on Transnationalism, Ethnicity and Identity.* Walnut Creek, Calif.: AltaMira Press.

Brito, Joaquim Pais de. 1982. "O Estado Novo e a Aldeia mais Portuguesa de Portugal." In *O Fascismo em Portugal: Actas do Colóquio, Faculdade de Letras, 511–32.* Lisbon: Regra.

———. 1991. "A Taberna: Lugar e Revelador da Aldeia." In *Lugares da Aqui: Actas do Seminário "Terrenos Portugueses,"* ed. Brian Juan O'Neill and Joaquim Pais de Brito, 167–99. Lisbon: Publicações Dom Quixote.

Buenaventura, Enrique. 1970. "Theater and Culture." Trans. Joanna Pottslitzer. *The Drama Review* 14, 2 (Winter): 151–56.

Burke, Peter. 1992. "We, the People: Popular Culture and Popular Identity in Modern Europe." In *Identity and Modernity,* ed. Scott Lash and Jonathan Friedman, 293–308. Oxford: Blackwell.

Cabral, Elisabeth. 1991. "O Trajo Popular: Texturas Perdidas do Nosso Quotidiano." In *Como Trajava o Povo Português,* xiv–xv. Lisbon: INATEL.

Cabral, João de Pina. 1986. *Sons of Adam, Daughters of Eve: The Peasant Worldview of Alto Minho.* Oxford: Clarendon Press.

———. 1989. "Sociocultural Differentiation and Regional Identity in Portugal." In *Iberian Identity: Essays on the Nature of Identity in Portugal and Spain,* ed. Richard Herr and John H. R. Polt, 3–18. Berkeley and Los Angeles: University of California Press.

———. 1991a. "A 'Minha' Casa em Paço: Um Estudo de Caso." In *Lugares de Aqui,* ed. Brian Juan O'Neill and Joaquim Pais de Brito, 120–40. Lisbon: Publicações Dom Quixote.

———. 1991b. *Os Contextos de Antropologia.* Lisbon: Difel.

Cardoso, José Maria Pedrosa. 1986. "O Papel Social de um Coro Amador da Area de Lisboa." *Associação Portuguesa de Educação Musical Boletim* 48: 44–50.

Cardoso, Tony. 2003. Interview by author. Audio recording. Newark, N.J., February 13.

Carlson, Marvin. 1989. *Places of Performance: The Semiotics of Theatre Architecture.* Ithaca, N.Y.: Cornell University Press.

Carriço, Manuela. 1989. "Visita Técnica ao Rancho Folclórico de Alenquer," Departamento do Conselho Técnico. Unpublished report, May 16, 1–2.

Carsten, Janet, ed. 2000. *Cultures of Relatedness: New Approaches to the Study of Kinship.* Cambridge, U.K.: Cambridge University Press.

Carvalho, Fátima Santos. 1996. Interview by author. Audio recording. Canados, Portugal, July 1.

Carvalho, João Soeiro de. 1990. "Ranchos Folclóricos: A Strategy for Identity among Portuguese Migrants in New Jersey." Master's thesis, Columbia University.

Carvalho, José Hermíno. 1996. Interview by author. Audio recording. Alenquer, Portugal, May 22.

Carvalho, Paul Archer de. 1995. "De Sardinha a Salazar: O Nacionalismo entre a Euforia Mítica e a Formidável Paranóia." In *Do Estado Novo ao 25 de Abril,* 79–123. Coimbra: Instituto de História e Teoria das Ideias, Universidade de Coimbra.

Caseiro, Carlos. 1995. *Marco Paulo: Na Estrada da Minha Vida.* Lisbon: Talento, Lda.

Castells, Manuel. 1989. *The Informational City.* Oxford: Blackwell.

Cerqueira, Joseph. 2002. Interview by author. Kearny, N.J., October 23.

———. 2003. Interview by author. Audio recording. Kearny, N.J., December 18.

Certeau, Michel de. 1984. *The Practice of Everyday Life.* Berkeley and Los Angeles: University of California Press.

Clifford, James. 1988. *The Predicament of Culture: Twentieth Century Ethnography, Literature and Art.* Cambridge, Mass.: Harvard University Press.

———. 1997. *Routes: Travel and Translation in the Late Twentieth Century.* Cambridge, Mass.: Harvard University Press.

Clifford, James, and George Marcus, eds. 1986. *Writing Culture: The Poetics and Politics of Ethnography.* Berkeley and Los Angeles: University of California Press.

Coelho, Bertino. 1990. "Visita Técnica ao Rancho Folclórico de Alenquer: Apreciação da Parte Musical," Departamento do Conselho Técnico. Unpublished report, May 21.

Coimbra, Rui. 1990. *Portugal.* Trans. Elizabeth Plaister. Florence: Casa Editrice.

Cole, Sally. 1991. *Women of the Praia: Work and Lives in a Portuguese Coastal Community.* Princeton, N.J.: Princeton University Press.

———. 1995. "Ruth Landes and the Early Ethnography of Race and Gender." In *Women Writing Culture,* ed. Ruth Behar and Deborah A. Gordon, 166–85. Berkeley and Los Angeles: University of California Press.

"Com Onze Tarefas para Cumprir: Conselho das Comunidades Portuguesas Reune em Lisboa de 8 a 13 de Setembro." 1997. *Luso-Americano,* June 25, 3.

Conquergood, Dwight. 1985. "Performing as a Moral Act: Ethical Dimensions of the Ethnography of Performance." *Literature in Performance* 5: 1–13.

———. 1991. "Rethinking Ethnography: Towards a Critical Cultural Politics." *Communication Monographs* 58: 179–94.

———. 1992. "Life in Big Red: Struggles and Accommodations in a Chicago Polyethnic Tenement." In *Structuring Diversity: Ethnographic Perspectives on the New Immigration,* ed. Louise Lamphere. Chicago: University of Chicago Press.

"Conselho das Comunidades Portuguesas: Reunião Amanhã e Sexta-Feira em Mass. Prepara Plenário de 26 a 28 de Junho." 2003. *Luso-Americano,* June 4, 4.

Constâncio, Vítor. 1994. "Lisbon, Cultural Capital of Europe: A Meeting Point of Cultures." *Lisbon 94 Official Programme.*

Coutinho, Bernardino, and Alberto Coutinho. 2002. Interview by Vanessa Marie Monteiro. Audio recording. Rutgers–Newark Ironbound Oral History Project, Newark, N.J., October 14.

Coutinho, Isabel. 1994. "Programação, Público, Números." *Público,* June 27, 28–29.

Cruz, Ana Bela Martins da. 1994. "O Olhar da Véspera." *Diário de Notícias,* February 26, 32.

Cruz, Manuel Braga da. 1988. *O Partido e o Estado no Salazarismo.* Lisbon: Presença.

———. 1992. "National Identity in Transition." In *The New Portugal: Democracy and Europe,* ed. Richard Herr, 151–62. Berkeley and Los Angeles: University of California Press.

Cunningham, John T. 1988. *Newark.* Newark, N.J.: New Jersey Historical Society.

Currais, Daisy. 2004. Interview by Diane Ruivo Currais. Audio recording. Rutgers–Newark Ironbound Oral History Project, Newark, N.J., November 10.

Cutileiro, José. 1971. *A Portuguese Rural Society.* London: Clarendon Press, Oxford.

DaCosta, Sónia. 2001. Interview by Maria DaSilva. Audio recording. Rutgers–Newark Ironbound Oral History Project, Kearny, N.J., April 16.

DaMatta, Roberto. 1992. *Carnivals, Rogues, and Heroes: An Interpretation of the Brazilian Dilemma.* Notre Dame, Ind.: University of Notre Dame Press.

Davis, Susan G. 1986. *Parades and Power: Street Theater in 19th Century Philadelphia.* Philadelphia: Temple University Press.

Debord, Guy. 1994 [1977]. *The Society of the Spectacle.* Trans. Don Nicholson-Smith. New York: Zone Books.

Deleuze, Gilles, and Félix Guattari. 1987. *A Thousand Plateaus: Capitalism and Schizophrenia.* Minneapolis: University of Minnesota Press.

Derrida, Jacques. 2000. *Of Hospitality: Anne Dufourmantelle Invites Jacques Derrida to Respond.* Stanford, Calif.: Stanford University Press.

Deutsche, Rosalyn. 1996. *Evictions: Art and Spatial Politics.* Cambridge, Mass.: MIT Press.

Dias, Jorge. 1970. "Da Música e da Dança como Formas de Expressão Espontâneas Populares aos Ranchos Folclóricos." *Colóquio* 2: 3–14.

———. 1990 [1955]. "Etnologia, Etnografia, Volkskunde e Folclore." *Estudos de Antropologia,* 65–80. Lisbon: Imprensa Nacional.

Dionísio, Eduarda. 1993. *Títulos, Acções, Obrigações: Sobre a Cultura em Portugal, 1974–1994.* Lisbon: Salamandra.

Douglas, Mary. 1995 [1966]. *Purity and Danger: An Analysis of the Concepts of Pollution and Taboo.* London: Routledge.

Drewal, Margaret Thompson. 1992. *Yoruba Ritual: Performers, Play, Agency.* Bloomington: Indiana University Press.

Duncan, James, and David Ley. 1993. "Introduction: Representing the Place of Culture." *Place/Culture/Representation,* 1–21. London: Routledge.

Enzensberger, Hans Magnus. 1989. *Europe, Europe: Forays into a Continent.* New York: Pantheon Books.

Escobar, Arturo. 1998. "Discourses of Place: From Globalization to Post-development." Paper presented at the Center for Humanities lecture series, Wesleyan University, November 12.

EuroRSCG. n.d. "Estratégia de Comunicação." Unpublished promotional handbook.

"Expositores Presentes na Feira 2002." 2002. *Feira da Ascensão XXI Edição.* Alenquer: Câmara Municipal de Alenquer.

Falassi, Alessandro, ed. 1987. *Time Out of Time: Essays on the Festival.* Albuquerque: University of New Mexico Press.

Federação de Folclore Português (FFP). 1978. "Estatutos." *Diário da República,* June 12, 54–55.

Feijó, Rui Graça. 1989. "State, Nation, and Regional Diversity in Portugal: An Overview." In *Iberian Identity: Essays on the Nature of Identity in Portugal and Spain,* ed. Richard Herr and John H. R. Polt, 37–47. Berkeley and Los Angeles: University of California Press.

Feldman-Bianco, Bela. 1992. "Multiple Layers of Time and Space: The Construction of Class, Ethnicity, and Nationalism among Portuguese Immigrants." In *Towards a Trans-national Perspective on Migration: Race, Class, Ethnicity and Nationalism Reconsidered,* ed. Nina Glick-Schiller et al., 145–74. New York: New York Academy of Sciences.

Feldman-Bianco, Bela, and Donna Huse. 1998. "The Construction of Immigrant Identity." In *Portuguese Spinner: An American Story,* ed. Marsha McCabe and Joseph D. Thomas, 60–73. New Bedford, Mass.: Spinner Publications.

Ferrão, Humberto Nelson de Jesus. 1991. "Folclore e Turismo: Limites Estruturais e Ideológicos no Ribatejo e em Portugal." In *Primeiro Congresso Internacional de Folclore.* Lisbon: INATEL.

Ferrão, João. 1996. "Três Décadas de Consolidação do Portugal Demográfico." In *A Situação Social em Portugal, 1960–1995,* ed. António Barreto, 165–90. Lisbon: Instituto de Ciências Sociais, Universidade de Lisboa.

Ferreira, Ana Paula. 1997. "Reengendering History: Women's Fictions of the Portuguese Revolution." In *After the Revolution: Twenty Years of Portuguese Literature, 1974–94,* ed. Helena Kaufman and Anna Klobucka, 219–42. Lewisburg, Pa.: Bucknell University Press.

Ferreira, Cristina, and Isabel Braga. 1994. "No Reino da Descoordenação." *Público,* January 27, 27.

Ferro, António. 1939. *Salazar: Portugal and Her Leader.* Trans. H. de Barros Gomes and John Gibbons. London: Faber and Faber.

———. 1940. "Exposição Mundial." *Diário de Notícias,* July 3.

———. 1982. *Salazar: O Homem e a Sua Obra.* Lisbon: Edições Fernando Pereira.

Figueiredo, António de. 1976. *Portugal: Fifty Years of Dictatorship.* New York: Holmes and Meier.

Foucault, Michel. 1973. *The Order of Things: An Archaeology of the Human Sciences.* New York: Vintage Books.

———. 1980. *Power/Knowledge: Selected Interviews and Other Writings.* Ed. Colin Gordon. New York: Pantheon Books.

Franklin, Sarah, and Susan McKinnon, eds. 2002. *Relative Values: Reconfiguring Kinship Studies.* Durham, N.C.: Duke University Press.

Freire, Gilberto. 1986 [1946]. *The Masters and the Slaves: A Study in the Development of Brazilian Civilization.* Berkeley and Los Angeles: University of California Press.

Fundação Nacional Para a Alegria no Trabalho (FNAT). 1945. *Dez Anos de Alegria no Trabalho.* Lisbon: FNAT.

———. 1958. *Regulamento Especial.* Compiled by the Gabinete de Etnografia, 1–4. Lisbon: pamphlet of regulations pertaining to *ranchos folclóricos.*

Gallagher, Tom. 1983. *Portugal: A Twentieth Century Interpretation.* Manchester, U.K.: Manchester University Press.

Garnier, Christine. 1952. *Férias com Salazar.* Lisbon: Edições Fernando Pereira.

Gaspar, Jorge. 1990. "Portugal between Centre and Periphery." In *The World Economy and the Spatial Organization of Power,* ed. Arie Shachar and Sture Öberg, 219–32. Aldershot, U.K.: Avebury.

———. 1993a. *As Regiões Portuguesas.* Lisbon: Ministério do Planeamento e da Administração do Território.

———. 1993b. "Geografia e Ordenamento do Território: Dos Paradigmas aos Novos Mapas." *Colóquio/Ciências* 13: 51–66.

Geertz, Clifford. 1986. "Making Experiences, Authoring Selves." In *The Anthropology of Experience,* ed. Victor Turner and Edward M. Bruner, 373–80. Urbana: University of Illinois Press.

Gillis, John R. 1994. "Memory and Identity: The History of a Relationship." In *Commemoration: The Politics of National Identity,* ed. John R. Gillis, 3–24. Princeton, N.J.: Princeton University Press.

Gilmore, David, ed. 1987. *Honor and Shame and the Unity of the Mediterranean.* American Anthropological Association 22. Washington, D.C.: American Anthropological Association.

Gilroy, Paul. 1993. *The Black Atlantic: Modernity and Double Consciousness.* London: Verso.

Girão, Aristides de Amorim. 1933a. *Esbôco duma Carta Regional de Portugal.* 2nd ed. Coimbra: Imprensa da Universidade.

———. 1933b. "Prefacio da Primeira Edição." In *Esbôco duma Carta Regional de Portugal.* 2nd ed. Coimbra: Imprensa da Universidade.

Glick-Schiller, Nina. 1999. "Transmigrants and Nation-States: Something Old and Something New in the U.S. Experience." In *Handbook of International Migration: The American Experience,* ed. Charles Hirschman, Philip Kasinitz, and Josh DeWind, 94–119. New York: Russell Sage.

Goffman, Erving. 1959. *The Presentation of Self in Everyday Life.* New York: Anchor Books.

Graça, Fernando Lopes. 1973 [1953]. *A Canção Popular Portuguesa.* Mem Martins, Portugal: Publicações Europa-América.

Gramsci, António. 1971. *Selections from the Prison Notebooks.* Trans. and ed. Quentin Heare and Geoffrey Nowell Smith. New York: International Publishers.

Grogan, Paul S., and Tony Proscio. 2001. *Comeback Cities: A Blueprint for Urban Neighborhood Revival.* Boulder, Colo.: Westview Press.

Grotowski, Jerzy. 2002 [1968]. *Towards a Poor Theater.* New York: Routledge.

Guardiola, Nicole. 1994. "Lisboa se Viste de Gala para Ser Capital de la Cultura." *El País,* January 4, 22–23.

Hall, Stuart. 1981. "Notes on Deconstructing 'The Popular.'" In *People's History and Socialist Theory,* ed. Raphael Samuel, 227–40. London: Routledge.

Halter, Marylin. 1993. *Between Race and Ethnicity: Cape Verdean American Immigrants, 1860–1965.* Champaign-Urbana: University of Illinois Press.

———. 2000. *Shopping for Identity: The Marketing of Ethnicity.* New York: Schocken Books.

Handelman, Don. 1990. *Models and Mirrors: Towards an Anthropology of Public Events.* Cambridge, U.K.: Cambridge University Press.

Harris, Marvin. 1964. *Patterns of Race in the Americas.* New York: Walker.

Harvey, David. 1989. *The Condition of Postmodernity: An Enquiry into the Origins of Cultural Change.* Oxford: Blackwell.

Herr, Richard. 1992. "Introduction: The Long Road to Democracy and Europe." In *The New Portugal: Democracy and Europe,* ed. Richard Herr, 1–19. Berkeley and Los Angeles: University of California Press.

Herr, Richard, and John H. R. Polt, eds. 1989. *Iberian Identity: Essays on the Nature of Identity in Portugal and Spain.* Berkeley and Los Angeles: University of California Press.

Herzfeld, Michael. 1980. "Honor and Shame: Some Problems in the Comparative Analysis of Moral Systems." *Man* 15: 339–51.

———. 1984. "The Horns of the Mediterranean Dilemma." *American Ethnologist* 11: 439–54.

———. 1987. "'As in Your Own House': Hospitality, Ethnography, and the Stereotype of Mediterranean Society." In *Honor and Shame and the Unity of the Mediterranean,* ed. David Gilmore, 75–89. American Anthropological Association 22. Washington, D.C.: American Anthropological Association.

Hobsbawm, Eric, and Terence Ranger, eds. 1983. *The Invention of Tradition.* Cambridge, U.K.: Cambridge University Press.

Holton, Kimberly DaCosta. n.d. Unpublished field notes documenting ethnographic research on *ranchos folclóricos.* Portugal, 1994–1996.

———. 1998a. "Dressing for Success: Lisbon as European Cultural Capital." *Journal of American Folklore* 111 (440): 173–96.

———. 1998b. "Like Blood in Your Mouth: Topographies of Flamenco Voice and Pedagogy in Diaspora." *Text and Performance Quarterly* 18: 300–18.

———. 1999. "Performing Social and Political Change: Revivalist Folklore Troupes in Twentieth Century Portugal." Ph.D. dissertation, Northwestern University.

———. 2002a. "Bearing Material Witness to Musical Sound: Fado's L94 Museum Debut." *Luso-Brazilian Review* 39 (2): 107–24.

———. 2002b. "Diaspora Dances: Performing Portuguese Folklore in Newark, New Jersey." Paper presented at the Society of Dance History Scholars, Philadelphia, June.

———. 2003. "Post-colonial Conflict and Community in a US Urban Enclave: Brazilian and Portuguese Immigrants in Newark, NJ." Paper presented at the Oral History Association annual meeting, Bethesda, Md., October.

INATEL (Instituto Nacional para Aproveitamento dos Tempos Livres dos Trabalhadores). 1991. *Como Trajava O Povo Português.* Lisbon: INATEL.

———. 1992. "VIII Estágio de Formação e Reciclagem de Directores e Ensaiadores Grupos e Ranchos Folclóricos." Unpublished program for regional folklore retreat, Oeiras, Portugal, November 9–21.

Ironbound Ties to Portugal. 1999. New Jersey Network video documentary.

James, Sharpe. 2002. Keynote speech given at the "Os Lusíadas" Rutgers–Newark Portuguese American Student Association anniversary dinner, February 23.

———. 2004. Welcome statement. The official website of the city of Newark, N.J., www.ci.newark.nj.us.

Jameson, Frederic. 1991. *Postmodernism, or the Cultural Logic of Late Capitalism.* Durham, N.C.: Duke University Press.

Jay, Martin. 1993. *Downcast Eyes: The Denigration of Vision in Twentieth Century French Thought.* Berkeley and Los Angeles: University of California Press.

Jenkins, Tony. 2001. "O Xerife Que Tramou os Sopranos." *Expresso: Vidas,* February 17, 12–14.

Kaplan, Marion. 1991. *The Portuguese: The Land and Its People.* London: Viking.

Karp, Ivan, and Steven D. Lavine, eds. 1991. *Exhibiting Culture: The Poetics and Politics of Museum Display.* Washington, D.C.: Smithsonian Institute Press.

Kaufman, Helena, and Anna Klobucka, eds. 1997. *After the Revolution: Twenty Years of Portuguese Literature, 1974–94.* Lewisburg, Pa.: Bucknell University Press.

Kirshenblatt-Gimblett, Barbara. 1991. "Objects of Ethnography." In *Exhibiting Cultures: The Poetics and Politics of Museum Display,* ed. Ivan Karp and Steven D. Lavine, 386–443. Washington, D.C.: Smithsonian Institution Press.

———. 1993. Foreword to *Performing the Pilgrims: A Study of Ethnohistorical Role Playing at Plymouth Plantation,* by Stephen Eddy Snow, xi–xviii. Jackson: University Press of Mississippi.

———. 1995. "Confusing Pleasures." In *The Traffic in Culture: Refiguring Art and Anthropology,* ed. George E. Marcus and Fred R. Myers, 224–55. Berkeley and Los Angeles: University of California Press.

———. 1998. *Destination Culture: Tourism, Museums and Heritage.* Berkeley and Los Angeles: University of California Press.

Klimt, Andrea C. 1992. "Temporary and Permanent Lives: The Construction of Identity among Portuguese Migrants in Germany." Ph.D. dissertation, Stanford University.

———. 2000a. "Enacting National Selves: Authenticity, Adventure, and Disaffection in the Portuguese Diaspora." *Identities* 6: 513–50.

———. 2000b. "European Spaces: Portuguese Migrants' Notions of Home and Belonging." *Diaspora* 9 (2): 259–85.

Klobucka, Anna. 2001. "Introduction: Saramago's World." In *On Saramago,* xi–xxi. Portuguese Literary & Cultural Studies, no. 6. [Dartmouth, Mass.]: Center for Portuguese Studies and Culture, University of Massachusetts–Dartmouth.

Kuin, Simon. 1994. "Alegria no Trabalho." *Expresso,* September 24.

Lavie, Smadar, and Ted Swedenberg, eds. 1996. *Displacement, Diaspora, and Geographies of Identity.* Durham, N.C.: Duke University Press.

Leal, João. 1991. "Ritual e Estrutura Social numa Freguesia Açoriana: As Festas do Espírito Santo em Santo Antão (São Jorge)." In *Lugares de Aqui: Actas do Seminário "Terrenos Portugueses,"* ed. Brian O'Neill and Joaquim Pais de Brito, 27–47. Lisbon: Publicações Dom Quixote.

———. 2000. *Etnografias Portuguesas (1870–1970): Cultura Popular e Identidade Nacional.* Lisbon: Publicações Dom Quixote.

Lefebvre, Henri. 1991. *The Production of Space.* Trans. Donald Nicholson-Smith. Oxford: Blackwell.

Leonardo, Micaela di. 1998. *Exotics at Home: Anthropologies, Others, American Modernity.* Chicago: University of Chicago Press.

Lepecki, André Torres. 2001. "Moving without the Colonial Mirror: Modernity, Dance, and Nation in the Works of Vera Mantero and Francisco Camacho (1985–1997)." Ph.D. dissertation, New York University.

Ley, David, and Kevin Olds. 1988. "Landscape as Spectacle: World's Fairs and the Culture of Heroic Consumption." *Environment and Planning D: Society and Space* 6: 191–212.

Lisboa, Maria Manuela. 2002. "An Interesting Condition: The Abortion Pastels of Paula Rego." *Luso-Brazilian Review* 39 (2): 125–49.

"Lisboa, Que Futuro." 1994. *O Independente.* January 14, 11.

"Lisboa 94 Já Tem Campanha de Imagem." 1993. *Semanário Económico.* May 21, 39.

"Lisboa—94 Vista pelos Dinamarqueses: Os 'Dias Gloriosos' de 'Pobre Portugal.'" 1994. *Público.* September 7, 28.

"Lisboa 94: Vítor Constâncio Explicou-se na Assembleia Municipal." 1994. *Jornal de Notícias.* February 18, 10.

Lloyd, David. 1997. "Nationalisms against the State." In *The Politics of Culture in the Shadow of Capital,* ed. Lisa Lowe and David Lloyd, 173–97. Durham, N.C.: Duke University Press.

Lopes, Isabel, and João Garcia. 1994. "Lisboa Entaipada." *Expresso Nacional,* February 19, 7.

Lopes, Teresa Rita. 1992. Prefácio to *Lisboa: O Que O Turista Deve Ver—What the Tourist Should See,* trans. Richard Zenith, 17–29. Bilingual ed. Lisbon: Livros Horizonte.

Lourenço, Eduardo. 1992. *O Labirinto da Saudade: Psicanálise Mítica do Destino Português.* 5th ed. Lisbon: Publicações Dom Quixote.

———. 1994. *Nós e a Europa: Ou as Duas Razões.* 4th ed. Lisbon: Imprensa Nacional-Casa da Moeda.

Lowe, Lisa, and David Lloyd. 1997. Introduction to *The Politics of Culture in the Shadow of Capital,* ed. Lisa Lowe and David Lloyd, 1–32. Durham, N.C.: Duke University Press.

Lowenthal, David. 1994. "Identity, Heritage and History." In *Commemorations: The Politics of National Identity,* ed. John R. Gillis, 41–57. Princeton, N.J.: Princeton University Press.

Lucena, Manuel. 1979. "The Evolution of Portuguese Corporatism under Salazar and Caetano." In *Contemporary Portugal: The Revolution and Its Antecedents,* ed. Lawrence S. Graham and Harry M. Makler, 47–88. Austin: University of Texas Press.

Luís, Claudia. 1996. Interview by author. Audio recording. Alenquer, Portugal, June 27.

Luís, Crispim. 1996. Interview by author. Audio recording. Alenquer, Portugal, June 18.

MacCannell, Dean. 1976. *The Tourist: A New Theory of the Leisure Class.* New York: Schocken.

Macedo, Helder. 1990. "Portuguese Culture Today." In *Portugal: Ancient Country, Young Democracy,* ed. Kenneth Maxwell and Michael H. Haltzel, 101–106. Washington, D.C.: Wilson.

Machado, Fernando Luis. 2002. *Contrastes e Continuidades: Migração, Etnicidade e Integração dos Guieenses em Portugal.* Oeiras, Portugal: Celta Editora.

Mahler, Sarah J. 1995. *American Dreaming: Immigrant Life on the Margins.* Princeton, N.J.: Princeton University Press.

Mano, Henrique. 2003. "Martins da Cruz Defende Consulados Itinerantes." *Luso-Americano,* September 24, 8.

Marcus, George E. 1989. "Imagining the Whole: Ethnography's Contemporary Efforts to Situate Itself." *Critique of Anthropology* 9 (3): 7–30.

———. 1992. "Past, Present and Emergent Identities." In *Modernity and Identity,* ed. Scott Lash and Jonathan Friedman, 309–30. Oxford: Blackwell.

Marcus, George E., and Michael Fischer. 1986. *Anthropology as Cultural Critique: An Experimental Moment in the Human Sciences.* Chicago: University of Chicago Press.

Margolis, Maxine. 1994. *Little Brazil: An Ethnography of Brazilian Immigrants in New York City.* Princeton, N.J.: Princeton University Press.

Marinho, Rita Duarte, and Elmer E. Cornwell. 1992. *Os Luso-Americanos No Processo Político Americano: Estudo Duma Situação Concreta.* Angra do Heroismo, Portugal: Gabinete de Emigração e Apoio às Açorianas.

"Martins da Cruz Quer Luso-Descendentes Mais Envolvidas na Vida Cívica e Política." 2003. *Luso-Americano,* April 30, 9.

Martins, Maria João. 1994a. "Coliseu dos Recreios: Pintado de Fresco." *Jornal de Letras,* February 22, 16.

———. 1994b. "Do Rato ao Cais do Sodré: A Colina da Saudade." *Jornal de Letras,* March 29, 8–9.

Martins, Moisés de Lemos. 1990. *O Olho de Deus no Discurso Salazarista.* Porto: Edições Afrontamento.

Martins, Rogério. 1993a. "A Vergonha." In *O Que Fica do Que Passa,* 255–57. Porto: Edições Asa.

———. 1993b. "Para Nossa Vergonha." In *O Que Fica do Que Passa,* 282–84. Porto: Edições Asa.

Massey, Doreen. 1994. "A Global Sense of Place." In *Space, Place and Gender,* ed. Doreen Massey, 146–56. Oxford: Polity.

Mateus, Augusto, J. M. Brandão de Brito, and Vítor Martins. 1995. *Portugal XXI: Cenários de Desenvolvimento.* Venda Nova, Portugal: Bertrand.

Mauss, Marcel. 1990 [1950]. *The Gift: The Form and Reason for Exchange in Archaic Societies.* New York: W. W. Norton.

Maxwell, Kenneth, and Michael H. Haltzel, eds. 1990. *Portugal: Ancient Country, Young Democracy.* Washington, D.C.: Wilson.

Medeiros, António. 1995. "Minho: Retrato Oitocentista de uma Paisagem de Eleiçao." *Revista Lusitánia,* n.s., 13–14: 97–123.

Melo, António de Oliveira, António Rodrigues Guapo, and José Eduardo Martins. 1989. *O Concelho de Alenquer: Subsídios para um Roteiro de Arte e Etnografia.* 2nd ed. Vols. 1–3. Alenquer, Portugal: Câmara Municipal de Alenquer, Associação para o Estudo e Defesa do Património de Alenquer.

———. 1991. "Pintar e Cantar Os Reis no Concelho de Alenquer." In *O Trabalho e as Tradições Religiosas no Distrito de Lisboa,* 241–60. Lisbon: Exposição de Etnografia, Governo Civil de Lisboa.

Melo, Daniel. 2001. *Salazarismo e Cultura Popular (1933–1958).* Lisbon: Imprensa de Ciências Sociais.

———. 2003. "As Marchas Populares: A Encenação da Cidade de Lisboa." In *Vozes do Povo: A Folclorização em Portugal,* ed. Salwa Castelo Branco and Jorge Freitas Branco, 307–21. Oeiras, Portugal: Celta Editora.

Melo, Francisco Soares de. 1990. "Um Rancho Folclórico num Meio Urbano: Estudo de um Caso." Paper given at the Colóquio Modernidade e Mudança na Música em Portugal, Lisbon, December 3.

Mendes, João. 1996. Interview by author. Audio recording. Alenquer, Portugal, June 19.

Mendes, Lourdes. 1996. Interview by author. Audio recording. Alenquer, Portugal, June 19.

Mónica, Maria Filomena. 1978. *Educação e Sociedade no Portugal de Salazar: A Escola Primária Salazarista, 1926–39.* Lisbon: Presença.

Moniz, Rita. 1979. "The Portuguese of New Bedford, Massachusetts and Providence Rhode Island: A Comparative Microanalysis of Political Attitudes and Behavior." Ph.D. dissertation, Brown University.

Moreira, Fernando João. 1994. *O Turismo em Espaço Rural: Enquadramento e Expressão Geográfica no Território Português.* Lisbon: Centro de Estudos Geográficos.

Moreira, Jessica. 2003. Interview by author. Audio recording. Newark, N.J., December 15.

Morley, David, and Kevin Robins. 1995. *Spaces of Identity: Global Media Electronic Landscapes and Cultural Boundaries.* London: Routledge.

Mourinho, António. 1983. *Grupo Folclórico Mirandes de duas Igrejas (Pauliteiros de Miranda).* Braga, Portugal: Oficinas Gráficas da Livaria Cruz.

Mulcahy, Maria da Glória. 2001. "The Portuguese in the US: An Overview." Invited paper given at Race, Culture, Nation: Arguments across the Portuguese Speaking World, conference at Brown University and University of Massachusetts–Dartmouth, March.

Murteira, João Luis. 1996. Interview by author. Audio recording. Algarve, Portugal, June 29.

Musical Traditions of Portugal. 1994. Smithsonian Folkways SF40435.

Myerscough, John. 1994. *European Cities of Culture and Cultural Months, Full Report: Unabridged Version.* Glasgow: Network of Cultural Cities of Europe.

Narayan, Kirin. 1993. "How Native Is a 'Native' Anthropologist?" *American Anthropologist* 95 (3): 671–86.

Nataf, Daniel. 1995. *Democratizations and Social Settlements: The Politics of Change in Contemporary Portugal.* Albany: State University of New York Press.

Nery, Rui Vieira, and Paulo Ferreira de Castro. 1991. *History of Music.* Lisbon: Comissariado para a Europália 91.

Neves, João César das. 1994. *The Portuguese Economy: A Picture in Figures, XIX and XX Centuries.* Lisbon: University Católica Editora.

Ó, Jorge Ramos do. 1987. "Modernidade e Tradição: Algumas Reflexões em Torno da Exposição do Mundo Português." In *O Estado Novo: Das Origens ao Fim da Autarcia, 1926–59,* 2: 177–86. Lisbon: Fragmentos.

———. 1992. "Salazarismo e Cultura (1930–1960)." In *Portugal e o Estado Novo (1930–1960),* ed. Fernando Rosas, 391–454. Lisbon: Editorial Presença.

Official Journal of the European Communities. 1985. Resolution of the Ministers Responsible for Cultural Affairs (Resolution 85 C, 153/02), June 22.

Oliveira, Ernesto Veiga de. 1966. *Instrumentos Musicais Populares Portuguesas.* Lisbon: Fundação Calouste Gulbenkian.

O'Neill, Brian Juan. 1991. "Espaços Sociais e Grupos Sociais no Nordeste Transmontano." In *Lugares de Aqui: Actas do Seminário "Terrenos Portugueses,"* ed. Brian O'Neill and Joaquim Pais de Brito, 141–66. Lisbon: Publicações Dom Quixote.

Ornelas, José. 2002. "The Fascist Body in Contemporary Portuguese Narrative." *Luso-Brazilian Review* 39 (2): 65–78.

Ozouf, Mona. 1988. *Festivals and the French Revolution.* Trans. Alan Sheridan. Cambridge, Mass.: Harvard University Press.

Pap, Leo. 1981. *The Portuguese Americans.* New York: Twayne Publishers.

Paulo, Heloisa. 1994. *Estado Novo e Propaganda em Portugal e no Brasil: O SPN/SNI e o DIP.* Coimbra: Livraria Minerva.

Pedro, Álvaro. 2002. Editorial. *Revista Feira da Ascensão XXI Edição.* Câmara Municipal de Alenquer, 2.

Peixoto, Rocha. 1967 [1904]. "A Casa Portuguesa." In *Obras.* Vol. 1, *Estudos de Etnografia e Arqueologia,* 89–132. Póvoa da Varzim, Portugal: Câmara Municipal de Póvoa da Varzim.

Pereira, António Luís. 1996. Interview by author. Audio recording. Alenquer, Portugal, July 3.

Pereira, Carlos. 1996. Interview by author. Audio recording. Alenquer, Portugal, June 23.

Pereira, Maria do Carmo. 1996. "Segundo Caderno: Um Século de Actividade Comercial Portuguesa em Newark, New Jersey." *Luso-Americano,* June 7, 25–63.

Pereira, Olinda. 1996. Interview by author. Audio recording. Alenquer, Portugal, June 23.

Peristiany, John G., ed. 1965. *Honour and Shame: The Values of Mediterranean Society.* London: Weidenfeld and Nicolson.

Pessoa, Fernando. 1992. *Lisboa: O Que O Turista Deve Ver.* Trans. Maria Amélia Santos Gomes. Lisbon: Livros Horizonte.

Pestana, Maria do Rosário. 2000. "Vozes da Terra: A Folclorização em Manhouce." Master's thesis, Universidade Nova de Lisboa.

Pinto, António Costa. 1995. *Salazar's Dictatorship and European Fascism: Problems of Interpretation.* New York: Columbia University Press.

Pitt-Rivers, Julian. 1968. "The Stranger, the Guest, and the Hostile Host: Introduction to the Study of the Laws of Hospitality." In *Contributions to Mediterranean Sociology: Mediterranean Rural Communities and Social Change,* ed. John G. Peristiany, 13–30. Paris: Mouton and Co.

"Plano Director Municipal do Concelho de Alenquer." 1991. Unpublished report.

Pocinho, Paulo, Consul Geral de Portugal. 2003. Interview by author. Audio recording. Newark, N.J., February 26.

Pomar, Alexandre. 1994. "Salvo Pelo Fogo." *Expresso,* July 2, 24–27.

Pomar, Alexandre, and Miguel Portas. 1994. "Para Quebrar o Consenso." *Expresso,* September 3, 44–46.

Portela, Artur. 1982. *Salazarismo e Artes Plásticas.* Lisbon: Biblioteca Breve.

Pratt, Mary Louise. 1992. *Imperial Eyes: Travel Writing and Transculturation.* London: Routledge.

Provan, Sarah. 1994. "Lisboa 94: Europe's 1994 Cultural Capital." *Europe,* February, 30–31.

Rabinow, Paul. 1986. "Representations Are Social Facts: Modernity and Postmodernity in Anthopology." In *Writing Culture: The Poetics and Politics of Ethnography,* ed. James Clifford and George E. Marcus, 234–61. Berkeley and Los Angeles: University of California Press.

Rae-Turner, Jean, and Richard T. Koles. 2001. *Newark, New Jersey.* Charleston, S.C.: Arcadia.

Ramírez, Olga Nájera. 1989. "Social and Political Dimensions of Folklorico Dance: Binational Dialectic of Residual and Emergent Culture." *Western Folklore* 48 (January): 15–38.

Rancho Folclórico de Alenquer. n.d. "Historial." Unpublished document outlining RFA history.

———. 1985. *Rancho Folclórico de Alenquer.* Musicália C-145.

———. 1996a. "Relatório de Contas 1996." Unpublished accounting documents.

———. 1996b. "Relatório de Contas Festival Folc. 1996." Unpublished accounting documents.

———. 2001. "Rancho Folclórico de Alenquer XVIII Festival de Folclore Nacional de Alenquer, 26.05.01." Unpublished document.

Reis, António. 1996. Interview by author. Audio recording. Alenquer, Portugal, June 29.

Rema, Luís. 2002. Interview by author. Audio recording. Alenquer, Portugal, May 22.

Ribas, Tomaz. 1982. *Danças Populares Portuguesas.* Lisbon: Biblioteca Breve.

Ribeiro, Marie Rosalie Teixeira. 2000. "Presença Luso-Americana nos Estados Unidos: Um Problema de Visibilidade." Ph.D. dissertation, University of Paris–Sorbonne, Paris IV.

Riegelhaupt, Joyce Firstenberg. 1964. "In the Shadow of the City: Integration of a Portuguese Village." Ph.D. dissertation, Columbia University.

———. 1967. "Saloio Women: An Analysis of Informal and Formal Political and Economic Roles of Portuguese Peasant Women." *Anthropological Quarterly* 40: 109–26.

———. 1979. "Peasants and Politics in Salazar's Portugal: The Corporate State and Village 'Nonpolitics.'" In *Contemporary Portugal: The Revolution and Its Antecendents,* ed. Lawrence S. Graham and Harry M. Makler, 167–90. Austin: University of Texas Press.

Rivas, Manuel. 1994a. "África: Capital Lisboa." *El País,* January 15, 6.

———. 1994b. "La Resistência Toma Lisboa." *El País,* January 15, 6.

Roach, Joseph. 1995. "Culture and Performance in the Circum-Atlantic World." In *Performativity and Peformance,* ed. Andrew Parker and Eve Kosofsky Sedgwick, 45–63. London: Routledge.

———. 1996. *Cities of the Dead: Circum-Atlantic Performance.* New York: Columbia University Press.

Robbins, Bruce. 1998. "Introduction: Part I: Actually Existing Cosmopolitanism." In *Cosmopolitics: Thinking and Feeling beyond the Nation,* ed. Pheng Cheah and Bruce Robbins, 1–19. Minneapolis: University of Minneapolis Press.

Rocha, Elza, José Eduardo Agualusa, and Fernando Semedo. 1993. *Lisboa Africana.* Lisbon: Edições Asa.

Rocha-Trindade, Maria Beatriz. 1990. "Portuguese Migration to Brazil in the Nineteenth and Twentieth Centuries: An Example of International Cultural Exchanges." In *Portuguese Migration in Global Perspective,* ed. David Higgs, 7–28. Toronto: Multicultural History Society of Ontario.

Rodman, Margaret C. 1992. "Empowering Place: Multilocality and Multivocality." *American Anthropologist* 94: 649–56.

Rodrigues, António. 1987. "Prefácio: António Ferro: Uma Modernidade Pronta a Viver." In *Obras de António Ferro: Intervenção Modernista I,* ix–xxvi. Barcelos, Portugal: Verbo.

Rodrigues, Armindo. 1996a. Interview by author. Audio recording. Camarnal, Portugal, June 18.

———. 1996b. Interview by author. Audio recording. Camarnal, Portugal, July 3.

Rodrigues, Fátima. 1996. Interview by author. Audio recording. Camarnal, Portugal, June 18.

Rodrigues, Fernando. 1996. Interview by author. Audio recording. Camarnal, Portugal, June 21.

Rosaldo, Renato. 1989. *Culture and Truth: The Remaking of Social Analysis.* Boston: Beacon Press.

Rosas, Fernando. 1986. *O Estado Novo nos Anos Trinta.* Lisbon: Editorial Estampa.

———, ed. 1990. *Portugal e o Estado Novo (1930–1960).* Lisbon: Editorial Presença.

Ruela, Rosa. 1993a. "Duzentos Mil Contos para 'Lavar a Cara.'" *A Capital,* September 1, 11.

———. 1993b. "Passa de Três Contos Vai Mostrar 'Lisboa Romântica.'" *A Capital,* September 1, 10–12.

———. 1994. "Coliseu de Mini-Saia." *Revista Visão,* February 10, 82–84.

Rumbaut, Rubén G., and Alejandro Portes. 2001a. "Conclusion: The Forging of a New America: Lessons for Theory and Policy." In *Ethnicities: Children of Immigrants in America,* 301–17. Berkeley and Los Angeles: University of California Press.

———. 2001b. "Introduction—Ethnogenesis: Coming of Age in Immigrant America." In *Ethnicities: Children of Immigrants in America,* 1–19. Berkeley and Los Angeles: University of California Press.

Russo Jorge, and Paulo Martinho. 1994. "Seminário em Planeamento Integrado: Alenquer." Unpublished report.

Sack, Robert D. 1986. *Human Territoriality.* Cambridge, U.K.: Cambridge University Press.

Sadlier, Darlene. 1989. *The Question of How: Women Writers and Portuguese Literature.* New York: Greenwood Press.

Said, Edward. 1983. "Traveling Theory." In *The World, the Text, and the Critic,* ed. Edward Said, 226–47. Cambridge, Mass.: Harvard University Press.

———. 1990. "Reflections on Exile." In *Out There: Marginalization and Contemporary Cultures,* ed. Russell Fereguson et al., 357–66. Cambridge, Mass.: MIT Press.

Samuel, Raphael. 1994. *Theatres of Memory: Past and Present in Contemporary Culture.* London: Verso.

Santos, Augusto Gomes dos. 1986a. "Apoios aos Nossos Emigrantes." *Raizes do Nosso Povo: Boletim Cultural da Federação do Folclore Português* 1 (1): 8–9.

———. 1986b. "Intróito." *Raizes do Nosso Povo: Boletim Cultural da Federação do Folclore Português* 1 (1): 5–6.

———. 1986c. "Observâncias Fundamentais para um Rancho Folclórico que se Propõe Representar a Sua Região com Base nos Usos e Costumes do Princípio deste Século." *Raizes do Nosso Povo: Boletim Cultural da Federação do Folclore Português* 1 (1): 24.

———. 1994. Interview by author. Audio recording. Arcozelo, Portugal, November 21.

———. 1996. Interview by author. Audio recording. Arcozelo, Portugal, June 24.

Santos, Boaventura de Sousa. 1993a. "O Estado, as Relações Salariais e o Bem-estar Social na Semi-periferia: O Caso Português." In *Portugal: Um Retrato Singular,* 17–56. Porto: Centro de Estudos Sociais e Edições Afrontamento.

———. 1993b. "Modernidade, Identidade, e a Cultura de Fronteira." *Revista Crítica de Ciências Sociais* 38 (December): 11–39.

———, ed. 1993c. *Portugal: Um Retrato Singular.* Porto: Centro de Estudos Sociais e Edições Afrontamento.

Santos, Brian. 2002. Interview by author. Audio recording. Kearny, N.J., May 19.

Santos, Fernando. 2002 "A Prática do Conselho das Comunidades Passará Sempre pela Capacidade de Afirmação dos Seus Membros." *Luso-Americano,* September 25, 2–3.

Santos, Gustavo Adolfo Pedrosa Daltro. 1996. "Sabiá em Portugal: Imigrantes Brasileiros e a Imaginação da Nação na Diaspora." Monografia de Conclusão de Curso, Centro de Estudos de Migrações Internacionais, UNICAMP.

Santos, José António. 1985. *Regionalização: Processo Histórico.* Lisbon: Livros Horizonte.

Santos, Vítor Pavão dos. 1987. *Amália: Uma Biografia.* Lisbon: Contexto.

Sapega, Ellen W. 1995. "Aspectos do Romance Pós Revolucionário Português: O Papel da Memória na Construção de um Novo Sujeito Nacional." *Luso-Brazilian Review* 32: 31–40.

———. 1997. "No Longer Proud and Alone: Notes on the Rediscovery of the Nation in Contemporary Portuguese Fiction." In *After the Revolution: Twenty Years of Portuguese Literature, 1974–94,* ed. Helena Kaufman and Anna Klobucka, 168–86. Lewisburg, Pa.: Bucknell University Press.

Sardo, Susana. 1988. "O Papel do Grupo Folclórico (Federado) no Contexto da Música Popular Portuguesa." *Associação Portuguesa de Educação Musical, Boletim* 58: 58–59.

———. 1990. "O Rancho Folclórico em Portugal e Seu Suporte Institucional." Paper given at the Colóquio Modernidade e Mudança na Música em Portugal, Lisbon, December 3.

———. 2003. "Cantar em Português: O Papel da Música na Reconstrução da Identitidade Goesa." In *Vozes do Povo: A Folclorização em Portugal,* ed. Salwa Castelo Banco and Jorge Freitas Branco, 579–97. Oeiras, Portugal: Celta Editora.

Sarkissian, Margaret. 2000. *D'Albuquerque's Children: Performing Tradition in Malaysia's Portuguese Settlement.* Chicago: University of Chicago Press.

Sassen, Saskia. 1996. "Identity in the Global City: Economic and Cultural Encasements." In *The Geography of Identity,* ed. Patricia Yeager, 131–51. Ann Arbor: University of Michigan Press.

Schechner, Richard. 1985. *Between Theater and Anthropology.* Philadelphia: University of Pennsylvania Press.

———. 1993. *The Future of Ritual: Writings on Culture and Performance.* London: Routledge.

Schmitter, Philippe C. 1975. *Corporatism and Public Policy in Authoritarian Portugal.* London: Sage.

Scott, James C. 1990. *Domination and the Arts of Resistance: Hidden Transcripts.* New Haven, Conn.: Yale University Press.

Seremetakis, C. Nadia. 1994a. "The Memory of the Senses, Part I: Marks of the Transitory." In *The Senses Still: Perception and Memory as Material Culture in Modernity,* ed. C. Nadia Seremetakis, 1–18. Boulder, Colo.: Westview Press.

———. 1994b. "The Memory of the Senses, Part II: Still Acts." In *The Senses Still: Perception and Memory as Material Culture in Modernity,* ed. C. Nadia Seremetakis, 23–43. Boulder, Colo.: Westview Press.

Seromenho, Margarida. 2003. "A Federação do Folclore Português: A Reconstituição do Folclore em Democracia." In *Vozes do Povo: A Folclorização em Portugal,* ed. Salwa Castelo Branco and Jorge Freitas Branco, 245–51. Oeiras, Portugal: Celta Editora.

Serrão, Joel. 1970. "Conspecto Histórico da Emigração Portuguesa." *Análise Social* 8 (32): 597–617.

———. 1977. *A Emigração Portuguesa: Sondagem Histórica.* Lisbon: Livros Horizonte.

Sheriff, Robin E. 2000. "Exposing Silence as Cultural Censorship: A Brazilian Case." *American Anthropologist* 102 (1): 114–32.
Sieber, R. Timothy. 2002. "Composing Lusophonia: Mulitculturalism and National Identity in Lisbon's 1998 Musical Scene." *Diaspora* 11 (2): 163–88.
Silva, Augusto Santos. 1991. "Tempos Cruzados: Um Estudo Interpretivo da Cultura Popular." Ph.D. dissertation, Instituto Superior de Ciências do Trabalho e da Empresa.
———. 1994. "Tradição, Modernidade, e Desenvolvimento: Portugal na Integração Europeia." *Revista Crítica de Ciências Sociais* 39: 147–62.
Silva, José Mário. 1993. "Coliseu Renasce em 94." *Notícias Magazine*, December 5, 32–38.
Silva, Manuel Deniz. 1999. "Musique et Fascisme: La 'Mocidade Portuguesa' dans les Années Trente." Ph.D. dissertation, Université VIII (Paris).
Silvano, Filomena, and Tereza Coelho. 1993. "Sobre a Construção de uma Casa." *Antropologia Portuguesa* 11: 59–65.
Skidmore, Thomas. 1993 [1974]. *Black into White: Race and Nationality in Brazilian Thought.* Durham, N.C.: Duke University Press.
Smith, Anthony D. 1993. *National Identity.* Reno: University of Nevada Press.
Soares, Mário. 1990. "Introduction: Portugal's Democracy." In *Portugal: Ancient Country, Young Democracy*, ed. Kenneth Maxwell and Michael H. Haltzel, 1–8. Washington, D.C.: Wilson.
Soja, Edward W. 1989. *Postmodern Geographies: The Reassertion of Space in Critical Social Theory.* New York: Verso.
Stallybrass, Peter, and Allon White. 1986. *The Politics and Poetics of Transgression.* Ithaca, N.Y.: Cornell University Press.
Stewart, Susan. 1993. *On Longing: Narratives of the Miniature, the Gigantic, the Souvenir, the Collection.* Durham, N.C.: Duke University Press.
Stone, Linda, ed. 2001. *New Directions in Anthropological Kinship.* Oxford: Rowman and Littlefield.
Strom, Elizabeth. Forthcoming. "Cultural Policy as Development Policy: Evidence from the United States." *International Journal of Cultural Policy.*
———. 2002. "Converting Pork into Porcelain: Cultural Institutions and Downtown Development." *Urban Affairs Review* 38 (1): 3–28.
Taft, Donald Reed. 1969 [1923]. *Two Portuguese Communities in New England.* New York: Arno Press.
Taussig, Michael. 1993. *Mimesis and Alterity: A Particular History of the Senses.* London: Routledge.
Taylor, Diana. 1991. *Theatre of Crisis: Drama and Politics in Latin America.* Lexington: University Press of Kentucky.
———. 1996. "'Damnable Iteration': The Traps of Political Spectacle." *Modern Language Quarterly* 57 (2): 305–19.
Teixeira, Carlos. 1999. *Portugueses em Toronto: Uma Comunidade em Mudança.* Açores: Direcção Regional das Comunidades.
Tomlinson, John. 1999. *Globalization and Culture.* Chicago: University of Chicago Press.

Turner, Victor. 1969. *The Ritual Process: Structure and Anti-structure.* Ithaca, N.Y.: Cornell University Press.

———. 1974. *Dramas, Fields and Metaphors: Symbolic Action in Human Society.* Ithaca, N.Y.: Cornell University Press.

———. 1986. "Dewey, Dilthey, and Drama: An Essay in the Anthropology of Experience." In *The Anthopology of Experience,* ed. Victor Turner and Edward Bruner. Urbana: University of Illinois Press.

———, ed. 1982. *Celebrations: Studies in Festivity and Ritual.* Washington, D.C.: Smithsonian Institution Press.

Vala, Jorge, ed. 1999. *Novos Racismos.* Oeiras, Portugal: Celta Editora.

Vala, Jorge, Rodrigo Brito, and Diniz Lopes. 1999. *Expressões dos Racismos em Portugal.* Lisbon: Imprensa de Ciências Sociais.

Valente, José Carlos. 1999. *Estado Novo e Alegria no Trabalho: Uma História Política da FNAT (1935–58).* Lisbon: Edições Colibri, INATEL.

Vasconcellos, J. Leite de. 1986 [1883]. *Tradições Populares de Portugal.* 2nd ed. Lisbon: Imprensa Nacional.

Vasconcelos, João. 2001. "Estéticas e Políticas do Folclore." *Análise Social* 36 (158–59): 399–433.

Ventura, Lídia Maria. 1996. Interview by author. Audio recording. Alenquer, Portugal, June 23.

Ventura, Luís Fernando. 1996. Interview by author. Audio recording. Alenquer, Portugal, June 23.

Viana, Abel. 1953. "Ranchos Regionais: Naturalidade e Estilização." *Mensário das Casas do Povo* 85: 12–13.

Vicente, António Luís. 1999. *Os Portugueses nos Estados Unidos: Política de Comunidades e Comunidade Política.* Lisbon: Fundação LusoAmericana Para o Desenvolvimento.

Wallerstein, Immanuel. 1974. *The Modern World System.* San Diego: Academic Press.

———. 1984. *The Politics of the World-Economy: The States, the Movements and the Civilizations.* Cambridge, U.K.: Cambridge University Press.

Wallis, Brian. 1994. "Selling Nations: International Exhibitions and Cultural Diplomacy." In *Museum Culture: Histories, Discourses, Spectacles,* ed. Daniel J. Sherman and Irit Rogoff, 265–81. London: Routledge.

Watts, Michael J. 1992. "Space for Everything (a Commentary)." *Cultural Anthropology* 7 (February): 115–29.

Wheeler, Douglas L. 1993. *Historical Dictionary of Portugal.* Metuchen, N.J.: Scarecrow Press.

———. 1994. "Letter to the Membership: 'A Moment of Personal Emotion.'" *Portuguese Studies Review* 3 (1): 3–4.

Whisnant, David E. 1983. *All That Is Native and Fine: The Politics of Culture in an American Region.* Chapel Hill: University of North Carolina Press.

Wiarda, Howard J. 1977. *Corporatism and Development: The Portuguese Experience.* Amherst: University of Massachusetts Press.

Williams, Gareth. 1998. "Democracy as Hatred: Accumulation, Affect, and the Rituals of State Formation in Central America." Paper given at the Center for Humanities lecture series, Wesleyan University. September 14.

Williams, Raymond. 1977. *Marxism and Literature.* Oxford: Oxford University Press.

Wilson, Rob, and Arif Dirlik, eds. 1995. *Asia/Pacific as Space of Cultural Production.* Durham, N.C.: Duke University Press.

Winkler-Hermaden. 1936. "Loisirs et culture populaire." *Compte Rendu du Congrés Mondial des Loisirs et de la Récréation, Hambourg-Berlin, 25–30 Jul. 1936.* Hamburg: Hanseatische Verlagsanstalt, 41.

INDEX

Page numbers in italics refer to illustrations.

KIMBERLY DACOSTA HOLTON is Assistant Professor and Program Coordinator of Portuguese and Lusophone World Studies at Rutgers University, Newark. She is also the founder and director of the Ironbound Oral History Project.